W9-DAX-460

MONEY IN
AMERICAN ELECTIONS

MONEY IN
AMERICAN ELECTIONS

FRANK J. SORAUF
University of Minnesota

Scott, Foresman/Little, Brown College Division
SCOTT, FORESMAN AND COMPANY
Glenview, Illinois   Boston   London

025415

Library of Congress Cataloging-in-Publication Data

Sorauf, Frank J. (Frank Joseph), 1928-
  Money in American elections.

  Includes index.
  1. Campaign funds—United States.   I. Title.
JK1991.S675   1988   324.7'8'0973   87-36955
ISBN 0-673-39784-X

1   2   3   4   5   6   7   8   9   10—PAT—93   92   91   90   89   88

Printed in the United States of America.

ACKNOWLEDGMENTS

The author and publisher are grateful for permission to quote from the following material:

Senator Brock Adams, "Dialing the Money Men Replaces Campaigning for Votes." *The Los Angeles Times,* June 24, 1987. Reprinted by permission.

Herbert Alexander, *Financing Politics,* 3rd edition. Reprinted by permission of the Congressional Quarterly Press.

Herbert Alexander, *Financing the 1976 Elections.* Reprinted by permission of the Congressional Quarterly Press.

Senator David L. Boren, "It's Time to Cut PAC Power." *The Washington Post,* June 10, 1987. © The Washington Post. Reprinted by permission.

David Broder, "Democratic Money—But Not for the Party." *The Washington Post,* October 29, 1986. © The Washington Post. Reprinted by permission.

The Center for Responsive Politics, *Money and Politics: Campaign Spending Out of Control.* Washington, D.C. Reprinted by permission.

Richard E. Cohen, "Spending Independently." *National Journal,* December 6, 1986. Copyright © 1986 by National Journal Inc. All rights reserved. Reprinted by permission.

R. Bruce Dold, "Private Percy Foe Spends Half-Million." *The Chicago Tribune,* October 22, 1984. Copyright 1984, Chicago Tribune Company, all rights reserved, used with permission.

Ronnie Dugger, "The Mating Game for '88." *The New York Times,* December 7, 1986. Copyright © 1986 by The New York Times Company. Reprinted by permission.

Thomas B. Edsall, "Democratic Party Skirted the Edge of Solvency at Mid-Year." *The Washington Post,* August 12, 1985. Reprinted by permission.

Thomas B. Edsall, "GOP's Cash Advantage Failed to Assure Victory in Close Senate Contests." *The Washington Post,* November 6, 1986. Reprinted by permission.

Alan Ehrenhalt, "The Natural Limitations of PAC Power." *Congressional Quarterly,* April 9, 1983. Reprinted by permission.

Dennis Farney and John J. Fialka, "His Ability as a Fund-Raiser Enhances the Power of California's Democratic Rep.

(continued on page 398)

For Shelly and Gerry,
in friendship

Preface

The plan of this book should be evident from its structure and text, even from its table of contents. But an author's hopes for a book may be less apparent. I have written this one to bring what have been disparate materials into a summary and interpretation of what we know about a single subject: the way we finance American election campaigns. I hope it will help to organize and define, both for research and for teaching, what can easily seem to be a mixture of arcane data, insiders' lore, and heated judgments.

I also want to acknowledge some debts. I could not have written the book without the help of three research assistants: David Linder, Tracy Tool, and Scott Wilson. Their hard work, mastery of the data, and ingenuity in the library made it possible to produce a manuscript without ending the rest of my personal and professional life. All the people at the Federal Election Commission have been unfailingly helpful, but I am particularly indebted to Bob Biersack, Kent Cooper, and Fred Eiland. Gerald Elliott was, as always, a peerless source of materials within the Beltway. Mary Ellen Otis effectively took care of formatting and printing the manuscript as deadlines loomed. I am grateful to my editor, John Covell, for his enthusiasm for the project and his continuing patience and support.

Finally, I am indebted to my fellow scholars in the field of campaign finance for their published research and their informal exchanges of opinions and ideas. Gary Jacobson read an earlier version of this manuscript and made very constructive suggestions. My colleague at the University of Minnesota, Ian Maitland, has helped me by commenting on parts of it and by generally responding to my thoughts and ideas. Even with such guidance, I have doubtless blundered into errors of various sorts in the book. For them and for the opinions and judgments in it, I alone am responsible.

Minneapolis, MN
September 1987

Contents

MONEY IN
AMERICAN ELECTIONS

1
An Orientation

Eras do not have specific dates of origin. The kind of massive, dramatic change that marks their onset is really a cluster of related changes happening only more or less at the same time. And so it has been with campaign finance in the United States. The stirrings of a new era, the contemporary era, began some time in the 1960s, but it arrived full-blown in the 1970s with the coming together of a number of trends and changes in American politics. It is not, however, the onset of the new era that marks it most indelibly, but rather the ways in which the current era differs from the one that preceded it.

Nothing characterizes the new era as vividly as the increase in the sheer sums of money spent in campaigns for public office. In 1972 all of the candidates for Congress spent a total of $77,305,769 in their campaigns; by 1976 the total had edged up to $115,500,000. By 1986 the total cost of congressional campaigns had jumped dramatically to $450,049,177, an increase of 482 percent since 1972.[1] Even allowing for the increase of 162 percent in the Consumer Price Index from 1972 to 1986 — that is, correcting for the effect of inflation — the increase in purchasing power dollars is still a very substantial 122 percent.

Other less visible, but scarcely less fundamental, changes

[1] The data for 1972 and 1976 come from Joseph E. Cantor, *Campaign Financing in Federal Elections: A Guide to the Law and Its Operation*, rep. 86-143 of the Congressional Research Service of the Library of Congress (Aug. 8, 1986). The 1986 data come from the reports of the Federal Election Commission.

1

altered American campaign finance in the 1970s and 1980s. In earlier years the large contributor — the fabled "fat cat" — had dominated it. Congress ended that domination in 1974; and at least partially in compensatory response, political action committees (PACs) began a period of unprecedented expansion. At bottom, however, the new system of campaign funding came to rest on the political generosity of millions of individual contributors, whether they gave their money directly to candidates or indirectly through PACs and political parties. Finally, a burgeoning of data and information marked the new era. Congress and a good many states began in the 1970s to require parties, PACs, and candidates to report their financial transactions; and a rich and detailed body of data on money in campaigns resulted. Drawing on those data, the mass media have reported the details of campaign finance for the American public in ways unimaginable in earlier years or eras.

I. The New Ways of Politics

All of these characteristics of the new era in American campaign finance are evidence of more fundamental changes in American politics. Most especially they are reflections of changes in the American way of campaigning. It is *campaign* finance we are talking about, and changes in American campaigns are bound to have an effect on the ways we fund them.

A very shrewd observer of politicians and campaigns wrote almost prophetically in 1961:

> The media have done to the campaign system what the invention of accurate artillery did to the feudal kingdom — destroyed the barons and shifted their power to the masses and the prince. A candidate now pays less attention to district leaders than to opinion polls.[2]

What seemed prophetic in 1961 seems commonplace in the 1980s. But in truth it is not only the media that wrought the changes. The technologies that revolutionized campaigning

[2]Stimson Bullitt, *To Be a Politician* (New York: Anchor, 1961), 65.

embrace all of the arts of modern communication and persuasion: the sample survey (i.e., the poll), computer-based information and analysis, specialized accountancy and legal advice, systematic fund-raising, and strategic scheduling and planning. The men and women who master these skills have become the new campaign technocrats, the campaign managers and consultants who so dominate contemporary electoral politics.[3]

In the decades after World War II, the major American political party slipped into decline. The fabled urban machines were ailing virtually everywhere; only Mayor Richard Dailey's in Chicago survived a few years longer. Party organization in places other than big cities were never models of vitality or effectiveness and now declined even further. Voters loosened their party loyalties a bit more in each decade after the war. The percentage of self-styled independents rose, and even voters who continued to profess a loyalty to a political party often became more casual about their commitment. Since loyalty to party governed a smaller part of the voting decision for millions of voters, split-ticket voting increased. Party lines in the Congress and many state legislatures also softened after World War II. Disciplined, cohesive legislators of one party faced similarly disciplined legislators of the other party less and less often. So, in a number of ways political parties began to count for less in the politics of the nation.[4]

Inevitably, the political parties were able to control less and less of the campaign for public office. Gone were the days when their ranks of local workers and committeemen canvassed the local voters — the equivalent of polling in those days — and gone, too, were the days in which party publications and party parades and rallies were the stuff and excitement of the campaign. The skills and labor the party mobilized were no longer the main resource of the campaign; they were

[3]For a good account of the rise and power of the campaign technicians, see Larry Sabato, *The Rise of Political Consultants: The New Ways of Winning Elections* (New York: Basic Books, 1981).

[4]On the decline of party, see Frank J. Sorauf, *Party Politics in America*, fifth ed. (Boston: Little, Brown, 1984), especially chap. 17. On the changing party loyalties of the American electorate, see Norman Nie, Sidney Verba, and John Petrocik, *The Changing American Voter* (Cambridge, Mass.: Harvard University Press, 1976).

increasingly replaced by the new media, the new technologies, and the new people with the new skills. In short, a new style of campaigning emerged; and the parties were less and less central to it.

Candidates increasingly found themselves free to run their own campaigns — provided they could raise the money to "rent" the new campaign expertise and media of the campaign. In the days of greater party control, the candidates had come by the resources for their campaigns by bartering their loyalty for the resources the party amassed. Candidates now found themselves in a cash economy. Fund-raising suddenly became a vastly more important part of the business of being a candidate or even of being a potential candidate. But for all this trouble in finding cash, candidates literally "purchased" a kind of political freedom. Campaigns were theirs to manage or, more accurately, to arrange the management of. The need to raise large sums of money was at once a weighty burden and a charter of independence from the party and its claims.

Behind all of these shifts and changes in the resources it takes to mount a campaign, there was also a shift in what one might call the resource constituency. In earlier eras the campaign resources, heavy in manpower from the locality, were mobilized by the political party. The resource constituency was, therefore, largely congruent with the electoral constituency. In the new era, the resource constituency is much more apt to be located outside of the party organization and, increasingly, outside of the electoral constituency. Candidates for Congress raise more money nationally or regionally; PACs and parties raise it centrally (i.e., nationally) and disburse it back to the candidates in the states and the congressional districts. The consequences of that divergence of electoral and resource constituencies have been momentous.

When Jesse Unruh, then the Democratic speaker of the California Assembly, laid down his dictum that "money is the mother's milk of politics," it had all the freshness of a new insight. That was in the early 1960s.[5] To be sure, some of the fundamental changes in American politics had begun before then. Extensive

---

[5]Mr. Unruh's office dates the earliest use of the phrase in print to the article, "Big Daddy's Big Drive," *Look* (Sept. 25, 1962).

TV coverage of campaigns was becoming common in the late 1950s, for example. Other changes were just beginning; the number of independents in the American electorate turned upward in the late 1960s. But by the time all the changes and developments were consolidated and shaped in the 1970s by a major body of regulatory legislation, a new era in campaign finance was upon us; and Unruh's dictum — still the most famous one-liner in campaign finance — had begun to seem almost commonplace.

Campaigns and their funding, in turn, reflect the broader context of the entire political system. Above all, the nature of campaigns and campaign finance reflects the centrality of the individual candidate in American politics. With very few exceptions, Americans nominate candidates not by some internal party process but by an election, a primary election. Especially in the states and localities, we choose public officials, such as public utilities commissioners and local assessors, not by appointment but by election. The resulting proliferation of elections and candidates in them extends campaigning to a scope no other democracy knows. And those campaigns are for candidates, not for a party. In much of the rest of the world, voters choose between or among political parties, largely because either parliamentary institutions or proportional representation in elections frame the combat in terms of party outcomes and party control of government.

Even more broadly than that, American campaign finance reflects American society, especially its voluntarism. Raising money for candidates, parties, and PACs has a great deal in common with raising money for the arts, for hospitals, or for charities. The ease with which a little persuasion can coax money from Americans for a worthy purpose has no parallel in the rest of the world, nor is there any parallel to the extensive and thriving American fund-raising industry. The skills and techniques of that industry — the art of the fund-raising letter and the use of computer-based mailing lists, for example — have nourished the new campaign fund-raising. While campaign finance may not replace apple pie in the American pantheon, it is every bit as indigenously American as a United Way campaign.

II. Actors and Events

The actors, the events, and the transactions in American campaign finance are all defined by legislative fiat. And as with all other things in American electoral politics, that means by 51 legislatures: the Congress and those of the fifty states. Congress regulates its own campaigns and those for the presidency, and the state legislatures regulate those for state and local office. (Some states do permit local councils and other governing authorities to exert some control over campaigns for local office.) But, unhappily, campaign finance is not even that simple. Legislation often defines different funding and regulation for different offices at the same level of government. Just at the national level, for instance, there are three systems of campaign finance: one for the two houses of Congress, a second for presidential candidates before the nominating conventions, and a third for the major party candidates for the presidency after the conventions. There is no public funding for the first, partial public funding for the second, and full public funding available for the third. Given all the options and varieties, no one really knows how many systems exist in the American states and localities.

Certainly the most celebrated, documented, and varied of the campaign finance systems is the one for congressional campaigns. It is the one this book will explore at greatest length; and it offers, therefore, the most useful "bare bones" model of the actors and events in campaign finance (Figure 1-1). Movement in the model is from left to right, as it is in all such flowcharts of a political process. The flow of money begins at the left with the willing individual. That person may give money to a PAC, to a party, or directly to a candidate; or he or she may decide to spend the money autonomously and independently to urge the election or defeat of a candidate. In reality, individuals spend virtually all of their money in the first three options; and among these three well over half of their money goes directly to candidates.

Political parties and PACs, for their part, may contribute funds directly to candidates; they also each have another, though different, political option. PACs may spend "independently" — in TV or newspaper ads or direct mail messages,

FIGURE 1-1
Major Actors and Flows of Money in Congressional Campaign Finance

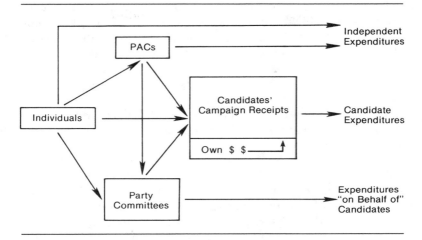

for example — to urge the election or defeat of candidates, just as individuals may. Political parties may spend directly in the election "on behalf of" candidates; in doing so, they are free to consult and coordinate with those candidates. (They may also spend money generally to promote the party itself.) Finally, of course, the candidates spend what they raise (or most of what they raise) directly in the campaign. In addition, they are free to add their own personal fortune to the funds they raise from individuals, PACs, and parties.

That schema prevails for most campaigns, with one exception: instances of public funding. In the presidential campaigns and various campaigns in less than a fifth of the states, money from some public treasury enters the system if candidates choose to accept the money and, usually, the attendant limit on their expenditures. In those instances one simply adds the treasury as one more source of candidate funds; and if public funds come on a matching basis, one would have to link it to the "trigger" of voluntary contributions from other sources. In the case of presidential campaigns for the general election, public funding is total and shuts out party, PAC, and individual contributions. Public funding in the states, however, is partial; and the public treasury in those campaigns coexists with the other sources of political money.

There are, to be sure, subtle and obscure transactions that so simple a representation cannot suggest. Figure 1-1 does not show, for example, that under federal law PACs may contribute to other PACs or to political party committees. Nor does it show that, in some states, corporations or trade unions may contribute money directly from their main assets to PACs, parties, or candidates. It also does not depict contributions (transfers) from one candidate to another. These, however, are details that do not alter the main contours of this dominant paradigm of American campaign finance.

Patterns of campaign finance vary a bit, then, from nation to state and from state to state; but the general structure is similar and one fundamental fact unites them. There are only five possible sources of the cash resources on which contemporary campaigning depends: a public treasury, individual contributions, party contributions, contributions by a PAC or some similar nonparty organization, and the candidate's own personal resources.[6] That fact is the hard reality no one can escape in thinking either about the status quo in campaign finance or about ways of changing it.

III. Judgment and Reform

Most Americans find it difficult, if not impossible, to view the funding of campaigns dispassionately. Small wonder, considering the messages about campaign finance that they regularly receive. Common Cause, the self-styled people's lobby, for instance has mounted a campaign against PACs ("People Against PAC$") in which a major piece of literature proclaims "It's a Disgrace . . . that our United States Congress is on the auction block. UP FOR GRABS to the highest PAC bidders." Much coverage of campaign finance in the mass media is similarly exercised, espe-

---

[6]Some states permit direct contributions by corporations, trade unions, and membership organizations, as we noted. (Under federal law and the law of other states, they would have to form a PAC to receive separate voluntary contributions for political uses.) One can argue, therefore, that there is a sixth source: organizations of various kinds.

cially in its treatment of PAC contributions. Nouns like "bribery" and adjectives like "obscene" mark the rhetoric of judgment about campaign finance. It is, in short, not a climate in which detached observation and analysis thrive.

Fear, outrage, and suspicion have, however, always dogged the use of money in American politics. It has always suggested images of bedrock bribery or corruption — the kind in which there is an exchange of favors for money, a quid for the quo. ("If they didn't expect something in return, why would they spend all that money?") It has also symbolized the tyranny of wealth and privilege in government and politics. And in the terms the turn-of-the-century Progressives favored, it has always represented the power of the narrow special interests over the public interests — the power of the greedy few over the many.

Certainly Americans have always been more suspicious of cash contributions than noncash contributions. Somehow we tend to look differently at the $1000 cash contribution than we do at the volunteer who gives $1000 worth of time and skills in the campaign. In fact, federal law makes the same invidious distinction. The $1000 cash contribution must be reported by the candidate as a contribution received, but the $1000 worth of volunteered effort need not be. Moreover, we celebrate the latter as doing one's duty as a citizen and exercising one's First Amendment rights. We do not so celebrate the cash contribution.

All of this is not to suggest a flight from judgment about campaign finance. Judgments about American politics are not merely useful; they are obligatory. But judgments are rarely useful if they spring from old assumptions and heated arguments rather than evidence and analysis. It is certainly important, for example, to consider what contributors — whether they are individuals, PACs, or parties — expect to gain or achieve by contributing money to candidates. It is equally important to try to gauge the impact of cash expenditures, especially different levels of expenditures, on the outcomes of elections. One could multiply the examples many times over. But, in all cases the effects or consequences of money in campaigns are not as easy to assess as received wisdom would suggest. To assess the motives of individuals, the goals and strategies of groups, and the effects of spending is no easy task, even after one has accumulated a great deal of evidence.

There is in fact no standard or measuring stick for some of the issues that trouble us in campaign finance. Take the question of the magnitudes of the sums spent in campaigns. It is a question of "how much is too much?" The average Democratic or Republican candidate for the House of Representatives in the 1986 general election spent $260,032. Is that too much, too little, or just right? How, in particular, does one decide? By the standards of middle-class personal finance, that total may indeed be appalling. By the standards of public entertainment (in which star baseball or basketball players earn five to ten times that much in a year, not to mention the "take" of rock music stars), the sum seems modest enough. (The salary of the *average* major league baseball player passed $300,000 back in 1984.) All of the Democratic and Republican general election campaigns for the House in 1986 when added together produce a figure ($210,626,146) less than a quarter of the annual advertising budget for Proctor and Gamble.

For many of the issues inherent in the American way of campaign finance, however, there is a clear and powerful standard for judgment: the imperatives and assumptions of democracy. In every sense it is the highest standard of them all. If one argues, for example, that competitive elections with the real possibility of "throwing the rascals out" are essential to a representative democracy, then one has a standard for judging campaign funding if it reduces that competitiveness. (It may not be easy, alas, to conclude if money is in fact reducing the competition.) One's understanding of the nature of representation — certainly a part of one's understanding of popular democracy — will lead one to judgment about the rise of national resource constituencies for members of Congress. Is it desirable or not, that is, that citizens outside of the voting district participate in the politics of the district and possibly win some measure of influence over its elected representative? It is not an easy question to answer, but it would be an impossible one without an underlying concept of representation in a democracy.

IV. The Discipline of Data

Congress's requirement that candidates, parties, PACs, and assorted other spenders report their campaign transactions in considerable detail has produced the most complete data on campaign finance known to modern democracy. Nothing in the states or the rest of the world match them. The Federal Election Commission (FEC) aggregates, publishes, and otherwise makes them available. Its data on congressional and presidential elections sustain the greatest share of the analysis and interpretation in this book. In fact, all data in this book have come from the press releases, printed reports, and computer tapes of the Federal Election Commission unless they are otherwise identified. Appendix A describes the data sources more fully.

The rows and columns of numbers that constitute the data are both a splendid resource and a formidable burden. As a resource they formulate the most complete record available of the campaign finance of a nation. They also have given rise to the largest body of scholarship on campaign finance among the democracies of the world. But they are a burden, too, because they are complex in definition, logic, and structure. They demand a high degree of care and precision even in making simple descriptive statements, and thus they impose a rigorous discipline on both author and reader. Nowhere is it truer that the answer you get depends on the question you ask.

For example, what did a race for the House cost in 1986? Well, the average cost of all campaigns in 1985–86 (the FEC measures in two-year periods called "election cycles") was $148,796. But that figure includes candidates defeated in the primary and even noncandidates who raised and spent money to "test the waters" or send up "trial balloons." (The language of American politics feeds on well-polished cliches.) It even includes candidates from 1984 who raised money in 1985 or 1986 to retire their campaign debts. However, the FEC publishes data limited to the expenditures of the candidates who ran in the general election.[7] The average cost for their campaigns was $218,975, but this includes independent candidates and the candidates of minor parties —

[7]These data include all expenditures over the two-year election cycle, including spending in the primary.

candidates who usually spend relatively little and who thus bring down the average. So, what is the figure for major party candidates in the general election? That average is $260,032. For argumentative purposes, critics of the status quo in campaign finance like to cite the average cost of a House campaign for the *winners* in the general election; that average in 1986 was about $355,000.[8] "You pays your money and you takes your choice," but it is supremely important to know exactly what the choice is.

The discipline of the data can also become a tyranny. In one very practical sense, the costs of campaigning for Congress are the costs the participants are required to report by law of Congress. Campaign costs are as Congress does. But it is important to keep in mind that Congress's definition, important as it is, is only one definition. And there are a good many costs it does not include. It assigns no value to the candidate's time and skills or to the time and skills of volunteer supporters, for instance. We tend to count cash costs and not to count noncash costs. Most controversially, federal statutes do not include as campaign expenditures any campaign to register voters or to get them out to vote. These activities are considered to be either nonpartisan or bipartisan. (That position does not convince Republicans who note that it is organized labor that spends the greatest resources on such activities.) That these are *some* part of the costs of contesting the election is less disputable. While some costs of campaigns may go unreported or uncounted, others are often overcounted. National committees of the political parties report total expenditures; for instance, does one wish to assign all the costs of the meetings and travel of the party bureaucrats to the campaigns?

Moreover, reporting — and the data it yields — is not equally demanding for all aspects of campaign finance. PACs must report every campaign contribution, no matter how small; individuals do not themselves have to report any contribution. Candidates must report the name of every PAC from which they receive a contribution; they must report only the names of contributors who give them more than $200. As a result we have far more data about PAC contributions than individual contributions; and

---

[8]The figure is a good approximation. The FEC's preliminary data for 1986 lists a rounded $155.4 million for the expenditures of House winners; that figure divided by the 435 winners produces a mean of $357,241.

given the effects of the "law of available data" on intellectual priorities, scholars and journalists write much more about PACs than they do about individual contributors. Americans thus know much more about PACs.

One could easily multiply the ways in which we become the prisoners of readily available data. Because federal law does not require full reporting about the objects and purposes of candidate expenditures, we know far less about what campaign money buys than we do about those who give it. And when one gets to the far sketchier laws and reporting requirements of many states, one is clutching often at fragments of data and only scattered pieces of the puzzle.

From all of this, one great lesson emerges: master the data or be mastered by them. Unless one understands their definitions and categories and treats them with care and precision, and unless one understands that their definitions are only one among a number of definitions of reality, one runs a great danger of falling victim to their tyranny.

V. Campaign Finance in the Bigger Picture

Depending on the scholarly idiom one prefers, intermediating political organizations such as parties and interest groups aggregate the influence of political individuals and bring those aggregates to bear on the institutions of government; or they link individual citizens to those institutions and the public officials who make policy in them. The process of aggregation or linkage is in fact a number of processes. In representative democracies it is accomplished for the largest number of individuals through the open election of public officials. Others are joined together to exert influence directly on the already chosen officials of government in processes we lump together as lobbying.

In a very rough but important way, political parties and interest groups in American politics long divided the domains of these two great aggregating processes — the parties dominating electoral politics and interest groups dominating the politics of lobbying. To be sure, the division of labor was approximate; but it was very real. And the two different kinds of political organizations seemed remarkably well adapted to their respective domains and to the different organizing tasks in them. Parties, large and omnibus organizations that tried to embrace majorities, were the organizations suited to contest elections. Interest groups, much narrower and more specialized and exclusive rather than inclusive, seemed better suited for the organization of diverse and specialized influence on policy-making.

All of the changes in campaign finance have threatened that great division of labor. Increasingly, interest groups and their offspring, the political action committees, are involved in election politics. And in states where it is legal, corporations, labor unions, and membership organizations are increasingly active directly in funding campaigns. In one sense that incursion is a reflection of the increased weakness of the political parties. But in another, more fundamental way, it reflects also some rudimentary changes in American politics. More and more Americans want to diminish their loyalty to an all-encompassing party; they prefer a more specialized election politics that permits them to pick and choose among candidates and issues. For that more specialized, more selective, more focused politics, the parties are blunter instruments than they want. The very idea of loyally voting a straight party ticket is exactly what the new election politics is *not* about.

The changing roles of the parties and groups have, of course, spawned a new one: the political action committee. PACs had been around in American politics since the 1940s, but only in the 1970s did they grow so dramatically in number and in influence. Most of them, indeed, became the electoral arms of parent organizations directly active in more traditional interest representation before legislatures and executive agencies. Their sharply increased importance reflects both the declining role of the parties in electoral politics and the changes in electoral politics to a politics of issues and volatile coalitions. Political action committees are, moreover, almost uncannily adapted for an election politics that is centered on candidates and that has cash as a medium of exchange.[9]

So, fundamental change in American campaign finance moves

[9]Frank J. Sorauf, "Parties and Political Action Committees in American Politics," a chapter in Kay Lawson and Peter Merkl, eds., *When Parties Fail* (Princeton, N.J.: Princeton University Press, 1988).

forward on two levels. On the most obvious one are the changes in the ways in which we raise and spend resources in campaigns, the changes that mark a new era in campaign finance since the early 1970s. But on another more fundamental level, the changes in campaign finance are part of a broader change in the ways in which we organize influence and consent in the American democracy. To describe and assess the changes on both of these levels are the chief tasks of this book.

2
A Little Bit of History

Before the new era in American campaign finance, there was no single old era. Neither campaigns nor their funding in 1950 or 1960 bore much resemblance to campaigns and campaign finance a hundred years earlier. In 1860 Abraham Lincoln never left Springfield, Illinois, during a campaign that probably cost no more than $100,000. It was his unsuccessful opponent, Stephen Douglas, who tried the unconventional strategy of barnstorming the country. In fact, throughout much of the nineteenth century, the messages of the campaign were carried either by highly partisan newspapers or by the workers of the parties; and voters voted their party loyalties in millions of straight tickets. To a considerable extent, campaigning in those decades was an exercise in activating both party loyalties and responses to party positions on the great issues of the day.

Campaigning evolved almost continuously in the twentieth century. The rise of charismatic candidates — some of them, like William Jennings Bryan, unsuccessful to be sure — resulted at least in part because of technological changes: railroads, photography, motion pictures, and then radio and television. Candidates, whether charismatic or not, began to take to the campaign trail. The growing power of organized business, farm, and labor groups began to break the monopoly the parties held on the political loyalties of Americans, as did the rise in literacy and education coupled with the explosion of sources of political information. Parties changed, too, as they slowly lost their vaunted cadres of ward and precinct workers as well as their armies of loyal voters. Campaigns slowly and fitfully became the candidate-centered events we know today.

Changes in the ways of financing campaigns over more than a century are, however, less easily described. Campaign finance has always been the *terra incognita* of American politics, a shadowy reality put together of sensational stories and the public's worst suspicions. From time to time, parts of reality emerged. The Progressive journalists at the turn of the century (the so-called muckrakers) detailed the financial interventions of business tycoons and the other wealthy. Occasionally, a congressional committee would expose a particularly scandalous episode. One discovered, for example, that insurance companies were drawing on assets standing behind the policies of their customers for political expenditures; those revelations led in 1907 to legislation prohibiting contributions by banks and corporations. But except for an occasional look into the seamy side of campaign finance, the shortage of information about it defeated even the most sedulous reporting.[1]

Two very fine political scientists, undeterred by the poverty of data, described twentieth century campaign finance as it was at two different times, a generation apart. Louise Overacker wrote her *Money in Elections* in the late 1920s, and Alexander Heard, in *The Costs of Democracy,* wrote in the late 1950s.[2] Their books report two soundings into the infinitely varied and ever-changing patterns of American campaign finance.

I. The Money World in 1930 and 1960

Campaign finance in the early years of this century still bore the marks of the previous one. There was a brashness and

---

[1] For a somewhat anecdotal, muckraking survey of early American campaign finance pre-1974, see George Thayer, *Who Shakes the Money Tree?* (New York: Simon and Schuster, 1973).

[2] Louise Overacker, *Money in Elections* (New York: Macmillan, 1932); and Alexander Heard, *The Costs of Democracy* (Chapel Hill: University of North Carolina Press, 1960).

rascality about it that suggested a simpler, more primitive electoral politics; and nothing suggested it more fully than the expenditures on election day. Direct "buying" of votes had not yet disappeared by the 1920s, but "treating" was more common. In Louise Overacker's words,

> Expenditures for cigars appear in the expense accounts of candidates in the Pennsylvania Republican Senatorial primary of 1926. Candidates in Massachusetts frequently return [sic] expenditures for "cigars and tobacco." In the 1930 senatorial campaign the Eben Draper Political Committee spent over $500 for this purpose.[3]

(Campaigns were also clearly a male occupation then.) But the major election day outlays went to the party workers who shepherded voters to the polls and instructed them about the course of duty or wisdom. Some cash also went to poll watchers and other party functionaries.

> In New York and many other cities on the Sunday or Monday before the election or primary the ward leader, who has received his slice of the funds from headquarters in bills of convenient denominations, distributes it to the precinct committeemen, who in turn hand it out to the workers. In New York State the Monday before election was long known as "Dough Day" for it was on that day that the cash was distributed among the "boys."[4]

When the duties of the recipients were light or even neglible, it was a practice that seemed very much like bribery.

As even these tawdry practices suggest, the political parties dominated the campaigns. They raised the money — a good deal of it from the people they put into elective or appointive office — and candidates were dependent on them. Indeed, the parties often required their candidates to raise a part of their campaign costs and give it to the party to spend on the campaign. But, as Overacker put it,

> The money which cannot be extracted from candidates or officeholders must be obtained from "the public" generally. This is

[3]Overacker, 35.
[4]Ibid., 37.

a very broad classification which includes groups as varied as
the organized criminal element of our large cities, corporations
and individuals who seek special favors, and those voters whose
gifts are prompted by an interest in the success of the party's
program . . .[5]

In short, party control of campaigns and campaign finance rested
on party control of government and, within that control, party
control of appointments and policy-making. When the party is
king, it rules over all the political realm.[6]

When the parties were forced to go outside of themselves for
money, Overacker found that they went to "big" contributors.
She repeatedly concluded that the "rank and file" contributed
little to party committees, that state committees relied on less
than 100 contributors, and that the great part of campaign
money came from "very wealthy individuals," from the "pluto-
crats" of campaign finance. In 1928's presidential campaign,

> Huge funds were raised by each party but in spite of urgent ap-
> peals for wide-spread support, intense interest in the campaign,
> and prosperity in most quarters, only 12.5 per cent of the Demo-
> cratic fund and 8.2 per cent of the Republican fund came from
> those who gave in amounts of $100 or less. More than half of the
> Democratic fund, and almost half of the Republican fund, came
> from contributions of $5000 or more.[7]

(In thinking about sums of money in 1928, it may help to keep in
mind that Henry Ford's basic family auto then cost about $500.)
This dependence on big contributors best indicates the persist-
ence of the nineteenth century traditions in campaign finance.

A new technology — the wireless radio — was, however, pulling campaigns into a new persuasive style.

---

[5]Ibid., 105.

[6]I am aware that in the entire period before the 1970s there is much more data
available on the financial affairs of party committees than there is on the finances
of candidates and nonparty contributors to them. Such a disparity in data could
lead one to a false impression of the central role of the parties in campaigning.
Even with all allowances made for these data imbalances, however, I think the
case is strong for these conclusions about the role of the parties.

[7]Overacker, 143. The general coverage of big sums can be found on pp.
119–143.

The radio played no part in the presidential campaign of 1924 but in 1928 it dwarfed all other campaigning agencies in importance and future campaigns are likely to be fought largely through the microphone. Something over $550,000, or eighteen percent of the funds used directly by the Democratic National Committee, went to bring Governor [Al] Smith's voice into every radio home in the United States.[8]

An hour of radio time on a nationwide hookup cost only something more than $10,000. Other media — newspaper ads, billboards, even buttons and stickers — remained important, too.

Finally, even so diligent a scholar as Overacker could not put together enough scraps and shards of data to venture an estimate of the total cost of campaigning in 1928.

> . . . in 1928, when the two parties were fairly equally financed and spent more than they ever had before, the total [in the presidential campaign] was $16,500,000. If the expenditures of county committees is estimated as equal to those of state organizations the grand total would be over $23,000,000. . . . [This summary] is admittedly incomplete, but it tells the [presidential campaign] story as far as it is available. One can only guess at what the total would be if we added to this all of the money spent by candidates for other national, state and local offices in the same election.[9]

Even today estimating the total cost of a year's campaigns, especially in the states and localities, is a daunting task.

More than a generation later, at the end of the 1950s, Alexander Heard portrayed a system of campaign finance much more complex and strikingly volatile. Television was beginning to work its revolution on American politics, and styles of fundraising and contributing were also in flux. The role of the political parties had begun to decline, at least in the Democratic party. It isn't clear whether the status quo Heard described was the end of an era or the transition to the next, but the distinction is probably not crucial. The evolution of funding patterns and styles is continuous, and the breaks with the past are neither clean nor abrupt.

[8]Ibid., 28.

In any event, the cross-sectional slice of campaign finance that Heard so skillfully described had at least six salient characteristics.

A LEXICOGRAPHICAL NOTE: "FAT CAT"

In matters of political jargon or vocabulary, William Safire is the authoritative source. His entry on "Fat Cat" in *Safire's Political Dictionary*, 3rd ed. (New York: Random House, 1978), begins this way (p. 220):

a man of wealth, particularly an important contributor to political campaigns. The phrase is both derogatory and respectful, since few politicians can go far without such supporters.

The phrase was popularized by Frank R. Kent of the *Baltimore Sun* in his 1928 book, *Political Behavior*: ". . . these capitalists have what the organization needs — money to finance the campaign. Such men are known in political circles as 'fat cats.'"

In politics, "fat" means "money." The word was used back in the last century: high-pressure fund-raising was called "fat-frying" in the campaign of 1888. Publisher Henry L. Stoddard wrote historian Mark Sullivan: "[Mark] Hanna was *a* fat-fryer. The fat-fryer was John P. Forster, President of the League of Young Republican Clubs. It was in 1888 that he wrote a letter suggesting 'to fry the fat out of the manufacturers.'"

The Domination of the Large Contributor. The years right after World War II clearly fell within the reign of the "fat cats," the big contributors in the argot of American finance (see box). Heard estimated, in fact, that "no less than one-half" of the $140 million raised and spent for all elections in 1952 came in chunks of $100 or more. Moreover, at the national level "around two-thirds" came in sums of $500 and over, and somewhat more than 85 percent in sums over $100.[10] (The 1952 sums of $100 and $500 are the equivalents of $413 and $2065 in 1986 when one corrects

[9]Ibid., 74.
[10]Heard, 49.

for the inflation of intervening years.) The major efforts to raise smaller sums of money from many more contributors had begun, but important successes at it were still to come.

The Vestiges of Patronage and Preferment. Patronage in its strictest sense — public jobs for the politically worthy — was at once a source of both cash and noncash contributions to campaigns. The patronage holders (and their families) worked for the parties and in the party campaigns, and they usually contributed a part of their salaries to the party coffers. The practice of securing part of the salary was known somewhat brutally as "macing the payroll." The magnitude of the macing differed, but Indiana provided a benchmark with itş well-known Two Percent Club. In the broader meaning of the word — preferment and access to governmental decision — patronage also provided cash to governing parties in return for building or insurance contracts, for permits and licenses, or for an indulgent governmental wink at illegality or irregularity. This source of funds, to be sure, existed unevenly in the United States, primarily in some states and localities.

Limited Group Participation. One gets the impression from Heard and others that group financing of electoral politics was largely limited to business and labor groups. And indeed Heard concluded that "the bulk" of American campaign activities was financed by "businessmen."[11] Businessmen are a diverse group; and labor's involvement, mature and important by the 1950s — the AFL and CIO merged in 1955 — added much more diversity. There are accounts in the '40s and '50s of other group involvement — the financial politics of the American Medical Association's attempts to forestall government medical insurance, for example — but Heard and his contemporaries focus on business and labor.

The Strength of Parties in Financing Campaigns. As late as the 1950s, the parties, especially the Republican party, still functioned as the major financial intermediaries. Candidates and their volunteer committees raised a good deal of money directly,

[11]Ibid., 119.

but the parties controlled the major share of it. Writing about senatorial campaigns, Heard concluded,

> Most funds reported as transferred to Republican Senatorial committees originated with the party's regular or finance committees at local, state, and national levels. In contrast, almost one-half such Democratic money came from separately organized labor sources and another substantial share came from "miscellaneous" groups.[12]

Even the early experiments of the 1950s in raising small sums of money — the door-to-door solicitations of Dollars for Democrats, for example — were those of the parties. The only systematic exception to the parties' brokering role appears to be that of organized labor; its money largely went directly to candidates.

The Importance of Solicitors. With face-to-face solicitation of substantial donors the dominant mode of fund-raising, the solicitor was a central figure in campaign finance. Well-connected men — for they were almost exclusively men — organized other well-connected men to fan out and shake the money trees. The skills were specialized, and many party organizations could not count on the ordinary party leaders to have them. Many parties, therefore, set up special finance committees for solicitations. It was, in short, a process in many states and communities not greatly different from organizing a public fund-raising program for a new hospital or art museum.

The Futility of Regulation. Congress had passed assorted, if somewhat forlorn, regulations of campaign finance beginning in the nineteenth century; so had some states. (A fuller discussion of that history follows shortly.) But none of the requirements for reporting or the limits on contributing or spending were effective. Often, only sketchy reports were required; usually, they were to be deposited with legislative officials. Enforcement or penalties were rarely provided for. Evasion and avoidance were widespread; ingenuity and illegality had become the custom. It

---

[12]Ibid., 308.

was widely conceded, for example, that corporation executives made financial contributions that their corporate employers (unable to contribute as a corporation under federal law) reimbursed by bonuses or expense account payments. Skepticism and cynicism, even wry amusement, about the regulation of campaign finance was the order of the day.

With the six characteristics noted, it is important also to say that we do *not* know very much about the mixture of noncash to cash resources that campaigning employed in the 1950s. That is, we really do not know the extent to which the system of campaign finance had evolved to a major reliance on cash. It is clear, however, that the answer involves another very central point: differences between Democrats and Republicans. Traditionally, Democrats had the greater noncash resources; they controlled the great majority of cities and states with the largest reservoirs of patronage opportunities. Among the great urban machines of the first half of the twentieth century, only the one in Philadelphia was controlled by Republicans. Even the postwar movement to new middle-class volunteers — many of them recruited by the literate presidential campaign of Adlai Stevenson in 1952 — largely involved Democrats. And when the parties tried to tap the small contributor, it was the Democrats who took the lead with a labor-intensive, door-to-door search of Dollars for Democrats. In one way or another, that is, the Democrats for a long time relied more than did the Republicans on the contributed energies of armies of volunteer workers.[13]

So, Heard's volume is full of evidence that Republicans were by 1960 raising more cash than were Democrats. As he wrote in an initial summary,

> It is safe to conclude that in the United States as a whole in 1956 Republican candidates benefited by at least 60 percent of all campaign expenditures made during the general election. The actual proportion was probably a bit higher, and it was no doubt higher than in 1952.[14]

---

[13]On the new volunteers in the Democratic party, see James Q. Wilson, *The Amateur Democrat* (Chicago: University of Chicago Press, 1962).
[14]Heard, 22.

But to what extent did the Democratic edge in noncash contributions (if, indeed, there was an edge) offset the cash advantage of the GOP? It is a tantalizing question — a very central question — but one never easy to address. But whatever the answer, it seems very likely that traditional Republican superiority in raising cash had put that party in a far better position to move successfully into the emerging cash economy of campaign finance.

II. The Transition to a New Era

The 1960s and early 1970s were a time of turbulent change, even transformation, for American campaigning and its funding. The seeds of change had in most instances been planted earlier, but many of them sprouted and matured more or less simultaneously in a single decade. On top of these ongoing and fundamental changes in American electoral politics, there happened one dramatic set of events that shook American confidence in electoral politics: the scandals of Watergate and Richard Nixon's presidency. With Watergate as the catalytic event, it all led to the most systematic attempts to reform campaign finance that the nation has ever experienced. But important as Watergate was, the less visible and dramatic changes at work were no less so.

Above all, television campaigning arrived in the '60s. Only 34 percent of American households had TV sets in 1952, but the percentage rose to 72 percent in 1956, 87 percent in 1960, and 92 percent in 1964. The number of television stations increased from 108 in 1952 to 661 in 1964.[15] The consequent revolution in campaign politics was anything but simple. The number and cost of media advertisements skyrocketed, but more importantly, the whole style and strategy of the campaign changed. Candidates planned a day's activities for a few minutes of exposure on the evening news; they increasingly were chosen for their TV appearance or skills (down to their smiles, their beards, and their hairlines or coiffures); and candidates perforce had to rely on the costly expertise of those who bought TV time, who filmed TV

---

[15]*Historical Statistics of the United States, Colonial Times to 1970*, Bicentennial Edition, Parts I and II (Washington, D.C.: U.S. Bureau of Census, 1975), 42, 796.

spots, and who arranged live TV guest appearances or confrontations.

At about the same time, parties and candidates began to achieve their first great successes in getting money from the proverbial "small" contributor. It was an old hope, this prospect of a "democracy of money." Henry Clay had wanted to create a national Whig organization in 1840 in which each member would contribute one cent a week; he apparently did not succeed. In 1916 William Jennings Bryan ("The Great Commoner") hoped for a million contributors by mail to his 1916 Democratic presidential campaign; only 20,000 responded, and he barely covered the costs of the project. The hope never died, though, and it was still alive in the 1950s. The Democrats raised considerable sums in grass roots, door-to-door solicitations in the 1956 campaign; after the election the party's national committee inaugurated direct mail solicitation for a Sustaining Fund.[16] But success eluded the parties until the 1960s, and then ironically it was three famous losers who achieved it.

Barry Goldwater, the Republican loser to Lyndon Johnson in 1964, attracted less than 39 percent of the popular vote; but he raised $5.8 million from 410,000 contributors through the U.S. mails. The average contribution was a shade more than $14. Goldwater's technique relied heavily on direct mail solicitation, drawing not only on lists of Republicans and his own personal supporters, but on rented lists of credit card members, brokerage house clients, and mail order customers. Four years later George Wallace's third-party candidacy for the presidency raised more than $5 million in amounts smaller than $100, a total that amounted to a staggering 76 percent of his receipts. The money was raised in a variety of ingenious ways, from traditional mailed appeals to $5-a-plate picnics. And still four years later, George McGovern — a loser who carried only Massachusetts and the District of Columbia in his race against Richard Nixon — raised close to $15 million in contributions from between 650,000 and 700,000 individuals, with an average contribution

[16]The two earlier examples are from Herbert Alexander, *Money in Politics* (Washington, D.C.: Public Affairs, 1972), 32–33. For a full review of the attempts to mine the small contributions in the 1950s, see Heard, 249–258. Heard refers to the technique of raising money by door-to-door or street corner solicitation as "panhandling."

of a bit more than $20. Contributors of $500 or less financed almost 60 percent of the cost of the McGovern campaign.[17]

Behind the new importance of television and the raising of small sums were important new technologies — those of the cathode ray tube and the computer that managed lists of contributors and addressed mail to them. Other kinds of new knowledge lay behind the development of reliable opinion sampling, an old art but one sufficiently reliable by only 1950 or 1952. (It was in 1948, after all, that the national polls had proclaimed the presidential election of Thomas E. Dewey almost a certainty.) The new arts of persuasion began to transform the candidates' speeches, the political messages on radio and television, and the written pitches in the letters soliciting money. And as masters of these new skills, there arose a new class of political technocrats: the campaign consultants.[18]

Finally, the health of the political parties continued to decline in the 1960s. Party organization in the states and localities lost its tone and vitality; the urban machines, especially, fell either to reformers or to impotence. Their patronage began to wither away — the victim of court suits, collective bargaining, and the inability to attract qualified workers with it. Perhaps nothing so vividly symbolized the decline of the centrality of political parties as the rise of the number of self-described independents in the American electorate. While independents were 23 percent of adults in 1960 by count of the University of Michigan's Survey Research Center, they were 35 percent by 1972. Moreover, the party loyalties of those who maintained them also softened; another 10 percent of the electorate dropped from "strong" to "weak" party loyalties.

The consequences of all of this were revolutionary. Candidates were inexorably becoming the central actors in the campaign and its finance, and the levels of getting and spending in campaigns began to rise steeply. The new dominance of the candidate was,

[17]The data for the Goldwater success in 1964 come from Herbert E. Alexander, *Financing the 1964 Election* (Princeton, N.J.: Citizens' Research Foundation, 1966); those on Wallace from his *Financing the 1968 Election* (Lexington, Mass.: Lexington, 1971). The McGovern data are from an article by Ben A. Franklin, "650,000 Donors Aided M'Govern," in *The New York Times* of Nov. 26, 1972.

[18]See Larry J. Sabato, *The Rise of Political Consultants* (New York: Basic Books, 1981).

in retrospect, inevitable. With the party's control of the campaign broken, who but the candidate would replace it? Candidates, furthermore, could command the new campaign technocrats just as easily as the party. The new visual media, moreover, put the focus of the campaign squarely on the candidates. Television cameras transmit a candidate's smile much more effectively than they convey an organizational abstraction like a political party.

Only one new condition limited the shift of the candidate into the political driver's seat: the need to raise cash. The new tools of the campaign and their masters were not volunteered or given; they had to be rented, often at a very dear price. At the same time, the candidates faced the reality of the sharp upturn in the rise of campaigning costs, caused both by the new media-based costs and the upward shift in the percentage of campaign costs that were paid by cash. So, the cash costs of campaigning shot upward, growing at a rate much greater than the rate of inflation for the first time in the postwar period (Figure 2-1). A new era in American campaign finance was in sight.

III. The Losing Struggle to Regulate

"Inadequate in their scope when enacted, they are now obsolete. More loophole than law, they invite evasion and circumvention." The words were Lyndon Johnson's, the date was May 25, 1967, and the occasion was a presidential message to the Congress proposing new election reforms. The reference was to the two chief pieces of congressional legislation about campaign finance then on the books: the Federal Corrupt Practices Act of 1925 and the Hatch Acts of 1939 and 1940. It would have been just as fit an epitaph for virtually any piece of legislation on campaign finance that Congress and the states had ever written.

The Johnson message was fashioned exactly 100 years after Congress began its essays in futile regulation. In 1867 it added a section to a bill on naval appropriations; the addition prohibited any naval officer or government employee from levying political assessments on workers in navy yards. In less than a decade, the same protection was extended to all government workers and

FIGURE 2-1
Total Campaign Spending in Presidential Election Years, 1952–1980

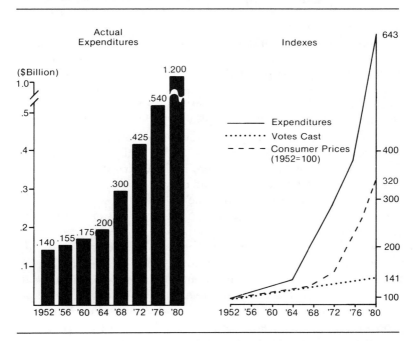

Source: Herbert E. Alexander, *Financing Politics*, 3d ed. (Washington, D.C.: CQ Press, 1984), 11.

broadened to include all forms of solicitation of political funds. Finally in the Civil Service Reform Act of 1883, other kinds of political demands were outlawed as a part of the general introduction of the merit system.

With the advent of Progressivism at the turn of the century, Congress once again confronted campaign finance. The issue was high on the reform agenda of the Progressives, and Teddy Roosevelt strenuously promoted it. In 1907 Congress, responding to the extravagant spending of the new industrial giants, made it a crime for any corporation or national bank to contribute to candidates for the Congress or the presidency. In 1910 and 1911, Congress tackled the issue of candidate expenditures for the first time; it established disclosure requirements and set spending limits for House and Senate campaigns. The same movement for openness and full information also succeeded in the states; there were publicity laws in fourteen states in 1905, but in forty-four states by 1920.

Campaign finance surfaced once again as a major issue, somewhat incongruously, in the relaxed and conservative years of the 1920s. It is perhaps proof that American political puritanism never really slumbers. A series of events — a Supreme Court decision casting doubt on Congress's power to regulate primary elections, rising levels of expenditure, the increasingly unrealistic expenditure limits of 1911, and congressional investigations into party and candidate finances — led to a successful codification and expansion of all federal law in the Corrupt Practices Act of 1925. It was Congress's first and only attempt at comprehensive legislation on campaign finance before the 1970s.

Bowing to the Supreme Court's limited definition of its powers, Congress excluded primary elections and convention proceedings from the coverage of the act. It strengthened the reporting requirements for nonparty political committees spending on campaigns in more than one state. (The substantial spending and political power of the Anti-Saloon League were apparently on the minds of many of the reformers.) Provisions on reporting were tightened to require regular reports. In recognition of population growth and the enfranchisement of women, Congress also adjusted the spending limits. Unless state laws set a lower limit, a candidate for the Senate could spend $10,000 or an amount equal to three cents per voter at the previous election, that total not to exceed $25,000. Candidates for the House by the same formula were limited to totals between $2500 and $5000. All of the other legislation on the books, including the ban on bank and corporation contributions, were folded into the new law.

The years before, during, and after World War II saw another spate of legislation on campaign finance. The very mixed nature of it suggests a variety of political motivations. The Hatch Act of 1939 (officially called the Clean Politics Act) outlawed active participation in politics by employees of the United States government and the political solicitation of people receiving relief funds from the federal government. A year later amendments to the act made three important innovations. First, they extended the 1925 legislation to primary election campaigns, the Supreme Court having changed its mind about Congress's power to regulate them.[19] Second, they established the first federal limit on contributions: individuals could give no more than $5000 to a candidate for federal office. Third, in recognition perhaps of the growing scope of government, the amendments prohibited any individual or business doing work for the United States government from contributing to a candidate or committee. In those years, too, Congress extended its prohibition on contributions by banks and corporations to labor unions (1943) and then extended all the prohibitions to primary election campaigns (1947).

Even before the flowering of federal legislation in the twentieth century, the states had begun to legislate. Virtually every state had legislation (and some had constitutional provisions) dealing with bribery and other election day inducements. Overacker quotes a Maryland statute of 1811–1812 that made it a crime to keep open any establishment at which "any victual or intoxicating liquors shall be gratuitously given or dealt out to voters."[20] Some states simply closed down the bars and taverns on election day, while others prohibited any wagering on elections.

By the 1950s the pattern of state legislation, inevitably complicated across 48 states, roughly mirrored federal legislation in most respects, although in all cases a few states had in fact preceded federal regulatory moves. California and Missouri enacted limits on candidate expenditures in 1893, for example, while Congress waited until 1911. In any event Alexander Heard could report in his 1960 book that

• by the late 1950s four states had limits on individual contributions, and those limits ranged from $1000 to $5000;
• by 1956 thirty-one states had limits on campaign expenditures, although in most cases those limits applied only to the

---

[19]Originally the Court had put primaries outside of the regulatory power of the Congress in *Newberry v. U.S.*, 256 U.S. 232 (1921). It reversed that position in *Smith v. Allwright*, 321 U.S. 649 (1944).
[20]Overacker, 290.

candidate and other expenditures made with his knowledge and consent; and

• by 1959 forty-three of the states had some requirement for reporting of campaign finance by candidates and/or party and other political committees.[21]

Of course, the extent and thoroughness of the laws varied greatly from state to state. And as Overacker lamented in 1930, "Some are so obviously sketchy on the enforcement side as to arouse the suspicion that the drafters must have hoped and expected that they would remain dead letters upon the statute books . . . "[22]

At both the national and state levels, the regulatory reality was defined by enforcement, not by the words of the statute books. And the reality was one of pervasive evasion and nonenforcement. The problems began with the failure of most statutes to create public authorities with responsibility for collecting reports, making them public, and pursuing unreported or illegal activity. The problems with the statutes of Congress are amply illustrative.

Reports of financial activity in federal elections were made to the Clerk of the House, who was required to keep them for only two years. The Clerk, moreover, had no staff or authority to enforce compliance with the statutes; neither he nor any other official was required to report violations of the campaign finance laws to the Justice Department, which in turn had no staff with expertise in campaign finance. Louise Overacker, writing in 1930 or so, describes the problems of the scholar or journalist in getting access to financial reports.

> When one asks for [old reports] one is taken into a tiny wash room where a series of dusty, paper-covered bundles repose upon an upper shelf. By climbing upon a chair and digging about among the bundles one usually finds what one wants if one persists in this "trial and error" method long enough, but there is no file and no system, and for some of the earlier campaigns no record of what is supposed to be there and what is not. When the strings are removed from the brown-paper parcels one is likely to find the oldest of these reports in a very mutilated condition.[23]

[21]Heard, 344–357 generally on the states.
[22]Overacker, 295.
[23]Ibid., 257.

It was a scenario repeated in many state capitals as well, and it persisted as normal experience well into the 1950s and '60s. Then there were the loopholes, the loopholes of which the laws were largely made. Much of the reporting legislation, for instance, required reporting for candidates and/or committees only during the campaigns proper. Clement Stone managed to give his $2.14 million to Richard Nixon in 1972 because he gave $2 million to the Nixon campaign before reporting became mandatory in April. Lesser contributors could be helped over the $5000 limit simply by creating additional committees to receive contributions up to that limit. Moreover, most of the limitations on candidate expenditure were undermined by provisions — either in the legislation or in judicial interpretations of it — that candidates could be held accountable only for expenditures made with their consent. Separate committees sprang up to spend on the candidate's behalf and outside of the expenditure limits. The reported total spending on all campaigns in 1960 equaled less than $30 million, but experts put the actual total at about $175 million.[24]

Beyond these and many other loopholes, there was a massive lack of will — no will to comply, no will to enforce. Contributors evaded publicity or contribution limits by giving through "dummy" contributors who made themselves available to channel money to a party or contributor. Corporations widely evaded the federal prohibition on their contributing by reimbursing corporate executives who contributed. "Under the table" gifts kept contributions from public sight. The prohibition against contributions by businesses contracting with the U.S. government was very widely ignored. And yet from the enactment of the Corrupt Practices Act of 1925 to its replacement in 1971, there is no record of even a single prosecution under its provisions. A conspiracy of cynicism and political convenience made it clear that, legislation aside, Americans were not really very serious about reforming campaign finance.

---

[24]For this datum and a general review of enforcement and compliance problems, see *Dollar Politics*, third ed. (Washington, D.C.: Congressional Quarterly, 1982), 6–7, and Heard, chap. 13.

IV. A New Era Begins: The Federal Election Campaign Act

Events and realities conspired in the late 1960s and the early 1970s to create a climate singularly favorable to real reform. But before reform would come, there was a period of ferment — growing dissatisfaction, false starts, reconsiderations, regulatory cul de sacs, and paths not taken. Indeed the few years from about 1960 — the year in which Heard's book was published — to 1974 were the most turbulent in the history of reforming American campaign finance.

Shortly after his inauguration in 1961, John F. Kennedy appointed a presidential commission on campaign costs in presidential elections. Alexander Heard was its chairman. The commission made a series of limited but innovative recommendations in its 1962 report. For example, it proposed removing the $5000 limit on individual contributions, but leaving the ceilings on campaign expenditures. The commission also proposed that individuals be able to deduct from their income taxes up to $1,000 a year for political contributions. The proposals received only perfunctory support from the president, and Congress brushed them aside without much consideration.[25]

Shortly thereafter, though, Congress took a first, if false, step in the direction of public funding for presidential campaigns. In 1966 it authorized a check-off plan for the federal income tax in which a taxpayer could divert one dollar of his or her taxes to a special fund for allocation to campaigns. But when Congress failed to come up with a plan for distributing the funds, the whole idea collapsed in 1967.

At the same time, the costs of campaigning were moving inexorably upward — and at increasing rates of acceleration (see Figure 2-1). The contributions of big contributors were becoming bigger; in 1968 Mrs. John D. Rockefeller spent $1.5 million on her stepson Nelson's quest for the Republican nomination, and Clement Stone gave $2.8 million — most of it to Richard Nixon's campaign for the presidency. At the same time, the costs of mass media campaigning climbed at a rate even greater than all costs: television costs in the general election of 1956 had been

[25]The official citation to the report of the Heard Commission is President's Commission on Campaign Costs, *Financing Presidential Campaigns* (Washington: Government Printing Office, 1962).

$6.6 million, but by 1968 they had shot up to $27.1 million.[26] Members of Congress in both houses began to be concerned that challengers with personal fortunes or access to large contributors might unseat them in media-based campaigns. And Democrats especially began to worry that easier access to money would make the Republican party a new majority party.

With all of that as background, the great wave of regulatory reform struck American campaign finance. Congress passed two major pieces of legislation on campaign finance in 1971. The Revenue Act of 1971 created a general campaign fund for presidential and vice presidential campaigns and permitted taxpayers to divert (i.e., "check off") a dollar of their tax liability to it.[27] In order to get the signature of a reluctant President Richard Nixon, Congress delayed implementation until the 1976 election.

Of greater ambition and immediacy was the Federal Election Campaign Act (FECA).[28] It had two main goals: tightening reporting requirements and limiting expenditures on media advertising. It made reporting of contributions and expenditures far more effective than it had been previously, especially in extending the requirements to primaries and other parts of the nomination processes. Indeed, so great was the confidence in reporting and the consequent disclosure of all financial transactions, that the bill repealed (as largely unenforceable) existing limits on contributions and expenditures. Only the old prohibition of contributions by corporations and labor unions was allowed to stand.

The FECA's attempt to limit media advertising was much more precisely targeted. Candidates for the House and the Senate were limited to a total spending on all media advertising — television, radio, magazines, newspapers, and billboards — of $50,000 or ten cents a voting-age resident of the district or the state, whichever total was larger. The effective limits ranged, therefore, from $50,000 to $1.4 million for California's senatorial candidates. Moreover, no more than 60 percent of the

---

[26]Herbert E. Alexander, *Financing the 1968 Election* (Lexington, Mass.; Lexington, 1971), 95.

[27]Pub. L. 92-178, 85 Stat. 562. This and subsequent statutes on the public funding of presidential campaigns are codified in 26 U.S. Code, chaps. 95 and 96.

[28]Pub. L. 92-225, 86 Stat. 3. The FECA and its subsequent amendments are codified at 2 U.S. Code, sec. 431–455.

maximum could be spent on radio and TV ads combined; the limits of these expenditures thus ranged from $30,000 to $840,000. The limits applied separately to primaries and the general election; the effective limits in a two-year election cycle thus were doubled. The bill also included a limit of ten cents a voting-age resident for presidential campaigns. The 1972 limit was $14.3 million, $8.58 million of it for radio and television ads.

To be sure, the FECA of 1971 had some successes in the 1972 campaign. Its reporting requirements brought the fullest disclosure of campaign transactions in American history; and while it did not curb the growth of campaign spending generally, it did limit the use of media advertising. But whatever it accomplished was overshadowed by the scandals of the campaign and its aftermath. And in fact it was the FECA itself that provided some of the information and the leverage about unreported information that helped to create the very Watergate scandals that overshadowed it. For, mixed in with all of the abuses of presidential power that eventually drove Richard Nixon from the presidency were a good many that had to do directly with campaign finance in the 1972 campaign. Indeed, the money that paid the burglars to break into the Democratic headquarters in the Watergate complex turned out to be misused campaign funds. And as revelation piled on revelation in the probes that followed Nixon's reelection, stories surfaced of attache cases stuffed with thousands of dollars, of illegal corporate contributions, and of elaborate "laundering" processes to hide the origins of substantial contributions (see box). Indeed, the head of the corporate gifts campaign of the president's reelection committee was eventually sentenced to jail for his activities.

Popular outrage over the Watergate revelations led to a wave of reform legislation in all American legislatures — legislation on conflicts of interest, on disclosure of assets by public officials, on lobbyists and lobbying, and on campaign finance. Propelled by that public mood, by organizations such as Common Cause, by a realistic assessment of the successes and the failures of the FECA of 1971, and by their own fears and concerns, the members of Congress in 1974 enacted massive amendments to the FECA.[29]

[29]Pub. L. 93-443, 88 Stat. 1263.

TALES FROM THE WATERGATE HEARINGS

Long after its most sensational discoveries — especially the existence of the Nixon tapes — the Senate Select Committee on Presidential Campaign Activities, chaired by Sen. Sam Ervin, Democrat of North Carolina, turned almost as an anticlimax to tales of wrongdoing in campaign finance. Journalist J. Anthony Lukas, drawing on the transcript of the committee's hearings, writes of one transaction involving Herbert Kalmbach, a principal fund-raiser for the Nixon reelection campaign, and George Spater, chairman and CEO of American Airlines.

At a dinner in New York on October 20, 1971, Kalmbach asked Spater for $100,000. Spater said he might be able to produce $75,000. Kalmbach said he hoped Spater would be able to do better than that. American Airlines was susceptible to such pressure because the company had at least 20 important matters pending before various federal agencies, among them a proposed merger between American and Western airlines. Spater says he and Kalmbach never discussed the merger or other airline business. But he was apprehensive; he knew that Kalmbach not only represented the President — who at that very moment had the merger matter on his desk — but also [in his private law practice] United Airlines, American's major competitor and a determined opponent of the merger. . . .

These terrors proved compelling and American paid its tithe. First $20,000 was paid out of personal funds. Then $100,000 was drawn on the airline's account at the Chemical Bank in New York and transmitted to the Swiss account of a Lebanese agent, Andre Tabourian (American had used him for other more legitimate transactions). The money was charged on American's books as "a special commission to Andre Tabourian in connection with used aircraft sales to Middle East Airlines." From Switzerland the money was transferred back to . . . New York. Later, Tabourian came to New York, withdrew the $100,000 in cash, and gave it to an American airlines official who put it in an office safe. In March 1972 Spater arranged for $55,000 — now "washed" of corporate contamination — to be removed from the safe, placed in an envelope, and delivered to the Nixon fund-raisers.

— *J. Anthony Lukas,* Nightmare *(New York: Viking, 1976),*
128–129.

In fact, they were so substantial that they dwarf the 1971 law they amended. In the "amendments" Congress scrapped the limits on advertising expenditures in the media and reimposed both contribution and spending limits; only the stiffened reporting requirements survived from 1971.

It is the consolidated legislation of the 1974 amendments that we know today as the FECA, the Federal Election Campaign Act. It still governs national campaign finance, for there have been very few important amendments to it. (Its most important provisions will be discussed at length in the chapters that follow; at this point a summary overview will suffice.) Its provisions, by major heading, were these:

• *Limits on Expenditures.* The FECA imposed extensive limits on what candidates for Congress and the presidency could spend in their campaigns. In addition, it limited what the candidates themselves could spend from their own resources on their own campaigns and what other groups and individuals could spend independently either to urge the election or the defeat of a candidate.

• *Limits on Contributions.* The FECA as amended set limits on individual contributions to candidates ($1000), on PAC contributions ($5000), and on contributions by party committees ($5000). It also set a total or overall contribution limit of $25,000 on individuals and complicated limits on the amounts party committees could spend "on behalf of" candidates of their party.

• *Enforcement.* For the first time, Congress created a special agency, the Federal Election Commission (FEC), to receive the reports of participants, to publicize data, and to enforce the statute by supplementary rules, by audits, and by various enforcement actions.

• *Public Funding.* Building on the 1971 creation of a fund produced by income tax check-offs, it designed two programs of public funding for presidential campaigns: one partial funding program during the presidential primary season and another program of full funding for the general election campaign.

• *Disclosure.* The 1974 amendments retained and strengthened the 1971 reporting requirements. Their effect and the usefulness of disclosure was, moreover, enhanced by the creation of the Federal Election Commission to gather and make the data easily available.

Most of the limits set in 1974 were "indexed" — that is, the amendments provided that they would rise as the Consumer Price Index (CPI) rose. The one major exception was the limits on contributions.

Finally, the Senate version of the bill had an additional provision for public funding of congressional campaigns. An amendment that would have added the same provision to the House bill lost on the floor of the House by a vote of 187–228. After a long battle in the conference committee, public funding for congressional campaigns was dropped from the final version, passed toward the end of 1974. Richard Nixon was no longer in the White House, and President Gerald Ford signed the bill.

V. The Buckley Decision and After

In its 1974 amendments to the FECA, Congress had provided for an easy challenge and expedited review of its handiwork by the federal courts. Very quickly an unlikely alliance of plaintiffs from the political right and left — including the American Conservative Union; James Buckley, Conservative senator from New York; Eugene McCarthy, pied piper of the Democratic left; and the New York Civil Liberties Union — obliged with a sweeping challenge in the U.S. District Court for the District of Columbia. In a matter of months, the Court of Appeals for the District of Columbia had upheld virtually all of the legislation; and the case was on its way to the Supreme Court. In January 1976 the Supreme Court handed down its decision, holding a substantial part of the amended FECA unconstitutional. Expedition had worked, at least superficially; the Supreme Court's decision came a little more than a year after the president signed the bill into law and well before it could take effect in even a single election campaign.

Nothing since the Court's decision in the case, *Buckley v. Valeo*,[30] approaches its significance in campaign finance. It is the only landmark case in the field. In deciding it, the Supreme Court for the first time swept campaign practices and the spending of money on campaigns under the protection of the First Amendment. In constraining those protected freedoms, the Court reasoned, Congress could act for only one purpose: to prevent corruption or the "appearance" of corruption. Applying its new-found explication of the First Amendment to the FECA before it, the Supreme Court

• struck down all limits on expenditures — whether by the candidate's campaign, by the candidate personally, or by others spending "independently" — as unacceptable restrictions on First Amendment freedoms;
• struck down the Federal Election Commission because the provision for Congress to appoint some of its members violated the separation of powers;
• upheld the constitutionality of the limits on PAC, party, and individual contributions to candidates and on party spending "on behalf of" them;
• upheld the constitutionality of the required reporting and then the making public of financial data on campaigns; and
• upheld the constitutionality of the two public funding programs for presidential and vice presidential candidates.

It was a decision that left a regulatory structure far different from one Congress had intended. The limits on contributions and the reporting requirements remained, but gone were all limits on campaign spending, on candidates' use of their own wealth, and on independent spending by people with no ties to the campaign (see Figure 2-2). Whatever the constitutional rationale, the Court left standing only a mangled torso of the FECA the Congress had written. Moreover, the decision had the effect of striking down expenditure limits in uncounted states, most of whose campaign finance laws, too, had been passed in the reformist zeal after Watergate.

[30]424 U.S. 1 (1976).

FIGURE 2-2
The FECA's Limits on Contributions and Expenditures in Congressional Campaign Finance

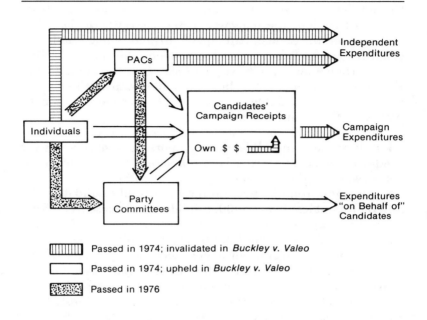

▦	Passed in 1974; invalidated in *Buckley v. Valeo*
☐	Passed in 1974; upheld in *Buckley v. Valeo*
▨	Passed in 1976

Note: A table with the amounts of limits can be found in Appendix B.

It was an easy matter for Congress to reconstitute the Federal Election Commission by providing that its members would be appointed by the president with the approval of the Senate, and it did so by spring 1976.[31] But as a way of maintaining some measure of congressional influence over the work of the FEC, it gave itself a veto over the rules of the commission. It also used the legislative opportunity to work some changes and adjustments in the FECA — altering and adding some contribution limits (e.g., a new limit of $5000 on individual contributions to PACs), tightening reporting requirements even further, and limiting PAC solicitations to members or to defined constituent groups.

[31]Pub. L. 94-283, 90 Stat. 475.

And there, for more than a decade, matters have stood with only a few changes. Attempts to stiffen the limitations on contributions, especially by PACs, have come to naught; one proposal to limit the total contributions any candidate could accept from PACs to $70,000 won narrowly in the House (217–198) but never passed the Senate. Attempts to extend public funding to congressional campaigns repeatedly failed. The only legislation of importance after 1976 was a series of amendments to the FECA passed in 1979; they passed because they were noncontroversial and thus supported by large majorities in both parties.[32] These amendments

• reduced and consolidated the reporting requirements for candidates and contributors, largely as a result of the burdens of "paperwork" in the elections of 1976 and 1978.

• exempted from the need to file reports all candidates who raised or spent less than $5000; candidates were also freed from the need to report in detail on contributions or expenditures of less than $200 (the earlier floor had been $100).

• exempted from reporting a set of activities by state and local party organizations that came to be known as "party building" activities; two of the most important were the provision of campaign materials such as brochures, buttons, bumper stickers, and similar materials, and the organization of attempts to register voters and get them to the polls.

The '79 amendments were, in short, both an exercise in fine tuning and the end of a legislative era.

In the absence of any genuinely major regulatory changes after 1974, one silent regulator was at work: inflation. Many of the limits in the 1974 legislation were indexed; but some were not, especially contribution limits and exemption limits. So the $1000 limit on individual contributions to candidates enacted in 1974 was twelve years later "worth" only about $450 in the purchasing power of 1986. And the reporting exemption for candidates raising or spending less than $5000, enacted in 1979 dollars, was "worth" only about $3,310 by 1986. The impact of

---

[32]Pub. L. 96-187, 93 Stat. 1339. As things have turned out, the party-building provisions are no longer noncontroversial; by 1984 they were at the center of the "soft money" controversy. More about that controversy later.

inflation on such "nonindexed" ceilings and floors from the middle '70s to the middle '80s was, of course, severe because of the severity of inflationary pressures. In just the dozen years between 1974 and 1986, the cost of living more than doubled; as measured by the CPI, it increased by 122 percent.

The absence of legislated change since the 1970s does not, however, mean the end of regulatory politics. Every session of Congress sees new bills and new hopes for a regulatory reform or innovation. We pick up their recent history in the last chapter of this book. But in a broader way, the entire remainder of the book is a spelling out of the history of American campaign finance after the mid-1970s.

3
The Source: Individual Contributions

Above all, the American way of campaign finance is voluntary and broadly based. To an extent unknown anywhere else in the world, it depends on the decisions of millions of citizens to channel some of their disposable resources into electoral combat. To be sure, there is a nonvoluntary element in the system — chiefly those campaigns financed in whole or in part with tax dollars — but it accounts for less than 10 percent of the money spent in national, state, and local campaigns in a presidential year.[1]0 All the rest comes as a result of decisions by a group of politically generous Americans. It is the largest group of American political activists and yet the one about which we know the least.

Contributing individuals put their money into the stream of campaigning in five ways (see Figure 1-1). The first three are in direct contributions to candidates, PACs, and political parties. The fourth is the route of independent spending, and the fifth is the contributions that individuals who are candidates give to their own campaigns. This rather simple set of options provides the structure for this and the following two chapters. All of the

---

[1]There may be other instances of nonvoluntary contributions to the stream of campaign finance — some "macing" of public salaries and some other contributions that are less than voluntary — but they no longer comprise very much of the money entering campaign politics.

options except the PAC and party options will occupy this chapter; PACs and parties will be the subject of the next two.

I. The Individual Contributors

Without question the greatest victory of the congressional reformers in writing the 1974 sections of the FECA was the end they wrote to the reign of the "fat cats." Individual contributors to congressional campaigns are limited to $1000 per candidate per election. In addition, they are subject to annual limitations: no more than $20,000 a year to party committees, no more than $5000 a year to a PAC, and a grand total of no more than $25,000 a year to all of the above taken together. At the same time, the means for reaching the small contributor blossomed and matured. So, restrictive legislation shares a role in ending the domination of the "big" contributor with the arts of computer-based mailing lists and direct mail solicitation.

Americans may argue whether a contributor of $25,000 to congressional campaigns or even the source of a single $1000 contribution can fairly be considered a "small" contributor. Suffice it to say that some small contributions are smaller than others. The changes worked since 1974 can perhaps better be expressed as an enormous broadening of the base of contributors in American campaign finance. Where there were once thousands, there are now millions of individuals contributing to parties, PACs, and candidates. We are, however, not sure how many millions — and we know even less about their motives and goals in giving.

Numbers first. The problem in counting the individual contributors to PACs, parties, and candidates begins with the FECA's requirement that recipients report only the names of contributors of $200 or more. Then, because of the sheer problem in aggregating and analyzing even those data, the FEC has reported totals only for contributions of $500 or more to candidates, PACs, and parties through 1984. Preliminary data for the 1986 cycle do not for whatever reason, contain even that information. The totals on receipts from individual contributors are reported only as undifferentiated totals. So, we have only limited information on individuals as sources of funds for candidates and their campaigns. Data in the states do not report total numbers of individual contributors, and in only a few instances do they report contributors above some threshold figure.[2]

Survey data ought to be a good deal more helpful; some are and some are not. In its survey of the American electorate, the Center for Political Studies (CPS) of the University of Michigan asked a sample of American adults this question in 1984:

> As you know, during an election year, people are often asked to make a contribution to support campaigns. During the past year did you give any money to an individual candidate, a political party organization, people supporting a ballot proposition, or to a particular issue or interest group?

A total of 242 respondents (out of 2,257) said they had.[3] That 10.7 percent of the sample, when applied to the voting age population of 169,963,000 in the country (according to Census Bureau estimates for 1984), yields a projected total of 18,186,000 contributors. If Herbert Alexander's projections that about $1.8 billion was spent in all of the 1984 elections — national, state, and local — are correct, that would mean an average contribution of a shade less than $100. This is a higher average than conventional wisdom would lead us to believe, but some reasonable adjustments can make the numbers credible.[4]

---

[2]Any author dreads making generalizations about the fifty states. This one and all that follow should be read as if they had a qualifying "to the best of my knowledge."

[3]*American National Election Study, 1984; Pre- and Post-Election Survey File.* These data and others from the various National Election Studies are made available through the Inter-University Consortium for Political and Social Research. Neither the Center for Political Studies nor the Inter-University Consortium bear any responsibility for the use I make of their data in this book.

[4]First, one can subtract ten percent or so from the $1.8 billion to account for the funds that enter the system by ways other than voluntary individual contribution. Then, realize the CPS data have traditionally overstated political activity in the United States; for example, they regularly show voting percentages some ten to twenty percentage points above the percentage of Americans actually voting, as measured by votes counted. So, one might reasonably reduce the reported contributors by at least ten percent. But on the other hand, the total expenditure estimates are for a two-year cycle, and the CPS question refers to "the past year." One then might inflate the total by twenty percent to account for the two years. A

"Yes" responses to CPS questions, however, have yielded some disturbingly varied data on contributions in the presidential years.

1952 —	3.7 percent	1972 —	12.9 percent
1956 —	7.0 percent	1976 —	9.4 percent
1960 —	11.5 percent	1980 —	11.2 percent
1964 —	9.0 percent	1984 —	10.7 percent
1968 —	7.6 percent		

The ebbs and flows aside, it is especially troubling that the percentage of self-identified contributors should be lower in 1984 than in 1960. All signs certainly point to an increasing number of contributors, even from 1976 or 1980 to 1984. Part of the problem may well be in the different wording of the questions about contributing money; a substantial part, too, may result from a very limited awareness about campaign finance on the part of many respondents. All this aside, the overriding issue is whether the data of the 1980s or those of the 1960s and 1970s are the more credible. The arithmetic of the last paragraph suggests that the more recent data are.[5]

So, it seems reasonable to talk of between 15 and 20 million contributors to all campaigns in the 1984 presidential election year. But who are they, personally and politically? Like other political activists, they are much better educated and wealthier than the average American (Table 3-1). In 1984, for instance, contributors were more than twice as likely to have completed a college degree than all respondents, and they came in significantly greater numbers from the highest status occupations. Not

ten percent decrease and a twenty percent increase nets to a ten percent increase. That increase in number of contributors would decrease the average contributor's outlay to an even more credible $60.20. Since many contributors give more than one contribution, that figure squares remarkably well with informal estimates of $40 or $50 as the size of the average contribution. Alexander's estimate is in his *Financing the 1984 Election* (Lexington, MA: Lexington, 1987), 83.

[5]In 1980 there was no single question on contribution, only separate questions on contributions to parties, PACs, and candidates. The percentage reported here is derived from those three questions for 1980. Ironically, it may well be the best indicator of contribution precisely for the reason of its more roundabout creation from more precise answers to more precise questions.

TABLE 3-1
Demographic and Political Characteristics of Contributors, Party Activists, and All Respondents: 1984

	Contributors	Party Activists	All Adults
1. % completing college	42.6%	31.1%	20.2%
2. % in professional, managerial occupation	40.5	29.0	20.8
3. % earning $30,000+	45.0	28.5	27.9
4. % white	92.6	85.5	73.7
5. % Republican	46.3	37.8	39.1
6. % very much interested in campaign	59.9	63.7	30.7
7. % voted in 1984	92.6	93.8	64.9
8. % seeing differences between parties	39.3	33.2	27.0

Source: Center for Political Studies, University of Michigan. Contributors are those responding positively to the question quoted in the text; party activists are those who said "yes" either to a question asking whether they attended a political meeting, rally, speech, or dinner or to a question about other miscellaneous activities in the campaign.

surprisingly, in view of their higher socioeconomic status, they are more Republican than the adult population as a whole. Finally, like the politically active of all kinds, contributors are more apt to be interested in politics and politically active in specific ways than adults in general.[6]

Just as interesting are the comparisons between contributors and the more traditional political activists (Table 3-1). The comparison leads to two conclusions. Contributors are, first, somewhat more middle or upper middle class than the usual political activists. In income, education, and occupation — the three surest indicators of socioeoconomic status — they are distinctly higher status than the activists. Second, their levels of political commitment and knowledge appear to be very similar to those of the traditional activists.

For all of the political activity that these millions of contribu-

[6]These findings for 1984 are entirely consistent with those from the 1980 CPS data reported by Ruth S. Jones and Warren E. Miller, "Financing Campaigns: Macro Level Innovation and Micro Level Response," *Western Political Quarterly,* vol. 38 (June 1985), 187–210.

tors engage in, there is precious little explanation. We know very little about how they come to give. Yes, they are increasingly solicited by mail, and their meals are increasingly interrupted by telephone solicitations. Data from 1984 suggest what we might expect about the incidence and frequency of various forms of solicitations. Of the 242 self-identified contributors in the University of Michigan national survey, 194 reported receiving mail solicitations, 55 were solicited by phone, and 61 in face-to-face contact. But while 34.5 responded to the mail and 36.4 to the phone, 72.1 responded positively to the personal solicitation.[7] But knowing the occasion for the contribution is not to know *why* it was given. We have no hard data with which to answer that question; but not knowing is, as always, an invitation to speculation.

Unquestionably the 15 million or more individuals who contribute cash to American electoral politics do so for a great variety of reasons. Even the individual contributor often gives for a curious mixture of reasons. For many of them, the nonpolitical reasons are potent, even dominant. Many give simply because they are asked, a premise on which a good deal of American fundraising of all kinds rests. The request for money activates some generalized, even vague, feeling of loyalty or sympathy, whether for the cause or the solicitor. Or for a number of reasons it may simply be hard to say "no." The data on the success rate of personal solicitation is apposite, and in their study of individual contributors Jones and Miller come to a similar conclusion.

> It must be recognized that while few contributions are forced or involuntary, the decision to contribute through one avenue rather than another may be less a matter of deliberate choice among alternatives and more a matter of ad hoc response to a direct solicitation from one of several competing organizations. [8]

For other contributors the nonpolitical motive springs from loyalty to a corporation, a membership organization, or a labor

---

[7]The data come from the 1984 study of the University of Michigan's CPS. The contributors were those responding positively to the omnibus question about giving to "an individual candidate, a political party organization, people supporting a ballot proposition, or to a particular issue or interest group."

[8]Jones and Miller, 200.

THE URGE TO CONTRIBUTE

A large number of PACs and party committees raising money by direct mail appeals concede that they raise disproportionately large sums of money from senior citizens. This fact invites speculation about reasons — greater disposable income, the voluntaristic ethos of their generation, deepening issue or ideological commitments, greater personal fears and insecurities. Every now and then a story surfaces about contributing that seems driven, almost compulsive. There is no reason to think they are anything but isolated instances, but they add a tragic footnote to the upbeat story of American political voluntarism.

> Cornelia Egan Alley, of Springfield, Ill., recently complained to the Washington Post that a flood of Republican and conservative fundraising letters persuaded her 84-year-old mother to spend all her savings.
>
> "For 30 years, my mother has given to the Republican Party," Alley said. "After my father died in 1979, she let the party interests fill a void left by him. For the past seven years, she . . . sent the requested donations to the tune of $20,000 annually."
>
> Now "bedridden in a nursing home," Alley's mother spends her time "in a constant scramble for money to send to those 'poor people' who supposedly need her help. She often spends hours in tears because she can no longer afford to help. Many of the letters are frightening and horrifying in their dramatic appeals for help. . . ."
>
> Alley said that in the spring she wrote to all 127 organizations asking that her mother's name be removed from their lists . . .
>
> The mail continues coming in at "a pound a day," however, and only two of the 127 organizations have written back to say they are taking her name off their mailing lists, Alley said.
>
> *From an article by Thomas B. Edsall, "Democratic Party Skirted the Edge of Solvency at Mid-Year," Washington Post (Aug. 12, 1985).*

union. PACs rely heavily on those motives. And for yet others, the reason for contribution may lie in the attractiveness of the fundraising event itself — the ambience, the entertainment, the food, opportunity to make business contacts, the small talk with the famous or near-famous.

For the politically motivated, the contribution may support a like-minded candidate or a cause passionately believed in (see box); or it may be made consciously to seek access to or recognition by the holder (or would-be holder) of a public office. But however political the individual contributor may be, it is unlikely that he or she approaches the strategic acumen that parties or PACs do at their greatest effectiveness. For one thing, individuals are much more apt to contribute to local candidates; thus they choose among a much more restricted set of choices. Moreover, PACs and parties have the expertise, political awareness, and long institutional memories that form a capacity for political strategies and tactics. That capacity is indeed one important reason why individuals organized into political aggregates for any reason are more effective and more influential than individuals acting alone.

One gets another insight into the distinction between "political" and "nonpolitical" contributions by looking at the differences among individuals who give to parties, to PACs, and directly to candidates (Table 3-2). The contributors to parties and candidates are in most ways similar; but the contributors to PACs seem to be atypical. All of the clues in Table 3-2 suggest that contributors to PACs ("groups") are less political than the contributors to candidates and to parties; it is very likely their motives for contributing are also less clearly political. The differences also suggest that the contributors who give to PACs may do so to limit the "costs" of contributing by reducing the extent of the political decisions inherent in the contribution. For them, that is, the contribution to a PAC may well be made for the very reason that the contributor can leave the political choices to the management of the PAC.

One important ingredient in the mix of motives and incentives for contributions to campaign politics was for long the tax credit individuals could claim on their U.S. income tax returns. Taxpayers could subtract from their income tax liabilities one-half of the value of political contributions to candidates, PACs, and party committees up to a total of $50 for individuals and $100 for married couples filing joint returns. The provision applied to

TABLE 3-2

Comparisons Among Contributors to Parties, Groups, and Candidates: 1982°

% Who:	Gave to Groups	Gave to Candidates	Gave to Parties	All Adults
Went to political meetings	18%	49%	37%	9%
Reported voting in 1982	78	91	94	60
"Very much" interested in campaign	45	60	65	26
"Very much" interested in outcome of cong'l'election	37	54	56	21
Followed gov't, public affairs "most of the time"	43	60	75	28

°The data are from the Center for Political Studies, University of Michigan. Since the original question used the noun "group" rather than "PAC," it is used here. Data for 1982 are used because of a fuller and more discriminating set of questions on contributions than the CPS has subsequently used. This table also appeared originally in Frank J. Sorauf, "Who's in Charge? Accountability in Political Action Committees," *Political Science Quarterly*, vol. 99 (Winter 1984–85), 597.

contributions at the state and local levels as well as the national.[9] The provision was, however, repealed in the massive overhaul of the Internal Revenue Code in 1986. We have no real idea of its effect in encouraging individuals to contribute — no idea of its role or impact in the system of campaign finance. We only know that in 1984 some 5.1 million taxpayers claimed a total credit of $257.4 million, which represented only half of their contributions up to an individual limit of $100. Whatever the value of these numbers as an incentive, it seems improbable that it was negligible. It may be, indeed, that the repeal of the tax credit will materially change American campaign funding. At the very least, it will probably accelerate the trend from smaller to larger individual contributions. We can only wait and see.

The individual's decision whether to contribute cash to a party, a PAC, or a candidate is a crucial one for the system of campaign finance, for it is a decision whether the individual contributor will maintain control over his or her dollar as it enters campaign politics. Money that goes to the parties and the PACs enters a second stage of political decision-making, one that is

[9] 26 U.S. Code, chap. 1, subchap. A, part IV, sec. 41.

more national than local, more political than nonpolitical, more purposeful than casual — one that is, to sum it up, more likely to be politically "rational." This distinction also organizes the rest of this chapter and the next two. The rest of this chapter deals with the money that individuals control directly, and the next two chapters deal with the funds of PACs and the parties.

II. The Candidates' Sources: an Overview

With all the rest of campaign finance, the total amount of cash entering congressional campaign politics has increased dramatically since the 1976 campaign. It has, in fact, more than quadrupled. Total receipts for all congressional candidates in 1976 were $104,870,597; the net receipts in 1986 were $471,448,960.[10] Even if one discounts for the increase in the Consumer Price Index from 1976 to 1986, that is a 133 percent increase in real dollars. (Expenditure totals do not differ much from totals on receipts, either in sums or in patterns of growth.) It is the increases in these totals that have so many people upset about the status quo in campaign finance.

The line of the increases in receipts has not, however, been straight (Table 3-3). A brief scanning of the receipt totals from 1976, the first year of FEC data gathering, to 1986 invites two observations. First, the rate of increases was considerably greater in the late 1970s than it was in the middle '80s. In fact, between 1982 and 1984, it appeared that the engines of American campaign finance were slowing down. The total receipts of candidates for the House increased in those two years only from $213.2 million to $222.5 million, and their expenditures actually dropped by one-fifth of a percent. Increases in Senate receipts continued, but at a rate slower than in previous two-year cycles. The rate of growth then picked up between 1984

[10]The FEC published only a single total for receipts in 1976. It was apparently a gross figure, and it included only major party candidates in the general election. In subsequent years it published both net and gross receipt totals for all candidates. For the years after 1976, I have used the more accurate net receipt totals, here and elsewhere in the text. In this case, in order to give a fuller picture of the total sums in national campaign finance in 1984, I have also shifted to a total for all candidates. The effect of using a less inclusive datum for 1976, of course, is to exaggerate the growth between that year and 1986 a little bit.

TABLE 3-3
Receipts of All Congressional Candidates, 1976–1986 (all figures in millions)

	Totals	Increase°	% Increase
1976	$104.9		
1978	199.4	$ 94.5	90.1
1980	248.8	49.4	24.8
1982	354.7	105.3	42.3
1984	397.2	42.5	12.0
1986	471.4	74.2	18.7

°The increase is the difference between receipts in the present and the preceding cycles.

and 1986, although it remained lower than it had been earlier. However, if one corrects for inflation, much of the difference disappears. In 1978 dollars, all receipts increased 20.2 percent from 1978 to 1982; and in 1982 dollars, they increased 16.6 percent from 1982 to 1986. Second, there is a decided pattern to the growth of funds available to congressional candidates. The growth is considerably greater in the off-years, those years in which there is no presidential campaign. This fact suggests that the funding of presidential campaigns and the attention they get diminishes the amount of money available to congressional candidates. In 1984, for example, even though the main campaigns for the presidency were publicly funded, individuals and PACs contributed $64 million to the candidates in the preconvention period.

And from where does the money come? It is certainly one of the better kept secrets of American politics that individual contributions made directly to them are and always have been the candidates' major source of funds (Table 3-4). Even in the absence of specific totals in 1978 on either individual contributions or those of the candidates themselves, one can accept the common estimate that the candidates themselves accounted for about 10 or 12 percent of their resources and then, by subtraction, conclude that individual contributors gave two-thirds of candidate receipts in 1978. PACs have always been in second place, followed by the candidate's own resources and the direct

TABLE 3-4
Funding Sources for All House and Senate Candidates, 1978–1986

	1978 sum (millions)	percent	1986 sum (millions)	percent
Individuals	°	65.0	$218.2	56.7
PACs	$34.1	17.1	105.3	28.0
Candidates	°	10.0	34.0	6.2
Parties	6.3	3.1	6.6	1.1

°The FEC did not separate individual and candidate spending before 1984. The percentages assigned to them are estimates and are explained in the text.

contributions of party committees. In the four elections since 1978, that pattern has remained stable — far more than one would imagine from much of the media coverage — but there has been a slow but steady shift in the percentages. The rise in the importance of PAC contributions has been matched by the compensating decline in the share provided by individual contributors. Party contributions declined, although party spending "on behalf of" candidates rose in the same period (that spending will be dealt with later). Candidate self-subsidy remained more or less the same.[11]

If one pares down the reports to those of the major party candidates running in the general elections, the totals are inevitably smaller; but the portions of the sources remain pretty much the same. The PAC percentage for 1984 does jump from 28 percent to 31.2 percent because PACs do not give much money to primary losers, noncandidates, and minor party contestants. The percentage accounted for by candidate contributions and loans drops significantly, from 6.2 to 1.8 percent. It is the reverse of the PAC effect — the candidates that PACs do not support must often pay more of their bills themselves.

[11]Quick arithmetic on the percentages in Table 3-4 will show that the totals equal something less than 100 percent. In fact the total for 1986 is only 92 percent. The rest is accounted for by a miscellany of other sources, the chief ones being transfers from other candidates, loans from sources other than the candidate, money from refunds (e.g., deposits refunded), and earned income (e.g., interest on campaign funds invested for the period between receipt and expenditure).

A NOTE ON THE NUMBERS

Ordinarily one buries questions of data and definitions deeply in foot-notes or abstruse appendices. Appendix A to this book serves that purpose in most instances. A certain amount of facing the realities of the numbers explicitly and "up front" is, however, necessary. This place serves well for one digression on the distinction between "all candi-dates" and various subsets of candidates, a distinction employed in the nearby text.

The Federal Election Commission's definition of "all candidates" is, not surprisingly, its most inclusive category; but one must be clear that it includes a number of "candidates" who never appeared on the gen-eral election ballot and, indeed, may never have appeared on any ballot. The "all candidates" category, that is, includes data from the re-ports of every individual who during the two years of an election cycle meets the FECA's definition of a "candidate" — candidates from the previous election cycle retiring debts, losers in the primaries, losers in the state conventions in those states still picking candidates in them, some candidates who sent up unsuccessful trial balloons, a few candi-dates who because of death never made it from a primary victory to the general election, *and* those candidates who did run in the general election.

The FEC also publishes data on "candidates in the general election," a limited and self-evident group. (It is possible in most of the data sets of the FEC to limit this group even further to *major party* candidates in the general election.) In any event, these totals do include candidates' fi-nance in the primary or other nomination struggle as well as their getting and spending in the general election. That is, the total includes all transactions the general election candidates made during the entire election cycle. It would even include activity in the cycle aimed at retir-ing debts from the last one.

Even though one complicates things for the reader by shifting from one set of data to another, different ones are more appropriate for differ-ent purposes. For instance, if one wants to describe the total sums of campaign money employed in a cycle, one uses the finances of "all can-didates." On the other hand, if one is interested in the average cost of contesting a seat for the House, one should probably limit oneself to the expenditures of major party candidates who made it into the general election. It serves no purpose to include candidates who never at-tempted to run in that year, and the inclusion of underfinanced independent and minor party candidates only lowers the average some-what misleadingly.

Aggregate totals, however, often conceal important varia-tions within the aggregate. One easily describes the contribu-tors to all races for the Congress (Table 3-4); but the mix of contributors to Senate and House races, for instance, differs considerably. In 1986 House candidates got 34 percent of their receipts from PACs; Senatorial candidates received only 21 per-cent. (The figures were 34 and 17 in 1984.) But on the other hand, campaigns for the Senate took in 65.4 percent of receipts from individual contributors; those for the House took only 49.5 percent. Such differences suggest diversities in the nature of campaigns and candidacies for the two houses; they also sug-gest that different kinds of contributors view races for each of the two houses differently.[12]

The diversities in fund-raising patterns between Democrats and Republicans are less dramatic, although the differences are not of the sort that popular political stereotypes would predict. Republicans get a significantly greater part of their money in party contributions. Democrats took only seven-tenths of a per-cent of their receipts from party committees in 1986, while Republicans took 1.4 percent. (Again, these percentages reflect only the parties' direct contributions to candidates and not their spending on their behalf.) Republicans also depended more on individuals, receiving 61.7 percent of their money from them, against the Democrats' 51.6 percent. On the other hand, Demo-crats depended more on PAC receipts (32.3 to 24.0 percent) and on their candidates' own resources (7.4 to 4.8 percent).

It is the differences among funding patterns for incumbents, challengers, and open seat candidates that are the genuine stun-ners. These are also differences that have the most profound implications for electoral politics and electoral competition. The differences for 1986 are shown in Table 3-5. There are small

---

[12]The differences between House and Senate campaign finance are explored at greater length in chap. 6.

TABLE 3-5

Sources of Receipts for All House and Senate Candidates, 1986 (in millions of dollars)*

Sources	Incumbents		Challengers		Open Seat	
	$$	%	$$	%	$$	%
Individuals	$132.4	55.2	$68.9	59.3	$66.1	57.4
PACs	89.5	37.3	19.2	16.6	23.5	20.4
Candidates°°	−1.5	.0	15.6	13.4	14.1	12.3
Parties	1.9	.8	1.9	1.7	1.2	1.0

°Percentages total to less than 100 percent because of other sources of campaign financing, the two most important of which are loans and interest earned on invested funds.

°°Candidate contributions are defined as candidate contributions to the campaign plus candidate loans to it minus candidate loans repaid. The negative figure in the Incumbents column results from the repayment of loans from earlier elections.

differences in reliance on individual and party contributions, but massive differences in PAC and candidate funding. Indeed, these two sources are virtual mirror images of each other; if the PACs do not provide, the candidates apparently have to. If one source of funding will not take political risks, others must.

All of these paragraphs, to recap, have described the receipts of the candidates themselves. In 1986 they totaled $471.4 million, of which $450.1 million was spent before the end of the two year cycle. While that $450.1 million dominates the direct political expenditures of the congressional campaigns, there were two other kinds (see Table 3-5). PACs, other groups, and individuals spent $8.5 million independently to urge the election or defeat of candidates, and party committees spent $23.2 million "on behalf of" candidates of their party. The PAC and party funds, of course, originally came from individual contributions. Candidate spending, in other words, accounted for 93.4 percent of the money spent directly on the 1986 campaigns for Congress.

III. Individual Contributions to Candidates

With the survey of the sources of candidates' money behind us, we return to the direct contributions of individuals to candidates. In the new era of campaign finance, these contributions have regularly accounted for more than half of the receipts of congressional candidates. The percentage has, however, slipped gradually in the 1980s; in the 1986 campaigns it stood at 56.7 percent. For House candidates individual contributors actually accounted for a bit less than half of all receipts. Nonetheless, they stand as the collective cornerstone of American campaign finance; their contributions a monument both to citizen participation and to the refinements of American political fund-raising.

Once again even an approximate count of individual contributors to specific campaigns does not come easily. Occasionally a candidate will make a fuller report on individual contributors; Sen. David Durenberger, a Republican from Minnesota, disclosed that in his 1982 campaign for reelection he received contributions from 34,200 persons, a number when divided into his receipts from individuals yields an average of about $120 per contributor.[13] But such scraps of data are rare, and they help us very little in assembling a broader picture.

For the individual contributions to congressional campaigns in 1984, we have only two guideposts: the grand total of all contributions was $218.2 million, and 110,108 individuals gave $500 or more for a total of $81.5 million. (Remember that candidates do not have to report the names of contributors or sizes of contributions smaller than $200 and that for practical reasons the FEC provided breakdowns of contributors and contributions only for sums of $500 or greater through 1984.) By subtraction, then, the individual contributions of less than $500 totaled $136.7 million. If one assumes that these contributions averaged at $50, there were 2,734,000 contributions. When one combines that total with the 110,000 "big" contributors and then reduces the total for contributors who made more than one contribution, one has a total of somewhat more than 2 mil-

[13]Senate Committee on Rules and Administration, *Hearings on Campaign Reform Proposals of 1983* (Jan. 26-27, May 17, Sept. 29, 1983); Senate Hearing 98-588; 98th Cong., 1st sess., 128–132.

lion individual contributors directly to congressional candidates. If one assumes an average "under $500" contribution of $30, the same arithmetic produces an adjusted total of more than 4 million contributors.

There are far more solid data, however, for saying that the average size of the individual contribution has increased in recent years at a rate much greater than inflation. House and Senate campaigners actually received smaller amounts of money in portions of less than $100 in 1982 than they did in 1978 after adjusting the totals for inflation. The drop was 17 percent among House candidates and 44 percent among those for the Senate. On the other hand, after similar adjustments, the $100 to $500 gifts rose 107 and 72 percents respectively, and those above $500 increased 84 and 75 percent.[14] More recent data find the decline of the individual contribution under $100 continuing in 1984 and 1986.[15]

The rising importance of larger individual contributions can be shown in another way. In 1978 individual contributions of more than $500 accounted for 16.5 percent of all money all congressional candidates received. By 1984, even though all individual contributions accounted for less of the total receipts, those over $500 accounted for 20.5 percent of all receipts of the congressional candidates.

How does one explain the decline of the "small" contribution? Without a doubt part of the explanation rests in reduced solicitation of the small contributor. The "costs" of raising money in small sums — whether one thinks of costs as time, cash, or energy — are simply too great for many candidates, especially when the cost-benefit ratio is so much more favorable in larger contributions from PACs and more generous individuals. Richard Conlon speculates that contributor cynicism is also at work. He cites the

[14]Richard P. Conlon, "A New Problem in Campaign Financing . . . And a *Simple Legislative Solution,*" paper delivered at the annual meeting of the American Political Science Association, Sept. 1, 1984. Mr. Conlon is the executive director of the Democratic Study Group (DSG) in the House of Representatives. His paper rests on DSG research into a sample of candidate reports to the FEC; the FEC reported data only on contributors of more than $500 in 1982 and 1984.

[15]Richard P. Conlon, "The Declining Role of Individual Contributions in Financing Congressional Campaigns," *Journal of Law and Politics,* vol. 3 (Winter 1987), 467–498.

growing feeling among average citizens that their small contributions are meaningless given the enormous sums needed to run a campaign, the flood of big contributions coming from Washington-based PACs, and the trend toward $1,000-a-person fundraising events.[16]

It may also be the case — to continue the speculation — that some individuals have reacted to these facts by increasing the size of their contribution, by "raising the ante" as the other bidders did. It is also possible that sheer affluence and increased expectations are at work here — that the $50 contribution has gone the way of the $50 hotel room.

Parallel to the question of the size of the individual contribution is the question of its geography. Again, the data are very meager. Traditionally one has thought of individual contributions as coming from the constituency of the candidate. Individual contributors thus were individuals who could vote in the race in which they were involved; out-of-state and out-of-district money was associated with PACs and "the interests." There is some reason to think, however, that greater numbers of individual contributions are now crossing state and district lines, especially in Senate campaigns. Senatorial races and their candidates achieve a national visibility that can translate into national fund-raising. In the 1984 senatorial race in North Carolina between Gov. James Hunt and incumbent Sen. Jesse Helms, both candidates, by all accounts, drew heavily on individual contributions from all over the country. Unquestionably, media-created celebrity and direct-mail solicitation techniques make it increasingly possible to reach generous individuals across state lines. Perhaps, indeed, that may explain part of the drift to larger sums in individual contributions.

There is little evidence of the goals and strategies of the individual contributors to congressional candidates. One certainly infers them with great difficulty from the patterns of their giving. They do tend to prefer incumbents, but so do all other contributors. Their support for incumbents, though, may be less purposeful than PAC support — it may result simply from the appeal of the well-known name and the visible personality.

The wisdom of campaigning has long claimed that individuals

16Ibid., 479.

tend to give later rather than earlier in the election cycle, because (so it has been said) the election and its campaign become salient only in the last, climactic months. In this instance the data do not support the working wisdom. By June 30, 1986 — at the end of the eighteenth month of the twenty-four month cycle — candidates for Congress reported receiving 58 percent of their receipts as of then from individuals. (Remember that by the end of the cycle individual contributions accounted for 56.7 percent of all receipts.) It may be, of course, that the eighteenth-month barrier is too late a measure of "early"; some PAC contributions do come in within the first four or six months of the campaign. For now, however, the case on the timing of individual contributions simply is not proven. The major drawback to individual contributions — from the candidate's viewpoint — remains their average size. The "costs" of raising $2,000 in ten or twenty pieces are, all other things being equal, much greater than raising it in a single contribution from a PAC.

One should keep in mind that individuals may also contribute their services to campaigns as volunteers. While a candidate must report receiving $1,000 in cash, or even the equivalent of $1,000 in the use of an airplane or auto, as a contribution to the campaign, the candidate does not have to report the gift of $1,000 worth of a volunteer's time or skills. The FECA excludes volunteer activity from its definition of a contribution.[17] The rationale for the distinction clearly has something to do with American suspicions of cash transactions and American celebrations of volunteer participation. Cash is bad and participation is good, even if it is not altogether clear why. Certainly one persistent rationale pivots around the assumption that the search for access or influence is more apt to accompany the cash contribution than it is the volunteered effort.

That key assumption is not, however, self-evident or very well supported. Many legislators have found the cash contributor no more demanding than the volunteer worker. Moreover, what we know about these two groups suggests that the activist is just as attentive to politics as the contributor (Table 3-1). The worker in the campaign will surely be from the district; the individual con-

---

[17]"The term 'contribution' does not include the value of services provided without compensation by any individual who volunteers on behalf of a candidate or political committee." 2 U.S. Code, chap. 14, subchap. I, sec. 431 (8)(B)(i).

tributor, especially the contributor to Senate campaigns, is increasingly likely not to be a voter in the election (or in future ones). The volunteer worker is, at the least, apt to persuade and mobilize other voters in the constituency.

IV. The Individual as Independent Spender

In writing the legislation of 1971 and 1974, Congress tried valiantly to close one of the great loopholes in the 1925 Corrupt Practice Act: the freedom from limitation of those expenditures made without the knowledge or consent of the candidate. It had been for almost a half century perhaps the largest of the loopholes, one that undid limitations on the sums of campaign money at all levels of government. First, Congress required every candidate to have a candidate's committee, the activities of which the candidate was required by law to be aware. Then, it placed limits on how much any other group or individual could spend *without* the knowledge, consent, or cooperation of the candidate. The FECA amendments of 1974 limited these makers of "independent expenditures" to the same limits an individual contributor had to observe: $1,000 per candidate per election campaign.

It was only one of a number of well-laid plans that the Supreme Court demolished in *Buckley v. Valeo* when it struck down all limitations on campaign expenditures.[18] Individuals and groups thus were freed to spend as much as they wished to urge the election or defeat of a candidate, as long as they did so without the knowledge or collusion of the candidate or the candidate's committee. As things evolved, independent spending from 1976 to 1986 was much heavier in presidential than in congressional campaigns and far more the province of groups (especially PACs) than individuals.[19]

---

[18]Actually, the Court only struck down the limits on independent expenditures in congressional elections in *Buckley*. Congress subsequently limited independent expenditures in presidential campaigns in which the candidate opted for public funding and thus invoked the spending limit on himself. The Court finally struck that limitation down in *FEC v. National Conservative Political Action Committee*, 470 U.S. 480 (1985).

[19]Independent spending by PACs is described in the next chapter, that in presidential campaigns in chap. 7.

Indeed, with one conspicuous exception, individual spenders account for virtually nothing of the independent expenditures in congressional campaigns (see box). The exception is a Los Angeleno named Michael Goland. Goland spent more than a

---

THE ENIGMATIC MICHAEL GOLAND

Although he is for now the record-setter in individual independent spending, Michael Goland's motives remain a matter of speculation. A report in Illinois' major newspaper at the time of the spending in the Percy-Simon race probes the question.

> Goland, 37, a childhood polio victim who lost the use of his left arm, is described as "very private" and "intense" by friends who know him, primarily through Jewish political and philanthropic organizations.
>
> "He's a very serious person. He has strong feelings on certain issues that couldn't be categorized by one political label," said Edward Robin, a Los Angeles attorney. . . .
>
> "It doesn't surprise me that he's so involved," Robin said. "Michael has had a high Jewish identity, and a lot of people in the Jewish community don't feel that Percy is a supporter of Israel."
>
> Yet Goland said Percy's stance toward Israel is not one of his top priorities.
>
> "That's a Percy-created smoke screen, that I'm a part of some Jewish-Israel conspiracy or Jewish-conservative conspiracy. I'm none of that," he said. . . .
>
> Goland said he is campaigning against Percy because of his own interest in aid to the handicapped and to education. . . .
>
> The [television] spot that has created the most controversy features a chameleon that crawls across the television screen and changes colors while an announcer says, "We haven't learned Percy's true colors, but we have learned that the U.S. Senate is no place for a chameleon."

— *R. Bruce Dold, "Private Percy foe spends half-million,"* Chicago Tribune *(Oct. 22, 1984)*

million dollars ($1,100,740, to be precise) to urge the voters of Illinois to defeat Sen. Charles Percy, a Republican, in his 1984 campaign for reelection. By the most reliable accounts, as an ardent supporter of Israel, he was unhappy with Percy's positions on the Middle East as chairman of the Senate Foreign Relations Committee. Goland himself denied the Israel connection, but neither he nor his campaign provided strong alternative explanations. Senator Percy lost the election to the Democratic challenger, Paul Simon, by less than two-tenths of a percent of the vote; but whether Goland's independent spending had anything to do with the outcome is impossible to say. It did, however, set a record; no individual spending in a congressional race has ever approached it. In fact, the next largest sum spent in 1983–84 was the modest $39,967 that James C. Moore spent urging the election of Lloyd Doggett as the next Texas senator.

Aside from Goland's million in 1984, independent spending by individuals is thus very sparse. There was a small upsurge in spending by a number of individuals in the Texas senatorial race in 1984 — two individuals spent a total of about $60,000 urging the election of two different candidates. They and Michael Goland do not, however, make a trend. Even with the extraordinary spending by Goland, all individuals spent independently only $1,172,439 in all 1984 elections for the House and Senate, only about 20 percent of all the $6 million spent independently on them. Excluding Goland's spending, other individuals accounted for just a bit more than a single percent of the $6 million. And in 1986 individual independent spending totaled only a paltry $36,288.

V. The Candidate Funds the Candidate

The candidate is the contributor of last resort. When all other sources of money fail, he or she unlocks the family checkbook or, worse still, remortgages the house or arranges loans from friends or the local bank. While candidate money in 1984 accounted for only 8.5 percent of the receipts of congressional candidates, it accounted for 14 percent of the resources of all challengers, 23 percent of receipts of open seat candidates, and

31 percent of the resources of losers in the primary. Incumbents, on the other hand, do not have to dip into the family treasury; in a balance of debts and payments, their own funds account for none of their receipts. Since incumbent candidates are usually winners, it follows that losers fund more of their own campaigns than do winners. The visibility and credibility of a candidate that we associate with probable victory is the same visibility and credibility that endears the candidate to financial contributors.

A close look at candidate self-financing for 1984, for example, shows that $13.8 million of the $34 million spent by all candidates from their own resources was spent by candidates who never reached the general election (Table 3-6). In the House races, in fact, the nongeneral-election candidates spent almost as much money of their own as did the House general election candidates. Among those candidates who ran in the general election, the major self-financing was by challengers for House seats and by Senate open seat candidates, a difference between the two houses that reflects the dismal prospects of House challengers and the vastly greater cost of a Senate open seat campaign.

TABLE 3-6
Reliance on Funds of Candidate, 1983–84°

	Gen. Elec. Cands.	Nongen. Elec. Cands.	Totals
House			
Incumbents	−$1,339,006	−$58,162	−$1,397,168
Challengers	6,033,875	3,064,448	9,098,323
Open Seats	1,949,533	4,459,095	6,408,628
Senate			
Incumbents	291,789	—	291,789
Challengers	980,419	3,051,045	4,031,464
Open Seats	12,229,658	3,287,917	15,517,575
Total:	20,146,268	13,804,343	33,950,611

°Candidates' funds are the net of candidate contributions to their own campaigns plus their loans to their own campaigns minus their reports of repayments of their personal loans.

The negative figure for House incumbents need some explanation. The FEC reports on self-financing include three totals: candidate contributions, candidate loans, and repayment of candidate loans. A net total is best approximated by adding the first two and then subtracting the third from that total. Apparently in the 1983–84 election cycle, House members retired enough debts from 1982, while obligating themselves scarcely at all in 1984, to produce the aggregate negative figure. It is just one more indication of the increasing ability of incumbents, especially in the House, to raise campaign money from sources other than themselves.

Once again there are data problems that deserve mention. First, the 1983–84 election cycle was the first one in which the FEC ventured totals for candidates' contributions and loans to their own campaigns. One cannot, therefore, make comparisons with earlier years. Second, there is undoubtedly an unavoidable degree of overestimation in the FEC's data on self-financing. The candidate loans do indeed largely become their own contributions as they are forced to pay them off themselves. But some candidates, especially those who have won, manage to retire them after the end of the reporting cycle with postelection contributions from PACs and individuals.

Candidate self-financing is also one of those special corners of American campaign finance in which one set of myths about money meets another set. Given the escalating costs of campaigning, men and women of great wealth (it is said) can draw on their own resources and "buy" their way into public office. In fact, a number of observers have suggested that this fear was a major motivation in Congress behind the FECA limitations on a candidate's use of his or her own resources to the same $1,000 per campaign limit of other individual contributors. (The $1,000 limit was, of course, struck down in *Buckley v. Valeo*.)

In 1970, for example, Rep. Richard Ottinger, a Democrat from New York, spent nearly a million dollars of his and his family's fortune in his unsuccessful race against better known candidates in the Democratic primary for the U.S. Senate. In the same year, millionaire Howard Metzenbaum, then a political unknown, defeated John Glenn for the Democratic Senate nomination in Ohio. In both cases the candidates spent large sums of their own money in media campaigns to make themselves and their names visible. Nor have such instances disappeared. In 1982 in Minnesota, Mark Dayton, young heir to a department store fortune and married to the granddaughter of John D. Rockefeller, set a record for self-financing by providing $6.8 million of his total receipts of $7.2 million. The record was soon eclipsed by a famous in-law, Gov. Jay Rockefeller of West Virginia, who spent $10.3 million of his own on a successful quest for a Senate seat.

The spending of millions of dollars on media campaigns for name (and face) recognition inevitably chills the candidate and office-holder without vast personal resources. But it is a great leap from that fear to a more general concern that personal fortunes buy their way into Congress. Three points are important. In the first place, Ottinger lost the primary and both Metzenbaum and Dayton lost in their respective general elections. The failure of a candidate to raise money from the usual external sources is often a reflection of potential contributors' assessments of the candidate's prospects for election in the first place. "Losers" often are self-financed, and self-financed candidates are losers. Second, the fears of the early 1970s resulted in great measure from an underestimation of the power of incumbents to raise campaign money to cope with challengers with personal fortunes. The rate of incumbent spending in the past decade has made that almost too clear. And finally, the whole concern about the challenger with money is often an incumbent's worry about competition of any kind. While we may not expect incumbents to cherish competition, the rest of us can; and the candidate's own resources may be one way to make the election competitive.

Data again provide the best antidote to the myth. Candidates simply do not often spend themselves to victory with their own money. In 1984 a total of seventeen candidates for the Senate spent $200,000 or more of their own money in the campaign; only two were elected (Rockefeller and John Kerry of Massachusetts), and eight of them never even survived the primary. Of the seven first-time winners of Senate seats in 1984, four spent none of their money (Gore, Gramm, Harkin, and McConnell) and one (Simon) spent $1,000. In that same year, eleven candidates for the House spent $200,000 or more of their resources; none won seats and six never even made it into the general election. All fifty-one of the first-time winners to enter the House in 1984 showed average receipts of $443,062, with an average sum of $32,539 from their own resources — some 7.3 percent of their receipts from themselves.

The reality of self-financing, therefore, suggests more modest fears and conclusions. In many cases challengers *do* have to provide their own resources, especially for "start up" costs. The sums they need are not usually the sums of millionnaires, but even appealing candidates with good prospects must provide the sums we associate with the affluent middle class. The prospect of losing $20,000, $30,000, or $40,000 of one's assets may well give potential candidates some pause. Moreover, there is the additional possibility that a challenger's money may "pay off" in later campaigns, that the initial self-financed and losing candidacy creates a name recognition and credibility that has subsequent electoral returns. Richard Ottinger and Howard Metzenbaum did ultimately win seats in Congress.

Related to the myth of the plutocrat spending his way into public office is the myth of the millionaire officeholder who perpetuates himself in office. Not to worry — millionnaire incumbents rarely have to dip into their own reservoirs. They raise their campaign funds pretty much as other incumbent members of Congress do. In fact, the self-financed campaigns of incumbents tend more often to be those of the unusual members of the House and Senate who run small, even old-fashioned campaigns of personal contacts and constituent service. Senator William Proxmire, Democrat of Wisconsin, and Rep. William Natcher, Democrat from Kentucky, are classic examples. Both profess to keeping campaigns small in order not to obligate themselves to contributors, and both spend very small sums in campaigns for reelection. Representative Natcher was, in fact, the only winner to spend less than $20,000 on a campaign for the Congress in 1984. He contributed $7,135 of the $7,245 his campaign took in.

When personal fortune meets the need for fortune, the meeting is often replete with irony, especially in the opprobrium that attaches generally to the candidate who uses his own wealth. It was a burden John F. Kennedy carried (with obvious success) throughout his career — the constant references to Jack's jack.

But if we fear the obligations that candidates incur in accepting money from others — especially the pressures contributors will exert on the public official — the candidate's own money, remarkably free from obligations, ought to seem less tainted and encumbered. Any interests that may attach to it are especially attenuated when the funds are inherited in the second or third generation. But it doesn't work that way with the public; one's own money has just as many stigmas attached to it as does the money of someone else.

VI. A Last Thought

How is it that we have been satisfied knowing so little about so common a political activity? Some 15 million Americans engage in it, making it the most common form of political activity beyond merely voting. Moreover, the neglect is all the more regrettable if one agrees that the broad-based voluntarism of those millions give the American system of campaign finance its most distinguishing quality.

The easiest answer is that the scholarly enterprise sets its priorities by the law of available data, and data on individual contributors are fragmented and fatally incomplete. In part that results from the sheer numbers of contributors and the awesome number of contributions they make. To record them and add them in the detail appropriate for analysis would take an administrative apparatus far greater than the Federal Election Commission can muster. It is a task that similarly defeats the capacities of state agencies.

In great part, however, the paucity of the record on individual contributors reflects the widespread American belief that they do not "threaten" the integrity of either electoral politics or legislative decision-making. The priorities of legislatures and administrative agencies are concerned with those who do. The purpose of reporting, record keeping, and disclosure is one of regulation, not one of basic research.

Finally, we just have not learned much about individual contributors because we have not thought them very important. They and their contributions have been the great unreported story in American campaign finance, too diffuse and undramatic to draw much attention. Moreover, individual money has increasingly gone to PACs and party committees rather than directly to the candidates — and then the PAC and the party becomes the story. Even candidates increasingly prefer to deal with organizations rather than individuals; it simply requires less time and energy that way. So, at a time when American politics is increasingly organized, it is the organizations we watch and even fear. It is indeed possible to lose sight of the trees for the forest.

4
Political Action Committees

They come in all shapes and sizes, and they come in all levels of political sophistication. Approximately 4000 of them are now registered with the Federal Election Commission, and uncounted others contribute to state and local campaigns. Although the federal statutes know them as multicandidate political committees, they are more usually called political action committees — or just PACs.

PACs also come bearing sinister myths and images. They are widely viewed as the new powerhouses of American politics, the latest mechanisms that "the interests" have perfected to work their selfish wills and ways in American politics. They have gained almost unlimited attention in the mass media since their growth in numbers and influence in the late 1970s, so much so that most Americans would be surprised to learn that they account for much less money in congressional campaigns than do the less celebrated individual contributors. Myths about the PACs have in fact achieved a form of reality. Of necessity one deals both with that reality and with the "real" reality. To separate them is no easy task.

I. Genesis and Growth

PACs originated in the American labor movement, specifically in the old Congress of Industrial Organizations (CIO). During World War II the U.S. Congress extended to organized labor the old prohibition that had long applied to corporations: none of the assets of the organization could be used for political activity. The CIO responded immediately in 1943 with what appears to have been the first American PAC. It was a separate political fund set up to receive and spend voluntary contributions, and it was called simply the Political Action Committee. So, a new kind of political organization was born and named at the same time. When the CIO merged with the American Federation of Labor (AFL) in 1955, the resulting AFL-CIO created its Committee on Political Education (COPE), the PAC that one scholar has called ". . . the model for virtually all political action committees."[1]

Other PACs began to spring up in the 1950s and 1960s, among them such formidable ones as the American Medical Political Action Committee (AMPAC) and the Business-Industry Political Action Committee (BIPAC). As these examples indicate, PACs tend to be officially named PACs, but the AFL-CIO's COPE is not alone in not having PAC in its name. When Congress got to the business of legislating on campaign finance in the 1970s, organized labor had almost 30 years of experience with PACs; and corporations and membership associations had less. Labor PACs were also more active and influential by any measure of comparison — sums of money contributed, influence exerted, voters mobilized.

All of this was prelude, however, to the great expansion of the 1970s, an expansion certainly promoted by the reform legislation of that decade. Virtually every major change in the regulation of campaign finance that Congress enacted in the 1970s spurred the growth of PACs.

● In 1971 Congress specifically authorized corporations and unions to spend their regular funds in establishing and adminis-

---

[1] Edwin M. Epstein, "Business and Labor under the Federal Election Campaign Act of 1971," in Michael Malbin, ed., *Parties, Interest Groups, and Campaign Finance Laws* (Washington, D.C.: American Enterprise Institute, 1980), 110.

tering — that is, in paying the overhead costs of — "separate segregated funds" to be used for political purposes. This provision was the first recognition of PACs and their legitimacy in federal legislation.

• In its drive to end the dominance of the "fat cats" after their very high profile in the two Nixon campaigns, Congress in 1974 put a limit of $1,000 per candidate per election on individual contributions. At the same time, it set the limit for a "multicandidate political committee" at $5,000 per candidate. Furthermore, individuals were limited to an aggregate of $25,000 a calendar year for all their contributions, while the multicandidate committees were subjected to no such aggregate limit.

• Congress in 1974 also removed the prohibition on the formation of separate segregated funds by contractors with the government of the United States. Many large corporations either were contractors or hoped to be.

• Finally, the creation of public financing for the presidential campaigns — again in 1974 — diverted organized money to congressional campaigns by closing off contributions to presidential campaigns. The diversion worked well for PACs that could coordinate their contributions to congressional campaigns with their parent organization's involvement in congressional lobbying.

Without a history as one of the problems in American campaign finance, PACs were not a target in the reforms of the 1970s; and they won advantages every time the reforms struck another target. They were unquestionably the beneficiaries of one of the fundamental laws of the mechanics of campaign finance: available money seeks an outlet, and if some outlets are narrowed or closed off, money flows with increased pressure to the outlets still open. It is the law that systems of campaign finance share with hydraulic systems.[2]

To the encouragements of the regulatory structure in the

---

[2]For a fuller recounting of the history and growth of PACs, see the Epstein chapter cited in footnote 1; Larry J. Sabato, *PAC Power* (New York: Norton, 1984), chap. 1; and Joseph E. Cantor, *Political Action Committees: Their Evolution, Growth, and Implications for the Political System* , report 84-78 GOV of the Congressional Research Service of the Library of Congress (Apr. 30, 1984).

FECA, the Federal Election Commission and the Supreme Court added their own. Responding to Sun Oil Company's request for advice in 1975, the infant FEC assured Sun that its political action committee (SunPAC) was a proper separate segregated fund, that SunPAC was free to solicit and spend political funds, and that Sun was free to pay its indirect and overhead costs. Whatever the ambiguities of the FECA about corporate PACs, they were resolved on the side of their legality.[3] Less than a year later, the Supreme Court created the final major opportunity for PACs in its decision in *Buckley v. Valeo* . When it struck down the severe limits on independent spending, it offered PACs one more viable and unregulated avenue of action, both in congressional and presidential campaigns. Individuals, PACs, and other groups were able to spend independently without limit, but only PACs were sufficiently organized to do so effectively.

While PACs undoubtedly benefited from the new regulations of the 1970s, they did not otherwise escape untouched by them. The new legislation required them to have a name, a treasurer, and a bank account; beyond that, their internal processes remained their own business. Their names, however, are not entirely of their choosing; PACs have to include the name of their parent organization, if they have one, in their own name. For example, the Better Government Committees and the Funds for an Enlightened Citizenry, are permissible names only for PACs without sponsoring organizations (for more on PAC names, see box). Their getting and spending also falls under federal control. A PAC may accept no more than $5,000 per year from any contributor, and it must report to the FEC all contributors (by name and occupation) of more than $200 in the year. The PAC is also limited in its contributions to $5,000 per candidate per election. (Since primary and general elections are two separate elections, the maximum total for an election cycle in effect is $10,000 per candidate.) On all of these transactions, the PAC must make copious reports to the Federal Election Commission.

---

[3]FEC Advisory Opinion 1975-23 (Dec. 3, 1975). The FEC divided 4–2 in deciding on its advice and set off something of a furor among Democrats and organized labor. The vote on the commission was along party lines, with the exception of Democrat Neil Staebler; the vote may well have cost him reappointment to the commission.

A PAC NOMENCLATURE

PACs have contributed their own, unforgettable share to political Americana. Their names are a veritable catalog of the diversity of American society and politics, as well as a reflection of the breezy, informal American style. To quote one of the leading scholars of PACs,

> The Peanut Butter and Nut Processers Association has its NUTPAC. The Beer Distributors have their SixPAC. Whataburger, Inc., operates Whata-PAC. There is a Bread-PAC (American Bakers Association), and EggPAC (United Egg Producers), a FishPAC (National Fisheries Institute), a Food PAC (Food Marketing Institute), and — to wash it all down — a Dr. Pepper PAC.
>
> Just about every classification of Americans has at least one entry. Blacks have the Parker-Coltrane PAC (named after founder U.S. Rep. John Conyears' favorite jazz saxophonists). . . . Women have several PACs dedicated to assisting their campaigns for public office, including the National Organization for Women PAC, the Women's Campaign Fund, and the National Women's Political Caucus Victory Fund-PAC.
>
> *Larry J. Sabato,* PAC Power *(New York: Norton, 1984), 25.*

Finally, PACs were enmeshed in complicated rules about their solicitations. As a result of the 1970s' reforms, corporate PACs may solicit their stockholders and their executive and administrative personnel without limit. Labor PACs may do the same for their union members. Each, that is, was given a prime constituency. Each may solicit the other's constituency by mail no more than twice a year. However, the PACs of associations — such as those of the American Medical Association and the National Realtors Association — may solicit only their members and their employees. And association PACs with corporate members may solicit the executives and stockholders of those corporations only once a year and only with the authorization of the corporation.

On the other hand, those PACs without parent organizations — the freestanding, unaffiliated PACs, like the National Conservative PAC — are unrestricted in their solicitations.

So, out of all the regulatory activity of the 1970s, there emerges a legal definition of a PAC, although the statutes of the United States never use the phrase "political action committee." What we think of as a PAC is a political committee that is not a party committee or a candidate's committee. In order to qualify for the $5,000 contribution limit, it must be a "multicandidate committee" — it must receive contributions from more than 50 people and make contributions to at least 5 candidates for federal office. (If it fails to so qualify, it becomes an "individual" and must observe the $1,000 limit on contributions.) And if it is the PAC of a corporation or labor union prohibited from making contributions directly from assets, it must be a "separate segregated fund" so that dollars collected for political purposes will be kept apart from regular corporate or union funds.[4]

So, in fits and starts the modern-day PAC was refined, defined, and launched. The launching was auspicious and success immediate. There were about 600 PACs registered with the FEC in 1974, and in just one decade that number had increased to about 4,000 (Table 4-1). Since 1984 there has been little growth. The growth post-1974 was initially greatest among the corporate PACs, but in the 1980s the unaffiliated PACs have grown at the fastest rate. The slowest rate of growth has been among labor PACs, both because of labor's head start in the 1950s and 1960s and because in a centralized labor movement the number of national labor organizations is limited.

The growth of PACs post-1974 can just as easily be gauged by looking at the rising curve of their contributions to candidates (Table 4-2). Again, the nonconnected PACs, starting from an insignificant sum, have shown the greatest rate of growth. The labor PACs, pacesetters at the onset of the new era in campaign finance, have expanded their contributions more than four-fold, and yet they have been surpassed by both corporate and association PACs. Overall, too, PAC receipts account for an ever (if slowly) increasing part of the receipts of congressional candi-

---

[4]The statutory provisions applying to PACs are scattered through Title 2, chap. 14 of the U.S. Code.

TABLE 4-1
Growth of PACs, by Type: 1974-1986

Year End	Corporate	Labor	Member- ship	Non- connected	Other[+]	Total
1974	89	201	318°			608
1975°°	139	226	357°			722
1976	433	224	489°			1146
1977	550	234	438	110	28	1360
1978	785	217	453	162	36	1653
1979	950	240	514	247	49	2000
1980	1206	297	576	374	98	2551
1981	1329	318	614	531	109	2901
1982	1469	380	649	723	150	3371
1983	1538	378	643	793	173	3525
1984	1682	394	698	1053	182	4009
1985	1710	388	695	1003	196	3992
1986	1744	384	745	1077	207	4157
1987°°°	1779	382	797	1044	209	4211

[+]"Other" includes the PACs of cooperatives and corporations without stock.
°These totals include not only membership PACs, but nonconnected PACs and PACs of cooperatives and corporations without stock.
°°The date for this year is Nov. 24, rather than Dec. 31.
°°°The data for 1987 are as of July 1, 1987.

dates, with the reliance of House candidates always outrunning that of Senate candidates. In 1974, 17 percent of all House candidate receipts came from PACs, and 11 percent of Senate campaign money came from them. By 1986 those figures had risen to 34 percent and 21 percent. PAC contributions, in other words, have been increasing at a pace somewhat faster than the contributions from other sources.[5]

While all of the legal changes of the 1970s may have been necessary conditions for the expansion of the PAC movement, they are not sufficient by themselves. The rise of PACs was a part of a broader rebirth of interest group politics. The number of lobbyists, group and individual, registered with Congress rose from 603 in 1972 to 1,970 in 1982. Even more fundamentally the PAC movement reflected changes in the American electorate — its

[5]See chap. 3, especially Table 3-4, for data on the relative importance of the sources of receipts of congressional candidates.

TABLE 4-2
Contributions by PACs to All Candidates for the House and Senate, 1974–86 (in millions of dollars)

Year end	Corporate	Labor	Member- ship	Non- connected	Other[+]	Total
1974	°	$6.3	°	$ .7	$1.0	$12.5
1976	°	8.2	°	1.5	2.8	22.6
1978	$9.8	10.3	$11.3	2.8	1.0	35.2
1980	19.2	13.2	15.9	4.9	2.0	55.2
1982	27.5	20.3	21.9	10.7	3.2	83.6
1984	35.5	24.8	26.7	14.5	3.8	105.3
1986	49.4	31.0	34.4	19.4	5.3	139.4

[+]An ambiguous and omnibus category in 1974 and 1976; after then it includes the PACs of cooperatives and corporations without stock.
°Specific figures not available.
Source: Adapted from Table 9, p. 88, of Joseph E. Cantor, *Political Action Committees: Their Evolution, Growth, and Implications for the Political System* , report 84-78 GOV of the Congressional Research Service of the Library of Congress (Apr. 30, 1984); data for 1984 and 1986 come from FEC reports.

breaking away from all-encompassing party loyalties, its intense involvement with single issues, and its increasing identification with politics beyond the local neighborhood or county. Finally, the rise of PACs reflected all that had happened to produce candidate-centered, high-tech campaigning in the United States. The political action committee was superbly adapted for the new cash economy of campaigning and for a limited politics of focused strategies.

Yet the relationship between the FECA reforms and PAC growth is powerful; moreover, it is replete with ironies and lessons for students of reform. When Congress began to reshape campaign finance in the early 1970s, liberal Democrats and organized labor favored legitimizing and strengthening the PAC movement. After all, labor PACs were then the dominant ones. In 1974 some Republicans in the Senate — led by Sen. Howard Baker of Tennessee — tried to prohibit political groups and committees from making political contributions. By the 1980s, after the totally unexpected growth in corporate and membership

PACs, the defense of PACs switched to the Republicans; and attempts to reform them were largely led by Democrats. That ironic twist, along with the unexpected PAC explosion, has led commentators to find in campaign finance reform their most striking illustration of the law of unanticipated consequences.[6]

II. Sorting Out the 4000

To begin, there are big and little PACs. In 1986 there were 16 PACs that made contributions to federal candidates in excess of a million dollars.[7] The Realtors Political Action Committee ($2.8 million), the American Medical Association PAC ($2.11 million) and the National Educational Association PAC ($2.1 million) headed the list. And at the same time more than a thousand of the registered PACs — 1,005 to be precise — made no contributions at all in the 1985–86 federal campaigns. The average PAC contributed $44,247 to federal candidates. Well under 10 percent of them contributed more than $100,000.

Of all the ways of sorting out PACs, however, the one approaching universal use is the classification scheme the FEC worked out in its early years. The FEC divided — and still divides — PACs into categories that describe their auspices: labor, corporate, trade/membership/health, cooperative, corporation without stock, and nonconnected. The first two, labor and corporate PACs, are self-evident categories. The fourth and fifth, cooperative PACs and those of corporations without stock, are equally self-evident, but relatively minor. They accounted for less than 4 percent of PAC contributions to federal candidates in 1986, and they are treated here (and most other places) either by exclusion or as an "other" category. The remaining two categories — trade/membership/health and nonconnected — raise the most

[6]Much of this political history of campaign finance legislation in the mid-1970s is told in great detail in the Federal Election Commission's two volumes: *Legislative History of Federal Election Campaign Act of 1974* and *Legislative History of Federal Election Campaign Act of 1976* , both published in 1977 by the U.S. Government Printing Office.

[7]That is, the 16 contributed more than a million to candidates for the Congress and the presidency. In a nonpresidential year, however, almost all of those contributions go to congressional candidates; PACs contributed only $73,761 to presidential candidates in the 1985–86 cycle.

serious definitional problems because they conceal a staggering variety of PACs within them.

The "trade/membership/health" rubric loosely covers the membership organizations; most authors, therefore, usually shorten it to a "membership" or "association" heading. There is a logic in the category; it includes the PACs of membership associations that are limited by the FECA to soliciting their members. But the associations are of all kinds: trade and business associations as well as professional associations, chiefly. Thus, if one wishes to talk about "business" money in a campaign, one clearly has in mind corporate PACs and *some* membership PACs (such as those, for example, of the American Bankers Association and the National Association of Home Builders). Even a more pointed attempt to define "oil" or "steel" or "retail food" money also involves the selecting of PACs from both the corporate and the membership categories.

The final FEC category, the nonconnected PACs, again has its logic: it includes all the PACs without sponsoring organizations — the "PACs without parents." And the distinction is fundamentally important. Since these PACs have no parents to pay the bills, for example, they must take their overhead and administrative costs out of their receipts from political solicitations. Yet, the fact that they are unattached to any founding or controlling organization frees them to solicit anyone in the country and thus to enjoy the benefits of direct-mail and computer list solicitations. But while these nonconnected PACs tend to have similar characteristics that result from being parentless, they are exceptionally varied in their political interests and goals. There are conservative PACs and liberal PACs; one-issue PACs (abortion, energy, environment, nuclear freeze, gun control, the gold standard, and the family farm among them); feminist PACs; ethnic and racial PACs; pro-Israel PACs; PACs of students and senior citizens, of political moderates, of socialists, of homosexuals, of artists, of business and labor interests — and one of California motorcyclists.

Despite all of these explanations and qualifications, however, the FEC typology works pretty well. In one sense it has to; it defines the categories in which the FEC aggregates and publishes data about PACs. To use any other system of categories, one has to disaggregate the FEC data, a process not unlike unscrambling scrambled eggs. Whatever may be the grumbling among scholars and journalists about the rigidities of the FEC categories, the law of available data dictates their widespread use.

But one kind of PAC does not fit the FEC's system very well: the personal PAC. The FEC groups them with the nonconnected PACs; and there they rest, categorically ill at ease. They are the PACs set up by officeholders and would-be candidates for purposes other than the direct funding of their own campaigns. Most commonly they permit the major figure whose PAC it is to distribute funds to the campaigns of other candidates. In the case of would-be presidential candidates, they also finance preliminary political travels and soundings before the candidate is forced to become an official candidate and form a candidate committee for the election cycle. The personal PACs will be discussed more thoroughly in Chapter 6.

Of the alternative ways of categorizing PACs, perhaps the most promising is the most simple: by size. Consider a few bits of data. Of all the 3,081 PACs making contributions or independent expenditures in 1986, fully 70 percent spent $20,000 or less. In fact, only 8.5 percent of them spent more than $100,000, and only 3.5 percent — 107 PACs — spent more than $200,000. To look at the distribution from the top, the 50 biggest political spenders (1.6 percent of the active PACs) spent 42.4 percent ($57.2 million) of all PAC dollars spent in federal campaigns in 1986. The list of the top 50, incidentally, includes only one corporate PAC (Lockheed PAC, number 50 on the list).

In addition to the sums they spent, the largest of the PACs are also marked by the numbers of candidates to whom they give. At the top of the 1986 lists was the Realtors PAC at $2,782,338 contributed to 533 candidates, an average of $5,220 per recipient candidate. Number two — the American Medical Association PAC at $2,107,492 — contributed to 465 candidates for an average of $4,532. (These figures suggest at least one explanation why these two PACs have recently increased their independent spending in congressional elections.) In fact, the ten flushest PACs in 1986 contributed to an average of 407 candidates for Congress, and the average of their average sized contribution was $4,215.

III. The Birth and Death of PACs

Even in the decision to create a PAC, one begins to see the differences between the connected and the nonconnected PACs, the PACs with parents and the orphan PACs. Where there is a founding organization of some kind — a labor union, a corporation, a membership association — the elected officers, aided perhaps by research and recommendations from the permanent staff, make the decision to establish a PAC. It is for most of them a decision not unlike the one to retain a Washington representative or to participate in a charitable fund-raising project. That is to say, it is a decision to seek the goals of the organization and its members by nondirect means, whether by generating political influence or by cultivating community respect and goodwill. It involves reaching outside of the traditional boundaries of the organization and into the public sphere. Some organizations have a longer history of doing this, and some are more skilled in making the cost-benefit calculations such actions involve. They inevitably come to different calculations of the costs and the benefits; fast-food chains, for example, have to worry about public reactions more than do the manufacturers of large turbines.

The nonconnected PACs, on the other hand, result from an entrepreneurial act. In some cases small groups of individuals and in others a single person see a political opportunity (or a "need," as they like to say) and organize to take advantage of it. Entrepreneurs define the interest or interests of the PAC, draw on their knowledge of elites and groups that share it, acquire or rent a few mailing lists, and begin to raise money. Newspaper accounts tell of Robert Samuel's role in founding Senior PAC (see box); there

---

A PAC IS BORN

Senior PAC has not become one of the Washington giants, but it did report spending almost $250,000 in independent expenditures in the 1984 campaign. It made no contributions to candidates in that year. Just two years earlier, its founder had high hopes for it; and a reporter for the *New York Times* was present.

In offices all over the capital on any given morning, scores of bright young men and women are trying to breathe life into newborn political movements. Most of them will fail, but a few of their offspring may survive to wield real influence, perhaps even to help shape a national election.

Robert Samuel is one of these venturesome parents. In a sublet cubicle seven blocks north of the White House, he is presiding over the creation of Senior PAC . . . In eight months, Senior PAC has raised only about $3,200 and has yet to invest in any campaign. . . .

To give his movement some credibility, Mr. Samuel has persuaded a group of prominent citizens to join an advisory board, among them Representative Claude Pepper, Democrat of Florida, chairman of the House Select Committee on Aging. . .

After a few abortive amateur efforts, Senior PAC has entrusted its fund raising to a San Francisco direct mail firm, Richard Parker & Associates, and a 30,000-letter test mailing will go out next month. The mail specialists have signed a three-year contract that does not require any initial investment by the client, strong evidence that older peoples' issues are professionally regarded as a good risk. . . .

At the age of 30, Mr. Samuel has seven years of relevant Washington experience, as legislative assistant to Representative James H. Scheuer of New York, a lobbyist for the National Council of Senior Citizens and political organizer for Concerned Seniors for Better Government, an arm of the A.F.L.-C.I.O.'s Committee on Political Education [COPE].

Just now he is without salary or staff, living on his savings until Senior PAC begins to acquire some assets. But he is confident that the volatility of the older peoples' issues and the absence of competition in his field will elevate his movement to prominence. "I can't believe it won't work," he says.

> Warren Weaver Jr., *"Political Action Group Focuses on the Elderly,"* New York Times *(Mar. 1, 1982).*

---

is no way to know how typical the specifics of his entrepreneurship are. In some instances the entrepreneurs may have an organizational background and yet want to create a PAC without formal ties. The powerful Business-Industry Political Action

Committee (BIPAC) was created by officers and officials of the U.S. Chamber of Commerce and the National Association of Manufacturers.

More interesting perhaps than the mechanisms of creation are the reasons for creating — or not creating. To begin, one gets a good deal of insight by looking at the PACs themselves and their parents. Labor unions and their PACs are the easiest; virtually every major national (or international) union has a PAC, as does labor's great umbrella organization, the AFL-CIO. The major unions outside of the AFL-CIO, the Teamsters and the National Education Association especially, also have PACs — with the result that virtually every member of a collective bargaining organization in the United States is involved in PAC activity at least to the extent of paying a PAC's expenses. This fact is only one more indication that the labor movement leads all economic organizations in its involvement in electoral politics. Its attempts to register and get out the vote are legendary, and it was present at the creation of the PAC.

However, fewer than 1,800 of the more than 3 million corporations in the United States have PACs registered with the FEC. The single most important characteristic of those corporations that do is sheer size. As early as 1979, Edwin Epstein reported that 66 percent of the 200 largest industrial corporations in *Fortune* magazine's listings had PACs; 40 percent of the first 500 had one, and only 24 percent of the second 500 did.[8] A more recent study limited to a group of large corporations still finds size relevant.

> . . . a firm's resource base significantly affects the likelihood of choosing to form an active PAC. Total employment base and assets each positively affect corporate participation in electoral politics.[9]

As for associations, the conventional wisdom, too, is that the likelihood of having a PAC relates to size. Probably not more than a

[8] "Business and Labor under the Federal Election Campaign Act of 1971," in Michael Malbin, ed., *Parties, Interest Groups, and Campaign Finance Laws* (Washington, D.C.: American Enterprise Institute, 1980), 128.

[9] Marick F. Masters and Gerald D. Keim, "Determinants of PAC Participation Among Large Corporations," *Journal of Politics* , vol. 47 (Nov. 1985), 1171.

few percent of the nonprofit associations have PACs; the *Encyclopedia of Associations* reported 21,370 of them in 1987.[10] Observers seem to agree that they are concentrated among the big ones. Regardless of the parent, size translates into capacity: assets for paying the PAC expenses, numbers of people for solicitation, and general political and administrative experience. Large size also means national scope and involvement with national issues.

Beyond the consideration of size, however, corporations and associations are more apt to create a PAC if their activities are subject to legislation by Congress. Epstein again in 1979 reported,

> In all likelihood PAC formation [among natural resource companies] has been influenced by the ongoing debate within Congress and the White House regarding this nation's energy policies. Similarly, PAC formation and activity among airlines increased during a time when an airline-related issue — deregulation — was on the congressional agenda. Further, paper and forest product companies are vitally affected by federal environmental decisions and the allocation of timberlands. So, too, drug firms, automobile manufacturers, aerospace companies. . . .[11]

More recently Masters and Keim find that corporations primarily in the "transportation, energy, and communications" industries are more likely to have PACs than those in other industrial sectors — those in construction, finance, or retail trade industries, for example.[12] Moreover, as the authors of one of the pioneering studies of corporate PACs point out, their greatest growth took place as a reaction to "a geometric progression of government regulation during the 1970s. . . . The future of the free-enterprise system [was] militantly proclaimed to hang in the balance, and bringing about change in the governing atmosphere in Washington [became] the central PAC purpose."[13]

This relationship makes good, even obvious, sense. The more immediate the political consequences, the more likely one is to

[10]*Encyclopedia of Associations*, 21st ed., (Detroit: Gale, 1987).

[11]Epstein, 136.

[12]Masters and Keim, 1165–1166.

[13]Edward Handler and John R. Mulkern, *Business in Politics: Campaign Strategies of Corporate Political Action Committees* (Lexington, Mass.: Lexington, 1982), 61.

engage in political activity. But the relationship need not be direct and immediate. PACs tend not to come in and out of activity according to the congressional agenda of the year; they often reflect a longer term view of the industry's relationship with public authority. To be sure, some PACs are founded for more general ideological purposes — corporations not subject to specific regulation may worry more generally about labor policy, foreign trade, fiscal and monetary policies, even their vision of economic health and survival. Organized labor's reasons are directly parallel and broadly ideological. And commitment to an issue or a set of issues — an ideology — is probably the major political reason for the founding of the nonconnected PACs. Their names often indicate as much.

All of this seems terribly rational and goal-oriented. PACs are created for political reasons, whether those of narrow interest or broad ideology; and they are created by organizations with skills and assets sufficient to make them go. And as their strength within organized labor suggests, they tend to be the product of long and secure political traditions. The circumstances of creation, however, are not quite that simple. Differences of size and relationship to government by no means fully explain the existence or nonexistence of PACs. One still hasn't explained, for example, why some corporations in the Fortune top 500 or some very large associations have PACs while other very similar organizations do not.

To explain these differences, it helps to go into the social-psychology and leadership of large organizations. It is an especially valid consideration in view of the fact that decisions about the creation of a PAC tend to be made by one person or a small group of people — by corporate CEOs or executive directors of associations, for instance. And so Larry Sabato reports the views of John Kochevar of the PAC of the Chamber of Commerce, who

> suggested, only slightly facetiously, that some chief executive officers from companies without PACs got the idea from PAC-company CEOs on the golf course. The PAC-less CEO, says Kochevar, would come back to the office saying "Goddammit, we've got to get one of those." Referring to the rapid proliferation

of business PACs, Kochevar remarked, "I can't explain how it happened any other way."[14]

To some extent, such a "keeping up with the Joneses" explanation suggests the question *"why* keep up with the Joneses?" In part it is a desire to be up-to-date and innovative, even politically fashionable — and not to be seen as stodgy and unimaginative. In part it is a desire to leave no political stone unturned, to explore every possible avenue of influence, and especially not to ignore a political weapon that one's adversaries are using. In the uncertain world of political combat, one may not be sure that a PAC will help greatly in achieving the organization's political goals, but many leaders of organizations will think it risky not to explore a possible advantage. The risk of not establishing a PAC will seem all the greater when one's fellow organizations have done so and especially when the mass media have been trumpeting its power over the members of Congress.

Because of the uncertainty about the influence PACs generate, it is not easy for a founding organization to engage in even the most approximate cost-benefit calculation. The cash costs are fairly clear. A parent of a PAC that raises and spends $200,000 or $300,000 in an election cycle may well find that the overhead and administrative costs — physical space, utilities, personnel, printing, and travel, among others — will run from 50 to 100 percent of the sums raised for political purposes. The nonmonetary costs are harder to calculate — the resentment of employees or members, or the resentments of consumers, for instance, when the PAC's political choices do not match theirs. A recent report of the Conference Board records the fears of several corporate public affairs officials:

> We are concerned with the negative publicity surrounding PACs. Our board doesn't think it is an appropriate activity for a consumer goods company.

> The potential for abuse inherent in a PAC's solicitation will inevitably be seized by some insensitive senior managers. And the

[14]Sabato, 31.

ensuing bad publicity will rub off on the companies — and on business in general.[15]

Beyond such specific fears, there is a common feeling in nonpolitical organizations that political activity is a matter best left to individual choice and decision. In those cases there are important psychic "costs" in violating norms about political role and political propriety.

It is the calculation of political benefits that is the intractable problem — as it is in all of campaign finance. The benefits, in fact, are often not apparent until the PAC is formed and in operation; at the moment of creation, there may be only a very hazy notion that PAC activity will lead to some form of "access" to the business of government. Realism sets in with experience, and all indications are that PAC managers see the benefits of operation in much more limited terms than does the broader public. One set of interviews with corporate PAC managers finds them unimpressed with PAC power; indeed, about a third of them have concluded that they have only "a minimal political impact." Says one manager,

> I do not feel that PAC contributions buy access or votes in most cases. It is a very expensive corporate activity and the money spent to administer it could be put to better use in direct lobbying activities.[16]

In some cases the managers blame PACs themselves, especially for inexpert spending decisions. In others there is a feeling that PACs are being exploited by the aggressive fund-raising of many members of Congress. But whatever the cause, disenchantment about the benefits of PAC activity is high, at least among corporate PACs.

The calculus behind the founding of a nonconnected PAC is almost by definition an entrepreneurial one. The PAC must be able to raise enough money to cover its expenses and yet have some left for political activities. Some PACs, indeed, have had none left; but they are exceptions. The truth for many, though, is that

[15]Catherine Morrison, *Managing Corporate Political Action Committees* , report no. 880 (New York: The Conference Board, 1986), 3.
[16]Ibid., 22.

direct-mail solicitation is a very expensive way to raise money, and for those who rely on it in nationwide solicitations, expenses may well absorb all but 10 or 20 percent of receipts. That does not necessarily mean, however, that the founders of the nonconnected PAC begin from scratch. There may be an organized, or at least a "natural" constituency available — opponents of abortion were organized in many states and localities before the emergence of national right to life PACs. And in some cases, the PAC without a parent may in fact have been founded by organizations who for some reason or reasons did not want to assume official sponsorship of the PAC. Even though they are not membership PACs, they can solicit lists of a friend's friends.

Given the problems and disenchantments in keeping a PAC alive, it is not surprising that a certain number each year slip into dormancy or even give up the struggle. That number is rising, and its share of the PAC total is increasing. In the 1979–80 cycle 2,155 of the 2,551 PACs registered with the FEC — 84.5 percent — contributed to a candidate for Congress.[17] In 1986 the comparable numbers were 3,152 active out of 4,157, an activity rate of 76 percent.[18] As for death, the FEC's annual totals of "terminations" give the basic count:

1977:	91	1982:	333
1978:	270	1983:	220
1979:	85	1984:	173
1980:	226	1985:	530
1981:	133	1986:	434

One can easily explain the increasing numbers in terms of the greater number of PACs and their lengthening lives. It is much less clear why the pattern of more terminations in the even-numbered years suddenly breaks in 1984 and 1985. What kind

[17]To be sure, a few PACs may have been active politically without contributing to candidates. They may have contributed to other PACs or party committees, or they may have made independent expenditures. There are, however, very few PACs who engage in one of those activities without also contributing directly to candidates.

[18]The early FEC data for 1986 provides data only for PACs that contributed to any federal candidate; that is, contributions to presidential candidates are included. In view of the very small number of them in an "off year," the percentage is inflated only by some fraction of a percent.

of PACs give up the ghost? Conventional wisdom says they are the smaller, less affluent ones. The FEC data do not easily speak to that question, but they do say that the deaths are fairly evenly spread over the various categories of PACs defined by parent organizations.

IV. The Internal Life of the PAC

The lives of political action committees are largely private. The reams of reports they make to the FEC include virtually nothing about the ways in which they make decisions, the people who make decisions, and the role of the people who give the PAC their money. And while scholars and journalists have devoted themselves to reporting the PACs' activities and finances, very few of them have ventured into their intraorganizational ways. Perhaps they have been daunted by the great range and variety of those lives, for the habits of some 4000 organizations of very different sizes, goals, and histories defy generalization of almost any kind.[19]

For the PACs with parent organizations (the connected PACs) knowledge begins with the fact that the parent organization can control the PAC — it can create it; define its organization and governance; select its personnel; and through them set its policies, goals, and strategies. Its control of the PAC knows only one important boundary: it cannot transfer its assets to the PAC, for the PAC's political funds must come from voluntary contributions specifically intended for political purposes. (That is, the PAC must be a "separate segregated fund" apart from the assets of the sponsoring organization.) Otherwise federal law puts no limits on the rights of the parent; having decided to bring its child into the world, the parent can subject it to whatever control and discipline it thinks appropriate. In very practical terms, for example, the parent is free to mesh and coordinate its PAC

---

[19]One great exception to these comments is the perceptive article on PACs as organizations by Theodore J. Eismeier and Philip H. Pollock III, "An Organizational Analysis of Political Action Committees," *Political Behavior*, vol. 7 (1985), 192–216.

strategies with its other political activities, especially its lobbying.

To put the matter the other way around, PACs are not participatory organizations. Although some PACs refer to donors as "members," they are not conventional membership organizations. Donors do not select the officers of the PAC and do not participate in making the crucial political decisions — nor do they select the people who do. The donors often are sedulously informed about the PACs decisions, and their opinions and preferences are often solicited and even taken very seriously; but very, very few PACs take the further step to give donors any direct or representational role. PACs are run generally by some combination or other of officers and permanent staff employees of an organization or a nonconnected PAC. As the Conference Board found in its study of corporate PACs:

> The most frequently employed practice is for a designated senior executive, usually the president or CEO, to appoint certain individuals to be officers or managers of the PAC. . . . Key PAC positions are open to volunteers in less than 10 percent of the cases in this sample. While PAC board members or officers may ratify the appointment of PAC executives, interviews indicate they are largely ratifying the choices of senior management rather than participating in a democratic selection process.[20]

As usual, systematic evidence seems to be limited to corporate PACs, but there is no reason to doubt the applicability of these observations to other kinds of PACs.

These two points — the power of the parent and the relative powerlessness of the donors — define the main outlines of PAC life. But the reality is softer and less distinct, more complex and less monolithic than these points by themselves would suggest. Within the organization there may be a number of views about the PAC. There is a classic divergence between the political goals and savvy of the elected officers and the professionals of the permanent staff. In corporate PAC terms that may mean a divergence between the board and/or chief executive officer and the permanent staff responsible for the PAC (often part of a vice

[20]Morrison, 12–13.

presidency for public or governmental affairs). If the parent has a Washington office or representative to handle its relations with the U. S. government, that person may well have different goals for the PAC than will the PAC managers and officials at the organization's headquarters. Washington representatives, for example, weigh in very heavily against any PAC decision that will anger a powerful congressional incumbent.

Moreover, the role of the donor — the contributor to the PAC — is only imperfectly summarized by the adjective "powerless." The donor is indeed powerless in a formal, participatory sense. If the PAC offends or disappoints its donors, however, they can withhold their funds. Moreover, their displeasure — especially in significant numbers — may cause the parent organization problems in morale and discipline, even in support and loyalty. PACs tend to be attentive, even responsive, therefore, to donor pressures. They often make contributions to candidates some donors favor even though such contributions do not comport with overall PAC goals. If they are national organizations — and most PACs are — that means placating a great many local pressures and wishes. Donor satisfaction is, in fact, one of the main reasons that PACs tend to spread their funds in large number of contributions of relatively small size.

Ultimately, the donor has the sanction of "exit" over the PAC, an ability that assumes that donor contributions are voluntary and thus can be ended voluntarily.[21] It is a point that popular myths would contest, for it has been widely asserted that individuals are pressured or coerced into contributing to PACs — especially corporate PACs — by their superiors in the parent organization. Even in the absence of much evidence, these charges are not easy to evaluate; indeed, coercion itself is not easy to define without a lengthy philosophical investigation of free will. But if one takes a simple operational definition — the threat of the imposition of substantial personal costs in rewards or status for failing to give — then the overwhelming majority of donations are voluntary. How does one come to such a conclusion? First, there is no substantial body of evidence that coercion is anything more than sporadic; the allegations that have been

[21]The term and idea of member "exit" in organizations comes from Albert O. Hirschman, *Exit, Voice, and Loyalty* (Cambridge, Mass.; Harvard University Press, 1970).

made in federal courts and before the FEC have never been up-held.[22] Second, what data we have on the PACs' successes in solicitations deny coercion; a survey of corporate PACs in 1985, for example, found that on the average only 31 percent of those executives and administrators who were solicited actually con-tributed. Even so effective a PAC as that of the National Association of Realtors has reported about a 30 percent return from its members.[23]

Perhaps surprisingly, donors seem not to press for participa-tion in most PACs. The explanation derives perhaps from their motives and reasons in becoming donors. Contributors to PACs may indeed be looking for more passive, less participatory forms of political activity. Making a contribution to a PAC as a political statement has much in common with a contribution to a United Way campaign. Or, to shift the metaphor, the PAC is a "political mutual fund."[24] One does not have to make dispersion decisions — the experts with the PAC or the United Way will do that — and so one does not have to take the time to collect infor-mation. Nor does one have to accept responsibility for those decisions if one's friends or acquaintances are unhappy about them. And if one is contacted by other supplicants for money, one can always say "I'm sorry — I gave at the office." The de-mands of time, expertise, and responsibility are thus compara-tively low. A more participatory role would inflate the "costs" of political activity enormously.

Moreover, donors to the connected PACs are motivated at least in part out of loyalty to and stake in the parent organization. Cor-porate PACs, for example, find that their donors come dispropor-tionately from upper echelons of executives and administrators. The further they solicit down into the lower regions of the corpo-

---

[22]The major litigation was the suit of the International Association of Machin-ists alleging coercion in fund-raising by a number of corporate PACs. The FEC dismissed the complaint and several federal courts did, too. *IAM v. FEC*, 678 F.2d 1092 (1982).

[23]Poll conducted in 1985 by Civic Service, Inc., for the Business-Industry PAC, the Chamber of Commerce of the United States, the National Association of Busi-ness PACs, the National Association of Manufacturers, and the Public Affairs Council. Data on the Realtors PAC come from a personal conservation with its former executive director, Richard Thaxton.

[24]Eismeier and Pollock, "An Organizational Analysis of Political Action Com-mittees," 196.

rate hierarchy, the lower the rate of participation.[25] Association PACs similarly find that members of longer standing are more likely to be donors. In part it is a matter of sheer financial ability to give, but there are also at play elements of success in the organization or occupation and a sense of sharing and identifying with the interests of the parent organization. Beyond supporting the interests of the parent organization, donors can give $50 or $100 as a sign of professional or workplace solidarity and can enhance their reputation for group responsibility. Contributing to a PAC is, in short, a low-cost way of seeking limited political goals while meeting both one's political and organizational obligations.

Where those ties to the parent organization have not been present, solicitation has failed. Neither corporations nor unions have had any success in their crossover solicitations — corporations on nonsalaried workers and unions on executives and administrators. Most indeed have not even tried them. Corporate PACs, in fact, have not even had conspicuous success in soliciting their stockholders, a failure that is possibly the most telling piece of evidence. Mobil Oil's attempts are perhaps indicative:

> Mobil, soliciting funds for last year's elections, mailed PAC brochures to the 160,000 individuals who own at least 100 shares of company stock; just 1,400 of them kicked in, and only 400 agreed to donate regularly by reducing their quarterly dividends. The $50,000 they contributed was an eighth of Mobil's PAC but cost the company $76,000 in postage and mailing. That made it five times costlier per dollar raised than soliciting Mobil executives.[26]

And Mobil's problems have hardly been unique.

So, the PAC with a parent draws on donors who act out of a combination of political and nonpolitical motives, who seem quite willing to leave the central political decisions to others, and who might even be frightened away by the necessity of participation. They hold the sanction of "exit" over the PAC, but most PAC

[25]See the data presented in Frank J. Sorauf, "Political Action Committees in American Politics: An Overview," Table 5-1, in *What Price PACs?*, report of Task Force on Political Action Committees (New York: Twentieth Century Fund, 1984).
[26]Burt Solomon, "Political Trawling Among Stockholders," *National Journal* (Mar. 7, 1987), 575.

managers report that their donor losses come not from the disaffected but from other reasons: death, leaving the organization, moving away. If the PACs attract the most loyal and involved donors in the first place, the ones who see their interests to be most congruent with those of the parent organization, their disinclination to exit clearly follows. In addition, the willingness of most PACs to placate the strongly held views of their donors reduces what dissatisfaction might arise.[27]

In fact, the whole idea of "exit" — of pulling out — perhaps misassumes the nature of PAC participation or loyalty in the first place. The one extensive set of data we have on PAC donors — a survey of Phillip Morris employees — suggests a continuous range of stable donor activity, not the dichotomous categories that entry and exit suggest. Some potential contributors give every year, some every few years, some every five or six years, some never. There is, in other words, a great deal of irregular, in and out, giving, a pattern that reflects varying levels of commitment and involvement more than approval or rejection of the PAC's political decisions. One sees a good deal more late-blooming and inconstant involvement than principled "exit." And that, again, reflects the fact that in the long run the individuals who decide initially to make a contribution to the PAC do so out of close sympathy with the goals and interests of the parent organization.[28] The chief problem for PAC leadership, therefore, is not to forestall exit, but to stimulate involvement and regular contribution in the first place. Indeed the fostering of supportive relationships with donors to the PAC is a task that concerns and involves many organizations that sponsor PACs (see box).

Not many of these observations, however, apply to the PACs without parent organizations. In fact, it is no exaggeration to say that most of them have no organizational life. Created by the initiatives of one or a few individuals, they are usually run by those individuals or their chosen successors. They may have broadly based boards of directors, but they are often "paper" boards little inclined to exert much control over the PAC. Donors to them

---

[27]On this kind of donor "voice" and on other matters of internal decision-making, Frank J. Sorauf, "Who's in Charge? Accountability in Political Action Committees," *Political Science Quarterly*, vol. 99 (Winter 1984–85), 591–614.
[28]Ibid., 604–605.

WORDS OF ADVICE

The corporate PAC movement has been sensitive to all of the ramifications of the relationship between corporate PACs and their donors. The Public Affairs Council, a Washington-based organization of corporate public affairs officers, has long been among the leaders of the movement; and its *Guidelines for the Operation of a Business-Employee Political Action Committee*, published in 1986, addresses PAC-donor relationships at a number of points.

1. . . . The spirit of volunteerism should be authentic in practice — no career rewards for contributing, no stigma for not contributing. All PAC records should be confidential to the extent possible under provisions of the law . . .
2. The business-employee PAC should . . . encourage its contributing members to involve themselves in a broad range of voluntary political activities at all levels of government. If conditions permit, it should provide opportunities for personal contact between the PAC members and the political decision-makers who receive, or perhaps wish to receive, the PAC's contributions. . . .
4. The business-employee PAC should, to the fullest extent possible, envision itself as a mini-political entity, separate from and independent of corporate management. Broad participation should be sought. PAC members should be encouraged through a variety of means to recommend support for various candidates of their choice in either major political party or in independent parties. . . .

are not only scattered all across the country, but they are not joined either by a common occupation or workplace or by loyalty to an ongoing parent organization. They are brought together only by an issue or ideology in most cases — and by the U.S. mails. They have little or no contact with the staff or the decision-making apparatus of the PAC.

It follows, therefore, that concepts of participation and exit have no real meaning in the nonconnected PACs. Solicitation by direct mail, in fact, lives with small return rates and substantial nonrepeat rates as a fact of the technology. But even the most regular contributors have no contact with the staff or decision-making of the PAC. These PACs, therefore, can draw on no organizational loyalty; there is only loyalty to a political cause or crusade. In a real sense they depend chiefly on their own prose, especially their letters of solicitation (the mailings) to maintain the attention and involvement of donors. And that dependence often means playing on political fears with catastrophic scenarios or dangerous threats of one kind or another. It is an unusually volatile relationship they must maintain, one requiring constant recruitment and reinforcement.

So, both the connected and the nonconnected PACs have stayed apart, as most interest groups have, from all of the participatory pressures that have transformed the American political parties. They encourage participation in the form of limited donor activity, but in their internal governance the relationship with their donors is at the most one of responsiveness. Participatory democracies they are not, for they mobilize a different kind of activity and a different kind of activist than do the parties. Intrinsic to the decision to contribute to a PAC is the decision to leave effective political decisions to others. Thus, PACs are political organizations of limited goals and of homogeneous and nondemanding political clienteles. Ironically, at least in a democracy, that limited involvement is a major source of their political effectiveness.

V. Strategies, Tactics, and Goals

No more than other political organizations do PACs publish or nail to the door of city hall lists of their goals and strategies. One largely has to infer them from PAC political activity. That activity is of two main kinds — contributions and independent expenditures (Table 4-3). Of their total political spending in 1982 of almost $103 million, a total of 94.4 percent went into contributions to various candidates and committees. Even though independent spending rose in the presidential year, contributions still accounted for 85.4 of PACs' political outlays in 1984. In 1986 they accounted for 93.6 percent. It is, therefore,

TABLE 4-3
Political Expenditures of PACs, 1982–1986

		1982	1984	1986
I.	*Contributions to*			
	other PACs	$ 3,671,149	$ 6,206,630	°
	parties	5,982,569	10,377,642	6,847,060
	pres'l cands.	106,637	1,519,562	73,761
	cong'l cands.	87,466,689	111,450,482	139,391,941
II.	*Independent Exps. in*			
	cong'l elections	5,681,579	4,796,880	8,668,843
	pres'l elections	88,126	17,353,928	840,288
III.	*Total Political*			
	Spending:	102,996,749	151,705,124	155,821,893°°

°Data not available by September, 1987.
°°Total does not include contributions to other PACs.

from the patterns of these contributions, especially the contributions to candidates from the Congress, that one best deduces what the PACs are trying to achieve.

The fact of the PACs' overwhelming support of incumbents probably says more about them than any other fact (Table 4-4). By 1986 almost 69 percent of their contributions to all candidates for Congress went to incumbents, and for House candidates it was more than three of every four dollars in both 1984 and 1986. Moreover, the fondness for incumbents has increased

TABLE 4-4
PAC Contributions to Incumbent, Challenger, and Open Seat Candidates for the Congress, 1978–1986 (in percentages of contributions to all candidates)

	House			*Senate*		
	Inc.	*Chall.*	*Open*	*Inc.*	*Chall.*	*Open*
1978	60.4%	18.8%	20.8%	48.0%	29.8%	22.2%
1980	65.8	20.8	13.4	49.7	38.0	12.3
1982	66.8	17.9	15.3	63.6	23.1	13.2
1984	75.6	14.9	9.5	60.4	21.3	18.3
1986	75.7	10.5	13.7	56.8	20.6	22.5

inexorably since the 1978 elections. That gain has sometimes been at the expense of challengers, sometimes at the expense of the open seat candidates. In 1986 for the first time, however, contributions to open seat candidates in both houses exceeded contributions to challengers.[29] Increased spending on open seat candidates may well be the PACs' acknowledgment that competitiveness in congressional elections is increasingly limited to them.

The partisan preferences of PACs are less clear-cut. But one preference is terribly clear: PACs contribute almost exclusively to the candidates of the two major parties. Their rise to prominence in American campaigns thus becomes just the latest disadvantage the minor parties face (Table 4-5). As for the choice between Democratic and Republican candidates, the picture is both mixed and volatile. In the aggregate, Democratic candidates get a larger share of PAC contributions (56.4 percent in 1986) than Republicans. Moreover that percentage was higher in 1986 than it was four cycles earlier; it was 52.3 percent in 1980, 54.3 in 1982, and 57.3 in 1984.

Different kinds of PACs, of course, display different patterns of party inclination. Labor PACs are and have been overwhelmingly Democratic; 94.7 percent of their money went to Democratic candidates in 1984 and 92.5 in 1986 (Table 4-5). (The figure was 93.6 percent in 1980 and 94.6 in 1982.) These are totals that confirm once again the close alliance of organized labor and the Democratic party; they demonstrate, too, that the alliance is crucial to Democratic candidates for reasons other than labor's ability to register and turn out a vote for its endorsed candidates. The other ideologically homogeneous category of PACs, those of corporations, have been consistently but much less overwhelmingly Republican; 61.1 percent in 1986 (Table 4-5) and 64.1, 65.7, and 61.8 percent respectively in the three previous cycles.

The other chief FEC categories — the associations and the nonconnected PACs — are much more various, and there is really no reason why one should expect strong party inclinations

---

[29]The share of the contributions going to open seat candidates is affected by the number of open seats in any election cycle. The open seats in the House, for example, fluctuated from 59 in 1982 to 27 in 1984 to 44 in 1986.

TABLE 4-5
Contributions to Congressional Candidates by Political Party, 1986

Type of PAC	Democrat	Republican	Other
Corporate	$19,178,451	$30,181,046	$4,900
Labor	28,641,991	2,331,517	4,300
Association	16,786,061	17,614,691	1,750
Nonconnected	11,197,480	8,173,735	6,093
Other°	2,827,685	2,441,991	250
Total:	$78,631,668	$60,742,980	$17,293

° Includes PACs of cooperatives and corporations without stock.

among them. There are Democratic and Republican preferences among the PACs within them, and by some accident or fortune they gave just about equal portions to Democrats and Republicans in 1984 and a small advantage to Democrats in 1986 (Table 4-5). Both were, however, less Democratic in the past; in 1980, for example, the nonconnected PACs gave only 29.5 percent of their money to Democrats, and the membership association PACs only 43.9 percent. In the case of the nonconnected PACs, the explanation appears to be the rise of new PACs more sympathetic to Democratic issue positions (feminist PACs, for example) or a more general liberal ideology (PACs such as Progressive PAC and the personal PACs of Democratic officeholders and officeseekers).

When push comes to shove in strategies, though, the cultivation of incumbents overrides the commitment to party. The "real" party preferences of many PACs surface only in the open seat races in which there is no incumbent (Table 4-6). Corporate PACs show overwhelming preferences for Republican candidates when they are not confronting an incumbent — when they are freer to follow their ideological "heart." The patterns of the association PACs also intensify in open seat races, although not so dramatically. Labor PACs become even more purely Democratic in their contributions in open seat races.

Even at the level of the individual PAC, there are important differences among the various kinds of PACs. In their study of 1349 larger PACs in the 1980 campaigns, Eismeier and Pollock find

TABLE 4-6
PAC Contributions in Percentages to Incumbent, Challenger, and Open Seat Candidates for Congress, by Party Affiliation: 1986

Type of PAC	Incumbent		Challenger		Open Seat	
	Dem.	Rep.	Dem.	Rep.	Dem.	Rep.
Corporate	31.8%	44.5%	3.6%	4.3%	3.5%	12.3%
Labor	50.7	6.9	24.4	.1	17.4	.4
Association	37.9	39.2	5.5	3.0	5.3	9.0
Nonconnected	27.0	23.6	17.2	7.8	13.5	10.8
Other°	42.4	37.9	6.3	2.6	4.9	5.9
Total of all PACs:	37.3	31.7	10.7	3.5	8.5	8.4

°Includes PACs of cooperatives and corporations without stock.

that 27 percent of the nonconnected PACs in their group gave either 80 percent or more and 50 percent gave less than 20 percent of their contributions to Democrats. So, 77 percent gave heavily either to one party or the other. The comparable percentage for labor PACs was 94 (93 percent of them heavily Democratic), but only 34 percent for corporate PACs and 30 for association PACs. The great majority of labor and nonconnected PACs, therefore, were heavily partisan; the great majority of corporate and association PACs were not.[30]

As these data begin to suggest, PACs singly and in the aggregate follow a complex mixture of strategies in their contributions to candidates. With the exception of a minority of single-minded PACs, they are seeking a number of goals and responding to a number of often conflicting pressures. Regardless of how well it is run or how politically sophisticated its management is, a PAC often cannot escape the need to balance and juggle a number of contradictory goals and strategies. There are numerous ways to categorize those strategies, most of them having a great deal in common. The one employed in this chapter groups them into four categories: the pragmatic (or legislative) strategy, the local

[30]Theodore J. Eismeier and Philip H. Pollock III, "Political Action Committees: Varieties of Organization and Strategy," in Michael J. Malbin, ed., *Money and Politics in the United States* (Chatham, N.J.: Chatham House, 1984), 130–131.

strategy, the ideological strategy, and the strategy of organizational maintenance.[31]

The Pragmatic (Legislative) Strategy. This is perhaps the dominant strategy for all of the PACs with parent organizations. It is reflected primarily in their overwhelming support for incumbents running for reelection. It is reflected as well in patterns of support for members of the leadership and members of specific committees. As a strategy it reflects the goals of pursuing and maintaining legislative access, of coordinating PAC contributions with the lobbying goals of the parent organization. In the words of one manager of a corporate PAC,

> PACs are important for doing business. They're a useful tool. But, an irreplaceable tool? No. You are not buying anything with your PAC money, but your lobbyists would be at a disadvantage if, after working for seven months with a staffer on a bill, the lobbyist (when approached for support) turned around and said: Sorry, we don't give to political campaigns.[32]

In short, this is the strategy of protecting lines of communication, of keeping doors and ears open, and above all, of not offending powerful incumbents by supporting their opponents.

One finds the pragmatic strategy among all kinds of PACs, and there is evidence that links it to other kinds of influence in Congress. It is clear that corporate PACs in which Washington representatives have a voice tend to pursue legislative strategies; it is less clear which way the direction of cause runs.[33] Do these PACs pursue a legislative strategy because their parents have lobbyists, or do their parents have lobbyists because they are committed more generally to a strategy of legislative influence? And the type of industry the corporate or association PAC represents appears also to make a difference. Pragmatic, legislative

[31]For other ways of categorizing strategies, see Theodore J. Eismeier and Philip H. Pollock III, "Strategy and Choice in Congressional Elections: The Role of Political Action Committees," *American Journal of Political Science*, vol. 30 (Feb. 1986), 197–213; and J. David Gopoian, "What Makes PACs Tick? An Analysis of the Allocation Patterns of Economic Interest Groups," *American Journal of Political Science* , vol. 28 (May 1984), 259–281.

[32]Morrison, 22.

[33]See Handler and Mulkern, 26–27; and Eismeier and Pollock, "Political Action Committees: Varieties of Organizations and Strategies," 125ff.

strategies are more common among those subject to old-style economic regulation and those close to administrative and agency politics — those with parent organizations in transportation, communications, banking, and defense.[34] Presumably, these industries have reached some kind of accommodation with the authority of Congress; in many instances, indeed, they accept the usefulness of the governmental role. There is, however, no underestimating the strain the strategy puts on corporate PACs, however; Democratic majorities in one or both houses of Congress force a substantial conflict with their fundamental party preferences. Labor PACs have faced fewer such hard choices.

It is perhaps the large, membership PACs that are the quintessential pragmatists. As Eismeier and Pollock write:

> . . . it is in the professional, Washington-based trade PACs that strategies of influence take purest form. In most of these committees, donor participation and influence are negligible. . . . In the absence of internal constraints, such PACs are free to weigh most heavily the staff's considered judgment about maximizing the political profits from campaign investments.[35]

That is, in these PACs, political professionalism reigns without having to pursue the mixed strategies that political and organizational realities force on other PACs.

The Local or Regional Strategies. These are the strategies that recognize the power of local political pressure of one form or another. Most large, connected PACs are to some extent or another local, if only because their parent organizations are federated and thus, in part at least, local. Often it is the donors rather who are local, and the PAC's localism thus is rooted in concern for the local candidate enthusiasms of donors. The localism of connected PACs has another root: this one in the alliances, formal or informal, that PACs and their parents have with local groups,

---

[34]Handler and Mulkern, 29–32; and J. David Gopoian, "Change and Continuity in Defense PAC Behavior," *American Politics Quarterly*, vol. 13 (July 1985), 297–322.

[35]Eismeier and Pollock, "An Organizational Analysis of Political Action Committees," 202.

officeholders, and voters in concern over a local industry, a local crop, or the more general local or regional economy. At times, localism as a strategy is not easy to distinguish from the pragmatic course; a PAC may support the local member of Congress in order to assure continuing easy working relationships. In part, too, this strategy may be a recognition of local political realities; the corporate PAC in a predominantly Democratic county does not want to close off access to dominant local political elites and officeholders, regardless of their political views.

Pressures to support local goals tend to be limited to PACs with parents. The nonconnected PACs are national in their appeals; and their donors have no local identity, no local interchange with other voters. But for the connected PACs, it is another and compelling kind of pragmatic strategy. One study, at least, suggests that it is a strategy common among PACs in the defense industries.[36] It is not a surprising relationship, especially in view of the importance of defense industries to their localities. For most PACs the local strategy simply reflects a combination of donor influence and a very practical desire to stay in touch with local political elites — reasons strongest among corporate PACs.

Ideological/Issue Strategies. Concern over an issue or a related issue dimension may also move PACs as they make their contributions. There are PACs whose decisions are governed by key votes on a specific issue, and there are PACs who respond to measures of the Americans for Democratic Action or the American Conservative Union on the liberalism or conservatism of candidates. The PACs following this strategy make their own calculation of the faithfulness or friendliness of candidates; for evidence they look at roll call analyses, the responses to candidate questionnaires, or the reports of lobbyists or PACs of similar convictions. It is, in short, the strategy of electing and protecting like-minded men and women in Congress. Its signs are overwhelming support for the candidates of a single party and a willingness to support challengers over incumbents.

The practitioners *par excellence* of this strategy are the labor PACs, with their almost complete support of Democrats, and the nonconnected, ideological PACs, with *their* commitment to the

[36]Gopoian, p. 305–307.

candidates of one party or the other. Among other kinds of PACs, the strategy appears to be more common among larger than smaller PACs.[37] It is also more common among corporate PACs subject to new forms of "social" regulation, for example, for protecting the environment or ensuring a continuing energy supply. Corporate PACs of the petroleum, chemical, and rubber industries afford good examples.[38] One can only speculate that they have not accepted or accommodated to the kinds of regulation represented by the Occupational Safety and Health Administration (OSHA) and the Environmental Protection Agency (EPA).

The Strategies of Organizational Maintenance. All social organizations engage in self-protective behavior, and PACs are no exception. For many PACs it means keeping harmony and sustaining participation levels in the PAC by satisfying donor opinion on contributions. (In that sense this strategy is often hard to distinguish from the strategy of localism.) PACs may also have to satisfy the political opinions and judgments of their "superiors" — corporate CEOs, labor executives, officials of membership organizations. They must protect the image and reputation of the parent organization, especially if it depends on a broadly based consumer satisfaction — a consideration that almost always weighs on the side of political caution and an aversion to political risk.

These self-protective considerations account in particular for two kinds of PAC behavior. First, they explain the inclination of some PACs to pad their "winning percentage," to give to candidates likely to win in order to be able to report stunning electoral victories — thus, wise and productive political "investments" — to their donors and superiors. One survey of a group of PAC managers reports that 93 percent of them consider a "record of backing winners" either very or fairly important in meeting the expectations of their donors.[39] It is, of course, a kind of organization building that relies on a certain lack of political sophistica-

---

[37]Handler and Mulkern, 24–25.

[38]Ibid., 31; and Theodore J. Eismeier and Philip H. Pollock, III, "The Microeconomy of PACs," paper delivered an the annual meeting of the American Political Science Association (Aug. 29–Sept. 1, 1985).

[39]Eismeier and Pollock, "An Organizational Analysis of Political Action Committees," 197.

tion, but it is effective nonetheless. Second, faced with the need to cover their own expenses, some nonconnected PACs use direct-mail solicitation to advertise the PAC (and its political efficacy) and to build up in-house contributor lists — all to maintain the organization rather than maximize the sums available for political expenditures.[40]

It is a rare PAC that can pursue just one of those strategies (see box). Most of them are navigating a maze of contradictory and compromising goals, accused often of timidity, political ineffectiveness, and cowardice on matters of belief and principle. The dilemmas of choice, moreover, set PAC against PAC; there has been continuing tension, for example, between corporate PACs giving money to incumbent Democrats (the pragmatic strategy) and those giving heavily or exclusively to Republicans (the ideological strategy). Compromise aside, the interesting analytical question on this point concerns the extent to which PACs drawn in so many strategic directions are capable of effective, "rational" political action.

THE BALANCING OF INTERESTS AND STRATEGIES

Sun Oil permitted a reporter for a national newspaper to sit in on a meeting of the contribution committee of its PAC (SunPAC); the committee decides which candidates will receive the PAC's money. His report began this way:

> The discussion turned to Indiana's Second Congressional District, which posed a special problem for the Sun Company. The committee chairman, Robert P. Hauptfuhrer, was the first to express an opinion.
> "His energy voting record isn't very good," he observed dubiously of Philip R. Sharpe, a four-term moderate Democrat challenged by a conservative Republican, Ralph Van Natta, a former state motor vehicle commissioner."
> But Clyde A. Wheeler Jr., Sun's chief lobbyist, observed that

[40]On this point, see the researches of Michael Malbin reported in Ronald Brownstein, "On Paper, Conservative PACs Were Tigers in 1984 — But Look Again," *National Journal* (June 29, 1985), 1504–1509.

Mr. Sharp was chairman of a key House energy subcommittee, and that he had been "very evenhanded" in presiding over a long series of hearings on natural gas this summer. Since the incumbent was "probably undefeatable," even in a heavily redistricted area, Mr. Wheeler said, it would probably not be worthwhile to help finance his opponent. . . .

In less than five minutes, the discussion was over. "Unless there's an objection, we're going to pass," ruled Mr. Hauptfuhrer.

—*Robert D. Hershey Jr., "$22,000 Plus a Long List of Races Equals a Busy Session for One Committee," New York Times (Oct. 13, 1982).*

The definition of "rationality" is certainly one of the oldest and deepest traps in political science. Most defensibly it involves some measure of the capacity, with limited means, of maximizing the attainment of one's political goals. In this context, therefore, it is a question of the ability of PACs to achieve the goals implicit in their strategies — to reelect incumbents, to elect or reelect like-minded public officials, and to build party majorities. All of these goals and their strategies share the need to elect the favored candidates. (Significantly, some of the local goals and many of the organizational goals do not depend on electoral victory; indeed a case can be made that direct-mail fund-raising is easier after defeat than after victory!) On this point Jacobson and Kernell suggest that the strategic calculus of contributors to congressional campaigns involves the interplay of two variables: the contributor's goals or motives and the direction of short-term party trends.[41] But both goals and the flow of partisan forces obviously change, often abruptly and with little warning. Are the PACs able to adjust their strategies to them?

The evidence is mixed. Eismeier and Pollock do find some movement of PAC contributions between 1980 and 1982 (especially among corporate PACs) in the direction that the theory of rational political expectations would predict. That is, faced with the likelihood of a Democratic year, 1980 supporters of Republican challengers shifted their contributions in 1982 away from

[41]Gary C. Jacobson and Samuel Kernell, *Strategy and Choice in Congressional Elections* , 2d ed. (New Haven: Yale University Press, 1983).

those ill-fated challengers and to the protection of threatened Republican incumbents. At the same time, however, pro-Democratic PACs did not seize the opportunities of 1982 to rush their money to Democratic challengers.[42] Other broader evidence also suggests that PACs do not change the pattern of their contributions over time, that they do not respond to gross political changes or even to changes in the behavior of officeholders. The contribution decisions of many PACs are incremental, with spending in the previous electoral cycle forming the baseline for the contribution decisions of the present one.[43] The evidence suggests once again, in other words, that some PACs do and some do not.[44]

The strategic complexity that PACs face may well be one important reason why they give such relatively small sums to so many candidates. In 1978 the average PAC contributed $23,906 to candidates for Congress; by 1984 that average had climbed to $37,088. The increase in six years was one of 55.1 percent. In the same years, the average contribution made by a PAC to a candidate rose from $722 to $1,065. The increase in average contribution was 47.5 percent. Not only did the more affluent PACs *not* use their new riches to make relatively larger contributions, but they actually increased the size of the average contribution at a slower rate than their average aggregate contributions. With greater resources in hand, they opted for an ever greater dispersion of their political contributions. Moreover, the differences among types of PAC are telling. In 1984 the average labor PAC contribution to federal candidates was $1,826, and the average from a nonconnected PAC was $1,544; in contrast, the average from a corporate PAC was $751 and $1,082 from an association

---

[42]Eismeier and Pollock, "Strategy and Choice in Congressional Elections: The Role of Political Action Committees," 198ff. The authors also point out that the resulting asymmetry works greatly to the Republicans' advantage; money flows to Republican challengers when their times are good, but money does not seem to shift to Democratic challengers in their sunny seasons. See pp. 212–213.

[43]See Handler and Mulkern, 18–20; and Gopoian, 313–314.

[44]The practice of "earmarking" is perhaps the ultimate in nonrational strategies. It permits the donor to earmark a PAC contribution for a specific party or PAC, thus taking the allocation decision out of the hands of the PAC. The practice is found almost exclusively among corporate PACs — the recent study of Catherine Morrison for The Conference Board finds that a third of them permit it. Few, however, encourage it, and the sums of money actually earmarked is in most cases small.

PAC. Thus, the average contribution is, as one would predict, smaller among those PACs that appear to be following the most mixed and diverse political strategies.

Finally, there remains one important issue of PAC tactic that is also an issue of effectiveness and rationality, albeit of another sort. The strategic considerations so far have honed in on the question of which candidates would be supported. *After* that decision, however, there is the emerging issue of assuring the greatest impact for every dollar contributed to the specified candidates. The great majority of PACs (e.g., more than 90 percent of corporate PACs[45]) give their contributions in cash, but a growing number of large PACs are making contributions "in kind" — in training classes for candidates and campaign managers, in fund-raising help and advice, in research and polling, and in advice on media buying and personal appearance. The effect of these contributions, of course, is to intrude the PAC into the campaign to some degree and to permit it to shape the people and the events of the campaign. In fact, some of the larger PACs have developed field staffs to help recruit attractive candidates, to identify the needy and worthy ones, and to negotiate and supervise the in-kind contributions. Such an organizational capacity and base of information, furthermore, moves these PACs to new levels of effectiveness and gives them the capacity, at least, for rigorously rational decisions that go beyond merely financing a campaign.[46]

VI. Independent Spending among PACs

The dramatic and sensational are easily exaggerated. If it is easy to overestimate the role of PACs in all of campaign finance, it is easier to mistake the importance of PAC independent spending. In 1986 for every dollar PACs spent in independent expenditures, they spent 16 in direct contributions to congres-

[45]Survey conducted in 1986 by Civic Service, Inc., for the Business-Industry PAC, the U.S. Chamber of Commerce, the National Association of Business PACs, the National Association of Manufacturers, and the Public Affairs Council.

[46]See Margaret A. Latus, "Assessing Ideological PACs: From Outrage to Understanding," in Michael J. Malbin, ed., *Money and Politics in the United States*, 159–161.

sional candidates (Table 4-3). That is, independent spending accounted for less than 6 percent of total PAC spending in the congressional campaigns of 1986. Independent spending is only a small part of total PAC spending; however, PACs usually account for more than 90 percent of the independent spending in congressional campaigns. In 1984, however, they accounted for only 80 percent, the result both of reduced PAC spending and of Michael Goland's $1.1 million intervention in the Illinois senatorial race.

Independent spending (by whomever) may be of two kinds: pro and con — urging the election or defeat of a candidate. It was in fact the con spending, the so-called negative spending, that brought independent spending its first notoriety. In 1980 the National Conservative Political Action Committee (NCPAC) spent heavily to defeat six liberal Democratic senators in their bids for reelection. Four lost (Birch Bayh of Indiana, Frank Church of Idaho, John Culver of Iowa, and George McGovern of South Dakota),[47] and NCPAC was quick to take credit. It probably took too much credit — each of the four losers had a good many reasons of ideology and constituency relationships to lose — but media fascination with the new gun in town gave credibility to its claims.

In any event, the growth of independent spending has happened rather quickly. In 1978 PACs reported spending only about $300,000 independently in congressional elections; the total rose to $2.2 million in 1980 and $5.5 million in 1982. (NCPAC accounted for more than half of the spending in 1980 and in 1982.) The total receded to $4.8 million in 1984, but bounced back to $8.7 million in 1986. It is a growth curve with three characteristics. First, it *is* one of growth. Second, it is one of decelerating growth after a very quick and steep rise from 1976 to 1982. And third, the curve dips in the presidential years, years in which (beginning with 1980) there has been substantial independent spending in the presidential campaigns.

Matters of growth aside, the independent spending of PACs for the last three election cycles has been marked by a concentration

---

[47]Two of the incumbent Democrats won: Alan Cranston of California and Thomas Eagleton of Missouri.

TABLE 4-7
Independent Spending by PACs on All Congressional Campaigns, 1982–1986
(in millions of dollars)

		1982		1984		1986°	
		For	Against	For	Against	For	Against
I.	House	$ .7	$ .9	$1.3	$ .1	$3.7	$ .3
	Senate	.4	3.5	2.1	1.2	3.8	.9
II.	Democrats	.3	3.9	.9	.4	3.3	.7
	Republicans	.7	.5	2.4	1.0	4.1	.4
III.	*Total*		$5.5		$4.6		$8.7

°Data for the party totals for 1986 come from candidate reports and total to approximately $200,000 less than the totals by house.

in senatorial races, a fondness for Republican candidates, and a volatile shifting among expenditures "for" and "against" candidates (Table 4-7). It has also been characterized by the domination of a small number of PACs. This domination, moreover, is doubly significant — both on its own account and as an aid to understanding the other three characteristics.

Preoccupation with the Senate. The reasons are not hard to imagine. Senate campaigns have greater visibility and greater political stakes; it is easier, therefore, for a national group to raise money for them (especially if it is a nonconnected PAC using direct mail) or to justify them to membership (if it is an association PAC). Senatorial races also afford the independent spender a greater opportunity to use mass media in the campaign. There is a narrowing of the spending gap over the years, and the growing importance of it in House races reflects the increasing participation of association PACs in 1984 and 1986.

Support for Republicans. "Support" for one of the major parties can usefully be reckoned as the sum of spending for the candidates of one party plus spending against those of the other party. By that measure the Republican advantage has narrowed from more than 5 to 1 in 1982 to 1.3 to 1 in 1986. The initial broad gap resulted largely from the dominance in early years of the conservative PACs, especially NCPAC. It was also concentrated in senatorial campaigns, in which all kinds of PAC activity have been less incumbent oriented. Thus the end of NCPAC's dominance has made a difference. Additionally, the increased spending of the membership associations has been in their best legislative/ pragmatic tradition; and that has helped Democratic incumbents. For most of the new era in campaign finance, however, there was a sizeable Republican advantage in independent spending, and it contrasted sharply with the small Democratic edge in the total of all PAC direct contributions.

Volatility of Pro and Con. Independent spending clearly is shifting from predominantly negative arguments to preponderantly positive. A substantial part of the shift is accounted for by NCPAC's reduced spending in congressional campaigns, but that observation begs the issue. There is no doubt that negative campaigning no longer seems as effective as it did in 1980. NCPAC suffered a humiliating defeat in the 1982 campaigns; it targeted more than a dozen House and Senate incumbents, and only one, Sen. Howard Cannon of Nevada, was defeated. (Senator Cannon also had two other reasons for losing: his Democratic party affiliation and allegations that he knew of union plans to offer him a bribe.) Since then, in fact, some candidates have been able to turn independent spending against them into vote-winning countertactics. Negative campaigning also appears to have failed as a fund-raising technique for NCPAC; at the very least it did not save it from the plague of debts and deficits that became public knowledge by 1986 and 1987.

In 1986 six PACs spent at least $400,000 independently; all of them are either association or nonconnected PACs.

1. National Committee to Preserve Social Security: $1,931,600.
2. Realtors Political Action Committee: $1,699,796.
3. American Medical Association PAC: $1,549,519.
4. National Conservative PAC: $1,079,814.
5. National Rifle Association Political Victory Fund: $792,516
6. National Right to Life PAC: $406,264.

Together they spent $7.5 million (or 86 percent) of the $8.7 million spent independently by PACs in the 1986 congressional elections. Their domination pales, of course, beside NCPAC's single-handed 58 percent of the 1982 total. It is substantial enough, though, to continue the generalization that the PAC role in independent spending is a role of the few.

The major players, if a small group, are not a homogeneous group. They come from only two of the FEC's categories, but therein lie some powerful differences. In 1986 nonconnected PACs made 53.3 percent of the PAC independent expenditures, and association PACs made 42.7 percent. (There obviously were very few players among the corporate and labor PACs.) The active nonconnected PACs were and are much more likely than the association PACs to engage in negative campaigning. In fact, in 1986 they made 84 percent of the expenditures urging the defeat of candidates; they accounted for 98 percent in 1984.

Clearly, the center of commitment has shifted from the nonconnected to the association PACs. NCPAC's declining role is probably the result both of its own fund-raising problems (which in turn may reflect the lowered level of conservative fears after six years of Ronald Reagan) and of its preoccupation with presidential politics. But why the *increased* role of a few large association PACs? One of the conventional explanations points to the necessity of finding a new outlet for PAC funds. The American Medical Association PAC and the Realtors PAC have funds far in excess of a million dollars to disperse (e.g., in 1986 they contributed $2.1 million and $2.8 million, respectively, to federal candidates). Furthermore, they already are making direct contributions to a very large number of candidates: 465 for AMPAC and 533 for the Realtors in 1986. If for whatever reason they are unwilling to raise substantially the size of their contributions — for fear of attracting too much attention and unfavorable publicity, for example — spending independently may be the most attractive outlet for new money. Their decisions certainly say that it is a more attractive option than giving money to party committees or other PACs — or than cutting back on receipts from their politically willing members.

But these PAC decisions are probably not that simple. Some PAC leadership certainly believes that independent spending opens an attractive new avenue for political action. It enables the PAC to participate in a more purely electoral strategy, one that supplements the parent organization's concern over issues in its lobbying. Says Peter Lauer of AMPAC,

> We don't believe that issues are the way independent expenditures should be promoted. Name identification and getting out the vote are the most important goals.[48]

This perhaps puts the point too narrowly. The PACs that have moved into independent spending are those that have outdistanced the limited tactic of direct contributions. They have developed the staff, the information, the sophistication — that is, the political capacity — to seek a wider political role.

These excursions into independent spending are not, however, without risk for PACs. Nonconnected PACs such as NCPAC face a burgeoning opposition to their spending in local congressional campaigns — and inevitably, as the word spreads, an increasing unwillingness of donors to give to campaigns that will be unpopular, or worse, will be turned into a winning issue for the candidates they oppose. But the parentless PACs at least have no parent or membership that will be embarrassed by aggressive political tactics or cheeky political language. Indeed, much-quoted expressions of political machismo such as those of NCPAC's Terry Dolan (on independent spending: "A group like ours could lie through its teeth and the candidate it helps stays clean,"[49]) may bring the group a certain useful celebrity.

For the PACs with parent organizations, however, independent spending can cause major internal problems within the organization. One very observant journalist reports about the Realtors' support of the Democratic candidate (Rep. James Jones) in Oklahoma for the Senate in 1986:

> Prominent local realtors and about a dozen Senate Republicans bombarded the group with telephone calls questioning why money was being spent on an opponent of [Republican Don] Nickles, who has one of the best Senate records in the group's annual vote ratings.

[48]Maxwell Glen, "Spending Independently," *National Journal* (June 21, 1986), 1537.

[49]Myra MacPherson, "The New Right Brigade," *Washington Post* (Aug. 10, 1980).

Those attacks were enhanced because Nickles had a double-digit lead over Jones and won with 55 percent of the vote. "You should never enter a race three weeks before an election unless it is really close and you can make an impact," said Jim Nicholas, president-elect of the Oklahoma Association of Realtors and a Nickles supporter . . .[50]

That was not the only membership trouble the Realtors' PAC had in 1986, and AMPAC took its share of flak, too. Their internal problems, it should be clear, were not spurred by negative spending; the money was all spent in support of candidates. It is too early to predict the future of organization PACs with independent spending, but such intraorganizational costs may be a more potent limit on their spending than the external issues of their impact and effectiveness in the campaign.

The shift to independent spending by association PACs will have one more important consequence: it will provide a different and probably more accurate measure of the magnitude of independent spending. The FEC has required PACs soliciting money for independent spending to include the solicitation costs if the mailed material urged the election or defeat of a candidate. The result has been reports of independent spending in which a great part of the spending is in the solicitation of the funds — and not in the kinds of campaign expenditures (media ads or mailings to voters) that one ordinarily thinks of as "campaigning." In some cases nonconnected PACs have even taken proceeds above costs entirely for the purpose of further prospecting and building of lists; in these cases the serving of organizational purposes supplants any political mission. Since the association PACs rarely use direct-mail solicitation and their parent organizations cover most of their overhead costs, their reports of independent spending are more purely expenditures in the persuasions of the campaign. In this sense a million dollars of AMPAC spending is "more" than a million by NCPAC by any conventional political indicator.[51]

[50]Richard E. Cohen, "Spending Independently," *National Journal* (Dec. 6, 1986), 2933.

[51]Malbin develops the point extensively, although largely in the context of spending in presidential campaigns, in an article by Brownstein, "On Paper, Conservative PACs Were Tigers in 1984 — But Look Again," *National Journal* (June 29, 1985), 1504–1509.

VII. In Conclusion and Speculation

For more than a decade, the growth of PACs — their money, their number, their influence — was the big story in American campaign finance. They came to symbolize the importance of cash in campaigns, and the zeal of the reformers focused most often on them. Now their growth seems largely over, and we really do not know why. The conventional explanation is that the "PAC movement" has "fulfilled its potential" or mobilized the political potential — but these are truisms rather than explanations. If there was a substantial element of faddism in the growth, is the fad now over, the victim perhaps of unfulfilled expectations and lost political chic? Or have sober cost-benefit analyses by founding organizations or entrepreneurs come to a bearish conclusion about PACs? Or has the combination of economic deregulation and the drying up of new government programs reduced the perceived need for political activity? The answers are by no means clear, and they will not become much clearer until we know more about the life histories and the internal decision-making of PACs and the potential parents of PACs.

No generalization about the approximately 4,000 PACs in existence fits easily. The stunning diversity among them defeats easy summary. At best, one can speak of modes and averages and major types, and even then one has to acknowledge all manner of exceptions. For a political science accustomed to generalizing about only two parties, it is frustrating not to be able to deal with PACs in simple statements. With all of that said and with all proper reservations, two sweeping generalizations about American PACs, one based on parentage and the other on size, do have a good deal of validity.

First, there are very important differences in the aggregate between PACs with parent organizations and PACs without them. PACs with parent organizations solicit funds from an organization's loyal clientele and with overhead and administrative funds usually provided by that organization. Their political strategies and tactics are set primarily by the parent in conjunction with the parent's other political activities — lobbying or voter registration efforts, for example. These strategies tend to be moderate, low-risk, and pragmatic, at least in part to protect the broader interests and image of the parent organization.

The nonconnected PACs, on the other hand, tend to raise money — both for political activities and for the ordinary expenses of the PAC and its fund-raising by mail solicitation of unaffiliated individuals. They are most commonly run by a few entrepreneurs who make the organizational and political decisions; donor input and preferences count for less. Their political strategies are bolder, featuring more ideological purity and greater funding of risky challengers in their direct contributions. Historically, too, a larger percentage of them have made independent expenditures in congressional and presidential campaigns.

Moreover, a good deal of the debate over the political responsibility of PACs also comes down to their parentage. Even though PACs with parents are not participatory democracies, they are bound to their donors and to the parent by common ties and loyalties. If not participatory, they are at least responsive — and that responsiveness constitutes an important kind of responsibility. No such ties characterize most nonconnected PACs, especially those that result from the entrepreneurial act and that define their own goals and tactics. At the most they are held responsible by the continuing need to raise money and to protect the PAC's ability to do so.

The distinction between PACs with parents and those without is heightened when one looks at the independent expenditures of PACs. In the case of direct contributions to candidates, the candidate is responsible for the ultimate spending of the money in the campaign. If the candidate's taste or tactics offend, voters can vote against that candidate. In the case of independent expenditures, the PAC makes the final allocation of the resources in the campaign; and displeased voters have no remedy. If the spending was truly independent, the candidate it was intended to help can hardly be held accountable. When connected PACs engage in independent spending, they are at least held responsible by the interests and leadership of their parent organization. When it is a nonconnected PAC, the lines of accountability for activity in a campaign are at their most attenuated and most troubling.[52]

Second, there are the differences that flow from size. The big PACs — that is, the ones spending the largest sums in the campaign — are more ideological and more willing to take risks than the small ones. They spend proportionately more of their political budgets on challengers and open seat candidates.[53] Furthermore, some of the most affluent are also becoming major independent spenders: AMPAC and Realtors PAC are two prime examples.

Even more important, perhaps, the largest PACs increasingly have been able to extend or expand their political role. Most are much more than checkbook PACs. Some have, for instance, begun to contribute major sums of "in kind" contributions, thereby insinuating themselves more actively into campaigns and their management. Others link their PAC activities to political programs of the parent organization, whether it be legislative lobbying or, in the case of labor, extensive programs of voter activation. In a real sense, the AFL-CIO's COPE was the first of them; its contributions to candidates and party committees melded with a well-established role beyond the funding of campaigns — the labor role in endorsing candidates, registering voters, instructing voters, and getting them to the polls. The great association PACs (and some nonconnected PACs) have moved in other directions, especially into more intensive and dominant roles in the campaign.

It is in these "superPACs" that the genus PAC has been developed to its most powerful form. Their broadened political roles and tactics undoubtedly reflect sheer resources, but they reflect more — staff, expertise, research, information, political memory, local ties, and political sophistication. The more they develop the capacity to do the political job well, the more they develop the capacity for doing a larger political job. In them one sees the essence of the "entrepreneurial style of American politics" in which

---

[52]For a fuller exploration of this problem, see Sorauf, "Who's in Charge? Accountability in Political Action Committees," 591–614.

[53]Eismeier and Pollock, "Political Action Committees: Varieties of Organizations and Strategy" in Malbin's *Money and Politics in the United States*, 132–136.

shallow mass participation may be combined with rationalized influence seeking. That it to say, the curious mixture of political passion and participatory indolence that seems to motivate many donors allows staff professionals to amass resources nationally and use them to advance group interests.[54]

The combination of relatively unincumbered resources and rational, skilled management produces in this most developed form a political organization of formidable effectiveness. It is also one of extraordinary appropriateness for a cash-based, candidate-centered campaigning.

---

[54]Eismeier and Pollock, "An Organizational Analysis of Political Action Committees," 211.

5

The Political Parties: Shadow or Substance?

On the surface, the party role does not amount to much. In 1985–86 all of the candidates for the House or the Senate received $4,950,326 from committees of political parties, whether national, state, or local party committees. That was a bit more than the combined contributions of the two largest PAC contributers: the Realtors PAC and the American Medical Association PAC. The party contributions accounted for a paltry 1.1 percent of the receipts of all candidates for Congress.

The parties also spent $22,753,193 on behalf of those congressional candidates — expenditures they coordinated with the candidates' campaigns but spent directly themselves.[1] But even when one adds contributions and expenditures on behalf of candidates, one has a total of only $27.7 million out of the total of $481.3 million spent directly in the campaign by candidates, parties, and independent spenders in the 1984 congressional elections — only a very modest 5.8 percent. (The comparable percentage two years earlier was 6.4.)

Such figures bespeak a party role in the nation's legislative elections that is in many ways a measure of the parties' decline

---

[1]Some scholars and practitioners refer to these expenditures "on behalf of" candidates as "coordinated expenditures." The FEC, in its published reports refers to them both as "441a(d) expenditures" and "on behalf of" expenditures. These are three ways of referring to precisely the same thing.

over the past half century. And yet, curiously, the parties are raising and spending more money than they did in their recent pasts. Some of their observers in fact see the revival, even the resurrection, of the national party committees in a new "sugar daddy" role. The truth is that the parties are both weak and strong — weak by any comparison external to themselves, strong by a comparison to their selves of 25 years ago. It is a classic case of good news and bad news, the glass both half full and half empty.

I. Party Domination in Other Times, Other Places

To put into perspective the role of the American parties in today's campaign finance, one has only to look at practices elsewhere or earlier in American politics. That, however, is not altogether easy, for full reporting of the details of finance such as the Federal Election Campaign Act (FECA) now requires is without parallel in other times or places. Legislated candor — in campaign finance, the registration of lobbyists, freedom of information acts, and conflict of interest statutes — is one of the refreshingly special characteristics of American government and politics, but it is a tradition we never legislated about very rigorously until after the Watergate scandals of the 1970s. Consequently, there are not many full-length studies of campaign finance in the other democracies or in earlier periods of the American experience. We do, however, have bits and pieces of a picture for many — enough to understand the contours of other practices and to contrast them with those of contemporary American politics.[2]

---

[2]One full-length study of importance is Michael Pinto-Duschinsky, *British Political Finance 1930–1980* (Washington, D.C.: American Enterprise Institute, 1981). Much of what we know about campaign finance elsewhere derives from three other sources: the American Enterprise Institute series on elections elsewhere (*Britain at the Polls, Canada at the Polls, Israel at the Polls*, etc., published in the 1970s and 1980s), many of them edited by Howard R. Penniman. Earlier Arnold Heidenheimer edited *Comparative Political Finance: The Financing of Party Organizations and Election Campaigns* (Lexington, Mass.: Heath, 1970); it presents snapshots of campaign finance in a number of countries and continents. For a brief comparative overview of campaign finance, see Khayyam Z. Paltiel, "Campaign Finance: Contrasting Practices and Reforms," in David Butler et al., eds., *Democracy at the Polls: A Comparative Study of Competitive National Elections*

Louise Overacker's study of American campaign finance circa 1930 has no chapter on the party role because it needed none. As the party governed virtually every aspect of campaign finance, it dominates every chapter. The chapter on "Filling the Campaign Chest" begins simply: "The dollars which a political party spends must be begged or borrowed from someone."[3] The chapter entitled "Why Men Give" opens more specifically:

> Why did the Standard Oil Company give $250,000 to the Republican National Committee in 1896? Why did Edward L. Doheny give financial support to both parties in 1920?[4]

In these and so many other passages, it simply is implicit but very clear that the parties controlled the raising and supplying of money for campaigns. Not only did the candidates not have a major part in this aspect of campaign finance, they were often levied a portion of the funds the party was raising for the whole campaign! Writes Overacker,

> The candidate is an interested party who is expected to contribute to his personal campaign fund, the general party fund, or to both. How much he pays may depend upon the importance of the office for which he is running, his financial resources and his liberality, the bitterness of the contest, and whether he sought the nomination or was a somewhat reluctant sacrifice upon the political altar. The size of his contribution may be left to his own conscience but in some cases a schedule of payments is worked out.[5]

It was the party or some party functionary who "worked out" that schedule. A passage like this one rings strangely these days, of course, and the reason is obvious: it reflects a relationship between candidate and party on matters of campaign finance that is almost completely the reverse from today's.

In the other democracies of the world, a substantial party role

---

(Washington: American Enterprise Institute, 1981), 138–172. The classic works on earlier times in American campaign finance, those by Louise Overacker and Alexander Heard, are discussed and noted in chap. 2.
   [3]Louise Overacker, *Money in Elections* (New York: Macmillan, 1932), 100.
   [4]Ibid, 169.
   [5]Ibid., 100.

persists, in part merely as a result of regulatory legislation. In Great Britain there are steep limits of about 4,500 pounds (about $7,200 in mid-1987) on constituency spending by candidates for Parliament; consequently, in 1983 the average major party candidate (Conservative, Labour, and the Liberal/Social Democratic Alliance) spent only about 3,000 pounds. The national parties are, however, under no such constraints; Labour spent 2,300,000 pounds ($3.45 million in 1983) and the Conservatives 3,830,000 pounds ($5.75 million). While interest groups are free to advertise their political views — not unlike American independent spending — the great bulk of their political spending flowed into party coffers. Seven trade unions alone contributed a total of almost 4 million pounds ($6 million) to the Labour party in 1983, and 14 companies contributed 50,000 pounds ($75,000) or more to the Conservative party.[6]

In Canada, to take another example, legal limits on the expenditures of both candidates for Parliament and on those of the parties also define the financial roles of each. In the 1980 election, the Liberal party spent $3,846,223 against its statutory limit of $4,546,192; its candidates spent $6,073,604 against their aggregate expenditure limits of $7,840,987.[7]

In other Western democracies, parties find a central role because public subsidies are paid to the parties rather than to candidates. Even in the 1970s the West German government provided subsidies worth 60 million U.S. dollars directly to the parties, a sum that accounted for about half of their receipts.[8] A later comparative study of campaign finance reports that of the 10 European countries making direct payments from the public treasury — Austria, Denmark, Finland, France, West Germany, Italy, Netherlands, Norway, Sweden, and the United Kingdom — only one (France) made payments to candidates. In the other

[6]Data from Michael Pinto-Duschinsky, "Trends in British Political Funding," *Parliamentary Affairs*, 38 (1985), 328–347. Note that the total receipts of the parties will far exceed their political expenditures since receipts must cover all overhead and operating costs.

[7]The figures are in Canadian dollars and come from F. Leslie Seidle and Khayyam Z. Paltiel, "Party Finance, the Election Expenses Act, and Campaign Spending in 1979 and 1980," in Howard R. Penniman, ed., *Canada at the Polls, 1979 and 1980* (Washington, D.C.: American Enterprise Institute, 1981).

[8]Generally on West German campaign finance, see Karl H. Cerny, ed., *Germany at the Polls: The Bundestag Election of 1976* (Washington, D.C.: American Enterprise Institute, 1978).

nine, the subsidies were paid to political parties and/or parliamentary groups.[9]

Behind these descriptions is a final point: parties elsewhere have sources of funds that American parties do not. Aside from the subsidies from the public treasury, many of them take in substantial sums in membership dues, either in the party itself or in some affiliated organization (e.g., a trade union). This has, in fact, been the traditional source of funds for the European parties of the left, and the fall-off in memberships they have experienced in the last generation has had the most serious financial consequences for them. In some instances parties still control appointments to local public employment (patronage), and those workers may be expected to return some of their income to the parties. Finally, parties elsewhere make money the old-fashioned way — they *earn* it.

> Many political parties, especially in Israel and Continental Europe, are actively engaged in quasi-commercial enterprises. Some own companies, and some operate through cooperatives or partnerships subject to party control. These include anything from party newspapers to travel agencies, import-export companies, banks, consulting firms, and even lotteries. Although found largely on the left wing of the political spectrum, such enterprises include the bingo games, lotteries, and advertising yearbooks organized and published by the British Conservatives, and printing plants and economic bulletins owned and published by the German Christian Democrats and Free Democrats . . .[10]

For all of these reasons and in all of these ways, then, political parties elsewhere have access to and control over the necessary cash for campaigns to an extent that their American counterparts can only hope and dream.

In the rest of the world, too, there are fewer alternatives to party money. Individual contributions are far less important, primarily because there is no lively tradition of political voluntarism outside the parties. Nor is there a tradition of group involvement

---

[9]Khayyam Z. Paltiel, "Campaign Finance: Contrasting Practices and Reforms," in David Butler, Howard R. Penniman, and Austin Ranney, eds., *Democracy at the Polls: A Comparative Study of Competitive National Elections* (Washington, D.C.: American Enterprise Institute, 1981).

[10]Ibid., 147.

in campaign finance, especially in groups other than those of business and labor. American campaign consultants are increasingly finding clients among the parties of the other democracies of the world, and some of them are trying to export American fund-raising techniques — even direct-mail appeals. They face a major challenge.

Nonetheless, to describe is not necessarily to explain. *Why* are political parties elsewhere able to establish such dominant positions in campaign finance? The explanation appears to rest largely in the nature of governmental and constitutional arrangements. In parliamentary democracies candidates are not at the center of politics; the parties are. Members of the parliament vote in cohesive, party-organized blocs to accept governmental power and to enact or oppose party programs. With so great a need for party cohesion, parliamentarians have less discretion and autonomy in their legislative votes than do the members of Congress; and any group that wants to shape public policy must attack party programs or seek influence within the party or party leadership circles. At election time the choice is thus one — and *seen* as one — involving parties: returning a party or parties to power or turning a party or parties out of power.

All of this, moreover, may be underscored by proportional representation systems in which the ballot (in many instances) presents the voter only the names of the contesting parties. In Israel, for one, the entire country is one constituency, in which each party runs a single party list with up to 120 candidates for the Knesset. The ballot, however, presents nothing more than the names of the contesting parties. Understandably, all Israeli laws and subsidies for campaign finance deal only with the political parties.[11]

Less central to government and politics, the American parties find it difficult to establish a substantial role for themselves in American electoral politics. They did, of course, have a larger role in earlier times; but that was a time of much smaller cash demands and much greater party control over both cash and noncash resources in American politics. Certainly the sheer magnitudes of the cash sums now involved stymie the American

[11]Leon Boim, "The Financing of Elections," in Howard R. Penniman, ed., *Israel at the Polls: The Knesset Elections of 1977* (Washington, D.C.: American Enterprise Institute, 1979).

parties — that combined with the exceptional availability of that cash from nonparty sources. So, too, does the parties' loss of their older monopoly of campaign information and skills. But the central problem for the American parties unquestionably rests in the absence of the institutional ties that bind together the fates of candidates and parties in so much of the rest of the world.

II. A Comeback for the American Parties?

Party committees spent in excess of 2.5 times more in the congressional elections of 1986 than they spent in those of 1978 (Table 5-1). (It should be clear that we are discussing here the total of contributions to candidates and expenditures made on their behalf.) While this 159 percent increase from 1978 to 1986 is certainly impressive, it is comparatively less stunning in a period in which all contributors to campaigns dramatically increased their commitments. In 1978, for example, PACs spent $35,468,202 in contributions and independent spending on the congressional campaigns, a figure 3.2 times that of the party committees. By 1986 PACs spent $143,404,122, a figure 5.2 times the $27.7 million of parties. It takes a lot of running to stay in the campaign finance race.

Two other central facts emerge from Table 5-1. First, the Republicans spend a good deal more money than do the Democrats. In fact, the better the Democrats got at fund-raising through 1982, the further they fell behind in the two-party competition. That would seem to be an anomaly, but the lines of Figure 5-1 make it clear that the Republicans were able to expand the distance between themselves and the Democrats even though their spending was increasing at a slower rate. The Republican downturns in 1984 and 1986 inaugurated a new era of greater interparty competition. They also beg for some explanation, which will appear later in this chapter.

Second, the data of Table 5-1 make it clear that both parties have expanded their spending in congressional elections entirely in their spending on behalf of candidates; their direct contributions have even declined somewhat between 1978 and 1986. The key fact behind this shift is the parties' control over the expenditures on behalf of candidates, even though in reality there is not much difference on that point between contributions "in kind" and many of the expenditures "on behalf." In either case the party controls the purpose of the expenditure — a tape for a television ad, perhaps, or a course in public speaking. There are, however, other trenchant reasons for preferring the "on behalf of" category: the statutory limits are more generous, it makes the party control of the expenditure clearer, and (for sensitive candidates) expenditures on behalf of a candidate do not increase the candidate's receipt and expenditure totals.

TABLE 5-1
Party Committee Spending in Congressional Elections, 1978–1986° (in millions of dollars)

	1978	1980	1982	1984	1986
Democrats					
Contributions	$1.8	$1.6	$1.7	$1.8	$1.6
On behalf of	.3	1.4	3.0	6.0	8.5
Total:	2.1	3.0	4.7	7.7	10.1
Republicans					
Contributions	4.5	4.4	5.5	4.8	3.4
On behalf of	4.1	7.8	14.2	13.1	14.3
Total:	8.6	12.1	19.8	17.8	17.7
Grand Total	$10.7	$15.1	$24.5	$25.6	$27.7

°Includes all party committees — national, state, and local — involved in the congressional campaigns.

All three of these facts about party role in campaign finance — the increasing sums of money, the Republican advantage, and the use of money for party (rather than candidate) directed spending — reflect a growth in the power and role of national party organizations. It began in the 1970s within the Republican party in what has come to be known as William Brock's revolution. While the Democrats were flexing national party muscle to open party processes to women and minorities and to control the selection of delegates to their national conventions, Brock and the Republicans marshaled national party strength for more traditional organizational business: recruiting candidates, winning elections, and strengthening the party's organization.

FIGURE 5-1
Democratic and Republican Party Spending, 1978–1986*

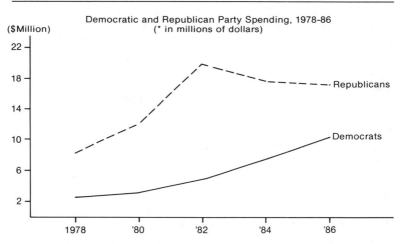

(*) Includes both contributions and on behalf of spending for national, state, and local party committees in Congressional campaigns.

The key to Brock's kind of party building was money. In the years after the passage of the FECA and the end of the "fat cat" era, he began the direct-mail solicitation of millions of Americans and the development of computer-based lists of proven contributors. He showed the skeptics in a few short years that a political party could raise substantial amounts of money in relatively small sums, just as Barry Goldwater, George Wallace, and George McGovern had showed that candidates could. While the party was not dormant before his tenure — the national party raised $6.3 million in 1974 and $8.9 million in 1975 — it was raising $17 million by 1979 and a very intimidating $37 million by

1980. In the latter years of the 1970s, 75 percent of the receipts came from direct mail solicitations.[12]

Meanwhile, the Democrats were floundering. Historically (and ironically) very dependent on large contributors, the party was slow to abandon that dependence. Moreover, it had little or no experience with the modern arts of list-building and fund-raising; and it could not muster the energy to acquire them. The national committee was understaffed and undernourished during the period, and during the Carter administration it functioned more as an adjunct to the Carter reelection drive than as a national party committee. During all of this period, moreover, it was shackled and demoralized by an enormous party debt, some of it carried ever since Hubert Humphrey's presidential campaign in 1968. What modest sums the party raised went to retire past debts rather than build a capacity for organization and more fund-raising. Indeed, it was not until the 1980s that the Democratic National Committee got serious about raising money. From then forward the plan was simple: catch up to the Republicans by doing what the Republicans had been doing.

With the augmented revenues, the national Republicans and, to a much lesser degree, the Democrats began to assert themselves in American electoral politics. Some of that increased affluence and influence is reflected in their growing spending in the campaigns (Table 5-1). It is the part of their activities governed by the FECA and reported to the FEC; it is the part, that is, that directs money into the statutorily defined campaign finance system. But party *receipts* indicate a growth of the national party committees beyond just their spending within the campaigns (Table 5-2). A quick comparison with the spending data of Table 5-1 indicates that spending fluctuates from 8 to 20 percent of receipts, depending on the party and the year — but on the overall

---

[12]Data from Xandra Kayden and Eddie Mahe, Jr., *The Party Goes On* (New York: Basic Books, 1985), 73–74. Chapter 3 generally describes these developments; its title is "Back from the Depths: Party Resurgence." On the revitalization of the national parties, see also John Bibby, "Party Renewal in the National Republican Party," in Gerald Pomper, ed., *Party Renewal in America* (New York: Praeger, 1980), 102–115; David Price, *Bringing Back the Parties* (Washington, D.C.: Congressional Quarterly, 1984); and A. James Reichley, "The Rise of National Parties," in John E. Chubb and Paul E. Peterson, eds., *The New Direction in American Politics* (Washington, D.C.: Brookings, 1985), 175–200.

TABLE 5-2
Net Receipts of National Party Committees, 1980–1986(*)

	1980	1982	1984	1986
Democrats	$30,957,805	$39,247,675	$90,223,959	$50,575,018
Republicans	163,496,231	215,046,541	289,241,446	209,794,719

*These totals include the National Committees and the House and Senate campaign committees of each major party.

it hovers around the 10 percent mark. (The Democrats in 1986 reached the 20 percent figure.)

The gap between receipts and political spending conceals some of the great unknowns of campaign finance. Some of the difference surely goes for direct-mail fund-raising costs — computer lists, prospecting for new names, postage, stationery — and some of it goes for general organizational costs — the building or renting of space, payroll, consultants, supplies and materials, and general overhead. Some, too, goes for field representatives, candidate recruitment, and assistance to state and local parties. Some also goes for the expertise and equipment to provide candidates (either as a contribution or at competitive costs) all kinds of services — polling, TV spots, sample press releases, fund-raising assistance, issue papers, research on opponents and constituents.[13]

The receipts, in other words, have gone to build national parties with increasing capacities to act as political parties. Some of that capacity, but by no means all, is captured in the data reported to the FEC on contributions and "on behalf of" spending. Well outside of these categories, for instance, was the institutional advertising — called "generic" advertising by some — that the Republicans began in 1980. The best known of these ads featured a Tip O'Neill look-alike as a set-up spokesman for

[13]In the words of Stephen E. Frantzich, these "service-vendor parties have taken the largely technologically based services which once dramatically weakened their role in contemporary politics, and began to use these services to rebuild the party organization." As for the candidates, they "find the party to be the vendor of choice if cost is the criteria." *Republicanizing the Parties: The Rise of the Service-Vendor Party*, paper presented at the 1986 meeting of the Midwest Political Science Association (Chicago: Apr. 10–12, 1986), 27, 29.

old-fashioned Democratic platitudes; it closed with the Republican slogan of the year: "Vote Republican — for a Change." In 1982's congressional elections, the Republican ads seized on one of Ronald Reagan's favorite exhortations and urged American voters to "stay the course" and vote Republican.

These generic ads came logically from the party's national committee. The congressional committees of the parties, the so-called Hill committees (for Capitol Hill),[14] have specialized more in the candidate-oriented politics of constituency research, knowing the opposition and sharpening the plans and skills of the campaign. Not encumbered with presidential politics and not involved with the rebuilding of state and local parties, they are the service vendors par excellence. They, too, have been energized in the late 1970s and the 1980s. In fact the reawakening of the national Democratic party apparatus happened initially in the congressional committees. Led by a then-unknown congressman from California, Tony Coelho, the Democratic Congressional Campaign Committee increased its receipts more than threefold between 1980 and 1982 (from $2.1 million to $6.5 million). So did the party's senatorial committee (from $1.7 to $5.6 million). The party's national committee revival did not "take off" until the 1983–84 period. By 1986, indeed, the congressional committees of both parties dominated the party role in congressional campaigns. Among the Democrats they accounted for 87 percent ($8.7 million of $10 million) of party contributions and spending in the congressional elections; among the Republicans it was 92 percent ($16.3 million of $17.7 million). Heading these committees, too, had become a splendid opportunity and a splendid burden (see box). So, the financial rebirth of the national parties offers hope of new influence for parties and a reversal of the much heralded "decline" and "decomposition" of the American parties. It is tangible evidence that the parties can adapt, however belatedly, to the new cash economy of American campaigning and that they can embrace the new technologies in information and persuasion. In these terms, indeed, the new

[14]Their official names are: Democratic Congressional Campaign Committee, National Republican Congressional Committee, Democratic Senatorial Campaign Committee, and National Republican Senatorial Committee. Like all other agencies and organizations in Washington, they are frequently called by their initials: DCCC, NRCC, DSCC, and NRSC.

COMMANDING THE SENATORIAL CAMPAIGNS

After setting spending records in bitterly contested campaigns for the Senate in 1986, both the NRSC and the DSCC found themselves with new chairmen in 1987: Sen. Rudy Boschwitz, a Republican from Minnesota, and Sen. John Kerry, a Democrat from Massachusetts. They immediately found themselves in controversy, although of very different kinds. As party fund-raising becomes more important in Congress, the chief fund-raisers become more visible and newsworthy.

Boschwitz inherited a committee shaken by the loss of eight seats and control of the Senate and compromised by some ill-timed bonuses for the committee staff after the election. Maxwell Glen writes that some critics charge that "the money raised by the campaign committee didn't get to the candidates it was intended to help . . . that it was spent on the high salaries and other expenses incurred by the NRSC's Washington staff." However, a

> more plausible explanation for the GOP failure, perhaps, is that the volume of money and aid available to Republican candidates made some of them complacent when they couldn't afford to be.
>
> "The opposition was thinner in funding, so they worked harder and smarter," Boschwitz said in a *New York Times* interview. "If this campaign proved anything, it is that money isn't everything."

From "Gaining Credibility," National Journal (Dec. 20, 1986), 3069.

Kerry's problem was more of his own doing. In the words of Maxwell Glen again, Kerry's biggest problem

> may be that he refused to take PAC money during his own campaign — a position that puts him in conflict with most of his colleagues as well as with the DSCC, which relied on PAC contributions for more than a fifth of its 1986 budget.
>
> Kerry, who has voted for Senate proposals to restrict PAC contributions, contends that his personal position will not interfere with the DSCC's fund-raising efforts. "You play by the rules that exist, even when you are trying to change the rules," he said in a recent *New York Times* interview.

From "Gaining Credibility," National Journal (Dec. 20, 1986), 3068.

financial capacity of the parties is as important for them and their new future as it is for the campaign finance of congressional candidates.

In these comparisons of receipts and campaign spending totals, one sees a great blurring of the boundaries of campaign finance. With greater party capacity for raising money, the distinction breaks down between the money the party committees give to and spend on behalf of candidates and the rest of the money they spend on the more traditional business and operations of a party. Certainly the institutional advertising of the Republicans gives some help or advantage to Republican candidates. Similarly, the candidate recruitment efforts of the parties affect the outcome of congressional elections just as surely as direct spending of thousands of dollars on the campaigns. The point is worth making for two reasons. First, it indicates that the party role in the campaign is much more pervasive than its formal role in campaign finance would suggest. And second, it underscores again that "campaign finance" has come to mean the moneys that Congress has regulated in one way or another. As a problem in boundaries, it is not much different from organized labor's registering voters and getting them to the polls — activities beyond the campaign spending that labor PACs report as their part in the campaign. And yet we *are* talking about campaign finance — and not about influence more generally in electoral politics. No one in touch with the reality of American campaigns would want to argue that money is the only source of influence in them. Our conventional concept of campaign finance — shaped especially by regulatory legislation — centers on the flow of resources to specific candidates and campaigns. It is candidate specific; and there are good reasons, both practical and conceptual, for drawing the definitional line in those terms. And by those terms, party resources in the United States are not yet a major factor in campaign finance. This is true whether one accepts as a measure the 5.8 percent for all congressional campaign expenditures (in 1986) that party spending accounts for or whether one looks at what the parties are permitted to spend under federal law.

In the 1974 amendments to the Federal Election Campaign Act, Congress set the same limits for all committee contributions, party and nonparty (i.e., PACs): $5000 per candidate per election, an effective limit of $10,000 for both primary and general election campaigns in a single two-year cycle. Then, Congress made a supportive concession to the parties by permitting additional spending on behalf of candidates. In the case of House campaigns, the limit per committee for those expenditures is $10,000 in 1974 dollars — that is, the current equivalent of that figure measured by the Consumer Price Index. For Senate campaigns the limit per committee is the greater of either two cents times the voting population of the state or $20,000. Both limits are indexed to the CPI.[15]

One more consideration complicates the legal limits even further: "agency." There are in fact two linked issues of agency. The limits, both of contribution and spending on behalf of, apply to the parties' state and local committees active in congressional campaigns. First, the state committees must function as agents for local committees in the state. Local spending in a campaign, that is, must be chalked up to the state committee's limit; and the state committee must make a consolidated report for all committees it has permitted to spend within its limit. Second, the state committee may make the national committees of its party the agent for spending within the state's limit; it may, in other words, cede its statutorily permitted spending to a national committee. The second kind of agency is, to put it mildly, the controversial one. Republicans originated the practice and won judicial approval for their interpretation of the statutes first in the FEC and then in the Supreme Court in a suit brought by a very displeased Democratic party.[16]

Some elementary arithmetic will illustrate the statutory limits and define, therefore, the outer limits of party participation in congressional campaign finance. By 1986's congressional elections, the "on behalf of" spending limits for House campaigns (originally $10,000) had inflated to $21,810. Those for Senate races ranged from a low of $43,620 (the $20,000 indexed to the CPI) to a high of $851,681 in California, the state with the

---

[15]Congress made another concession to the parties in the FECA; individuals were limited to $5000 in their contributions to PACs, but the limit on individual contributions to party committees was set at $20,000. All of these limits are governed, though, by the overall, aggregate limit of $25,000 per year on individual political contributions.

[16]*FEC v. Democratic Senatorial Campaign Committee*, 454 U.S. 27 (1981).

largest number of voters.[17] So, taking House campaigns as the easier example, the computation of party spending limits goes this way: direct contributions of $10,000 each (not indexed) by the party's national committee and its House campaign committee and a combined limit of $21,810 in expenditures on behalf of the candidate, for a total of $41,810. The contribution and "on behalf of" authority of the state committee (totaling $31,810) may be spent by that committee or ceded to the party's national committee.

One final calculation is central. That total party spending limit of $72,620 is just about 28 percent of the average expenditure ($260,032) made in the 1984 House campaigns by all of the Democratic and Republican candidates in the general election. Even if the parties spent up to the limit — "maxed out" in the jargon of the money men — the party role in congressional elections would be less than impressive by world standards.

In reality, spending to the statutory limit is by no means the rule. Of the 33 Democratic candidates for the Senate in 1984, 22 received $15,000 or more in contributions; 6 received more than $20,000. Of the 32 Republicans in the general election, 30 received $15,000 or more and 9 received more than $20,000. More telling are the data on spending on behalf of candidates. Democratic spending for 10 of the 33 exceeded 90 percent of that variable limit, and Republican committees exceeded 90 percent for 26 of their 32 candidates.[18] At least for the Republicans one is probably safe in saying that everyone who needed help got it to the statutory limit.

III. Party Goals and Strategies

In a very important sense, the American "political party" is an elegant fiction. The singular noun suggests a single organiza-

[17]Gary C. Jacobson, "The Republican Advantage in Campaign Finance," in John E. Chubb and Paul E. Peterson, eds., *The New Direction in American Politics* (Washington, D.C.: Brookings, 1985), 154, provides the arithmetic on which these calculations for 1986 are based.

[18]Data on the "on behalf of" spending in 1984 come from Joseph E. Cantor, *Data on Political Party Coordinated Expenditures in Congressional Elections: 1980–1984*, report No. 86-768 of the Congressional Research Service of the Library of Congress (July 3, 1986).

tion with a single set of goals and a single set of means to reach them. There are many good reasons for maintaining the fiction of the party's unity and singularity, but there are also good reasons for understanding that it is in fact a fiction. The major American parties are loose coalitions of individuals and groups with quite different interests. Much of the history of the American political parties can indeed be told in terms of the battles between the party organization and the party's officeholders for control of the resources and the symbols of the party. The battle is also fought every two years on the fields of campaign finance.

The competition begins with the struggle of party incumbents and party committees for some of the same funds. Granted that they are not competing for precisely the same sum of money — what an incumbent raises is not necessarily denied a committee, and vice versa — but funds for a party and its candidates are finite, and some of them could go either to the party or the incumbent candidates for reelection. In such a competition, of course, almost all advantages are on the side of the incumbents. Their positions of legislative influence are central to their fundraising capacity, and that capacity is further buttressed by their high probability of reelection — House incumbents are more than 95 percent successful these days. The party committees, whose purpose is to some degree redistributive, suffer in the competition, and so, therefore, do the party's needy challengers and open seat candidates. The problem is all the greater in the Senate where incumbents who are *not* up for reelection raise money in competition both with their colleagues who are and with their party's committees. Writing late in the 1986 campaign, David Broder noted the problem among the underfunded Democrats and quoted a "leading authority" on it:

> "It's obviously a problem," said Sen. George J. Mitchell (D-Maine), chairman of the Democratic Senatorial Campaign Committee. "Many people who have been asked for these early contributions have told me, 'You ought to ask people who are running in future years to delay their solicitations.' But it's difficult to ask senators to put aside their personal interests."[19]

[19]"Democratic Money — But Not for the Party," *Washington Post* (Oct. 29, 1986).

The problem was less pressing for the Republicans because their Senatorial Campaign Committee had raised enough money to fund all of their competitive Senate campaigns to the legal limit.

Behind these struggles are different political goals, even in the politics limited to congressional campaigns. Party organizations — here chiefly the two party campaign committees in the House and the two in the Senate — want to maximize the number of victories, the number of seats won. The incumbent members of Congress are interested primarily in their own political futures. In fund-raising terms that means raising *more* than enough money for a winning campaign. It may mean raising intimidating sums to frighten away strong competition, sums that will show their fund-raising and vote-getting capacities for a race for higher office, sums for the unforeseen campaign crisis, or sums merely to build additional name recognition and political support. Simply put, the incumbent often seeks more than mere victory, but those political goals are personal. The broader, common interests of the party are less salient, especially in the years in which control of the chamber does not hang in the balance. So, candidates define their "need" for money quite differently than will a committee looking for electoral victory.

Incumbents, therefore, stand in the way of a rational allocation of available party resources in the campaign. Their campaigns are, by the standards of electoral "need" defined by party committees, greatly overfunded, while the campaigns of the party's challengers and open seat candidates are in the aggregate badly underfunded. (The campaigns of challengers are almost certain to be underfinanced, regardless of party or other circumstance.) So, in the words of Gary Jacobson, the party confronts

a collective good problem; rational individual behavior produces inferior collective results. The problem is all the more severe because recruitment and campaign finance practices reinforce one another. The availability of money attracts strong candidates; promising candidates attract campaign contributions. Contributors ignore weak candidates; the shrewder potential candidates choose not to run if they are not assured of sufficient funds. A party would be better off, collectively, if it could mount candidacies that counteract rather than reinforce contrary national forces. But this is only possible to the degree that recruitment and campaign funding do not depend on strategic individual decisions.[20]

The strategic problem for the party would be eased if it accounted for a larger share of the campaign outlays, but the parties — not to mention the maximum role the FECA defines for them — fall far short of that goal. "Even a party as well-heeled as the Republican cannot, therefore, supply a sufficient share of the necessary campaign funds to guarantee their efficient distribution."[21]

So, in 1982, for instance, Democratic incumbents, obsessed especially by the fate of some fellow incumbents in 1980, raised and spent record sums far beyond the needs of an election year in which political currents were running in their direction, the result primarily of a recession during the first two years of the Reagan presidency. (Indeed, 32 House Democrats had more than $100,000 left over after the campaign.[22]) Democratic challengers languished, and the Democratic National Committee lacked sufficient funds to help them. The Republicans were able to fund the 1982 campaigns more efficiently and thus minimize their losses in an unfavorable year.

Ironically, 1982 was the first year in which the ambitious chairman of the Democratic Congressional Campaign Committee, Representative Tony Coelho, shifted that committee's spending strategy away from an even-handed one that made no distinctions:

> Among his first management decisions was to insist that during the 1982 elections DCCC funds be used selectively: test-marketed, as it were. Previously the committee had handed out a set amount, usually a thousand dollars, to every Democratic candidate regardless of need. This was both an attempt to avoid intramural bickering and an admission that the committee had no larger blueprint. Coelho decided to ignore those Democrats with "safe" seats and concentrate resources on close races.
>
> Many in the party old guard were furious. Senior incumbents

[20]Gary C. Jacobson, "Party Organization and Distribution of Campaign Resources: Republicans and Democrats in 1982," *Political Science Quarterly* , vol. 100 (Winter 1985–1986), 609.

[21]Ibid., 611.

[22]Ibid., 615.

who had served faithfully found themselves rewarded with no party funds; green or little-known candidates got the legal maximum of $50,000 [*sic*] in intra-party help. It was a controversial decision, and Coelho took the heat for it — "I still have enemies in Congress because of it," he says . . . [23]

It was a course of action that saved something for the Democrats in a very promising year. The making of enemies, moreover, was not fatal to Coelho's career in the House; he was chosen his party's whip in early 1987, at least in substantial part because of his role in the revival of the DCCC.

Whatever may be the inability of the party committees to achieve a perfectly "rational" electoral strategy (largely as a result of their need to placate powerful incumbents), they invariably pursue a more efficient strategy in the campaign than do the party's candidates taken together. Therefore, the

> greater the share [of campaign resources] controlled by the party and the freer its officials are to pursue collective ends, the more efficiently the party will deploy campaign resources, and therefore the more seats it should win. The more resources controlled by the party's stronger candidates, the less efficient and collectively successful it should be.[24]

All other things being equal, then, the larger the party share of total campaign costs, the more electorally efficient those total expenditures will be. The greater fund-raising abilities of the Republicans not only provide more money for the campaign, but a more effective pursuit of the party's goals of controlling as many congressional seats as possible.

The central assumption behind the argument is, of course, that the parties are freer and more able to make the hard strategic decisions on behalf of the collective interests. And there is evidence that they are. For one thing, the parties do appear to fend off the importunings of incumbents in safe seats. What money they give

---

[23]Gregg Easterbrook, "The Business of Politics," *Atlantic Monthly* , vol. 258 (Oct. 1986), 32.
[24]Gary C. Jacobson, "Parties and PACs in Congressional Elections," in Lawrence C. Dodd and Bruce J. Oppenheimer, eds., *Congress Reconsidered*, 3rd. ed. (Washington, D.C.: CQ Press, 1985), 139.

TABLE 5-3
Party Committee Support for House Incumbents in 1984 General Elections by Competitiveness of Outcome

General Election Vote:	Democrats		Republicans	
	Avg. Direct Contribution	Avg. o.b.o. Spending°	Avg. Direct Contribution	Avg. o.b.o. Spending°
71–100	$83	$147	$8,270	$1,323
61–70	646	1,214	10,616	13,519
51–60	6,309	6,361	12,452	28,087
41–50	9,275	20,871	16,700	38,767

°The o.b.o. expenditures are those made "on behalf of" candidates; they are sometimes referred to as "coordinated" or "441a(d)" expenditures.

incumbents goes largely to the incumbents in competitive districts (Table 5-3). Conversely, the parties spend far less than the average on the most secure incumbents, although the more affluent Republican committees can give larger contributions to the less threatened. This same capacity to choose among candidates is indicated by the parties' abilities to channel a substantial part of their funds to nonincumbents. In 1984, Democratic incumbents in the House and Senate got only 30 percent of the money Democratic committees gave and spent on behalf of candidates; in 1986, Democratic incumbents got only 23 percent. Among the wealthier Republicans, it was 36 percent in 1984 and 45 percent in 1986.

In addition to spending disproportionately on marginal, competitive races, the parties time their spending to assure its strategic value. In particular, they manage to delay their on behalf of spending to the latter part of the campaign — to a time when the closeness or outcome of an election is most predictable. In 1982, for example, the Democrats had made 83 percent of their contributions to Senate candidates by June 30th, and the Republicans 56 percent. But by the same date the Democrats had made only 5 percent of their on behalf of expenditures, the Republicans only 6 percent. So, the increasing reliance on the on behalf of spending not only assures the party greater control over the spending of the funds in the campaign, but it permits the

TABLE 5-4
Percentages of Democratic and Republican Spending on House Incumbents, Challengers, and Open Seat Candidates, 1982–1986

	1982		1984		1986	
	Contribs.	*o.b.o.*°	*Contribs.*	*o.b.o.*°	*Contribs.*	*o.b.o.*°
Democrats						
Incumbents	35.7%	34.1%	50.1%	52.4%	36.1%	31.4%
Challengers	44.1	41.3	31.8	29.0	41.7	44.0
Open Seats	20.3	24.6	18.0	18.5	22.2	24.6
Republicans						
Incumbents	45.5	37.2	36.7	24.4	42.6	34.9
Challengers	32.3	35.4	50.0	58.8	33.2	31.5
Open Seats	22.1	27.4	13.3	15.7	24.2	33.6

°o.b.o. refers to the expenditures "on behalf of" candidates.

parties to spend them more efficiently. The ability to function effectively in the last months of a campaign is, incidentally, also a reflection of the parties' capacity for polling and otherwise tracking the campaign.

Finally, the party committees show at least some ability to direct their spending into the prevailing political winds (Table 5-4). In the 1982 House campaigns, waged in an economic recession that created opportunities for the Democrats, that party shifted resources behind challengers and open seat candidates, while the Republicans moved to protect vulnerable incumbents, some of whom had come into office in the sweep of 1980. But the political breezes shifted in 1984. Early in the campaign another substantial Republican victory seemed likely, and the Republicans shifted support to nonincumbents. The Democrats moved to protect their vulnerable House members. Then in 1986, with the tides again running to the Democrats, they shifted resources to challengers and open seat candidates, while the threatened Republicans circled the wagons around their incumbents. The shifts are perhaps modest in their magnitudes, but they are all in the direction one might expect in a party strategy that adapts to the short-term political trends of the time.

All of these signs and portents indicate an ability to make hard political choices, to pursue a collective electoral strategy that will maximize — or will work toward maximizing — the number of victories for a given expenditure of money. But strategic choices are more complex than even these data would suggest, for not all campaigns and constituencies are equal. The differences are, of course, greater in the Senate. It may take x units of scarce resources to win one race, but five or ten times that to win another; yet each senator elected has one vote and each makes up the same fraction of a party majority in the Senate. The dilemma is at its most dramatic when the candidate comes from the most populous state with the most expensive campaigns (see box).

THE CRANSTON CASE

The 1986 campaign of Sen. Alan Cranston, a Democrat, posed the strategic dilemmas a party faces in responding to large-state campaigns. The report of Phillip J. Trounstine in the *San Jose Mercury News* of August 3, 1986, ("Cranston hits Democrats in pocketbook") needs no comment or introduction.

California Sen. Alan Cranston's bid for a fourth term in the face of a tough and expensive challenge is casting a pall over the campaign finances of his fellow Democratic Senate candidates from coast to coast.

Although Democratic Senate campaign officials have yet to decide precisely how much to give him, Cranston could receive up to $1.7 million. That would be more than a third of the $5 million total the Democratic Senate Campaign Committee expects to parcel out this fall to candidates in the close contests among the 34 Senate seats up for election. . . .

"The question is, 'Where can the money be of best use?' And it's clearly in a smaller state where $100,000 can go a hell of a long way," said one Democratic source. . . .

Few Democratic campaign managers deny the California senator's need for assistance in his race against [Republican Ed] Zschau. And they recognize that Cranston, who has raised huge sums over the years for other Democrats, also is responsible for raising much of the $5 million the Democrats' Senate committee expects to distribute nationally.

Moreover, some party leaders regard Cranston and California as far more than just another Senate seat.

"It's a megastate," said Paul Tully, executive director of Sen. Edward Kennedy's political action committee. "What's happening in the megastates is a significant measure of the health and well-being of the Democratic Party." . . .

As its strategic activity indicates, the political party is a special kind of player in campaign finance. Like other "investors" in campaigns the parties pursue victory; but they seem less sure why they pursue it. This uncertainty of purpose stems largely from their domination by their incumbent officeholders, their "parties in government." Even though the national committees play an increasing financial role in the campaigns, they still tread very lightly around the goals and interests of congressional incumbents; thus their money comes largely without strings attached. They have an electoral strategy, but they have not yet developed a policy strategy. If they ever turn their growing financial role and their electoral strategies to the service of a party program or ideology, if they begin to apply those tests to the recipients of their aid, then their role in the campaigns will transform them and, with them, much of American politics.

IV. The Party as Money Raiser

The FECA has worked an almost complete transformation on all fund-raising, including that of the parties. Historically, they depended on very large contributors and, to a lesser extent, on thinly veiled evasions of the laws that prohibited direct contributions by banks, corporation, and labor unions. The reforms in the 1970s limited individuals to a maximum contribution of $20,000 a year to a national party committee; they were further constrained by a gross, overall limit of $25,000 a year for all of their contributions. Moreover, the "big" economic interests organized their own PACs; and enforcement of the statutes began

TABLE 5-5
Net Receipts of Party Committees by Source, 1985–1986

	Totals	Parties	PACs	Individuals
Democrats				
DNC	$17,235,406	0	$1,252,997	$12,554,500
DSCC	13,397,809	35,500	2,418,736	8,875,626
DCCC	12,322,969	41,997	2,063,794	8,297,039
State°	18,797,696	1,536,319	n/a	13,845,537
Total:	$61,753,880	1,613,816	5,735,527	43,572,702
Republicans				
RNC°°	$83,866,969	73,480	375,326	76,931,950
NRSC	86,130,776	97,616	433,745	74,870,667
NRCC	39,796,974	199,505	302,462	34,303,461
State°°°	42,638,196	9,091,020	n/a	31,076,929
Total:	$252,432,915	9,461,621	1,111,533	217,183,007

°Includes local committees and the receipts of Dollars for Democrats.
°°Includes a category of "other national Republican," which reported receipts of only $86,813.
°°°Includes local committees.

in earnest. Fortunately for the parties, the arts of raising small sums by direct-mail solicitation had begun to flourish.

The revolution in party fund-raising is reflected in the receipts of the party committees reporting to the Federal Election Commission for 1985–86 (Table 5-5). Democrats and Republicans both rely heavily on individual contributions, but one difference stands out between them. Democrats, especially the committees in the House and Senate, depend more on PAC contributions (almost all from labor PACs) and, therefore, less on individual donors. As recently as 1980, the Democrats relied more than Republicans on contributors of $500 and more, but by 1984 their dependence (15 percent) had dropped below the Republicans (18 percent).[25]

The totals, especially those for the national party committees

[25]The funding sources in the columns of Table 5-5 do not account for all of the net receipts. The contributions from parties, PACs, and individuals account for only 82 percent of the Democratic total and for 90 percent of the Republican total. The remainder is accounted for by loans, interest and dividends, and proceeds from the sale of services.

— the national committees, the congressional committees, and the senate committees — reveal that receipts for 1986 were down significantly from those in 1984. For the national committees of the Democrats, the total dropped from $65.9 million to $50.6 million; and the Republicans went from $246.1 million to $209.8 million. It was a surprising falloff, especially in view of the hopes that many friends of the parties had for their renaissance as campaign funders. Even more surprising, perhaps, was the paucity of comment about and explanation of the decline.

Embedded in the totals are some clues to an explanation. Both national committees declined sharply in money raised between 1984 and 1986 — the Democrats from $46.6 million to $17.2 million, the Republicans from $106.2 million to $83.8 million. But three of the four Hill committees *increased* their receipts; only that of the Republicans in the House turned downward. The problems of the two national committees, of course, happened in an off-year congressional election following a presidential cycle; but in the past Republican fund-raising had surmounted the lesser motivations of the off-years. According to reports well into 1987, the problems at the RNC continued into the 1988 election cycle. In summer 1987 the RNC was forced to lay off 40 of its 275 staff members, while the Democratic committees were a bit ahead of past performance early in the two-year cycle.

In any event, speculation over the declines stimulated a number of explanations, none of them necessarily incompatible with any other one. Was it donor fatigue (the pros call it "burnout")? Republicans especially had been working the same contributor lists over and over, often competitively, and even some of the loyal contributors had begun to complain. Or was the Republican party the victim of success? It was harder to make those letters of solicitation bristle with outrage or make the donor tremble with fear when Ronald Reagan was in the White House. Or were the problems of the Reagan administration in the second term a cause for donor disenchantment? These explanations were, however, limited to one party; and both faltered. Had the parties simply expanded their lists of donors to the outer limit of their potential? The pool of potential givers was perhaps finite after all. Or had the party organizations lost out in the fevered competition with PACs and candidates for the favor of contributors? Or was there a pervasive image of parties and candidates awash in cash and, therefore, not needing more very badly? Whatever the causes of the parties' drop-off in 1986 — and they are probably many — it makes one pause. Especially coming after the leveling of PAC growth and a flattening of spending in House campaigns only two years earlier, it suggests a new volatility in American campaign finance. Perhaps donors are becoming selective, more sensitive to short-term political forces. (The one Republican committee to increase its receipts in 1986 was the one desperately trying to hold onto a slim majority in the Senate.) Perhaps individuals are giving to candidates and PACs instead. Or are they more realistic about the political benefits and accomplishments that flow from ample spending? In specific terms, have their letters of solicitation promised more than the parties could deliver?

Yet, the fact remains that the parties do raise very substantial sums, ones that are so similar to the amounts PACs raise as to tempt comparison. In 1986, a year without the complication of presidential campaigns, all PACs reporting to the FEC raised $352.9 million; the party committees reporting in the same year raised $314.2 million. In the previous cycle the parties had "out-raised" the PACs, $396.4 million to $288.7 million. But close comparison ought to be resisted for at least two major reasons. First, parties must take administrative and overhead costs out of their receipts; most PACs (with the exception of the nonconnected ones) can rely on a parent organization to pick up most or all of those costs. Understandably, then, a larger share of PAC receipts are free to go into political expenditures. Some 53 percent of PAC receipts in 1984 were spent in federal elections; the share was 42 percent in 1986.[26] Both for 1984 and 1986, the party committees spent only 9 percent of their receipts in contributions to federal candidates or spending on their behalf. Second, since PACs are exclusively campaign participants, all of their political expenditures go into the campaigns. Not so for the parties, which try at least to function more broadly as political parties. We do know that almost 10 percent of their resources go into the FECA's definition of campaign finance; we do not know how

---

[26]There is no way of knowing how much of the remaining percentages went for overhead; some certainly went into state and local political expenditures.

much goes into other, obviously related, political purposes. These issues aside, the final line for 1986 is that all parties spent $28,360,942 of their receipts in the congressional elections, the PACs a more substantial $148,060,784, a figure more than five times greater.[27]

There is another, final, revenue-raising side to the parties: their role as broker. The four committees on Capitol Hill have become increasingly adept at mating candidates with prospective contributors, especially PACs. In a format informally known as "the meat market," candidates are introduced to those who control the contributions; they may even have a chance to make a short speech in order to display some of their political wares. Moreover, if the party has decided to support Candidate Jones, its decision serves as a cue to other contributors that the party leadership considers the candidate a viable prospect; its failure to provide anything more than token support, conversely, is a silent warning that the candidate or his situation is without great hope. One observer quotes Rep. Guy Vander Jagt of the NRCC:

> "If we smile on a candidate," he says, "that candidate's fortunes zoom. If we frown, his fortunes plummet. When we say, 'Do something,' they pretty much do it.... It's almost frightening the impact we have. It's awe-inspiring."
>
> Vander Jagt has been known to wax hyperbolic at times, but he is more right than wrong. With year-round professionalism and huge budgets . . . the campaign committees are the center of the congressional campaign system.[28]

The key position as an allocator of campaign monies comes in part to the parties by reason of their being parties; but part, too, results from the infrastructure they have built with those funds that do not register as expenditures in the campaigns proper.

Furthermore, affluent committees, especially those of the Republican party, have devised and perfected ways of channeling money they cannot use. Some of it is channeled to avoid FECA restrictions; labor unions or corporations, both forbidden to make

---

[27]This party total includes both contributions and expenditures "on behalf of" candidates; the PAC total includes both contributions (to candidates, parties, and other PACs) and independent expenditures.

[28]Alan Ehrenhalt, "Political Parties: A Renaissance of Power?" *Congressional Quarterly* (Oct. 26, 1985), 2187.

contributions under federal law, may be guided to states in which their direct contributions to candidates for state office are legal or to state or local voter mobilization projects that are outside the scope of campaign finance as the FECA defines it. This is the much touted "soft money." At the same time, party committees may channel funds directly to candidates by "bundling" — by convincing donors to write checks directly to candidates and delivering the checks for them. The beauty of these arrangements, of course, is that the funds do not register as receipts or expenditures for the party committees.[29]

V. Is There a Permanent Republican Advantage?

Republican and Democratic candidates for Congress have in the aggregate raised similar sums of money for their campaigns in recent years. Taken as two groups of partisans, indeed, their competition for campaign resources has been closer than their competition for votes. In the presidential campaigns, a system of public funding (voluntary but pervasive through its first three elections) assures the candidates equal funding and the parties equal spending rights. But as soon as one gets outside of candidate controlled finance, a very substantial Republican edge appears. Independent spending is heavily pro-Republican, both in congressional and presidential elections. And the receipts and spending of party committees, documented in this chapter, weigh heavily in favor of the Republicans. In 1986 national Republican committees raised $209.8 million to the $50.6 million of the Democrats; those Republican committees spent $16.8 million in the congressional campaigns, the Democrats $9.1 million.

In part this Republican advantage results from the Republican head start. The Brock successes of the 1970s gave the Republicans an advantage in more than just the sums of money raised. It led to advantages in technology, trained personnel, the size of contributor lists, and even the reduction of fund-raising overhead. In fact, Republicans claimed their fund-raising costs had

---

[29]These practices will be discussed more fully in chap. 10.

dropped to a very slim 19 percent of receipts by 1980.[30] It is, in other words, a race in which the front-runner keeps improving its performance while the contender struggles not to let the gap widen.

The Democratic problem may well be more fundamental than even that. As David Adamany has argued,

> Contributing to politics is disproportionately an activity of the well-educated, higher-income groups, and those who engage in other political activities as well. These groups are primarily Republican. Even contributors to the Democratic telethons of the early 1970s were drawn from these groups, leading the authors of a major study of telethon givers to suggest that the failure of the Democrats' fourth telethon may have reflected the exhaustion of a narrow base.[31]

By any measure one wants to adopt, the average Democratic loyalist has less disposable income than the average Republican, and that is a crucial fact in a system of campaign finance that rests ultimately on the voluntary contributions of individuals. Moreover, the Democratic edge in the number of loyalists has shrunken considerably since the 1960s.

Beyond that somewhat self-evident difficulty, other problems haunt the Democrats. There are those who think that the internal ideological divisions within the party — the gulf between the ideological left and the moderates, especially — make support harder to mobilize behind a unified appeal for funds, particularly in the somewhat strident, even demagogic pitch that is the productive norm in direct-mail solicitations. The appeals that result aim largely at the party's traditionally liberal wing, leaving centrist Democrats to give their money to PACs or candidates of a stripe they prefer. Because Republican candidates are more homogeneous, a contributor to a party committee abandons choices of lesser significance.

Finally, there is the more elusive matter of different party cultures. The Democrats have always reveled in a political individu-

---

[30]David Adamany, "Political Parties in the 1980s," in Michael J. Malbin, ed., *Money and Politics in the United States* (Chatham, N.J.: Chatham, 1985), 77.

[31]Ibid., 105. The study Adamany refers to is by Elwood and Spitzer; see note 107 on p. 120 of Malbin.

alism that defies party discipline and looks, at worse, like political chaos. Their national conventions, for instance, have always been bumptious, rowdy, and argumentative in contrast to the orderly, somewhat staid, and largely predictable meetings of the Republicans. It is just possible that a Republican tradition of social discipline and organizational authority helps the party organization hammer out and enforce some kind of treaty among the competitors within the party for scarce campaign funds.

It seems safe to say that the Democratic party will not catch the Republicans in the race to the bank. It is probably safe to surmise, furthermore, that they do not expect to and that they will settle for raising "enough" money. But "enough" masks any number of uncertainties and obscurities. It obscures the question of just how great an electoral advantage the extra Republican spending "purchases," which in turn raises the entire problem of assessing the effect of the elements of a campaign that money buys. One quickly returns to the mysteries of what "works" in campaigns and what does not. And one faces, too, the difficult questions of marginal utilities, especially the question of estimating the curve of the diminishing returns.

Any calculation of "enough" also requires a decision about the range of political influence one is trying to compare. Does one simply compare Republican money and Democratic money, or does one tote up a full account of all Republican and Democratic bases of political power? That is, does one consider, in addition to money, the number of party loyalists, the strength of group support, the advantage in the representational system of the Senate or districting for the House, and all the other myriad bases of political influence? Or does one judge "enough" simply in terms of the ability to maintain an overall competitiveness for the two house of Congress?

The calculus of party advantage must finally deal with one more two-edged consideration: the effect of holding office. For candidates in office, power confers enormous fund-raising leverage; and incumbents are almost always in a position to outspend their challengers. It is this advantage that has kept the larger number of Democratic incumbents in the Congress financially competitive with the Republicans. *Party* fund-raising, on the other hand, rests heavily on direct-mail solicitation, and that system works better for the party out of power. Appeals based on fear and anxiety have greater force when the "enemy" has already come through the gates. In these curious and ironic ways, then, being in power helps the party's incumbents, but being out of power may well help the party committees. It is one more reminder of how complex an organization the political party is when winning or losing affects its various parts in different ways.

VI. A Final Thought

The activities of party committees are among the most puzzling aspects of American campaign finance. For one thing, they are — along with the well-kept secrets about individual contributors — among the least reported of them. The mystery surrounding them also results from the fact that the "parties" are many party committees with often differing capacities and goals. Thus, the old and intricate relationships between state parties and their national committees lead to the complicating "agency" agreements. And the watchful, even tense, relationships between the legislative campaign committees and the national committees of the parties reflect persistent divisions that are almost as old as the party system itself.

In part, too, the puzzlements and perplexities stem from the very nature of a political party. Its political ambit is not as limited and defined as that of a PAC. Its involvements in campaign finance are only one reflection of a broader political role. It is in fact very arbitrary to separate its campaign activities from the other business of a political party. Expenditures for party building, candidate recruiting, and generic advertising — to take only three examples — do not fall within the scope of the FECA, since the FECA's accounting is candidate centered and such spending cannot be easily assigned as costs or expenditures in specific candidates' campaigns. Nonetheless, it is hard to imagine that they will not affect election outcomes — if party labels and party loyalties mean anything in our politics. The parties pose a constant challenge, therefore, to the usual definitions of "campaign finance."

The parties fascinate and perplex for yet another reason: it is only with them that one sees the campaign spender pushing hard against the statutory constraints of the FECA. To be sure, a few individuals and PACs are forced to limit their contributions, even to devise strategies for avoiding the limits of the law. They are, however, relatively rare in large universes. But the number of national party committees is a small one, and at least one of them — the National Republican Senatorial Committee — has been increasingly restricted by the limits of the FECA. This fact underlies and joins together the assorted controversies over agency, bundling, and soft money. In other words, the efficacy of statutory regulation is tested here because the pressures to find new outlets for blocked money are the strongest. The challenge to legal constraints is all the firmer because the parties are such persistent, sophisticated, and "politicized" actors in finance. They do not flee in timidity or embarrassment from the frustrations of statutory limits.

So, amid all of this perplexity it is appropriate that one find it hard to assess the party role in campaign finance. (It is not easy to assess the party role in *any* aspect of American politics.) Certainly that role is more substantial than the totals of contributions and "on behalf of" expenditures would suggest. Beyond the hard figures of confirmed expenditures is the party role as conduit: the fund-raising cues to other contributors and the ability to direct and divert funds (the bundling and the sending of soft money to the unregulated states). Moreover, there are the activities of the party generally — the candidate recruiting, the party as vendor of choice, the general party building — that supplement, even prepare, their direct impact on the campaigns. But if, in 1986 terms, the impact of party committees is greater than the $27.7 million they spent on the congressional campaigns, it is surely less than their receipts of $314.2 would suggest. "Somewhere in between" seems the safest hedge, its imprecision a sign of the difficulty we have in taking the measure of the American parties.

6
Raising the Stakes

There are givers and takers in campaign finance. "Takers," however, might not be exactly the right word. The acquisition of campaign funds suggests active verbs — to solicit or to raise money, perhaps. Indeed, there are increasingly bitter contributors (givers) who would prefer terms more like "extract" and "put the bite on." For candidates increasingly do not wait passively for others to lay contributions at their feet. They ask for money, they beg and compete for it, and they devise ever more inventive ways of cajoling prospective contributors into surrendering it.

In providing the necessary resources for a campaign, there is a push and a pull; and the balance between them shifts over time. In the early years after the passage of the FECA, contributors and spenders dominated the dynamic; they were aggressive and confident of their role in campaign finance's new order. Increasingly in the 1980s, however, candidates have become more aggressive, even importunate, in raising the money they think they need for campaigning. And among the candidates none have been more confident and aggressive than the incumbent legislators who seek reelection. The consequences of this shift in power in the financial nexus is the pervasive theme of this chapter.

I. The Incumbents

The ability of incumbents to raise ever-increasing sums of money has without any doubt raised the stakes in campaign finance over the period of the late 1970s and early 1980s. In the campaigns for Congress, the best documented of incumbent successes, the incumbent share of the total campaign funds has increased even as those sums have grown appreciably. In 1978 incumbents accounted for 38.4 percent of the receipts of all candidates for the House and Senate. This percentage rose to 45.0 in 1980, to 47.0 in 1982, to 55.5 in 1984, and then slipped back to 50.9 percent in 1986. These percentages take on their real meaning when one notes that incumbents accounted for only 25.5 percent of the major party candidates in 1986.

As do the data on receipts, those on expenditures show the same rapid development of incumbent superiority. At the same time expenditure data better reflect the events of the campaign, especially if one brings the data down to the level of individual contests for congressional seats. In doing so, it is preferable to use average expenditure data that include only the major party candidates in the general election. This way, one eliminates the impoverished minor party and independent candidates and all primary losers in the major parties; if they are included in the calculations, they will depress the averages much more than the realities of congressional campaigning justify. Within this carefully defined group of candidates, the incumbents (who are, after all, all major party candidates) increased their domination in spending over the period from 1977–78 to 1985–86 (Table 6-1). Only the Republican challengers in the Senate have shown a spending increase of the magnitude of that of the incumbents — and only because of their great surge in the 1986 campaigns. Since 1982 the open seat averages have led the average spending in both parties in both houses.

The data in Table 6-1 have their dips and rises. The upward curve of greater incumbent superiority, that is, is not a smooth one. There are at least two explanations. First, in the Senate the seats up for election in any year differ from those of the preceding and the following year. The electoral vulnerabilities of incumbents differ from election year to election year, and so do

TABLE 6-1

Average Expenditures of Major Party, General Election Candidates in
Campaigns for Congress, 1978–1986

	1978	1980	1982	1984	1986
HOUSE					
Democrats					
Incumbents	$103,104	$157,326	$245,327	$279,192	$312,258
Challengers	75,677	78,421	126,803	102,338	142,974
Open Seat	206,910	188,381	266,569	359,843	418,962
Republicans:					
Incumbents	127,115	176,976	287,039	282,000	366,485
Challengers	74,628	113,045	129,933	144,919	110,010
Open Seat	191,297	227,737	318,222	401,196	456,477
SENATE					
Democrats					
Incumbents	618,211	1,402,677	1,606,717	1,755,055	2,712,713
Challengers	788,720	787,634	1,516,015	1,348,950	1,678,774
Open Seat	760,695	1,104,416	4,330,489	5,799,368	2,846,622
Republicans					
Incumbents	2,065,674	1,233,834	2,123,089	2,999,804	3,598,965
Challengers	602,935	872,125	999,694	639,628	1,871,706
Open Seat	826,208	1,134,936	3,953,352	3,400,450	3,836,240

the sizes and political traditions of their constituencies (i.e., the
states) at contest in a given year. Second, the bumps in the curve
reflect short-term changes in party fortunes and the consequent
shifts in patterns of contributions by some PACs and some party
committees. With all indicators pointing to a Democratic tide in
1986, Democratic money went to challengers; and Republican
money went to help embattled incumbents. But at the same time,
Republican money generally went into all Senate races in an attempt, futile as it turned out, to keep a Republican majority in the
Senate. And yet, despite all the blips in the curve, the surge of the
incumbents is clear, if clearer in the House than in the Senate.

In fact, there are those who would argue that incumbents have
managed to finance their campaigns for reelection well beyond
need and into the ranges of avarice or profligacy. These critics
have on their side the increasing sums that candidates have left
over after reelection and that they have available for the next

TABLE 6-2
Cash on Hand as a Percentage of Total Receipts for Candidates in General Elections, 1978–1986

	1978	1980	1982	1984	1986
House	5.5%	6.2%	6.7%	9.5%	13.5%
Senate	1.0	.7	1.7	2.2	4.2

election cycle (Table 6-2). It is only the incumbents who have these surplus funds to carry over into the next election cycle. On January 1, 1985, House incumbents had a total of $30,639,410 in cash on hand; challengers and open seat candidates had a total of only $333,578. In the Senate the incumbents who would run for reelection in 1986 had about $7.7 million on hand at the opening of 1985; nonincumbents had less than $100,000. In fact, only in the House in 1982 and 1986 have the nonincumbent candidates accounted for more than a single percent of all the cash on hand at the beginning of a cycle; and in both years it was only a shade over a percent.

The incumbents of the House have always been the candidates with the early cash on hand (Table 6-2). They ran for office every two years, and for that reason they could most easily justify the constant campaign. Their surpluses from one campaign conveniently became a starting stake for the next. Members of the Senate, less harried in a six-year term, stood apart from the early cash race until recently. With them it is more a case of early fundraising than a carrying over of surpluses; and because of their staggered terms, such early fund-raising means that those not facing an immediate campaign compete with those who are. In the 1985–86 election cycle, Senators whose terms were to end in 1988 and 1990 raised more than $25 million. Since their collective cash balances at the end of the year were well below that figure, they apparently spent significant amounts either on fundraising or on continuing political expenditures. So the continuous campaign comes to the Senate.[1]

Even as late in the campaign as the end of June of election years

[1]The data of the paragraph are from Maxwell Glen, "Early-Bird Fund Raising," *National Journal* (June 20, 1987), 1589.

— at the end of the 18th month of the cycle — the challengers still have not caught up, even in relative terms. Leaving aside the different sums incumbents and challengers raise, by June 30, 1986, Democratic incumbents in the House had raised 62.1 percent of the funds they raised in the entire cycle; Republican incumbents had raised 58.6 percent. But Democratic challengers in House races had raised only 39.6 percent of their receipts and Republican challengers 41.7 percent. If early money is "better" money for all of the reasons of the campaigning lore, then incumbents maintain those advantages that result from the timeliness of money. They raise more money, and they raise more useful money.

Taken as a whole, these early and massive incumbent resources seem to confirm the charges of incumbent hoggishness — raising money for their campaigns without regard for any reasonable sense of what they need for reelection and, worse, competing for scarce funds with other candidates of the party who need the money. Moreover, there is the heated issue of what candidates do with what is left over; not all of it goes into the next campaign. While that is not directly an issue of campaign finance, it is an ethical question of some heat and emotion.[2]

In a superficial sense, incumbents raise large sums of campaign money because they can. And they can for two central and interlocked reasons. First, they hold public office, and they make public policy that affects the lives and livelihoods of millions. Their ability to raise PAC money — 69 percent of which went to incumbents in the 1986 election cycle — reflects the widespread PAC perception of campaign contributions as a part, an

[2]In Congress's 1979 legislation on campaign finance, it confronted the issue. For all members of Congress elected for the first time in 1980 or after, it provided that excess campaign funds could not be diverted for personal uses and that, aside from funding future campaigns, it could be used only for purposes such as scholarships/fellowships, charitable donations, the political costs of holding office, or contributions to other political committees. (The funds could also be refunded to their contributors.) Members of Congress elected before 1980 were "grandfathered" out, and they were still free to use the funds more broadly. Most of them, to be sure, carry excess funds over to the next campaign, give them to other candidates or party committees, or fund their noncampaign political expenditures (e.g., trips back to the home district). Occasionally newspaper and magazine stories document instances of diversions for personal use, especially when members of Congress must liquidate their campaign funds after defeat or retirement. (The candidate must, however, pay income taxes on any funds diverted to personal uses.) See 2 U.S.C. sec. 439a.

integral part, of a broader program of lobbying and legislative influence. Second, incumbents are very likely to win reelection if they seek it. The safety of incumbents, in fact, reached new heights in 1986. More than 98 percent of all incumbent House members seeking reelection won another term; that is, only six of 390 lost. In the states outside of the South, moreover, incumbents received more than 60 percent of the vote in about 80 percent of the congressional districts.

The ability to raise money, however, does not address the nagging question of the need for it. Why should congressional incumbents, more and more secure in their seats (especially in the House), feel so great a need for more and more campaign resources? Why, especially in view of the enormous advantages of incumbency? Men and women in office have easy access to the media, and far more of the electorate knows their names and faces than knows those of their challengers. Their staffs and offices provide an ever-widening variety of services for the people of the constituency: information on government programs, pamphlets of various kinds, help in seeking benefits and finding errant social security checks, for example. Their mailings and newsletters reach into every home in the state or district. For these and other reasons, then, congressional elections are less and less competitive and, by any measure of election results, incumbents more and more secure.[3] Why do they not reflect that security in their campaign finance?

Blessed with their comparative advantages in raising funds, incumbents are free, first of all, to define their campaign needs

[3]The literature of political science has studied and documented the safety of incumbents and the decline of competitive elections (the "marginals") at great length. See, inter alia, Albert D. Cover, "One Good Term Deserves Another: The Advantage of Incumbency in Congressional Elections," *American Journal of Political Science*, vol. 21 (Aug. 1977), 523–542; Morris P. Fiorina, *Congress: Keystone of the Washington Establishment* (New Haven: Yale University Press, 1977); Gary C. Jacobson, "The Marginals Never Vanished: Incumbency and Competition in Elections to the U.S. House of Representatives, 1952–82," *American Journal of Political Science*, vol. 31 (Feb. 1987), 126–141; John R. Johannes and John C. McAdams, "The Congressional Incumbency Effect: Is It Casework, Policy Compatibility, or Something Else?" *American Journal of Political Science*, vol. 25 (Aug. 1981), 512–542; Thomas E. Mann, *Unsafe at Any Margin* (Washington: American Enterprise Institute, 1978); David Mayhew, "Congressional Elections: The Case of the Vanishing Marginals," *Polity*, vol. 6 (Spring 1974), 295–317; and Diana Yiannakis, "The Grateful Electorate: Casework and Congressional Elections," *American Journal of Political Science*, vol. 25 (Aug. 1981), 568–580.

broadly and protectively. At the beginning of an election cycle, no candidate or contributor knows how close the margin will be 22 months later; incumbents often do not even know who their opponents will be. Nor do they aim for a narrow, even a "normal" electoral margin; they aim to win big to enhance their political reputations and to scare off future competition. They deal not in modal probabilities, but in worst case scenarios. In this context candidates raise money early to discourage would-be challengers both by displaying their financial prowess and by setting a financial hurdle for any challenger. Even in short run terms, incumbents raise large sums as a form of catastrophe insurance against the sudden emergence of a strong and well-financed challenger and, later in the campaign, against an unexpected last-minute flurry or "coup de campagne" by the challenger.[4]

To be sure, some estimates of the closeness of the coming election do enter the getting-spending calculus. Goldenberg and Traugott, in their study of a group of campaigns for the House in 1978, found that campaigns whose managers thought the election would be relatively close greatly outspent those whose managers saw their candidates as sure winners or sure losers.[5] Interestingly, though, the same study reported that 75 percent of the campaign managers for incumbents saw their candidates as "sure winners"; the other 25 percent thought them "vulnerable." These campaign managers made their estimates, however, no earlier than September of election year; and early fund-raising and spending may have caused them to be more optimistic than they were a year earlier.

Beyond these expanded understandings of electoral need, however, the incumbent may be pursuing other fund-raising goals. What is, by one reckoning, the raising of excessive money

[4]In fact, Gary Jacobson reports that the declining number of marginal House seats in the 1960s and 1970s was not matched by a declining rate of reelection for incumbent House members. In other words their incidence of defeat remained constant even though their victory margins went up, a circumstance that reflected greater volatility in congressional elections and a greater candidate responsibility for the outcome of the vote. See his "The Marginals Never Vanished: Incumbency and Competition in Elections to the U.S. House of Representatives, 1952–82," *American Journal of Political Science*, vol. 31 (Feb. 1987), 126–141. In 1984 and 1986, however, the incumbent success percentage in House elections advanced appreciably.

[5]Edie N. Goldenberg and Michael W. Traugott, *Campaigning for Congress* (Washington, D.C.: CQ Press, 1984), 85ff.

may rather be, by another strategy, the building of contributor lists for the future. Or it may be the building of both a nest egg and candidate credibility for the pursuit of another office in the future — a seat in the senate or a governorship, perhaps, for a House member. The incumbent may also simply be saving for a future campaign for the present office; House members, for example, want to be prepared for an unfavorably altered constituency after the decennial reapportionment.

Such fund-raising is indeed self-interested, and it may very well complicate a party's attempt to allocate resources rationally and productively. But whether the parties like it or not, it too is rational behavior by incumbents whose main goal is the furthering of their political careers. As cash becomes more important in the mounting of campaigns, the ability to raise cash becomes a cardinal qualification for candidacy. The "war chest" of the cliches thus becomes a token of prowess in the new martial arts of campaign politics. And since predictions about campaigns are so fallible — about the strength of opposition, about the popularity of a president and the parties, even about the likely success of a campaign strategy — it is clearly rational to abandon the calculus of "enough" and conclude as Mark Twain is said to have concluded about good bourbon: "Too much is barely enough."[6]

II. The Challenging Candidates

Facing the awesome political advantages of incumbency, the challenger depends heavily on campaign money as the great equalizer. To counter all of the advantages of incumbency is no easy task. The challenger may be aided by national political forces — the consequences of a downturn in the economy, perhaps — or by the particular vulnerability of a specific incumbent in a certain constituency. But in most cases, in order to compete with the incumbent, the challenger must campaign more aggres-

---

[6]I am indebted to Charls Walker for bringing the Twain quote to my attention. I cannot locate its source in Twain's writings; Walker tells me he heard it from Gabriel Hauge, the economist, who was an advisor to President Dwight Eisenhower in the 1950s.

sively, more extensively, and thus more expensively than the incumbent.

It follows, as Gary Jacobson has argued, that the more a challenger spends on the campaign, the better the chances of winning. In the face of all the advantages of incumbency, the challenger's battle for name recognition and for an agenda of issues cannot be waged without ample sums of cash. For incumbents, on the other hand, spending tends to vary *inversely* with electoral success; the more they spend, the worse they do! It is not that spending loses votes for them, but that they spend increasing sums of money when they see their careers threatened by a close or losing campaign.[7]

Challengers, however, do not often find the funds they need to mount competitive campaigns; indeed, the margin of the incumbents' financial superiority grows election cycle by election cycle (Tables 6-1 and 6-2). The picture seems even gloomier for challengers if one brings campaign finance down to the level of the individual race. In 1984 no challenger for a seat in the Senate spent as much as the incumbent, and only three of them spent 70 percent or more of the incumbent's total. Of the 390 challengers for House seats in that year, 27 (7 percent) spent more than the incumbents they were opposing. If one goes back to averages, Senate challengers in most years come somewhat closer to the expenditures of their opponents than do challengers in the House, undoubtedly a reflection of the basic fact that Senate challengers have a better chance of winning (Table 6-3). But the differences are not consistent (e.g., 1984), and they appear to disappear in the face of strategic spending by one or both parties in response to short run political forces.[8]

How does a challenger raise the necessary campaign money? Obviously with great difficulty. Perhaps the question is more usefully put another way: Why do some challengers succeed in raising more money than others? Why can some challengers

[7]Gary C. Jacobson, *Money in Congressional Elections* (New Haven: Yale University Press, 1980). The Jacobson findings about the relationship between money and votes are discussed more fully in chap. 10.

[8]On the differences between the financing of House and Senate campaigns, see Frank J. Sorauf, "Varieties of Experience: Campaign Finance in the House and Senate," in Kay L. Schlozman, ed., *Elections in America* (Boston: Allen and Unwin, 1987), 197–218.

TABLE 6-3
Average Expenditures of Major Party Incumbents and Challengers in General
Elections, 1980–1986

House	1980	1982	1984	1986
Incumbents	$164,453	$263,434	$280,241	$334,223
Challengers	99,633	128,409	131,108	124,739
Ratio, I:C	1.7:1	2.1:1	2.1:1	2.7:1
Senate				
Incumbents	$1,357,232	$1,796,054	$2,484,715	$3,303,547
Challengers	845,570	1,189,012	1,041,577	1,743,085
Ratio, I:C	1.6:1	1.5:1	2.4:1	1.9:1

threaten the incumbent while others cannot? From the point of
view of the potential contributor — whether that be a PAC, a
party committee, or an individual — money will in most cases go
to challengers with chances of winning. The central question
then is: what makes a challenger with a chance of winning? There
are three chief considerations:[9]

1. *An attractive candidate.* Attractiveness is many things: name
   recognition as an officeholder, a former candidate, or a celebrity; an attractive personality and family; a confident persona
   in public or on television; skills in meeting people and speaking in a variety of settings.
2. *The district factors.* One might just as appropriately call
   these the "incumbent factors": the closeness of the incumbent's margin in the last election; the general party preferences of the district; the relationship of the incumbent's
   voting record to the preferences of the district; the incum-

[9]The literature on considerations affecting challenger funding is large. See,
for example, Jon Bond, Cary Covington, and Richard Fleisher, "Explaining
Challenger Quality in Congressional Elections," *Journal of Politics*, vol. 47 (May
1985), 510–529; Gary C. Jacobson and Samuel Kernell, *Strategy and Choice in
Congressional Elections* (New Haven: Yale University Press, 1981); Lynn
Ragsdale and Timothy E. Cook, "Representatives' Actions and Challengers' Re-
actions: Limits to Candidate Connections in the House," *American Journal of
Political Science*, vol. 31 (Feb. 1987), 45–81; and John C. McAdams and John R.
Johannes, "Determinants of Spending by House Challengers: 1974–1984,"
American Journal of Political Science, vol. 31 (Aug. 1987), 457–483.

bent's skills in dealing with constituents and with the rigors of campaigning.

3. *National political trends.* These are the tides of national politics that (*ceteris paribus*) favor one party or the other in a given year; they reflect primarily the impact of some issue (often that of the health of the economy) or the perceived success or failure (i.e., the popularity) of the president and his administration.

It goes almost without saying, also, that the challenger's skill at fund-raising — or the ability to rent the services of someone with them — makes a difference. But while this is a necessary condition for financial success, it is hardly sufficient by itself.

In these relationships among challenger, money, and election outcome, however, there are puzzling questions of simultaneous cause. Is money raised because the prospects of victory are great, or does the money produce the votes and thus the victory? Does the availability of money for the campaign attract strong challengers, or do strong challengers attract the ample resources? Common sense suggests these are false dichotomies; cause runs in both directions. The sequence or the dominant direction of the cause, however, does not yield as easily to common sense. Jacobson and Kernell have argued that the pivotal decisions are those of "strategic actors" in the fund-raising process — the contributors of all kinds, the financial brokers, and more generally the political elites.[10] It is their estimation of the chances of victory — based largely on the surge of national political tides — that provides the money, entices the strong challengers into the race, and ultimately propels the challengers into competitiveness in the campaign. That much is certainly true. Yet not all contributors pursue such a rational, modulated political strategy; effective candidates may get their funds on other overriding appeals. And in their activities in recruiting candidates, party committees are increasingly determining the strength of candidates. However one views the interaction of these actors — candidates, contributors, and political organizations — there is a powerful self-fulfilling prophecy at work here. If the major political actors think an election can or will be close, they will make

[10]Jacobson and Kernell, *Strategy and Choice in Congressional Elections.*

decisions (i.e., spending in the campaign) that in turn will make it close.

There is also another less obvious way in which the challengers struggle at the business of raising funds. Amounts aside, they have to spend more time and money at it. PACs have an overwhelming preference for incumbents (see Chapter 4); therefore, that relatively easy way of raising money in large bites is more often denied to challengers. They finance a larger percent of their expenditures from their own savings and equity, often after fruitless attempts to raise it in other ways. (More than 15 percent of the receipts of House challengers in 1986 came from their own resources.) We have no systematic data on person-hours spent raising money; but every bit of evidence we have suggests that challengers spend, dollar for dollar, a good deal more effort than incumbents at it.

Whatever may be their difficulty in raising the sums in contributions that the incumbents do, the House and Senate challengers do far better, ironically, in the spending they do not control — the spending that does not funnel through their personal campaign committees. When one totals independent spending and party "on behalf of" spending in the 1986 cycle, challengers approach the totals of incumbents (Table 6-4). In 1986 the challengers benefited from 43.4 percent of these expenditures; in 1984 it was an impressive 58.2 percent. So, the challenging candidates get badly needed help from the risk-takers in American campaign finance — in these cases primarily from the unconnected, ideological PACs; a few very large association PACs; and committees of the major parties. One may have some doubts about the efficacy of the independent spending; but the party spending brings needed cash and, often, campaign expertise. Unquestionably these expenditures are crucial in sustaining some measure of electoral competitiveness in congressional politics.

III. Wild Cards: the Open Seats

Amid the fascination with the struggle between incumbents and challengers, the candidates for open seats (those seats

TABLE 6-4

Independent Spending for and against and Party Spending "On Behalf of" All Candidates for Congress, 1986

House	Independent Spending°	Party Spending
Incumbents	$1,751,138	$2,050,102
Challengers	1,048,023	2,134,645
Senate		
Incumbents	1,611,487	6,224,133
Challengers	1,335,445	5,441,145

°Independent spending for incumbents is the total of spending "for" incumbents plus the total spending "against" challengers; the total independent spending for challengers is the obverse.

for which no incumbent contests) have become the "great forgotten." There is very little about them in the scholarly literature. For that oversight, though, there are some mitigating circumstances. There is a small number of these seats in any given year, and thus the special circumstances in any one of them greatly affect totals and averages. (For example, there were three open Senate seats in 1982, four in 1984, and six in 1986.) Moreover, the universe of open seats in either house of Congress differs greatly every two years, making comparison over time very risky.

Open seat campaigns for the Senate are now on the average the most expensive campaigns for Congress — an average of $4.1 million for major party candidates in 1982, $4.5 million in 1984, and $3.3 million in 1986. They are increasingly national campaigns with national attention and substantial national funding. And because of the party battle over control of the Senate in the 1980s, they took on a particularly ideological and partisan quality. But they are by no means a single kind of campaign. Expenses do differ, for instance. Both the high and the low were set in 1984 in West Virginia; the successful candidate, Jay Rockefeller, raised $12.1 million; and his defeated opponent, John Raese, mustered only $1.2 million. Even in that single year, candidates differed in where the money came from. Rockefeller contributed $10.3 million from his own fortune; the loser in Massachusetts, Raymond Shamie, anted in close to a million of his own. His successful adversary, John Kerry, spurned PAC funding; but PACs contributed about $2.3 million to Lloyd Doggett and Philip Gramm in Texas, accounting for close to 15 percent of the money in that race. Most of the campaigns did, however, reflect the usual reliance on individual contributions. Aside from the Rockefeller campaign, individuals contributed more money than any other source in all the campaigns.

Even in the more stable realm of House open seat campaigns, there is considerable variation in the number of open seat campaigns. From 1978 through 1986, there was an average of 46 in any given year. The average, however, concealed the range of totals; the numbers for those five election years were 58, 40, 59, 27, and 44. To put the matter another way, over that period there have been eight or nine incumbent-challenger races for every one open seat. Despite the meager numbers — and *because* of the success of incumbents seeking reelection — more than two-thirds of the members of the 98th Congress originally entered the House by winning a race for an open seat. For this reason alone, open seat campaigns attract the strongest and best-financed candidates. The reasons are exactly the same as those for the happy few challengers with a very good chance of winning.

Taken as a whole the open seat campaigns are considerably more competitive than the incumbent-challenger battles. In 1984 almost half of the winners (46 percent) won with less than 55 percent of the vote. Beyond their competitiveness they have another distinctive characteristic. Because there are no "stabilizing" incumbents in these races, they are much more susceptible to national political trends than are the incumbent-challenger races.

The open seat candidates face competition of a second kind: competitors in the primary election of their own party. It is competition that weighs heavily on the campaign finance of open seat candidates. In 1984, for example, 99.3 percent of the expenditures of all incumbent candidates for the House were spent by those who reached the general election; 82.8 percent of all challenger monies were spent by those challengers who made it to the November general election. But for open seat candidates, it was only 54.3 percent. To use another index, from 1978 through

1984 a candidate who lost in the primary outspent at least one of the two candidates in the general election in 36 percent of the open seat races. "Competitiveness" has at least two layers of meaning in the open seat races.[11]

There is, however, one important parallel to the incumbent-challenger campaigns. While open seat candidates do not run against powerful incumbents, they do run against an opposing party and its normal strength in the district. Moreover, the greater the long-run strength of the opposing party, the more money the open seat candidate needs to be competitive. Apparently, too, potential contributors and their mentors — the strategic politicians, that is — adjust their calculus about chances of winning to substitute party strength for incumbent strength. As David Linder has written,

> The party advantage in open seat races acts much like the incumbent advantage. The reigning "incumbent" — be it individual or party — can raise greater amounts of money because of his/its strength and thus performs better in the election. In either setting, an incumbent proves a good investment.[12]

Indeed in recent years about three of four open seats in the House have gone to the candidate of the previous incumbent's party.

IV. Passing the Hat and Plate

Someone once said that politicians are like chain smokers; they light a new campaign from the butt of the old one. Indeed campaigning is virtually continuous for members of the House, and so is their raising of money. In recent years, too, the pace of campaigning has quickened in the Senate, so much so that a rash of stories in the nation's newspapers in 1986 pointed out that senators whose terms did not expire until 1988 or 1990 were

---

[11]These data and the material of the following paragraphs rely very heavily on David C. Linder, "Money and Competition in House Open Seat Elections," a thesis for the baccalaureate degree summa cum laude in political science at the University of Minnesota (Spring 1986).

[12]Ibid., 76.

raising funds almost as sedulously as the class of 1986. The *New York Times* reported that the class of 1990 already had, by the end of 1986, more than $7 million in cash on hand. The *Times* also reported that potential donors resented the increased fund-raising pressure and, more generally, being "hounded" for contributions for campaigns yet years away.[13]

In whatever legislative body one chooses, it is unquestionably the incumbents who are the most insistent raisers of money. It is they who have perfected and rely heavily on that lucrative happening known simply, if ambiguously, as "the fund-raiser." It is an event of some kind — a dinner, a lunch, a reception, perhaps even an outing — for which the attendees buy a ticket, ostensibly for the chicken, crab dip, liquid refreshments, and good fellowship. Tickets are pressed upon possible attendees — proven individual contributors, lobbyists, or PAC representatives, chiefly — with varying degrees of firmness, and the size of the tab varies largely with the celebrity of the political beneficiary. The going rate for Washington fund-raisers seems to extend these days from $250 to several thousand dollars. The price varies with the office (House incumbents at the lower end of the scale) and the celebrity and seniority of the host. Incumbents hosting such occasions have on their side the power of incumbency as well as their personal charm to encourage people to come. Challengers, too, can hold fund-raisers; but it is more common for them to be guest-beneficiaries at an event some incumbent or other political celebrity hosts for them.

Far less dramatic a way of fund-raising is the direct-mail appeal. For most congressional incumbents, it is limited to the state or district in contest; attempts at national fund-raising have failed for all but a very few of the most visible senators. (It should be noted, though, that occasionally a challenger parlays a "notorious" incumbent opponent into a national appeal; Gov. James Hunt of North Carolina did so in his unsuccessful challenge of Sen. Jesse Helms in 1984.) Building the list for such solicitations is indeed one of the most important tasks and byproducts of a political career. Each new campaign adds more names of contributors who can be solicited for further contributions, for volunteer

[13]Richard L. Berke, "Raising 1990 Funds And Some Hackles," *New York Times* (Feb. 23, 1987).

work in the district, or for attendance at an event. Such methods, in short, are systematic ways of cultivating the individual contributor; and the fact that individual contributors remain the chief source of campaign funds vouches for their success.

Beyond these two conventional techniques, the only limit is imagination. Congressman Jack Kemp, a Republican from Buffalo, capitalized on his career as a pro quarterback and led a three-day fund-raising party to the 1987 Superbowl. The trip featured talks about his campaign for the Republican presidential nomination as well as football chit-chat with Don Shula and O. J. Simpson. Other candidates have tapped into sympathetic national networks; women candidates hit women's organizations and events hosted by prominent women activists, and others raise money in ethnic or religious communities (e.g., Sen. Paul Sarbanes of Maryland in the Greek-American communities, Sen. Howard Metzenbaum of Ohio and Sen. Rudy Boschwitz of Minnesota in the Jewish communities). And there is always one of the most potent devices of them all: the phone call from the candidate.

The ways of raising money are legion; and they become a matter of public commentary chiefly because of claims of coercion, especially claims that candidates — particularly well-placed incumbents — will not take no for an answer. Insistent follow-up notes, phone calls, and even personal visits from staff to chivy the invitees into acceptance are the ingredients of which newspaper stories are made and have increasingly *been* made. Lobbyists and PACs do say "no" even to such urgent entreaties, but some do not feel they can. The result is a rising chorus of complaint that solicitations have made a mockery of voluntarism. Such donor unhappiness reaches its zenith in the states over invitations to fund-raising events during short and intense legislative sessions. There have been attempts to forbid the solicitation of funds during legislative sessions in a number of states, and at least one — Texas — prohibits legislators from accepting contributions during a period from 30 days before a session through its final day.

In the search for money and monied sources, the candidates are not alone. Challengers especially rely on help from party committees and incumbents of their party. But candidates of all kinds are increasingly helped by the least visible of the major actors in American campaign finance: that diverse group called simply the "fund-raisers." The FECA guarantees their obscurity, for if they are individuals, it does not require that they report their activities. They are conduits, and since money neither originates nor ends with them, they are invisible under the law.

V. Brokers and Agents

In a literal sense, all actors in campaign finance except individual Americans and the candidates are fund-raisers. That is, they are intermediaries in campaign finance. But that is not how the FECA sees it. PACs and parties are defined primarily as contributors, perhaps because they stamp their political goals and priorities on the money they raise. This leaves as "brokers" those who are not themselves statutory contributors, those who serve as conduits or agents or intermediaries in the raising of campaign funds. With one significant exception — the personal PACs — the FECA does not require them to file public reports because it does not consider them contributors. Thus they fall between the sections and clauses of regulatory legislation, forced into public scrutiny only by an occasional bit of journalistic curiosity.

Brokers are of all kinds and shapes; more importantly, they have greatly different goals and motivations as the midwives of campaign finance. Within their splendid diversity, one sees at least a number of general types or varieties.

The Professionals. The fund-raisers who are for hire are a part of the same profession that raises money for hospitals, colleges, and dance companies in the United States. They know how to do it, when to do it, and why to do it; their expertise extends from preliminary studies on the possibility of raising money to the final stages of collecting pledges and promises. But there is a peculiarly political variant among them, one best typified by the conservative direct-mail whiz Richard Viguerie. While most professionals work for the income, Viguerie works also for the triumph of conservatism. His computer list of proven conservative contributors — rented but never given to customers — was considered one of the jewels of American conservatism until it seemed to lose its sparkle in the middle 1980s.[14]

The Lobbyists. A number of free-lance lobbyists, especially the well-connected members of Washington's political law firms, help candidates raise money in Washington by steering them to contributors, hosting small occasions for them, and making their own political ties and connections available. The "payoff," of course, is access to them for their clients if the candidates win the election. In discussing why Jack Valenti and his Motion Picture Association of America are among Washington's most influential groups, a piece in the *National Journal* notes that Valenti "arranges Hollywood fundraisers [and] lends celebrities to Members' campaigns . . ."[15] In fact, Washington recently has seen the growth of all-purpose political consultants — "clout merchants," one source calls them — who lobby, organize grass-roots campaigns, mount public relations campaigns, devise media strategies, organize direct-mail campaigns, monitor issues, take polls, *and* manage political fund-raising.[16]

The Officeholders. Incumbents help other candidates raise money by hosting fund-raisers for them, by giving them access to their mailing lists, or simply by making an appearance at their fund-raising events. Only the most visible of them succeed in the latter "drawing card" role; the most successful of them all undoubtedly is the president of the United States. Well into the 1986 campaign, Ronald Reagan was said to have raised more than $25 million for Republican candidates, more than $10 million of it for senatorial candidates. Incumbents also transfer funds to other candidates in two ways: by contribution from their own surplus funds (subject to the same limits that apply to all individual contributors) or from their own personal PACs (in which case the limits are those that apply to PACs). The goals of fund-raising incumbents are complex; many are partisan and/or ideological, but

---

[14]On the troubles of Richard Viguerie, see for example, David Brooks, "Please, Mr. Postman: The Travails of Richard Viguerie," *National Review* (June 20, 1986), 28–32.

[15]Burt Solomon, "Measuring Clout," *National Journal* (July 4, 1987), 1708.

[16]Burt Solomon, "Clout Merchants," *National Journal* (March 21, 1987), 662–666.

among them are the creation of gratitude and obligation that will help the officeholder secure and hold positions of legislative leadership.

Groups and Networks. Their goals are those of policy and ideology and access — the same goals as groups organized into PACs. In recent years one of the best publicized sets of them has been a women's political network, led by a bipartisan Women's Campaign Fund in many states. Acting at least in part on the belief that traditional fund-raising sources are not available to women candidates and that that fact explains the dearth of women candidates, they have staged fund-raisers for candidates across the country.[17]

Wealthy Individuals. As fund-raisers they represent a tie to the old regime of campaign finance. Much of their work is done in one-on-one solicitation within a circle of friends and associates — just as it was done in the old days. Some of them were indeed among the big contributors in those times. As Herbert Alexander has remarked, "One of the most important impacts of the Federal Election Campaign Act is that it has exchanged the big giver for the big solicitor."[18] Their fund-raising secret is simple; they know or know of other wealthy people with similar political involvements — people like themselves. They are especially potent figures in presidential politics, and as such they will be discussed in the next chapter.

Celebrities. Star power raises money for just about any cause, including politics. The celebrity attracts paying people to some kind of event — the principle is as simple as that. Geraldine

[17]On the subject of the conventional wisdom about the financial problems of women candidates, two careful studies find that when one controls for incumbency and other political differences, women raise about as much money as men. But they find it harder to become candidates in the first place, and that may in part result from perceptions that they will not be able to raise campaign funds. See Carole J. Uhlaner and Kay L. Schlozman, "Candidate Gender and Congressional Campaign Receipts," *Journal of Politics*, vol. 48 (Feb. 1986), 30–50; and Barbara C. Burrell, "Women's and Men's Campaigns for the U.S. House of Representatives, 1972–1982," *American Politics Quarterly*, vol. 13 (July 1985), 251–272.

[18]Quoted in Tom Watson, "Networks of Rich Texas Money Brokers Help Turn on Floods of Campaign Cash," *Congressional Quarterly* (Apr. 14, 1984), 876.

Ferraro and Walter Mondale have that ability in Democratic circles despite their loss in the 1984 elections. The stars of the popular arts traditionally have lent their celebrity to political causes; Los Angeles and Hollywood have always been profitable stops on the fund-raising tour. In the 1986 campaign, for instance, the Hollywood Women's Political Committee threw a party at Barbra Streisand's ranch near Malibu for six Democratic senatorial candidates. Tickets at $5000 per couple were by invitation only. The entertainment featured songs by Ms. Streisand, who had not sung in public in the previous six years, it was said. The net "take" was more than a million.

The PACs. A few PACs act as fund-raising brokers, and they do so in a number of ways. Some, the Business-Industry PAC (BIPAC), for example, provide information and political expertise to smaller PACs and thus guide their contribution decisions. Expertise is a prime source of influence in the politics of campaign finance. Some PACs collect money from other PACs for their own distribution; the classic example is the AFL-CIO's COPE, which in 1983–84 received 86 percent of its receipts from other like-minded PACs. Still other PACs raise money by "bundling"; they encourage individual contributions to specific candidates by facilitating the contributions and by transmitting them (in a bundle, apparently) to the chosen candidates.

And then among the PACs as financial intermediaries, there are the personal PACs. They are part precampaign committee (especially for would-be presidents), part ordinary nonconnected (ideological) PAC, and part financial broker. As a very special case, they require separate treatment.

VI. The Personal PACs

All personal PACs have at least two characteristics in common: they are nonconnected PACs (they have no parent organization), and they are the creation of a single, visible individual. In almost all cases — and this is central to their role as brokers — sponsoring individuals are raising and giving money at least in part to support their own political careers, positions, or goals. It is thus a relationship to the candidate not unlike the one of the fund-raising lobbyist. It differs, of course, in that these *are* PACs even if they are like no other PACs; they raise money, spend it, and account for it under the FECA's regulation of PACs.

Any history or accurate counting of the personal PACs defies scholarship. There is no documenting of the first one, although they are widely thought to be a post-1974 phenomenon. That uncertainty results at least in part from the bland, nondescriptive names they carry; one rarely can tell from the name that it is a personal PAC. Americans for the National Interest jockeys with The Volunteer Committee, and the Fund for America's Future competes with the Committee for Freedom. From the group names one cannot tell the name of the founding personage, nor can one discern their party affiliations. (These four are, in the order above, the PACs of Democrats Bruce Babbitt and Gary Hart and of Republicans George Bush and Pat Robertson.) For that reason it is not always easy to count the personal PACs, but by 1987 there were more than 40 of them registered with the FEC. There were also dozens of them in the states.

Most of the personal PACs registered with the FEC fall into one of two groups: the PACs of would-be presidential candidates and those of congressional incumbents who hold or yearn for leadership positions. For the individual hoping to win a party nomination for the presidency, the personal PAC is a useful, pre-candidacy device. It enables one to travel about the country making contacts, being seen, giving speeches, planning an organization, hiring staff and consultants, and making fund-raising contacts. Just the process of raising money for the PAC by direct mail has the serendipitous benefit of building a list of proven contributors for a future campaign; it wages one more battle in the war for names. The PAC covers administrative or overhead expenditures, at least for the purposes of reporting to the FEC; and from the remaining funds the PAC (that is, the "founder" of the PAC) may also make contributions to candidates, thereby winning well-placed gratitude and obligation. All of this goes on under the polite fiction that the person of the personal PAC is not yet a candidate, since a personal PAC may not be used to advocate directly any candidacy.

Indeed, it is hard to think of the early stages of a presidential candidacy without such a PAC. By the end of 1986, Democrats Bruce Babbitt, Joseph Biden, Richard Gephardt, Gary Hart, and Edward Kennedy had one, as did Republicans Howard Baker, George Bush, Robert Dole, Alexander Haig, Jack Kemp, Pat Robertson, and Donald Rumsfeld. Having one is no guarantee of success; but in a presidential politics in which the early pre-convention stages — those about the time of the Iowa caucuses and the New Hampshire primary — are increasingly important, the personal PAC carries the potential candidate through an awkward early period in the development of candidacy. Not having had one is just one more disadvantage that the late-starting candidate has to overcome.

THE FUND-RAISING OF HENRY WAXMAN

A Democratic member of the House from the monied precincts of Hollywood, California, Rep. Henry Waxman has become a major fundraiser for fellow Democrats. He works through a PAC called "the 24th Congressional District of California PAC." The following are excerpts from an article by Dennis Farney and John J. Fialka, "His Ability as a Fund-Raiser Enhances the Power of California's Democratic Rep. Henry Waxman," in the *Wall Street Journal* of November 10, 1983:

> "Henry Waxman represents the closest thing to a Democratic political organization we've got right now," says Washington political consultant Leon Billings. "Henry is doing individually what the Republican party is doing institutionally."
>
> It's true. Incumbents like Rep. Waxman have flourished as fundraisers in the last decade, even as the Democratic party itself has struggled with creeping atrophy. They have become political warlords, building their personal band of followers. . . .
>
> [Waxman's] first big coup came early in 1979, when his colleagues on the full Energy and Commerce Committee elected him subcommittee chairman. In a 15-to-12 vote, he upset North Carolina's Richardson Preyer, a Southern patrician favored by the House Democratic leadership. Some colleagues say that Mr. Preyer lost the contest by failing to hustle for votes. Nevertheless, it couldn't have hurt that, in the months preceding the vote, Mr.

Waxman had given his Democratic committee colleagues about
$24,000 in campaign contributions.

Mr. Waxman thinks too much is made of the money. "I've always
been insulted by the suggestion that those people voted for me because I gave them money," he says. "It was more an ideological
thing. And if I were only exercising power for the sake of power,
people might justifiably raise their eyebrows. But I feel I'm
deeply involved in issues."

The other kind of personal PAC — those of the congressional
incumbents — must also be kept apart from the incumbent's candidate committee. Their purposes differ from the PACs of the
incipient presidents. The incumbents raise money for their PACs
with the power of incumbency; this power may also be enhanced
by a leadership position or the possibility of acquiring one. And,
indeed, one of the major goals of such PACs is precisely the bol-
stering of leadership or the recruiting of support for a bid for it.
Put more broadly, such PACs exist and spend heavily to mobilize
peers — peers in the party, on a committee, on a subcommittee
(see box). Like the PACs of the candidates thinking about the
presidency, they may also exist to further the political careers of
their principals.

If one leaves aside the PACs of congressional incumbents considering a presidential race (e.g., those of Dole and Kemp), then
the personal PACs in Congress are much more common among
Democrats than Republicans. In the House in 1986, Speaker Tip
O'Neill, Majority Leader Jim Wright, and Whip Tom Foley all
had them, as did Tony Coelho, a successful aspirant to Foley's position when Foley and Wright "moved up" following Tip
O'Neill's retirement. The Democratic leader in the Senate,
Robert Byrd of West Virginia, had one; and so did a major challenger for his position, Bennett Johnson of Louisiana. There
were a few Republicans with personal PACs, but except for Jesse
Helms's National Congressional Club, they raised small sums.
The explanation for the relative absence of Republicans probably

rests on the differences between the two parties — between the organized and disciplined Republicans, who care not for competition with the party fund-raising committees, and the relaxed and undisciplined individualism of the Democrats.

Those PACs of incumbents pursue their goals — whether it is a leadership career or the building of a party majority or a more cohesive majority — the same way that all PACs do: by making contributions to candidates. The same contribution limit of $5000 per candidate per election applies to them. Members of Congress can and do give their surplus campaign funds directly to other candidates; but when they do, the FECA's contribution limits on individuals apply: $1000 per candidate per election. The total sum of those contributions, also known as candidate "transfers," is unknown but probably substantial; the FEC does not aggregate and report them. The personal PAC, however, has at least three advantages: (1) the PAC can absorb some noncampaign political costs (e.g., issue development, travel, staff development) as a part of its overhead, (2) the PAC is subject to contribution limits five times greater than those on the candidate's campaign committee, and (3) PACs can receive contributions of $5000 from individuals, while candidate committees are limited to gifts of $1000.

Inevitably, there are some personal PACs that do not fit either of the two categories. Pamela Harriman's Democrats for the 80's is one. In many ways it is very similar to the other ideological PACs in that it raises money for Democrats and to advance a mainstream Democratic philosophy; moreover, Mrs. Harriman, widow of Averill Harriman, is advancing no political career through it. The case for including it here rests entirely on its place in her fabled fund-raising activities for Democrats, not only in her Washington home but in other parts of the country. Her PAC is an extension of the activities and contacts of a wealthy individual fund-raiser. The HHH Fund exemplifies another variant of the personal PAC. Established by the widow and son (Hubert Humphrey III) of the late senator and vice president, it raised a modest sum in 1986 for a few Democratic senatorial candidates. Humphrey, then the attorney general of Minnesota, was considering a race in 1988 for the Senate seat held by Republican David Durenberger.[19] Generalizations come easily about the receipts and expenditures of the personal PACs. A study of 20 of the PACs of congressional members in 1983–84 makes that clear.[20] In that election cycle, they raised a total of $19,617,294, an average of just a bit less than a million a PAC. (The median, however, was about $143,000.) Their receipts ranged from the $5.7 million of Jesse Helms's National Congressional Club to the $2000 of Congressman William Thomas's 96th Club. Of the $19.6 million in receipts, $16.7 million came from individual contributors and $1.6 million from PACs. (While the sum coming from PACs is less than 10 percent, it is still a much larger percentage than any other group of PACs raises from other PACs.)

There are easily discernible differences in fund-raising among the personal PACs. The largest among them rely heavily on direct-mail solicitation and thus raise far higher percentages of receipts from individual contributors (Table 6-5); with the exception of Jesse Helms, they serve possible candidates for a presidential nomination who are building a list of proven donors. The personal PACs raising the largest percentage of funds from PACs, on the other hand, are those (with the exception of Walter Fauntroy) of the leadership. Their PACs raise money very much as powerful incumbents do in other circumstances.

Similarly, the largest PACs give the smallest portion of their receipts in contributions to congressional candidates. In part this is because they are spending a large portion of the receipts to finance direct-mail solicitation and to build lists of new donors in the war of names. In the case of Helms's PAC, a substantial part of

[19]Information about personal PACs is largely limited to reporting in elite newspapers and in the Washington magazines. For examples of the latter see Bob Benenson, "In the Struggle for Influence, Members' PACs Gain Ground," *Congressional Quarterly* (Aug. 2, 1986), 1751–1754; and three articles by Maxwell Glen in the *National Journal*: "Elite Group of Members of Congress Are Doling Out Political Contributions" (Aug. 18, 1984), 1566–1568; "Starting a PAC May Be Candidates' First Step Down Long Road to 1988" (Feb. 16, 1985), 374–377; and "A Formidable Fund Raiser" (Apr. 19, 1986), 938–941. The last of the three describes the activities of Pamela Harriman and her PAC.

[20]The 20 are those PACs active in 1983–84 that were on the list of 28 members' PACs listed in the later article (from mid-1986) of Benenson, "In the Struggle for Influence, Members' PACs Gain Ground."

TABLE 6-5
Twenty Personal PACs of Members of Congress in 1983–84: Receipts and Contributions to Congressional Candidates

Sponsor of PAC°	Net Receipts	% Receipts from PACs	% Funds Given°°
Sen. Howard Baker	$4,469,645	8.0%	9.3%
Sen. Robert Byrd	171,302	51.0	65.4
Rep. Tony Coelho	31,250	39.2	66.9
Sen. John Danforth	141,439	23.5	9.9
Sen. Dennis DeConcini	112,102	23.2	2.7
Sen. Robert Dole	1,180,888	27.6	34.4
Rep. David Drier	32,250	18.6	86.5
Rep. Walter Fauntroy	25,038	93.3	28.4
Sen. John Glenn	106,480	3.8	28.4
Sen. Jesse Helms	5,703,035	—	1.8
Rep. Jack Kemp	2,179,573	2.1	9.8
Sen. Edward Kennedy	3,556,016	6.4	5.7
Rep. Thomas O'Neill	117,654	64.6	45.1
Rep. Stephen Solarz	68,588	6.5	48.6
Sen. Ted Stevens	112,184	26.3	30.2
Rep. William Thomas	2,000	—	200.0
Rep. Morris Udall	917,931	12.7	10.4
Rep. Henry Waxman	222,376	16.2	51.2
Sen. Pete Wilson	145,279	38.9	23.8
Rep. Jim Wright	322,264	48.6	69.3

° For a list of the names of the PACs, see the Benenson article cited in footnote 19.
°°Percentage of net receipts given to congressional candidates.

the expenditures is going into independent expenditures, especially in the presidential race. (Helms's PAC is the only one of the nonpresidential PACs seemingly uninterested in the mobilization of influence in Congress.) In the case of presidential PACs, a good part of the receipts are going to support the travels of the potential candidate and the development of other political assets for a presidential candidacy.

Personal PACs differ also in their relative support of incumbents, challengers, and open seat candidates. There appears to be a special calculus at work in each PAC, but in the aggregate only a shade over half of their contributions go to incumbents, with 33 percent going to challengers, and the rest to open seat candidates.[21] Conventional wisdom has had it that the PACs of the powerful in Congress gave much more than that to fellow incumbents. Moreover, personal PACs calculate with external political forces in mind. In 1984 the PACs of Democrats in Congress gave overwhelmingly to endangered incumbents, while the PACs of Republicans invested a substantial majority of their funds in challengers and open seat candidates. Revealingly, then, while the personal PACs of congressional incumbents seek different goals than do the party committees, the exigencies of American politics force them into similar contribution strategies.

VII. In Conclusion

The intermediaries in all social transactions are inevitably the least visible participants. They help to arrange the transaction; but because they are not formal parties to it, they slide easily from sight. This has certainly been the case in American campaign finance. The media have recently begun to discover the brokers, but their official invisibility under the FECA discourages even the sharpest journalistic curiosity. About them we know only a few names and a few anecdotes; most of their role and influence is left to speculation.

In view of their relative obscurity, it is not easy to tell whether the role of the broker/fund-raiser is on the increase. But the contributors in the process — especially the PACs active in congressional campaigns — certainly have that impression. So, while millions of Americans, tutored by Common Cause and the daily newspaper, worry about the demands contributors put on successful candidates, there are growing numbers of contributors unhappy with the demands of phone and direct-mail appeals, lobbyists resentful of the hard sell that accompanies invitations to money-raising events, and virtually everyone uneasy about incumbent candidates for reelection who raise far greater sums than they spend. We have always feared the pressures of the contributors, but now the impression grows that

---

[21]These calculations are based on the same 20 personal PACs employed in the paragraphs above.

there is also a reverse pressure on contributors to give compliantly and repeatedly.

Moreover, there is evidence that the greater aggressiveness in fund-raising has created a backlash. The softness of direct-mail returns testifies to the increasing oversolicitation of those lists. The leveling off in the growth of PACs and the recent setbacks in party fund-raising may be straws in the same wind. All in all, we may very well be in the early years of a contributor resistance to the raising of money for campaigns. If we are, it will establish a very central fact that has not been clear in the heady days of rising campaign outlays: that there *are* limits to the sums of money that can be raised to pay for American campaigning. It will also serve as a reminder that in the voluntary marketplace of American campaign finance some equilibrium will be struck between the supply of cash and the demand for it, some accommodation made between the goals of the suppliers and those of the demanders.

For now, however, incumbents in Congress are able to dominate the system of campaign finance. In considerable part their fund-raising prowess derives from the facts of their incumbency: their perquisites, their role in policy-making, their probabilities of winning campaigns for reelection. Above all, the ease with which they raise money, especially early money, permits them to act preemptively rather than reactively. Early receipts, even without early spending, discourage competition in the primary and attractive challengers in the general election. The weight of the incumbent's financial advantage — made a weapon of intimidation, ironically, by the law's requirement of full disclosure — adds to all of the other advantages of incumbency that discourage competition. In the broadest sense, of course, all fund-raising is reactive — reactions to past elections, to real or perceived insecurities, to imagined possible turns of fortune and worse case scenarios. But the effect is preemptive if it determines the behavior of other present candidates, real or potential.

For all the success the incumbents have had in raising money, there is an unmistakable unease about its burdens in Congress. No doubt it influenced some of the support for proposed reforms in Congress in 1986 and 1987. Members complain about the time and energy that fund-raising absorbs; and some, too, express a distaste for its rituals and pleadings. Others note that contributors expect "access" and that such expectations translate directly into demands for time on their already crowded schedules. The impression grows, in other words, that while the sums of money given and taken rise steadily, the process pleases no one (see box). We seem at last to have achieved a parity of displeasure about the getting of money with which to fund the nation's campaigns.

THE LAMENTS OF THE INSIDERS

Displeasure with campaign finance from the public and outside observers has not been uncommon. Much of American journalism and the movement to reform the system reflect it. But the widening displeasure of insiders is increasingly on the public record. A few indications follow.

Brock Adams, elected as a Democratic senator from Washington in 1986, on the allocation of his time in a campaign challenging an incumbent:

> I remember waking up at 5:30 a.m. in Goldendale, Wash., to begin another day of "dialing for dollars" . . . making phone calls not to potential constituents but to political action committees asking for thousands of dollars. During 1986 I began most of my days this way. . . .
>
> I never imagined how much of my personal time — at least 50 percent — would be spent on fund-raising. Most of the time I was not talking to constituents about contributions; I was talking to professionals who control PACs and lobbyists who were far removed from the voters of Washington state. I was campaigning for money, not campaigning for votes."

From "Dialing the Money Men Replaces Campaigning for Votes,"
Los Angeles Times *(June 24, 1987)*

Commenting on the frequent pilgrimages of senatorial candidates to Florida to raise money, a Miami developer and fund-raiser, Jeffrey Berkowitz, observed that it was getting harder and harder to find contributors for them:

> "The opportunity to be in proximity to a living Senator,"

Berkowitz said, choosing his words carefully, "has become less than overwhelming."

Maxwell Glen, "Early-Bird Fund Raising," National Journal
(June 20, 1987), 1588.

Finally, Bonnie Reiss, treasurer of the Hollywood Women's Political Committee, testified before the Senate Committee on Rules and Administration in favor of proposals to limit the growth of campaign spending.

On the one hand, we are happy that you and your colleagues are making frequent trips to Los Angeles, because it affords us an opportunity to meet and discuss issues of mutual concern. On the other hand we can't help but worry about the overwhelming amount of time spent raising money — yours and ours. . . . It is clear to us all that far too much of your time, energy and intellect is spent in demeaning pursuit of the almighty campaign buck. Can't we find a way to free you from all this, so that you can spend more time addressing the crucial issues facing our nation and our world, not to mention spending time with your families, reading a good book, playing a set of tennis, or even seeing a movie?

From testimony of Apr. 22, 1987

For all of this, the metaphor of an arms race is increasingly apt. In the dynamics of the escalation of campaign costs, a strong and aggressive set of actors (i.e., the incumbent candidates) seek a new electoral advantage or protection. Their adversaries feel compelled to add resources with which to redress the lost balance (the lost competitiveness). All participants, moreover, act in an increasingly unstable environment. The decay of party loyalties has made voters less predictable and more sensitive to very short term political appeals; new campaigning skills and technologies can — or candidates *believe* can — produce almost overnight turns in electoral fortunes. Electoral threats of new severity, in other words, can develop with new speed; and reaction times have sharply diminished. The need grows to adopt preemptive strategies in pursuit of an evermore elusive security. And since no one really knows what "works" in a campaign — or what retaliatory measures a given move will provoke — there is the additional pressure to arm oneself for every contingency.

Moreover, economizing in the every day sense of the word has not been necessary. In the steep climb of campaign costs, as in the upward spiral of arms costs, the supply of available resources with which to pay for security has until now seemed almost unlimited. There has been an implicit assumption in American campaign finance that contributors and potential contributors do little to constrain the steep rise of costs. Thus far the only effective constraint of "cost" has been that of the time and effort going into the raising of the money. But if the sources of campaign money are in fact beginning to resist or contract, we will surely see a new and effective constraint and thus a fundamental change in the dynamic of the campaign finance system.

7
Presidential Campaigns: The Public Funding Option

There is a pervasive uniqueness about the American presidency and its politics. The office itself, especially in the extent of its powers, defeats comparison. Election to it involves a many-phased campaign without parallel in its scope and length, the last part waged within a baroque, and surely unique, institution called the electoral college. As if to match all of this specialness, Americans have devised a two-part system of public funding for this extended campaign that again has no peer or precedent.

Public funding for presidential campaigns differs in the two parts of the campaign. For the first part — the period of the presidential primaries and the selection of delegates to the nominating conventions — there is a system of partial public funding triggered by private, voluntary contributions. It covers the period from the beginning of the new election cycle to the national nominating conventions of the election year, and it is defined and hedged about with provisions of daunting complexity. For the second part of the campaign — the two- to three-month general election campaign after the nominating conventions — there is full public funding in which the candidate choosing it may not raise or spend funds other than those coming from the federal treasury. Public funding is voluntary to be sure, but both major party candidates in 1976, 1980, and 1984 accepted it and its restrictions. It is also the only instance of full, 100 percent public funding in all of American politics — national, state, or local.

Public funding for the presidential campaign, like most of the other reforms of the 1970s, is rooted in the excesses and illegalities of the years immediately preceding. Indeed the full weight of public and congressional wrath over the Watergate revelations fell on the presidential campaign. It was, after all, the Nixon campaign in 1972 that had initiated the Watergate break-in; the burglars who broke into the headquarters of the Democratic national committee were paid with funds given to the Nixon reelection campaign. It was also the Nixon campaign that received the illegal corporate contributions and the secret $100,000 from Howard Hughes (secreted by a confidant of the president). It was this campaign that bypassed the contribution limits of the 1971 FECA by raising enormous sums before the act's implementation date and then fought long (and unsuccessfully) in the courts to conceal the fact.[1]

But Watergate is hardly the entire background to public funding of presidential campaigns, for Congress began edging in that direction as early as 1966. In that year it passed the so-called "Long bill," named after its sponsor, Sen. Russell Long of Louisiana. It created an income tax checkoff plan, in which citizens could divert a dollar or two of the taxes they owed into a special fund from which payments would be made to political parties whose presidential candidates in the previous election got at least 5 million votes. The plan came to naught when Congress failed to enact legislation to spell out the details and implement it. At least in part, it was the victim of fears of party power when the members of Congress began to realize the implications of giving money to party organizations rather than to candidates.

After the spending totals of the 1968 presidential elections were toted up, reform broke out again. President Richard Nixon vetoed a first attempt to limit media spending in 1970. Congress then revised the limits upward, and the president signed the 1971 Federal Election Campaign Act into law. In addition to instituting the strict reporting requirements that are still in effect today, the 1971 act attempted to cap expenditures by limiting

---

[1]For a good summary of the background to and history of the reform of presidential campaign finance, see *Dollar Politics*, 3d ed. (Washington, D.C.: Congressional Quarterly, 1982), 8–15.

the amounts candidates could spend on media advertising — a clear reflection of the belief that escalating campaign levels in the 1960s were primarily the result of the new media campaigning. The limit on media spending in the presidential election was set at 10 cents an eligible voter; in 1972 the overall media limit was fixed at $14.3 million, with a "limit within the limit" of $8.5 million for radio and TV expenditures. These limits did help to slow down the increase in campaign spending in 1972, but they were scrapped when Congress legislated much broader and more inclusive spending limits in the 1974 amendments to the FECA.[2]

More important certainly was the creation in late 1971 of a fund financed by income tax checkoffs of one dollar from single returns and two dollars from joint returns.[3] It was intended for presidential candidates — not the parties — but the specifics were never detailed. At the insistence of President Nixon, the statute did not go into operation until 1973, with no payments until the 1976 elections. These dates freed him from its coverage and also left a good deal of time for reconsideration in the Congress and for challenges in the courts. But in buying that time, ironically, Richard Nixon had not counted on the most momentous happening of all: the popular reaction to the scandals in his own campaign for reelection.

Finally, these stirrings of reform were at all points intertwined with party politics. The Republican superiority in fund-raising was well established by 1970, and the gap between the two parties' resources was growing. The availability of the newly powerful mass media made the Republicans' financial superiority all the more threatening. For their part the Democrats were still mired in debt from the campaign of 1968. Watergate's revelations about a Republican president and a Republican presidential campaign turned a somewhat precarious Democratic program of reform into a mandate that swept even hesitant Republicans into its cause. And so Congress fleshed out a plan for full public funding of presidential campaigns in 1974 and added

---

[2]These limits were struck down in 1976 in *Buckley v. Valeo*. It seems safe to say that had the 1971 limits on spending on the media not been repealed in 1974, they, too, would have been invalidated in *Buckley*.

[3]The Revenue Act of 1971, of which the checkoff provisions were a part, was Public Law 92–178.

to it the new idea of partial public funding for the preconvention period.[4]

I. Finance Before the Nominating Conventions

For the purposes of federal law, the first phase of the presidential campaign begins at some undetermined time in the previous election cycle and continues until the national nominating conventions of the two major parties officially anoint their candidates in the summer before the election. In the 1984 elections, for example, the candidates for the major party nominations reported raising a total of $4.5 million before the 1984 election cycle began on New Year's Day of 1983. Such contenders for the party nominations qualify for support from the treasury when they raise $5000 in at least 20 states in sums of no more than $250 from any individual contributor.[5] When they qualify (become eligible), the U.S. treasury matches all individual contributions of $250 or less, dollar for dollar, up to a maximum of $5 million in 1974 dollars. That is to say, the $5 million aggregate limit is adjusted upward in each presidential campaign to reflect increases in the Consumer Price Index. (The first of the 1988 candidates to qualify for the matching grants, Democrat Richard Gephardt, did so on April 1, 1987.)

With the public money, however, comes a set of limits on spending that establish records of some sort for complexity. The restrictions include:

- a limit of $50,000 on the candidate's use of personal and family resources.
- a limit of $10 million on the total expenditures of the prenomination campaign, the limit being adjusted upward every

---

[4]The 1974 provisions initiating public funding for presidential campaigns were a part of the amendments in that year to the 1971 Federal Elections Campaign Act. Those amendments were contained in Public Law 93-443.

[5]They can later lose that eligibility for public funding if they win less than 10 percent of the vote in two consecutive presidential primaries; they *then* can regain the eligibility if they win at least 20 percent of the vote in a subsequent primary.

four years to reflect changes in the CPI. (Candidates may also raise an additional 20 percent above the ceiling to cover fund-raising costs.)

• limits on spending in specific states. The limits are again de-fined in 1974 dollars (and thus adjusted upward every four years) in a pair of alternatives: $200,000 or 16 cents for each eligible voter, whichever is the larger. In 1984 that meant state limits that ranged from $404,000 (the 1984 equivalent of $200,000) in a number of states, including pivotal New Hampshire, to $6.0 mil-lion in California.[6]

Candidates may, finally, spend money beyond these limits to cover legal and accounting costs in the campaign.

This system has operated now in three searches for the presi-dential nominations: 1976, 1980, and 1984. Only one candidate has made the decision not to qualify for federal matching money: John Connally, the Texas Republican, in 1980. Drawing on his own resources and those of his wealthy supporters, he raised and spent $12.72 million, unencumbered by any spending limits. His campaign fizzled for reasons having little to do with campaign fi-nance, and he got only a single vote in the Republican nominating convention of 1980. It was undoubtedly the single most "expen-sive" convention vote in the history of presidential nomination politics. Other candidates have, of course, tried and failed to qualify for the matching funds; none of them seemed at the time to be credible candidates.[7]

In these three presidential cycles, only one third-party candi-date — Sonia Johnson of the Citizens Party in 1984 — qualified for federal funds. Lyndon LaRouche also qualified in the same year, but the FEC considered him a Democrat; despite his use of a party name special to his cause and despite his rejection of the Democratic party "mainstream," he was officially a candidate for the Democratic nomination. In 1980 John Anderson, eventually

---

[6]Note that the individual state spending limits add to a figure more than twice the overall limit of $10 million in 1974 dollars; candidates therefore must limit their spending in some states to a figure well below the statutory limit.

[7]In 1980 the candidate with the largest total of receipts who failed to qualify was the Libertarian candidate, Edward Clark, who raised $1.1 million. In 1984 it was again the Libertarian candidate (this time David Bergland) who raised more than $600,000.

TABLE 7-1
Sources of Receipts for Presidential Preconvention Campaigns, 1980–1984
(all dollar figures in millions)

Sources	1980		1984	
Individuals	$74.1	(56.5%)	$64.4	(59.7%)
Public funds	30.1	(22.9%)	36.5	(33.9%)
Loans	16.1	(12.3%)	4.3	(4.0%)
PACs	1.6	(1.2%)	1.3	(1.2%)
Total	$131.2		$107.8	

Notes: 1.) The percentages do not add to 100 percent because candidates have other receipts (e.g., interest, their own contributions, contributions from parties and other candidate committees). 2.) The 1984 data differ in two important ways from those for 1980. The cut-off date for 1984 is the end of 1985; the data for 1980 are only for the 1979-80 cycle. (That later cut-off undoubtedly explains, at least in part, the lower debt figure in 1984.) The 1984 data are also for "adjusted receipts" and thus reflect rebates, refunds, and other corrections in the totals.

an independent candidate in the general election campaign, also qualified for federal funds, but as a Republican who unsuccessfully sought his party's presidential nomination. Public funds, however, account for only about one-third of the money raised and spent in preconvention campaigning by those candidates qualifying for them (Table 7-1). By far the most important source of funding is individual contributions. PACs, on the other hand, account for a consistently small part of major campaigners' receipts — only 1.2 percent in 1984.

The paucity of PAC money in these preconvention campaigns is easily explained. From the candidates' perspective, PAC money is "worth" less than money coming from individual contributors; it cannot help them qualify for matching money, and it is not matched by federal funds once eligibility is established. For their part, most PACs prefer to avoid the high-risk politics of nominations; PAC contributions in contested primary elections for the House and Senate are also negligible. Campaigns for nominations divide people of the same party or ideological persuasion, and they also run a good probability of being losing campaigns. What little PAC money going to candidates before the conventions tends to go late in the primary season to candidates who have virtually sewed up the nomination. It is these late contributions to almost certain nominees that explain why corporation PACs, ordinarily wary of battles for nominations, accounted for almost half of all PAC contributions ($742,293 of $1,506,892) in the 1984 preconvention period.

So, it is the contributions of individuals that fuel the campaigns for the party nominations, both for the sums they give and for the matching funds they trigger. Indeed, there is little money available from any other source. PACs contribute little, party committees do not give to contestants for their nominations (except to help them pay off debts later), and the statutes limit candidates accepting federal funds to $50,000 from their own fortunes and those of their immediate families. Moreover, a candidate functioning outside of the federal funding system raises money pretty much as do those in it. Of John Connally's $12.7 million in 1980, $11.6 million came from individual contributions (91.5 percent). He received only $205,000 from PACs.

The picture, then, is one of individual voluntarism triumphant. In 1984 all of the candidates of all parties reported a grand total of $64,438,612 in individual contributions in the preconvention period. Encouraged by a funding program that matched contributions only to $250, the candidates took almost 60 percent of their individual contributions in chunks smaller than $500. Only two candidates, Democrats John Glenn and Alan Cranston, raised more than half of their individual contributions in sums of $500 or more.

There is no way of saying how many individuals volunteered their cash for presidential nomination politics in 1984, but we do have one clue. The 11 candidates eligible to receive matching money submitted a grand total of 793,565 contributions totaling $38,007,033 for matching — with the average contribution thus a little less than $48. The almost 800,000 contributions do not, however, translate directly into contributors. Some individuals may well have given more than once to the same candidate or given to more than one candidate. On the other hand, the figure does not include the small informal contributor (e.g., the one who puts cash in the plate or bucket passed at a rally), nor does it include the contributions to candidates not eligible for matching.

The logic of it, though, suggests there were at least 800,000 contributors active in the preconvention period.[8]

Overall, money from the U.S. Treasury was the candidates' second source of receipts. It is a source that is stable over time (see Table 7-1) and reasonably constant at any one time (Table 7-2). There are two explanations for the candidates' differing reliance on public funds in 1984. The LaRouche candidacy is the great outlier in the distribution of Table 7-2; in his case a very substantial part of his campaign (38.1 percent) came from loans. LaRouche aside, those candidates raising money in small contributions matched a greater percentage of them with federal funds and, thus, show a greater percentage of receipts from federal funds. For example, Sonia Johnson raised 92.5 percent of her individual contributions in sums under $500; George McGovern raised 85.8 percent of his in those small amounts.

TABLE 7-2
Public Payments to 1984 Candidates

	Party	Federal Funds	% of Total Receipts
Askew, Reubin	D	$975,901	36.5%
Cranston, Alan	D	2,113,736	35.4
Glenn, John	D	3,325,383	27.1
Hart, Gary	D	5,328,467	35.5
Hollings, Ernest	D	821,600	33.3
Jackson, Jesse	D	3,053,185	37.1
Johnson, Sonia	C	193,735	45.8
LaRouche, Lyndon	D	494,146	11.4
McGovern, George	D	612,735	42.3
Mondale, Walter	D	9,494,921	35.4
Reagan, Ronald	R	10,100,000	37.2

Finally, there is a very strong correlation between raising money and winning the party's nomination for the presidency. In rough terms, in fact, it is a perfect correlation. In 1980 and 1984, three of the four major party nominations were contested;

[8]Not all of the amount submitted was certified for matching by the FEC, and what was certified was later reduced by the return of some funds to the treasury. The result is the final net payment of $34.9 million in matching money from the U.S. treasury.

Ronald Reagan won his in 1984 without opposition. In 1980 the Democrats were led in fund-raising by Jimmy Carter ($18.6 million in receipts) and Edward Kennedy ($12.3 million), the Republicans by Ronald Reagan ($21.4 million) and George Bush ($16.7 million). Among the Democrats in 1984 the leaders were Walter Mondale ($26.3 million) and Gary Hart ($14.5 million). In all three instances, that was the order of finish in the balloting of the nominating conventions. Although the perfect correlation of money and place in the race does not continue — John Glenn, with fewer delegates than Jesse Jackson, raised $12.1 million to his $7.9 million in 1984, for instance — the perfect relationships in first and second places are more than coincidence.

THE BROKERS: WHAT DO THEY WANT?

The participation of the very successful money raisers in the nation's presidential politics inevitably raises questions of their goals and motives. A recent newspaper article addresses that question squarely for a group of Democrats.

> "It's an expensive little hobby," Nathan Landow says of his fund raising. "I don't get anything out of it as far as anything to do with business. I never have." [James] Calaway agrees: "It doesn't help my business at all. Zero. It is a negative in that it's taking so much of my time and my energy."
>
> There are many other prices to be paid. Says J. Livingston Kosberg, the savings and loan executive, "There probably are business opportunities that you are excluded from. It's a lot easier to make a deal with a businessman at a Republican fund-raiser than it is with a migrant worker at a Democratic barbecue."
>
> The motives of the Democratic collectors [fund-raisers] are many and varied. "They want to be a part of the process," says Walter Mondale in his law office in Washington. "They're not narrow people. They worry about their country. I'd put that center. I think some of them enjoy the excitement and combat of politics, and they want to be a part of it in an influential way. A lot of them are in it because they want something. I just don't like to be around people like that."

When raising money for a Presidential [candidate], [Robert] Farmer says, "the issue is simply this: Is this guy going to win?" What do the collectors want if their candidate does win? "A lot of them," Farmer replies, "want to change their first name to 'Ambassador' or 'Secretary'. A lot of them want the candidate's attention. A lot of them would like to sleep in the Lincoln Bedroom, or be on the board of the Kennedy Center, or go to a state dinner at the White House, or ride on Air Force One. Some of them want to be appointed to Federal positions in their state. Some of them just like to know the candidates on a first-name basis."

—*Ronnie Dugger, "The Mating Game for '88," New York Times (Dec. 7, 1986).*

Even though the FECA has displaced the big contributor from presidential politics, the need for the big fund-raiser is as great as ever. Enormous sums of money must be raised nationally under the most arduous circumstances. Candidates seek money for a campaign that is not a general election campaign, but rather a campaign for the right to run for election — and at a time that is a year or more before that general election. Given the task at hand, people with contacts among the affluent and politically involved are almost literally worth their weight in gold. Candidates line up to coax them to their campaigns, for they are the new "kingmakers" in American politics (see box). Their methods are simple and even time worn. Duane Garrett of San Francisco, a prominent Democratic fund-raiser, claims to have some 3700 names of potential donors on file cards. His preferred method is the persuasive personal phone call, but others employ a wide range of social events and blandishments.

In the early days of the 1988 campaigns, the new sensation of the fund-raising fraternity was a group of 45 Democratic money men banded together as Impac '88. Headed by Nathan Landow, a Maryland real estate developer and Mondale supporter in 1984, they originally hoped to unite on a single Democratic candidate for 1988. That hope faded, and by early 1987 some 15 of the 45 had committed themselves to various contenders. At that time 17 of the uncommitted approached Sen. Albert Gore of Tennessee who had earlier removed himself as a possible seeker for the party nomination. They pledged to raise $250,000 apiece ($250,000 × 17 = $4,250,000) if Senator Gore would become a candidate. In spring of 1987, the senator reconsidered and said he would be a candidate.[9]

Finally, disbursement totals inevitably approximate receipt totals; but, it turns out, spending greatly outruns disbursement. The difference between the two is debt. Candidacies for presidential nominations have always involved a good deal of financial prestidigitation. The FEC, for instance, issues formal certificates of eligibility for matching funds in the year before the election, even though the payments do not begin until January of election year; candidates use those certificates as collateral for early loans. The magic fails for many of the hopefuls, however, and the creditors line up. Gary Hart emerged from the end of the 1983–84 cycle with a campaign debt of $3.6 million, John Glenn with one of $2.9 million; as of 1987 they and Alan Cranston, Jesse Jackson, Ernest Hollings, and Lyndon LaRouche also reported lingering debts from 1984's campaign.

The Hart debt is something of a classic case. It is in fact two debts, one from 1984 and one from 1988. Newspaper sources had estimated the 1984 debt at close to $4.7 million by the end of the primaries; apparently fund-raising later in the year (with matching from the treasury through calendar year 1984) reduced that total to the reported $3.6 million. Between then and mid-1987 more fund-raising and settlements with vendors (some reported to be for only 10 cents on the dollar) had reduced the debt to $1.3 million. At that point some receipts from a Hart fund-raising event in Los Angeles — receipts intended for the 1988 race — were seized under federal court order to pay off insistent creditors from 1984, and Hart asked the Federal Election Commission to permit him to use money contributed to his 1988 campaign to pay off the 1984 debts.

While the FEC auditors were reviewing the Hart reports from

[9]Again, for information on the fund-raisers, one has to go to the Washington journalists. See, inter alia, two articles in the *National Journal*: Ronald Brownstein, "The Money Hunt" (June 7, 1986), 1375–1379; and Maxwell Glen, "Kennedy's Early Departure from Race Frees Up Donations for Rest of Field," (Jan. 25, 1986), 208–212.

1984 prior to an FEC decision, Hart withdrew from the 1988 campaign, done in by a shipboard and Washington-weekend friendship with a young model. (The decision to withdraw was in part forced by the impact of the friendship on Hart's fund-raising for 1988.) The 1988 campaign ended with a small debt of $300,000, which when added to the 1984 obligations produced a total of $1.6 million. To liquidate both debts, Hart requested the matching money he had already qualified for ($900,000) before he dropped out of the race. In June of 1987, the FEC ruled 5–1 that the Hart campaign was not eligible for federal money because he was no longer an active candidate. It left unresolved the question of whether the 1988 money could have been used to retire the debts from 1984.

One last point on spending in the preconvention period is necessary. Those candidates accepting the public funding may spend no more than $10 million in 1974 dollars, not counting the exempt spending for fund-raising, legal, and accounting costs. The limit climbed to $20.2 million in 1984; and for the first time in the statute's history, candidates almost brushed the limit. Ronald Reagan spent $20.1 million in disbursements subject to the limit, even though he was unopposed for his party's nomination; Walter Mondale spent $19.9 million in his campaign. The next highest total in limited expenditures was Gary Hart's $12 million.

II. The Politics of Preconvention Finance

Campaign finance in the preconvention period is a very special case in American politics. It funds not a single campaign but a series of campaigns (in both the primary and the caucus states) strung out between January and June. The search for pledged delegates, state by state and week by week, interacts with the search for money. Candidates enter state contests in part to boost their credibility as candidates so that they can raise money to contest more state primaries or party processes. So, in a very real way, candidates win because they have raised money; and they raise money because they are already winning. In such an extended, interactive, multicontest race, an impressive correlation quickly builds between the sums of money raised and the

FIGURE 7-1
Sources of Receipts of Glenn, Jackson, Hart, and Mondale Campaigns in Different Periods of 1983–84

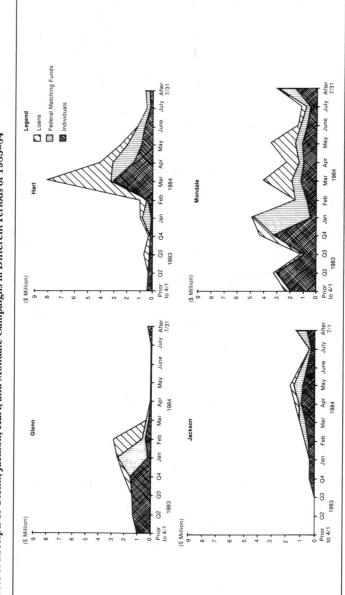

Source: FEC Report on Financial Activity 1983–1984; *Final Report, Presidential Pre-Nomination Campaigns* (Apr. 1986).

number of delegates pledged to one's nomination. But when the system of campaign finance and the various rules of selection interact in a series of "elections" — as they do for a few months in the preconvention period — it is not easy to separate the effect of one from the effect of the other.[10]

The interaction of votes and money is easy to see in the flows of money into the Mondale and Hart candidacies of 1984 (Figure 7-1). Walter Mondale, the front-runner throughout, raised very substantial sums before election year and was poised to receive major payments from the treasury at the beginning of 1984. After a slow start, Gary Hart's funding reached a peak in March of 1984 after his upset victories in New Hampshire (February 28) and Florida, Massachusetts, and Rhode Island (all on March 13). Hart was thus for a few brief and financially productive weeks a new media celebrity, both a new "face" and a David stalking a Goliath. His victories dramatically boosted his ratings in the polls, and suddenly he looked like a very possible nominee. But as they say on the sports pages, he lost the momentum quickly as Mondale pulled ahead in the delegate count, aided especially by successes in lining up the delegates not selected in presidential primaries (i.e., the ex officio "superdelegates" and the delegates chosen in the states employing caucuses and other party processes). The consequent decline in the Hart receipts began very quickly.

The "window of opportunity" for Gary Hart in 1984 was thus a fairly narrow one. For 1988 it will be even narrower for candidates who are not front-runners. The states have rushed to move their delegate selection processes earlier in the year so as not to be left out of the action of those weeks in which candidacies are made or broken. So, while only 20 percent of the major party convention delegates were chosen by mid-March in 1984, more than one-third of them will be in 1988. "Super Tuesday" in 1984 (March 13) featured primaries in five states; in 1988 it (March 8 — already being hyped as "Mega Tuesday") will have at least 14, including 9 in states of the Confederacy.

As the crucial decision-making period moves up in the year,

---

[10]For a good survey of finance in the preconvention period, see Michael J. Malbin, "You Get What You Pay for, but Is That What You Want?" in George Grassmuck, ed., *Before Nomination: Our Primary Problems* (Washington, D.C.: American Enterprise Institute, 1985), 72–86.

the crucial fund-raising period does, too. There is less and less time for the kind of candidate "bootstrapping" that Gary Hart did in 1984 as the period of interaction between votes and money narrows. Conversely, fund-raising in the year before election year becomes more important and so does the lining up of experienced fund-raisers in the major states and regions. Candidates also face increasingly difficult decisions about how to "spend" their money in this brief but crucial time. Above all they have to pick and choose the states whose delegate selection they will contest. They have always done so for political reasons; it has never made any sense for a nomination seeker to spend scarce resources in states likely to go to other candidates. Now candidates also have to select for reasons of campaign finance. In part they pick and choose because money is scarce, but in part they do so because the state-by-state spending limits add up to more than twice the aggregate limit candidates can spend in the preconvention period (if, of course, they are receiving matching funds).

Increasingly, though, the need to spend early has overtaken any strategic mapping of spending through the whole of the campaign — which in turn will encourage more states to move their delegate selections into the brief period of intense spending. In 1984, Gary Orren reports, the major candidates concentrated their spending in the early processes:

> Mondale spent between 90 and 100 percent of the legal maximum in early Iowa and Maine caucuses and the New Hampshire primary. Two weeks later he spent about 40 percent of the limit in Alabama and Massachusetts and 28 percent in Georgia. Thereafter Mondale never spent more than 26 percent of the limit in any state . . . In the crucial Illinois, New York, and Pennsylvania primaries his campaign spent about 12 percent of the individual state limits. Although to a less extent, Hart also spent nearly 67 percent of the limit in Iowa, 90 percent in New Hampshire, and 34 percent in Massachusetts. His outlay was less than 20 percent of the allowable level in more than half the states.[11]

Well-financed front-runners will almost inevitably pursue an

[11]Gary R. Orren, "The Nomination Process: Vicissitudes of Candidate Selection," in Michael Nelson, ed., *The Elections of 1984* (Washington: Congressional Quarterly, 1985), 45–46.

early knockout strategy, and the other candidates have no alternative but to respond as best they can. Certainly they cannot afford a strategy of evenly paced spending through the June primaries. Both Hart and Mondale had spent more than 80 percent of their total preconvention sums before the end of April. There is a substantial danger in that strategy, of course; if the front-runner doesn't score the knockout, his and a number of the other campaigns may founder because they can't raise money or because they aren't permitted to spend it. There is already concern that the concentration of delegate selection by Mega Tuesday in 1988 makes that scenario more credible.

Alas for the candidates, Congress's limits on spending in the states take none of this into account. The limit for the New Hampshire primary campaign in 1984 was $404,000 — the same as the limit for Guam and 7 percent of the limit ($6,019,276) for the very late and far less important primary in California. The limits, therefore, encourage candidates into the most elaborate strategies for cirmcumventing the spending limits on campaigns in the small states with strategically early selections. Both in 1980 and 1984, candidates in the New Hampshire primary took out TV advertising on Boston stations, housed staffs just beyond New Hampshire borders, and contracted for printing and other services in adjoining states — all to keep spending in New Hampshire within the statutory limit.

Under such circumstances pressures on the regulatory limits are intense. This is, in fact, one of those few points in the system at which the limits are in actuality confining. In 1984 Walter Mondale permitted would-be delegates pledged to him to form separate and independent delegate committees that would raise money (substantially from labor sources) to finance "their" campaigns as delegates in states such as New Hampshire. Gary Hart and much of the media challenged the independence of those delegate campaigns from the Mondale campaign, and eventually Mondale acknowledged their expenditures as part of his campaign and counted them against the state spending limits that bound him.[12] With the pressure to spend to the limit in the early

[12]After lengthy negotiations the Mondale campaign agreed, after the election, to return some $30,000 to the U.S. treasury, the part of the excess spending by the Mondale campaign and delegate committees assignable to federal matching funds.

FUNDING THE OUTSIDER: MORE THAN PEANUTS

Jimmy Carter, erstwhile peanut farmer and governor of Georgia, started the groundwork for his campaign funding much before the 1975–76 cycle. He worked hard on the 1974 campaigns for the DNC, and, as Herbert Alexander explains it,

> The position introduced the unannounced presidential candidate to party leaders as he stumped for congressional candidates in 32 states. The governor's aides meticulously copied names and addresses of the party faithful who would later receive pleas for funds. In December, Carter mailed contribution requests to about 30,000 Georgians and 500,000 other Americans whose names were taken from lists of Carter contacts, McGovern 1972 backers and contributors to the Democratic National Committee.
>
> In 1975, with his gubernatorial term completed and his younger brother minding the family peanut business, Carter could campaign full time. He traveled more than 250 days in the year, making appeals for funds and trying to improve a name recognition factor of 2 percent. In the first six months of the year, Carter raised $331,605. To supplement candidate appearances, "Project 20" was launched, a program concentrating mailings and personal solicitations in the southern and early-primary states so that Carter would qualify for matching funds. He attained eligibility for federal monies in August. From January through December of 1975, the campaign raised approximately $850,000.
>
> After November, the Carter organization began to utilize a few fund-raising techniques that offered public relations value. . . . In February 1976 Carter participated in a "Georgia Loves Jimmy" telethon carried by TV stations in his native state. The four-hour program combined speeches by the candidate and reports from campaign officials with appearances by singers Gregg Allman and James Brown, baseball stars Hank Aaron and Phil Niekro, and comedian and one-time presidential candidate Pat Paulsen. The telethon, which cost about $100,000, raised about $328,000 with matching funds.

—*Herbert E. Alexander,* Financing the 1976 Election
(Washington, D.C.: CQ Press, 1979), 234–235.

state processes all the greater in 1988, the statutory regulations will be even more severely tested while the candidates struggle to achieve take-off for their candidacies.

Just as important as these consequences for the campaigns are the consequences for candidates and the parties. On this point, partial public funding that matches small individual contributions and the accompanying spending limits open a route to nomination for political "outsiders," the candidates without connections to the party's networks of contributors and brokers/fund-raisers. The route is especially available if the candidate is otherwise unoccupied and can invest months and months of time in the pursuit of small contributors and funding eligibility. Jimmy Carter is the example-extraordinaire (see box). Carter spent a great part of 1975 "on the road" for the presidency, winning enough local support to generate a good showing in statewide polls such as those of Florida and Iowa. The low spending limits in the early state races, such as those in Iowa and New Hampshire, also help the outsiders and the dark horses because they protect them from massive spending by affluent front-runners. The need for intensive early campaigning further helps the outsider by disadvantaging the candidates with heavy responsibilities; senatorial leaders such as Howard Baker and Robert Dole have found it hard to build the necessary national following. Moreover, the spending limits offer some protection against campaigns funded by the candidate's own resources; even Nelson Rockefeller in 1976 felt compelled to accept public funding and thus its restriction of his own funds to a mere $50,000.

At the same time the new financing of presidential nominations would appear to work against late starters. It now seems much more difficult to make the promising late entry that Robert Kennedy did in 1968, a candidacy of growing strength until his assassination. The need for a strong early impact works against it. So does the limit of $1000 per individual contribution. Last-minute candidacies need money more quickly than can usually be raised in sums of three figures.

There is also some reason to think that the funding of the preconvention battles has increased the number and length of candidacies for the nominations. If that is so, strains on party cohesion and harmony will multiply. Stephen Wayne points out that the program of matching grants

> has enabled candidates to continue to seek the nomination even after disappointing showings in the early primaries. Moreover, it has required the fiction of an active candidacy right up to the convention in order to remain eligible for federal funds. This new staying power is well illustrated by the contrast between the Muskie campaign of 1972 and the Udall campaign of 1976. As the front-runner, Senator Edmund Muskie had raised over $2 million by January 31, 1972, before the primaries even began, and eventually spent over $7 million in his campaign. Nonetheless, he was forced to abandon his quest for the nomination in part because of lack of funds after only five primaries (two months). Representative Morris Udall, on the other hand, was not nationally known and had not demonstrated substantial fund-raising capacity. Yet, he was able to raise over $4.5 million, including almost $2 million from the Treasury, and to compete actively in more than one-third of the states without winning one primary or controlling one state delegation other than his own.[13]

The personal organizations and followings developed in those lengthy candidacies often persist long after the struggle is over as independent centers within the national party. More than 10 years after the 1976 campaign, Udall's PAC, Independent Action, was still raising money by direct mail. More threatening to party harmony is the likelihood that public funding will enhance challenges to incumbent presidents seeking reelection. Ronald Reagan's challenge to Gerald Ford in 1976 and Edward Kennedy's to Jimmy Carter in 1980 both relied heavily on the U.S. Treasury.

Last but not least among the immediate impacts is the administrative burden that results from so complicated a set of provisions for so fast moving a set of campaigns. The candidates are forced to set up elaborate and centralized control over their state campaigns, both to meet the reporting requirements and to stay within expenditure limits in the states and in the country as a whole. The accountants, lawyers, and managers set the rules; spontaneous "amateur" activity in the localities must be discour-

---

[13]Stephen J. Wayne, *The Road to the White House*, 2d ed. (New York: St. Martin's, 1984), 45.

aged. For a late-blooming campaign such as Jesse Jackson's in 1984, the problems are particularly nightmarish. Of course, the lot of the regulator is not happy either; the preconvention phase of the presidential campaign has always been the FEC's biggest headache.[14]

Beyond these fairly immediate consequences, the financing of preconvention politics has accelerated the centralizing and nationalizing of American politics. The need for comprehensive administration and control of the campaign for compliance with eligibility requirements and spending limits is just one more reason for centralization. Joined with others — the nationalization of issues, the increasing nationalization of fund-raising, the rebirth of the national party committees, for example — they are working a very fundamental change on the American political landscape.

Finally, by making available the means with which to contest the preconvention period state by state, the system of finance enlarges the importance of those months and thus pounds one more nail into the coffins of the national party conventions. Again the reasons for the rising importance of the selection of delegates are complex — jet airplane travel, television campaigning, greater media attention, the increased number of primaries, the decline of state parties and their independence — but the emergence of a viable way of funding the preconvention politics must be among them. The result is to settle party nominations in most instances before the doors of the convention halls open in midsummer of election year. Not once since 1952 in either major party's convention has it taken more than one roll call of the delegates to determine the presidential nominee.

III. Financing the Presidential Campaign

Full public funding awaits the nominees of the Democratic and Republican conventions — if they choose to take it. All six major party candidates took it in 1976, 1980, and 1984. Ronald Reagan's decision was the only one to occasion surprise, since he

[14]For examples of the regulatory problems and a detailed analysis of the preconvention system as it worked in 1984, see Herbert E. Alexander and Brian A. Haggerty, *Financing the 1984 Election* (Lexington, Mass.: Lexington, 1987).

had earlier opposed public funding. The 1974 statute makes a grant of $20 million to each major party campaign for the post-convention period, the sum being indexed to the Consumer Price Index. By 1984 the total was $40.4 million.

When candidates accept public funding, they also accept a set of very stringent limits on fund-raising and spending, limits that effectively restrict the campaign to the sum from the federal treasury.

- Candidates may raise privately only the funds necessary to cover their legal and accounting costs.
- Candidates may use only $50,000 of their own personal resources and those of their immediate family.
- Candidates may spend only the contemporary equivalent of $20 million ($40.4 million in 1984) plus the small amounts they raise for compliance costs and they contribute from their own resources.
- The candidate's national party committee is also limited in its spending on the candidate's behalf to a total of two cents for every American of voting age, that total adjusted for increases in the CPI ($6.9 million in 1984).

If a candidate in the future decided not to accept public funding, the usual limits on contributions (e.g., $1000 on individual contributions and $5000 on PACs) would apply. There would be no limit on the candidate's use of personal resources, nor would there be limits on either the candidate's spending or spending by the party. (In neither case — public funding or not — is there a limit on independent spending in support of or in opposition to a presidential candidate.)

While the candidates of the major parties qualify automatically for the postconvention subsidies, the candidates of other parties are less fortunate. They qualify by winning 5 percent of the popular vote in a presidential election after having been on the ballot in 10 or more states. If they do, they receive *after the election* a sum from the treasury that is prorated against the full payments to the major party candidates. Only John Anderson's independent candidacy in 1980 has so far qualified; Anderson received $4.2 million dollars in postelection payments on the strength of his 6.6 percent of the popular vote.[15] The public payment came too late, of course, to help the Anderson campaign; and its likelihood was not certain enough to serve as collateral for bank loans. Had Anderson run in 1984, though, he would have begun the campaign with that partial eligibility for federal funding already established.

This particular public funding plan is thus no friend of minor parties or independent candidacies. Indeed in creating it Congress tried very hard not to encourage an explosion of third-party candidacies. Legislatures in the United States have long operated on that fear in drafting election laws of all kinds, and in this particular instance the concern was heightened by the effect of third-party candidacies in the electoral college — that is, the possibility that by winning a few electoral votes a third candidate might prevent both of the major party candidates from winning a majority of votes and thus throw the election into a special meeting of the House of Representatives.

Whatever the persuasiveness of the reasons, many observers thought its treatment of minor parties was the most likely part of the FECA to fall in the Supreme Court. The Court, however, upheld the distinctions between the major parties and others in *Buckley v. Valeo.*

> Third parties have been completely incapable of matching the major parties' ability to raise money and win elections. Congress was, of course, aware of this fact of American life, and thus was justified in providing both major parties full funding and all other parties only a percentage of the major-party entitlement. Identical treatment of all parties, on the other hand, "would not only make it easy to raid the United States Treasury, it would also artificially foster the proliferation of splinter parties."[16]

The Constitution, noted the justices, did not require Congress to

---

[15]The formula for the prorating is as follows: The Anderson percentage (.066) divided by the average percentage of the major party candidates (.458) times the full allocation ($29.4 million) they each received. The total is $4,237,000.

[16]425 U.S. 1 (1976) at 98; the quote embedded in this quotation is from the opinion of the Court of Appeals in the same case: 519 F. 2d at 881.

fund "every nascent political group" just because it financed the major parties.[17]

That, then, is the "first campaign" for the presidency, as Herbert Alexander has called it. "Publicly financed and legally limited," it is "within the control of the major party nominees and their campaign organizations." It is, moreover, "supplemented by funds raised privately by each of the major national parties for spending on behalf of its presidential ticket."[18] The second (and simultaneous) campaign is much less well defined.[19] It consists of the presidential campaign activities of party and nonparty committees, some of them within the scope of federal legislation and some of them not. It is in fact something of a residual category of activities, and it helps perhaps to take it up after a consideration of the "third" campaign, the campaign of the independent expenditures.

TABLE 7-3
Independent Expenditures by Party of Candidate Aided, 1980 and 1984

	1980°	1984
Republican		
For Republican candidates	$12,581,957	$15,830,043
Against Democratic candidates	736,772	486,998
Total:	$13,318,729	$16,317,041
Democratic		
For Democratic candidates	123,058	806,417
Against Republican candidates	47,868	343,835
Total:	$170,926	$ 1,150,252

°In 1980 there were also independent expenditures against John Anderson ($2635) and on his behalf ($199,438).

In 1976 Congress belatedly tried to limit sharply (i.e., to $1000 per election) the amount of money that persons or groups

[17]424 U.S. at 98, quoting *American Party of Texas v. White*, 415 U.S. at 794.

[18]Herbert E. Alexander, *Financing Politics*, 3d ed. (Washington D.C.: C.Q Press, 1984), 125. Alexander and Haggerty use the same division of the presidential campaign into three "campaigns" in their *Financing the 1984 Election*.

[19]I have altered Alexander's categories a bit. He includes the private funds to cover legal and accounting costs in the "second" campaign. Because they are in the control of the presidential candidate, I have included them in the first.

might spend "independently" on a candidate accepting public funds and all of the restrictions that came with them. Even though the Supreme Court had struck down the FECA limitations on independent spending in congressional elections in *Buckley*, Congress tried to justify the limitations in presidential campaigns as an integral part of that public funding plan. Lower courts held the limitation unconstitutional, using the logic and precedent of *Buckley*'s invalidation of the other clause on independent spending, thus preventing the Federal Election Commission from enforcing it in the 1980 and 1984 elections. The Supreme Court finally settled the question in 1985 by striking down the clause.[20] At almost exactly the same time, the FEC was announcing that $17.5 million had been spent independently in the presidential election of 1984 (Table 7-3).

Two facts above all mark independent spending in the 1980 and 1984 races: the size of the Republican advantage and the dominant spending of a small number of PACs. (Data on 1976 are incomplete and even suspect; the FEC estimate of $1.6 million in the presidential campaign is probably high.[21]) Spending on campaigns is, of course, both "for" and "against" candidates; if one considers spending "against" a candidate's opponent to be "for" the candidate, one can easily calculate totals for the two parties (Table 7-3). In 1984, therefore, Republicans benefited from – $16.3 million of the $17.5 spent on the candidates of the two parties — a giant 93.4 percent. They enjoyed a margin of 98.7 percent in 1980. These are margins greater than the Republicans have enjoyed in independent spending on congressional races. Spending on the candidates of other parties was nominal: $202,000 in 1980 and $1049 in 1984.[22]

Four of the independent spenders accounted for $14,662,938

[20]*FEC v. NCPAC*, 470 U.S. 480 (1985).

[21]For a discussion of the 1976 data problems, see Joseph E. Cantor, *The Evolution of and Issues Surrounding Independent Expenditures in Election Campaigns*, Report No. 82-87 of the Congressional Research Service of the Library of Congress (May 5, 1982), 24–25.

[22]The aggregated data of the FEC, unfortunately, does not separate independent spending into the preconvention and postconvention periods. One would have to undertake a lengthy, report-by-report review in order to do so. There was almost no independent spending before the nomination in 1984, but there was $2.7 million spent in 1980 before the conventions. Expenditures for and against Edward Kennedy account for $.6 million and those for John Connally total $.3 million; most of the rest was for Ronald Reagan.

or 84 percent of all money spent independently on the 1984 presidential campaign by individuals, PACs, and other groups: the National Conservative PAC (NCPAC), the Fund for a Conservative Majority, Ruff PAC, and Jesse Helms' National Congressional Club. All of their spending went either for Reagan or against Mondale, except for an inexplicable $209 that NCPAC reported in support of Walter Mondale. NCPAC, at $10.13 million, alone accounted for 58 percent of the total. Five "pro Republican" PACs led the independent spending in 1980: Americans for an Effective Presidency, Americans for Change, the Congressional Club, the Fund for a Conservative Majority, and NCPAC. The Congressional Club led with $4,601,069 spent to support the election of Ronald Reagan; all spending of the five was either in support of Reagan or in opposition to Jimmy Carter or, in the preconvention phase, Edward Kennedy.[23]

A wealthy Texan, Cecil Haden, set the individual spending mark in 1980 with $182,726 in support of John Connally and then $413,221 in favor of Reagan. His total outlay was $595,947. Haden again led the list of individuals in 1984, but with a sharply reduced total of $40,386. In 1980 and 1984 the connected PACs — those of labor unions, corporations, and membership organizations — accounted for 3 percent and then 2 percent of the independent spending in all of presidential politics.

In 1980 the extensive spending by Americans for an Effective Presidency, Americans for Change, and the Fund for a Conservative Majority raised another issue. All three had no previous history or parent organization. Moreover, they spent independently only in support of Ronald Reagan in 1980, and two (Americans for an Effective Presidency and Americans for Change) made only nominal contributions to candidates. In short, they appeared to be largely ad hoc organizations to collect and spend what would in earlier years have been direct contributions to the presidential candidate or his national party committee. Moreover, Democrats accused them of such close ties to the Reagan camp and the Republican National Committee — especially in shared vendors for fund-raising and media advice — that

---

[23]Independent spending for the Democratic candidates has been of a much different order. In 1984 the largest total was that of Senior PAC: $221,137. Various state organizations supporting a nuclear freeze (i.e., the Freeze Voter organizations) spent more than $175,000, and The Woman's Trust spent $170,635.

their spending was not genuinely independent. Only the Fund for a Conservative Majority reappeared in 1984; the other three leading spenders in that year were more traditional conservative PACS: NCPAC, RuffPAC, and the National Congressional Club. The accusations of coziness with the Reagan-Bush campaign also reappeared.

These independent spending totals are hefty numbers, and they make striking headlines. The $17.5 million spent independently on the 1984 presidential campaign caught a good deal of attention. But that total and the totals of the big PACs that make it up are more than a little suspect. Michael Malbin's research makes it clear that some of the largest spenders actually "spend" primarily for fund-raising costs; 85 percent of NCPAC's independent spending in 1983–84 and 93 percent of RuffPAC's went for fund-raising costs. In fact political advertising of whatever form accounted for no more than 10 percent of the independent spending of those two PACs and the Fund for the Conservative Majority. Clearly their reported expenditure totals exaggerate their political activity, but in a curious way the greater truth perhaps is the fact that the press reports the inflated numbers, that they are taken without question, and that they become a truth in themselves.[24]

Finally, Alexander's "second" campaign is being waged and financed simultaneously with the "first" and "third." This part of the campaign includes spending "permitted but not limited under the law."[25] Two kinds dominate it:

● Spending by state and local party committees on volunteer, grass-roots activity on behalf of the party's presidential ticket. Such spending had not been permitted in the 1974 legislation, but amendments in 1979 authorized it as a way of restoring a campaign role to the local parties.

● Spending by private organizations (unions, corporations, membership organizations) of two kinds: communications

[24]Malbin's analysis of the PAC independent spending in support of Ronald Reagan in 1984 is reported in Ronald Brownstein, "On Paper, Conservative PACS Were Tigers in 1984 — But Look Again," *National Journal* (June 29, 1985), 1504–1509. The groups claim that FEC rules require them to list solicitation costs as independent expenditures because their letters of solicitation urge the election or defeat of specific candidates.

[25]Alexander, *Financing Politics*, 125.

urging their members or constituents to vote for a particular presidential candidate and nonpartisan campaigns to register voters and get out the vote.

The presidential candidates and their national committees are free to channel money to such activities and to coordinate them with their own campaigns. Not surprisingly, they work a great deal more closely with state and local party committees than they do with nonparty organizations.[26]

Putting dollar figures on the second campaign entails serious problems of data and definition. As for the data problems, Alexander and Haggerty estimate the following totals for 1984.[27]

	Reagan	Mondale
State and local party comms.	$15.6 million	$6.0 million
Labor/corporations/assns.	3.5 million	20.1 million

The totals of the state and local party committees are reported to the Federal Election Commission. Of the expenditures by nonparty organizations, however, only the internal communications in excess of $2000 need be reported to the FEC. The value of communications below that threshold and the value of registration and get-out-the-vote drives are Alexander's own well-informed estimates. Of the estimated $20.1 million spent for the Mondale campaign, all but $100,000 was accounted for by organized labor's extensive political activities within its membership.[28]

---

[26]The money channeled by national party committees, always mindful of their own tight spending limits, to state and local party committees not under any such limit is one kind of money in the stream of campaign finance that it has become fashionable to call "soft money." The entire question of soft money diversions will be explored more fully in chap. 10.

[27]Alexander and Haggerty, *Financing the 1984 Election*, 331. To repeat, Alexander has always included the candidate's compliance expenditures in this "campaign"; I have moved them to the first.

[28]The only part of that labor spending on the Mondale campaign in 1984 that was reported (and was required to be reported) to the FEC was $4.4 million in communication costs; labor accounted for about 98 percent of the communications in support of the Mondale-Ferraro ticket. There was only $214,417 reported in communication costs pro and contra the Reagan-Bush ticket, 72 percent of it by labor unions.

The concept of the second campaign touches again the problem of the boundaries of the campaign finance system. It is, in short, the question of "what we count" in toting up the bill for a campaign — the presidential campaign in this instance. State and local party committee expenditures must be reported under federal law since they are considered as campaign expenditures. Registration and vote turnout campaigns are not, as long as they are nonpartisan. Labor has long been confident that nominally nonpartisan programs would overwhelmingly turn out Democratic voters, but union members' desertion of Democratic presidential candidates in the 1970s and 1980s has begun to undermine that assumption.

As soon as one seeks definitions beyond the statutorily defined system of campaign finance, there seems to be no logical place to stop. Why not include, for instance, some estimate of the value of incumbency in a congressional or presidential election? Why not include the value of volunteer citizen labor in a campaign? Is there any logic in including some party activist's money but not time and skills? Do we not include such campaign resources simply because we find it hard to put a price tag on them? Or are we more interested in tracking money than in accounting for all of the resources the campaigns employ? And if we are, why?

All of this is more than scholarly semantics, for there is a politics behind the definitional issue. Republicans, in defending their party's superiority in presidential campaign spending, have long contended that the accounting stopped short of the pro-Democratic expenditures by labor outside of the system of campaign finance defined in the statutes. Obviously, including those expenditures in the accounting produces a more nearly equal set of totals for the two parties. "Advantage" or "imbalance" in American campaign finance is in part the result of what one counts; and when there is uncertainty over what to count, there is argument over who is advantaged and by how much. Ultimately, the entire argument suggests how important a symbol in American politics "equality" of resource and opportunity is. It has animated much of the legislation on campaign finance, and it still weighs heavily as a reform issue.

IV. The Consequences of Public Finance in the Campaign

After Congress acted in 1974, presidential campaign finance was never to be the same again. The spending limits in effect as a result of public funding have slowed the rise of campaign outlays. Since the limits are indexed, they have risen only as fast as the Consumer Price Index; spending in congressional campaigns between 1974 and 1984 increased much more steeply. Furthermore, public funding has largely eliminated the rigors of fund-raising in the general election campaign. Gone are the hasty trips and sleepy-eyed appeals to potential contributors that used to interrupt the campaign. And with a good idea from the beginning of the resources available to them, candidates and their managers can work out a more long-sighted plan for the campaign. These consequences ought, logically, to produce a "better" campaign — at least a more rational and focused one.

Perhaps so, but perhaps not. Critics of the new era in presidential campaign finance repeatedly charge that one of its major consequences has been a reduction of the scope and effect of the campaign. The charge really comes down to the allegation that the candidates do not have enough money to conduct an intensive and extensive campaign throughout the 50 states. It is a charge not easy to evaluate. Certainly larger and larger portions of the campaign are geared to television, both in political advertising and in the candidates' maneuvering for "free" TV news and documentary coverage. Political buffs and junkies testify that campaigns no longer spend very much on the campaign buttons, stickers, and posters that will become political memorabilia. But the question of how much presidential campaigning is enough appears to be just another of those important but unanswerable questions that haunt contemporary campaigns for public office.

It seems much clearer that the new campaign finance has in fact stimulated the growth of independent spending on presidential campaigns. The data are eloquent: from an estimated $1.6 million in 1976 to $17.5 million just two elections later in 1984. It also seems clear that at least some of that increase resulted from the cap on private fund-raising that accompanies the federal funding. The development of nonconnected, ideological PACs spending all or virtually all of their money on the presidential race is persuasive evidence. So once again, money closed off at one outlet seeks an open one, and in *Buckley* the Supreme Court provided a very large one.

In assessing the impacts or consequences of the public funding of presidential campaigns, one cannot avoid the matter of winners and losers. The Democrats unquestionably were the winners. Not only did they lag far behind Richard Nixon and the Republican party in funding the campaigns of 1968 and 1972, but they borrowed so heavily just to stay within hailing distance of the Republicans that they seemed destined to labor under a permanent debt. To be sure, the heavy favoring of Republican candidates in the independent spending and the Republican advantages in national and state/local party committee outlays add up to a Republican advantage in all-over presidential spending, even if one factors in the labor spending in voter mobilization. But the Republican advantage would undoubtedly be greater without public funding and its attendant limits on spending, and in their heart of hearts Democrats really hope only to stay "fairly" or "reasonably" close to the more affluent Republicans. Full parity is for the land of wishes and dreams.

Finally, there is the tricky question of the impact on minor (third) parties and independent candidates such as John Anderson.[29] On the surface of it, the public funding plan seems to discriminate against minor parties. The statute explicitly sets up three different categories of political party:

● the major political party, a party which received 25 percent or more of the vote at the last presidential election and which is therefore entitled to a full subsidy.

● the minor political party, which received between 5 and 25 percent of the vote the last time and which is entitled to a partial subsidy. (John Anderson's campaign in 1980 is the best and only example.)

[29]In 1980 the FEC faced the question whether to consider John Anderson's "independent candidacy" a minor party for the purposes of public funding. Despite Anderson's reluctance to think of his candidacy as a third party, the Commission did declare it eligible for funding. The result was to give Anderson the best of both worlds in the semantics of parties and independents.

• the "new" party, one that did not meet the 5 percent standard and will receive a subsidy *after* the election if it exceeds the standard in the present election.

So, parties are indeed treated differently, and a new party or candidacy such as John Anderson's suffers through a campaign without any subsidy until after the votes have been cast. Anderson's plight would have been more serious had he not had funding as a Republican preconvention candidate and the organization, visibility, and contributor lists he developed as a candidate for the Republican nomination. In addition, only a major party is entitled to a subsidy for the costs of a party convention.[30]

But is it that simple? To be sure, parties other than the two major parties do not share fully in the public funding, but there is more to presidential campaign finance than that. The limits on major party candidates' spending that accompanies their public funds improves the relative position of the minor party candidate. That candidate is also free to raise money from private sources, to use personal resources, and to spend in the campaign without limits. The vice presidential candidate for the Libertarian party in 1980, David Koch, contributed $2.1 million of the $3.5 million the party's ticket spent in the campaign. More to the point perhaps, George Wallace of Alabama raised $7 million in 1968 and carried over a surplus of more than a million at the end of the campaign.

In brief, the effect on the minor parties depends on how one frames the question. Does the new system bring parity to the minor parties? No, but it is less clear that it adds to the existing disparity between them and the major parties. And what minor parties or candidates does one have in mind? Clearly public funding offers little to the congenital "small" minor party — such as the Socialist Workers or the Prohibitionists. But for a larger, more credible party able to meet the 5 percent threshold, the effect is not clearly harmful. One can easily project a scenario in which a candidate such as George Wallace in 1968 raises $7 million and

---

[30]The subsidies to the parties for their national conventions were originally set at $2 million in 1974 dollars; the sum was later raised to $4 million. The payments to the Democratic and Republican parties in 1984 were $8.1 million apiece. The citation on these parts of the code is 26 U.S. Code sec. 9002.

gets about 15.5 percent of the popular vote. That candidate would certainly be strengthened for the future by the program now in place. The statutes do, however, erect a formidable barrier to the established minor party (the one with between 5 and 25 percent of the vote) becoming a major party — but then no American minor party has even approached that barrier for a long time.

Finally, raising money is not necessarily the minor party candidate's worst problem; election law, for example, can be a more serious one. In fact, John Anderson in 1980 spent almost as much money seeking a place on the ballots of the states ($2 million) as he did on media advertising in the entire campaign ($2.3 million).

V. The Source: the Income Tax Checkoff

The U.S. Treasury paid out almost $132 million for the pre-convention campaigns, the conventions, and the general election candidates in the 1984 election cycle. The source is a special fund created by Congress and supplied with dollars by payers of U.S. income taxes who choose to divert a dollar (two dollars for joint returns) of their income tax liability to the special fund. Taxpayers accomplish the contribution by checking a box on their income tax returns — hence the term "checkoff" for the funding mechanism. If that seems on first blush to be a roundabout way of providing the funds from the treasury, it was intended to be. Opponents of public funding argued that Americans ought not to be taxed to pay for the political campaigns of parties and candidates they opposed. The device of a fund created by voluntary decisions of individual taxpayers was the answer to the objection.

The use of the checkoff involves a gamble that enough Americans will divert their dollars to keep the fund solvent. So far the gamble has worked — so far. The funds have more than covered the public funding obligations, and under present conditions they seem likely to continue to do so (Table 7-4). There are, however, imaginable conditions under which the fund would be threatened. One is double-digit inflation in which the indexed payments to candidates would rise when the sums contributed through the checkoff (one and two dollars) would not. A second is the rise of the number of eligible candidates in the preconvention phase of the campaign, a circumstance most likely when, as in 1988, there is no incumbent president running. Finally, the newly revised income tax code introduces another element of uncertainty into the fund, since it will for 1987's taxes reduce the number of people having to file returns and pay income taxes.

TABLE 7-4
Financial Status of the Tax Checkoff and Presidential Election Campaign Fund, 1974–1984 (dollars in millions)

| | Tax checkoff | | Presidential election campaign fund | |
	Money Designated	% of Returns	Disbursements	Year-end Balance
1974	$27.6	—	0	$27.6
1975	31.7	—	$ 2.6	59.6
1976	33.7	—	69.5	23.8
1977	36.6	27.5%	.5	60.9
1978	39.2	28.6%	0	100.3
1979	35.9	25.4%	1.1	135.2
1980	38.8	27.4%	101.4	73.8
1981	41.1	28.7%	.6	114.4
1982	39.0	27.0%	0	153.5
1983	35.6	24.2%	11.8	177.3
1984	35.0	23.7%	120.1	92.7

Note: The checkoff data on money designated are for tax returns filed in that year, but the percentages reflect returns processed in the fiscal (as opposed to the calendar) year. Inconsistencies in year-end balances reflect in part the repayments that result from postelection audits.

Source: Joseph E. Cantor, *The Presidential Election Campaign Fund and Tax Checkoff*, Report No. 85-180 of the Congressional Research Service of the Library of Congress (Sept. 17, 1985), 28.

More generally unsettling is the unwillingness of Americans to support the fund. The fact is that never in its short history have as many as 30 percent of income taxpayers "checked off" (Table 7-4). Since the checkoff boxes were moved to the front page of the tax return form for 1974, the percentage has fluctuated between 24 and 29 percent. (Only between 40 and 45 percent of the taxpayers check the "no" box; the rest check neither.)[31] In part these figures must reflect the belief among some taxpayers — words on the tax return to the contrary — that they increase their tax liability by participating. But it must also reflect millions of little acts of rebellion against either public funding or, more likely, against the perceived excesses and extravagances of contemporary campaigns and campaign finance.

VI. In Conclusion: The Politics of Public Funding

The great American experiment in public financing is now more than three presidential campaigns old. It is hard to say specifically what kind of system of campaign finance the reformers thought they were fashioning. Different proponents had different goals and expectations, and alternative futures were not clear to anyone. Perhaps it is enough to say that they shared in various degrees a reaction against many aspects of presidential campaign finance as it had been practiced in the 1960s and in 1972. Moreover, it is hard to assess or summarize the results of the "great experiment" because it was in fact two experiments, two very different systems of campaign finance contrived for the parts of the campaign before and after the nominating conventions.

Whatever may have been the hopes of the reformers, the main results or accomplishments of the "new order" in financing presidential campaigns are less ambiguous. It has slowed the growth of spending by candidates after the nominating conventions to the pace of inflation. It has sharply reduced the role in presidential politics of the big contributors (the "fat cats") and the business and corporate interests that had dominated much of the fundraising in both parties in earlier elections. It has established a central role for the small individual contributor in the matched public funding system of the delegate selection processes. It has brought relative parity in the funding of the campaigns of the two major parties and their candidates. And it has virtually eliminated the illegal contributions that had become almost common-

---

[31]The data of this paragraph and the data and format of Table 7-4 come from Joseph E. Cantor, *The Presidential Election Campaign Fund and Tax Checkoff*, Report No. 85-180 of the Congresssional Research Service of the Library of Congress (Sept. 17, 1985).

place before 1974. Its accomplishments have retained the support and loyalty of its original champions, most especially of Common Cause and political liberals generally. There still remains a considerable body of opposition and skepticism, however. It generally reflects a mixture of three concerns: (1) concern that public funding penalizes the Republicans in the area of their resource advantage without affecting the advantages of the Democrats, (2) concern over the general wisdom of using tax resources to subsidize and then regulate political activity, and (3) concern that the limited expenditures that result will not communicate the message of the campaign fully enough. Given these positions, it is not surprising that opposition and skepticism are and have been greater within the Republican party. But there are other broader indications of skepticism — the lack of support for extending public funding to congressional elections and the slipping rate of "checking off" to provide money for the public funding.

Still, public funding persists. More remarkable than its mere survival has been the virtually unanimous voluntary participation of all major party candidates in three campaigns — John Connally being the only exception. The states with public funding report a much higher frequency of candidates who decide to go their own ways in raising money.[32] Is there then some support or perceived support out there? Do candidates fear the wrath of a mass media that has been largely supportive of public funding? Or do they merely opt for public funds because they find it to their own interests in managing their campaigns — to avoid the hated tasks of fund-raising and to have a predictable flow of money on the basis of which to plan?

If there is some residue of support for public funding, it bears asking again why the experiment in reform has not led to public funding of congressional campaigns. The immediate and shocking stimulus of a Watergate is missing. Whatever one may think about congressional campaign finance since 1974, it has been largely free of scandal and corruption. There are still the partisan and philosophical objections to public funding; and at a time of

---

[32]This difference, though, may simply reflect the fact that the public funding programs in the states offer a much smaller percentage of the permissible expenditures in public money. State programs of public funding are discussed in chap. 9.

record deficits and suppressed spending on domestic programs, it has acquired a new objection. Beyond all of that, there is the growing feeling that public funding in presidential campaigns is a special case. The position of the challenger is greatly different from that of challengers in congressional elections; name recognition and media attention come far more readily and make it easier for the potential presidential nominee to raise the funds for matching. It seems less likely, for instance, that a challenger in a noncompetitive congressional district could raise enough money to meet even modest matching requirements. Public funding in presidential campaigns is a special case in one last and very important way: the expenditure limits that go with it run little risk, contra the case in Congress, of entrenching incumbents in office. Presidential incumbents have become notoriously insecure since the 1950s, and when they aren't, the Twenty-Second Amendment to the Constitution limits them to two terms.

In short, Americans are ambivalent about their experiment in the public funding of campaigns for public office. They don't really warm to the idea, but they don't like the alternatives either. And they do like the expenditure limits that accompany public monies. No one, perhaps, symbolizes that ambivalence better than Ronald Reagan. Long an outspoken opponent of public funding, he and Nancy Reagan are reliably reported never to have checked the "yes" boxes to send a few dollars into the fund for paying candidates. Moreover, his first recommended revision of the income tax code sent to Congress in 1985 would have abolished the checkoff altogether. Yet in 1976, 1980, and 1984, Ronald Reagan accepted a total of about $90 million in public money for his three campaigns for the presidency, far more than any other single candidate has received in the short history of public funding.

Public funding persists in a particularly unfriendly political climate. Ambivalent feelings about massive public subsidies of election campaigns are not surprising in a time of deregulation, tax reduction, and reduced role for government. Perhaps it is testimony to the strength of the idea of public funding — and to the glaring absence of alternatives — that it should have survived without impairment in so unfriendly a time.

8

The Other Players: The Media, the Supreme Court, and the FEC

Contributors, spenders, candidates, and fund-raisers conduct the principal business of campaign finance. Apart from them, the flow of cash, and the whirlwinds of the campaign, however, are the institutions that react to the events and transactions of campaign finance. Through those reactions they shape future options for the active participants. Chief among them are the legislatures that construct a pervasive web of regulation for the nation and the states; their work is woven through all of the chapters of this book. Here we examine three others: the mass media, the United States Supreme Court, and the Federal Election Commission.

To shift the image somewhat, the major actors and activity in American campaign finance are framed and bounded by an extensive and enveloping "environment." That environment defines both the outer extent of the campaign finance system and the choices for the principal actors in the system. Its chief element is the regulatory legislation — national, state, and local — that pervades any analysis of what goes on in American campaign finance. But the environment is more complex and richly textured than that. There are the constraints of the Constitution, for

222

which the Supreme Court speaks; there are the constraints that the FEC introduces in its applications and interpretations of statutory regulation; and there are the political constraints of mass opinion and those in the media who inform and shape it.

I. The Mass Media and Public Opinion

Gaffes and blunders have plagued the media's reporting of the facts and events of campaign finance. It staggers the imagination to think that millions of Americans heard Tom Brokaw on the NBC nightly news explain the Supreme Court's decision that Congress could not limit independent expenditures (by PACs and others) in publicly funded presidential campaigns.

> In this country, PACs are political action committees, and they were organized to end the practice of individuals giving huge amounts of money, sometimes millions of dollars, to presidential campaigns. Under current law, PACs are limited to contributions to individual campaigns of $1,000, but today the Supreme Court ruled that is a violation of free speech. Now the PACs can give as much money as they want to campaigns.[1]

While there are some accurate phrases in the report, there are substantial errors in each of the three sentences. How frequent are such blunders in American journalism? It is simply impossible to know. Certainly they are the exception, no matter how frequent; in this instance the other two national TV networks did accurately report the story that Brokaw botched. But the gaffes are plentiful, and many people involved with campaign finance have their own collections of bloopers.[2]

[1] Quoted by Larry Sabato in his article, "PAC ruling misunderstood," *Baltimore Sun*, Mar. 24, 1985. The Brokaw broadcast in question was that of Mar. 18, 1985.

[2] My own collection includes one favorite that involves the same story Brokaw was reporting. It appeared in *The Washington Times*, Washington's "other" newspaper on Mar. 19, 1985, and was written by Tom Diaz. Its headline read "Court voids limit on PAC donations," and it began

The Supreme Court opened the way yesterday for political action committees to pour as much money as they like into presidential campaign war chests.

In a major victory for the country's two biggest conservative PACs, the high court struck down a federal law that put a $1,000 ceiling on contribu-

In newspaper reporting the Achilles' heel is the headline. Reporters and editorialists for the elite newspapers and wire services generally understand their subject, but headlines for their pieces are written by editors far less versed in the intricacies of campaign finance. Hence the errors that confuse PAC contributions with their independent spending, the gross receipts of PACs with their political spending, congressional with presidential finance, voluntary finance with public funding.

Errors of fact are understandable. Campaign finance is a notoriously obscure and complex subject, even for the initiated; and very few news organizations can afford the luxury of an in-house expert on so specialized a subject. The more serious issue is the *direction* of the error. Almost invariably it is — as it is in the Brokaw script — in the direction of exaggerating the sums of money going into campaigns, of overstating the unfettered power of PACs, of denying the efficacy of statutory limits on American campaign finance. The effect is to report a picture that "fits" and reinforces the worst suspicions that countless Americans have about money in politics.

Even when reporting is factually accurate, it tends to reinforce those suspicions. The repeated accounting of PAC spending for the first year of the election cycle, the first 18 months, and then the end of the cycle undoubtedly creates a picture of PAC dominance of campaign finance. So, too, do stories of direct-mail fund-raising by ideological PACs that do not make clear that substantial proportions of their receipts and expenditures will cover operating and fund-raising costs. By the same token, the stories on individual contributions above $500 or at $1000 give the impression that the wealthy "fat cats" continue their reign. The genuine dominance of candidate finance by millions of smaller individual contributions, conversely, remains an unreported story.

Occasionally, careless journalism will bracket what it thinks

tions by "independent PACs" to presidential candidates who take federal campaign funds.

Not only are contributions and independent spending hopelessly confused in both headline and text, but the writer has also misunderstood the program of federal funding of presidential campaigns. Facts may be almost completely wrong in stories such as these, but the message about the dangers of unbridled PACs comes through clearly, no matter how mistakenly.

are the excesses of campaign finance with "other" scandals and illegalities in American life. In reporting the indictment of Ivan Boesky for illegal activities in the financing of corporate take-overs, *Newsweek* let it all out:

> It [the Boesky case] follows what seems a chronic scandal in the defense industry, where virtually all of the top contractors have been caught cheating the government. Washington is awash in PAC money, and presidential crony Michael Deaver is only the most conspicuous of the capital's influence peddlers.[3]

The fact that PAC contributions are unassailably legal expressions of First Amendment freedoms does not save them from inclusion with cases of illegality and alleged illegality. In sum, there is a pattern and a direction to reporting on American campaign finance — a "bias," that is — and it is simply too obvious to escape notice.

"Bias" is a word that carries too many meanings, and it is perhaps best to begin by eliminating some of them. There is no reason to think there is an intentional political bias at work here. The men and women of the media do not go about willfully distorting reality, nor do they try to weigh in on one or the other side of the battles between Democrats and Republicans, liberals and conservatives, business and labor. The explanation lies rather with what scholars have come to call "structural biases": the biases rooted in the very nature of journalism, in the professional norms of its practitioners, in their political worldviews, in the need to sell papers and attract audiences, and in the constraints of communicating about a complicated subject to an unsophisticated and often uninformed audience.

In the most immediate sense, structural biases affect the campaign finance story in journalistic ways. To be interesting the news must have identifiable actors (people), understandable and dramatic activity, and elements of conflict or disagreement, even threat or menace. The stories, especially on television, must be short; and they must avoid any complexity, whether of structure, language, or argument. Any statistics beyond a few dollar totals and a percentage or two are usually out of the question. The

[3]Newsweek (Dec. 1, 1986), 49.

ultimate criterion is appeal to the reader, viewer, or listener — a report that the consumer of the news will attend to and perhaps even understand.

Campaign finance, with all of its arcane complexities and endless numbers, does not easily lend itself to the imperatives of mass media journalism. Perhaps the "NCPAC story" has come closest in the last decade. It has involved large sums of money (well across the important threshold of "millions"); a gutsy, no-holds-barred "negative campaigning"; the conflict between NCPAC and its outraged "targets"; and the outrageous and unrepentant persona of its late executive director, Terry Dolan. But for the most part, the campaign finance story defeats the journalistic imperatives. It is one of confusing trends, figures, legislation, and court decisions, all of them hobbled by the need for important definitions and distinctions. The one persistent connection to the mass public is dollars — money. In an era in which personal finance has become a national obsession, when tax reform laws are discussed largely in terms of how they will affect "your" tax bill, and OPEC decisions are evaluated by how much more "you" will have to pay at the pump, campaign finance, too, is a money story in which larger and larger dollar totals *are* the story.

The other part of the "systematic bias" of American journalism is the view of politics and the political system that its journalists share. As scholars such as Austin Ranney and Herbert Gans have pointed out, American journalists widely reflect a view of politics, and more generally of power and influence in American society, that is "a revised and updated version of the 'progressive' outlook that dominated American politics from the 1890s to the 1920s."[4] As Ranney explains,

> Progressive journalists and political activists believed that the decent core of America consists of the ordinary good citizens who genuinely seek what is good for the general welfare. The great enemies of society are the big political machines, the business "trusts," and the other special interests that try to advance their selfish goals at the public's expense by buying elections and corrupting public officials.

[4]Austin Ranney, *Channels of Power* (New York: Basic Books, 1983), 52; see also Herbert J. Gans, *Deciding What's News* (New York: Vintage, 1980).

The way to save America, the progressives proclaimed, is to reform our political system: First, let the muckraking press dig up and publish all the sordid facts about the greed and lawlessness of the special interests so that honest citizens will know the full extent of the evil they do. . . . Finally, when the system is thus reformed and purified, it will no longer be the tool of the special interests but will become what it was meant to be: the people's instrument for promoting the general welfare.[5]

In short, the men and women of the media have a distinctive political worldview, and it shapes and colors the way they report political reality. It also defines the political role of the media in reporting that reality; contemporary investigative reporting is certainly the lineal descendent of Progressive muckraking.

In the realm of campaign finance, the Progressive worldview often transcends even the gulf between political liberalism and conservatism in the media. So staunchly tory a newspaper as the *Wall Street Journal* reflects fully the dominant worldview of the media elites in its news columns. And even crustily conservative small town and city newspapers reflect the same views in outraged editorials about the status quo in campaign finance.[6]

What survey data we have on the political outlooks of American journalists support these general observations. A 1979–80 survey of "media elites" (240 journalists and broadcasters at "the most influential media outlets") offers evidence of persistent Progressive values. In assessing the relative influence of seven groups in contemporary American society, the respondents identified two clusters of groups: three "very influential" (business, the media, and unions, in that order) and four "relatively disadvantaged" (consumer groups, intellectuals, blacks, and feminists). When the respondents were then asked what distribution of influence they would prefer, the ranking was different. The media elites

would strip both business and labor of their current perceived power, while raising the status of all the other groups. In the media's preferred social hierarchy, business leaders fall from first

[5]Ranney, 53.
[6]For a sampling of the views of editorialists around the country, see the collection reprinted in the *Congressional Record* for Feb. 4, 1986, pp. S990 and following.

to fifth position, and unions drop to the very bottom of the ladder. Feminists would move up only slightly, but blacks, intellectuals, and consumer groups would all have more influence than either business or labor.[7]

One can also infer patterns of preferences from the decisions American journalists make on what to report and how to report it.

The American way of campaign finance is, of course, beautifully suited to excite, confirm, and reinforce the Progressive worldview. The cash that flows through it is a temptingly easy measure of influence; and the PACs are perfect manifestations of the special, narrow, or vested interests. (It is in fact common for the media to identify PACs as special interest groups.) The corrupting power of money is easily confirmed; why would banking interests give money to members of the Senate Banking Committee if not to secure their votes on matters of importance to them? And the ability of money to influence elections is just as easily established; is it not true that winners spend a good deal more than losers?[8]

And so the two systematic biases — those intrinsic to the successful operation of the media and those springing from the political outlooks of their practitioners — work their predictable ways. Even without a painstaking content analysis of the last decade's reporting, the results are easily apparent. The vocabulary of reporting campaign finance itself offers plenty of cues — "special" or "narrow" interests "pour" or "funnel" their obviously liquid cash into the "war chests" or the "campaign chests" (and occasionally the less aggressive "coffers") of willing candidates. The sheer quantity of reporting on PACs and individual contributors (and the use of candidates' own personal fortunes) is in the same vein. The same is true of the emphases on the growth of the sums of money involved — larger receipts and greater expenditures — all with little or no discounting for the effects of inflation.

---

[7]S. Robert Lichter and Stanley Rothman, "Media and Business Elites," *Public Opinion*, vol. 4 (1981), 59–60.

[8]Again, these matters of the influence of money and its spenders on legislative decision-making and on the outcome of elections will be discussed fully in chap. 10.

PACs provide especially ample targets for the more determined forms of investigative reporting, and indeed something like "PAC bashing" often results. Inevitably, perhaps, the country's most famous investigative reporters, those on CBS's "60 Minutes" program, took on the PACs in September of 1984. The results were not to everyone's taste. Richard Armstrong, the president of the Public Affairs Council, was particularly outraged.[9] Armstrong had been interviewed for the story by Morley Safer. The long interview was mined for the few moderately critical comments it contained, and minutes and minutes of Armstrong's favorable views were left on the proverbial cutting room floor. There was no resolution to the controversy, but Armstrong has set the relevant materials on the record for public scrutiny.[10]

One gets a hint of the effects of systematic bias also in the sources the media turn to for data, cues on newsworthiness, and "twist" or "spin" on the story. By far the most popular is Common Cause, the very organization present at the creation of the FECA and still a powerful advocate for reform, especially the extension of public funding. Common Cause, of course, reflects and organizes the same political values and outlooks as American journalism reflects. In the words of its biographer, it can be

> placed within the reform tradition of the Progressives. . . . [It is] a recent manifestation of the mobilization of elements of the American middle class who attempt to enhance democracy and effective government through the adoption of procedural reforms supported for reasons other than clear-cut economic gain.[11]

[9]The Council is a national association of corporate officials in charge of public and/or governmental affairs programs. Since those officials most usually are responsible for the corporation's PAC, the Council has taken a prominent leadership role in the corporate PAC movement. Armstrong has also been one of the most tireless and aggressive defenders of PACs and their political role. He had in fact earlier dueled with CBS over its reporting of PACs on its regular evening network news. The Council's *Corporate PAC Newsletter* often carries examples of what it believes to be failures in treating campaign finance in all of the media.

[10]Richard A. Armstrong, "Give PAC Proponents a Hearing," *Campaigns and Elections*, vol. 5 (1984), 44–48.

[11]Andrew S. McFarland, *Common Cause: Lobbying in the Public Interest* (Chatham, N.J.: Chatham House, 1984), 23. McFarland also observes, p. 82, that "the major national newspapers and television networks have a concept of the government reform agenda that is similar to the Common Cause definition. Items

The point is not that Common Cause's facts and data are wrong — they are not — but that its definition of which facts are remarkable and thus newsworthy reflect a particular view of political influence in the United States.

Conversely, a catalog of stories not reported also points to the same biases. The mass base of American campaign finance — the sheer numbers of people contributing to PACs, parties, and directly to candidates — goes unreported. So, too, do declines in receipts or spending, not to mention slowdowns in the rates of growth, such as those in the totals raised and spent by House candidates in 1984. The contribution patterns and strategies of less visible PACs and the fund-raising of less visible members of Congress remain largely unknown. The responses of journalists to such observations are either that those stories are not "news" or that they aren't "what the public wants to read" (or watch or hear). And that is precisely the point of structural bias.

For all of this, the reporting of the end of PAC growth provides a splendid illustration. Twice each year all the way back to the end of December 1974, the Federal Election Commission has released counts of the numbers of PACs registered with it. In the years of increases in the numbers of PACs, 1974 through mid-1984, America's newspapers and news services leaped on the rising totals and reported them widely. The number of PACs had grown from 608 in 1974 to 4009 just 10 years later; and given the reporting of that growth, it verged on common knowledge. The growth curve had, to be sure, begun to moderate in 1982 — without appreciable comment in the media — and in 1985 it leveled off to an even 4000 in midyear and even took a little dip to 3992 at the end of the year. After the PAC explosion of the preceding decade, the downturn surprised even most PAC observers and scholars. The FEC press office presented the totals in news releases of August 19, 1985, and January 20, 1986. The data were clearly set out with, as always, a full listing of the PAC totals back to 1974.[12]

The country's three elite daily newspapers — the *Los Angeles*

such as public financing of elections, reforming the congressional seniority system, permitting public attendance at almost all legislative committee meetings, and requiring top government officials to disclose financial holdings get mentioned repeatedly in the press."

[12]The data of the FEC press releases are those of Table 4-1.

Times, the *New York Times*, and the *Washington Post* — responded with apparent skepticism. The *Los Angeles Times* reported nothing of the new totals or either FEC news release. The *New York Times* responded to the FEC's news release of August 19th with a two-paragraph item on August 24, 1985, in its collection of items entitled "Washington Talk":

> Political action committees, those special interest groups sponsored by business and labor that help finance campaigns of favored political candidates, declined in number in the first six months of 1985, from 4,009 to 4,000, according to a report by the Federal Election Commission. While the decline was modest, it was the first since the commission began keeping records of these groups in 1974.
>
> The figures also show, however, that more members of Congress are accepting and spending more PAC contributions in order to win re-election, so the drop in committees should probably be regarded as only a seasonal blip.

As proof that the Progressive spirit lives, the story is almost too perfect. In the first sentence, there is the reduction of the complexity of the PAC movement to the clash between business and labor. Then in the second paragraph, there is the denial of the story in the first. There is also the introduction of "the figures" on spending with the misleading suggestion that they are a part of this FEC report. And finally there is the gratuitous comment about "a seasonal blip" when the data of the FEC release (data that go all the way back to the beginning) show no previous seasonal declines. That much reported and explained, the *New York Times* did not report the further decline to 3992 PACs that the FEC disclosed in January of 1986.

For its part the *Washington Post* failed to report the first of the FEC releases, but it did carry the second. On January 20, 1986, in a story headlined "FEC Reports Fewer PACs In Late 1985" it reported the drops from 4009 to 4000 and then to 3992 "following a decade of rapid growth." But in the third paragraph of the story, the *Post* put things into its perspective:

> The slight retrenchment does not mean PACs are spending less. In fact, they set a record in the last congressional elections by

providing House and Senate candidates $105 million, 26.5 percent of all money raised. PAC contributions have tripled since the 1978 elections.

As in the single story in the *New York Times*, there is no suggestion that the growth of PAC contributions was at a decelerating rate between 1982 and 1984. Finally, the *Post* story concluded by further minimizing the story it was reporting:

> Fred Wertheimer, president of Common Cause, which is lobbying to abolish PACs, said he took no comfort from the new figures.
> He predicted that PAC contributions will climb again in this year's elections. The FEC did not say which PACs folded, but Wertheimer speculated they were "not significant givers."

There was no attempt to speculate why PAC growth had stopped so suddenly. As for the speculation about the significance of the dead, one can only say that the press never pondered the significance of the newcomer PACs in the years it was reporting the upward growth curve. (In defense of Common Cause, moreover, it has *not* been campaigning to abolish PACs, a course that would be futile in view of the Supreme Court's holding that they are exercising First Amendment rights.)[13]

There are, not surprisingly, signs that American public opinion about campaign finance also comes from the Progressive mold. A Louis Harris poll of November 1982 found that 54 percent of a sample of American adults considered environmental PACs "good." Women's PACs enjoyed the approval of 53 percent, but support for labor PACs was only at 27 percent and "big company" PACs won the approval of a meager 20 percent. In its ordering and selectivity of approval, mass opinion is almost identical to the social preferences of elite journalists cited previously. The Harris poll also made quite clear the problem in interpreting poll data such as these: do we see attitudes about campaign finance, or do we see more basic views about groups and the distribution of influence in American society?[14]

---

[13]For a fuller documentation of the treatment of this and two other stories, see my article, "Campaign Money and the Press: Three Soundings," *Political Science Quarterly*, vol. 102 (Spring 1987), 25–42.

[14]Reported in William Schneider's column "Opinion Outlook" in *National*

But more specifically about campaign finance, 84 percent of the respondents in the same poll agreed that "those who contribute large sums of money have too much influence over the government."[15] (One wonders what the response would have been to a question that stipulated "those millions of Americans who contribute money . . ."; we risk a confusion between attitudes about campaign finance and those about the power of wealth.) In the same poll, 62 percent of the respondents found "excessive campaign spending in national elections" a "very serious problem." (Again, one wonders what the response would have been to a question that reported sums instead of the adjective "excessive.") On the subject of PACs generally, a Roper poll of December 1982 found (in a much more neutrally worded question) that 41 percent of its respondents thought PACs a "bad thing"; 23 percent saw them as a "good thing."[16]

So, what to do? General public opinion seems clearly agreed on only one course of action: limit campaign spending. Given a group of suggestions for reform by the Roper organization in December 1983, the most favored course of action was "limits set on the amount of money that can be spent on political campaigns"; 60 percent of the sample selected it.[17] Similarly, a Civic Service survey of February 1985 proposed a $240,000 limit on "general election" spending for "congressional campaigns" (noting that the limit had been proposed in the Congress). More than two-thirds of its national sample approved.[18] It matters not to pollers or the mass public, apparently, that the Supreme Court held statutory limits on spending unconstitutional in 1976.

The transcendence of the idea of limits, either on contributing or spending, appears also to explain the contradictory results different polls get on the issue of public funding. Civic Service found 65 percent disapproval in early 1985 for this formulation:

Journal (Feb. 26, 1983), 472–473. Schneider reports a Roper poll on the group influence in his column in the *National Journal* for Dec. 21, 1985. The results are strikingly similar; labor and business groups have too much influence, farmers and senior citizens too little.

[15]Ibid.

[16]Ibid.

[17]"Opinion Roundup," *Public Opinion*, vol. 7 (Apr./May 1984), 31.

[18]Reported in *Attitudes Toward Campaign Financing*, a report by Civic Service, Inc., Feb. 1985.

> It has been proposed in Congress that the federal government provide public financing for congressional campaigns for the U.S. House of Representatives and Senate. Would you approve or disapprove of the proposal to use public funds, federal money, to pay the costs of congressional campaigns and how strongly do you feel?[19]

But the Gallup poll found only a half-year earlier (in July 1984) that Americans favor public funding in the Gallup proposition:

> It has been suggested that the federal government provide a fixed amount of money for the election campaign of candidates for Congress and that all private contributions from other sources be prohibited. Do you think this is a good idea or a poor idea?

Against 36 percent who thought it was a "poor idea," 52 percent thought it a "good" one. Democrats approved at the rate of 56 percent, Republicans by 45 percent.[20] Clearly the difference between the two questions is the elimination of private contributions in the Gallup formulation. (To speculate again: what would the response to a public funding proposal be if "strict limits on campaign spending" were included?)

In short, the American public appears to want a campaign finance system in which the funds will be provided by individual contributors of small sums (who are not motivated by economic self-interest) and in which the sums spent will be sharply limited. It is, ironically, a vision of campaign finance not unlike that which animated many in the Congress when it passed the FECA in 1971 and 1974. It is this vision that the Supreme Court rejected in favor of its First Amendment vision in 1976 in *Buckley v. Valeo.*

Systematic bias in the media and the contours of public opinion thus meet in a great analytical conundrum. They are very similar in their outlooks about power and influence and thus about American campaign finance. But how are they related? The media must attract consumers, and they do so by telling the stories their public likes to hear. The public, for its part, is not born with its attitudes about political power and campaign fi-

---

[19]Ibid.
[20]George Gallup, Jr., *The Gallup Poll: Public Opinion 1984* (Wilmington, Del.: Scholarly Resources, 1985), 122–123.

nance. Do the media shape those opinions or merely tap them in defining newsworthiness? Certainly it is some of both and enough to certify an independent opinion-shaping role for the media.

II. The Nine Justices and the Judicial Power

The Supreme Court's modern jurisprudence on campaign finance begins and virtually ends with *Buckley v. Valeo*.[21] There have been cases since it, but they have done little more than elaborate or embroider on *Buckley*. For more than a decade, the Court has remained fixed and firm — some would say rigid and unyielding — in the constitutional interpretations it framed in that first test of the FECA.[22]

At the center of *Buckley* was the Court's announcement, for the first time, that the giving and spending of money in election campaigns was a form of political expression protected by the First Amendment. In some of the words of the Court,

> A restriction on the amount of money a person or group can spend on political communication during a campaign necessarily reduces the quantity of expression by restricting the number of issues discussed, the depth of their exploration, and the size of the audience reached. This is because virtually every means of communicating ideas in today's mass society requires the expenditure of money.[23]

The electorate's increasing dependence on the mass media for its political information, said the Court, "has made these expensive modes of communication indispensable instruments of effective political speech."[24] For the first time, a number of wags have pointed out, the old aphorism that "money talks" has been

---

[21]424 U.S. 1 (1976).

[22]Much of the material of the following paragraphs is treated more fully in my article "Caught in a Political Thicket: The Supreme Court and Campaign Finance," *Constitutional Commentary*, vol. 3 (Winter 1986), 97–121.

[23]*Buckley v. Valeo*, 19. In discussing the majority opinion in *Buckley*, one is discussing a per curiam opinion that runs, including Appendix, to 235 pages in the U.S. Reports.

[24]Ibid.

elevated to a constitutional principle. And because in the Court's judgment spending involved the expression of ideas more clearly than the giving of money to candidates, it struck down the FECA's limitations on expenditures while upholding those on contributions.

As it does with restrictions on any right or freedom protected by the First Amendment, the Court announced it would subject legislative restrictions on campaign finance to rigorous scrutiny and review. But while ordinarily the Court merely states that principle and warns legislatures that they will have to bear a heavy burden of justification, in *Buckley* it undertook to sift out and specify the grounds on which the Congress could justify limitations. It was a search almost without precedent; even in its first and classic statement of the "clear and present danger" doctrine, the Court did not undertake to define or list all of "the substantive evils that Congress has a right to prevent."[25] Why it chose to do so in this instance, especially since it was assessing a comprehensive piece of legislation with which there was so little experience, only the Court knows. But in a lengthy exercise in weighing and weeding out possible grounds, it settled on one and only one: corruption or the appearance of corruption. If Congress or a state legislature were to limit any campaign transactions, it would have to be justified on that ground alone.

When it invoked the danger of "corruption," moreover, the Court was not using the word in any allusive or metaphorical way — it meant plain old corruption, the "buying" of subsequent legislative votes with campaign contributions. "To the extent that large contributions are given to secure a political *quid pro quo* from current and potential office holders, the integrity of our system of representative democracy is undermined."[26] Nine years after *Buckley*, the Court reaffirmed that definition:

> Corruption is a subversion of the political process. Elected officials are influenced to act contrary to their obligations of office by the prospect of financial gain to themselves or infusions of money into their campaigns. The hallmark of corruption is the financial *quid pro quo*: dollars for political favors.[27]

[25]*Schenck v. U.S.*, 249 U.S. 47, 52 (1919).
[26]*Buckley*, 26–27.
[27]*FEC v. NCPAC*, 470 U.S. 480 (1985), 497.

In that same case, a synonym for "quid pro quo" also appeared: "exchange of political favors."[28] But whatever the operative phrase, it seems clear that the Court's concept of corruption is very close to the ordinary meaning of bribery and very far from looser meanings that suggest "only" misuse or degradation of an institution or process.

Not only did the Court define the range of a legislature's regulatory authority in *Buckley*, but it also undertook to reject some others that the plaintiffs (and the lower court) proposed. After noting that those plaintiffs asserted a legitimate government interest in equalizing the opportunities for groups and individuals in electoral politics by putting limits on contributions and expenditures, the Court rejected it with an absolute and magisterial sentence:

> [T]he concept that government may restrict the speech of some elements of our society in order to enhance the relative voice of others is wholly foreign to the First Amendment, which was designed "to secure 'the widest possible dissemination of information from diverse and antagonistic sources.'"[29]

In a literal sense it was "equality" the Court rejected in deferring to freedom under the First Amendment. In a more significant sense, it rejected the Congress's interest in fostering what it believed to be a healthy and credible working of the democratic processes. (For a dissenting view of *Buckley*, see box.)

MR. JUSTICE WHITE DISSENTING

In *Buckley* and after, only Justice Byron White of the nine justices of the Supreme Court has consistently upheld the power of the Congress to pass legislation such as the FECA. It is worth noting that Justice White is the one member of the Court with substantial experience in campaign

[28]Ibid., 498.
[29]*Buckley* at 48–49. The Court was quoting *New York Times v. Sullivan*, 376 U.S. 254, 266, 269 (1964), which in turn was quoting *Associated Press v. U.S.*, 326 U.S. 1, 20 (1945) and *Roth v. U.S.*, 354 U.S. 476, 484 (1957).

politics; he coordinated the presidential campaign of John F. Kennedy in the Mountain States in 1960. Two excerpts from his dissent in *Buckley* (424 U.S. 1, [1976]) follow.

Let us suppose that each of two brothers spends $1 million on TV spot announcements that he has individually prepared and in which he appears, urging the election of the same named candidate in identical words. One brother has sought and obtained the approval of the candidate; the other has not. The former may validly be prosecuted . . .; under the Court's view, the latter may not, even though the candidate could scarcely help knowing about and appreciating the expensive favor. For constitutional purposes it is difficult to see the difference between the two situations. I would take the word of those who know — that limiting independent expenditures is essential to prevent transparent and widespread evasion of the contribution limits. (pp. 261–262)

. . . [M]oney is not always equivalent to or used for speech, even in the context of political campaigns. I accept the reality that communicating with potential voters is the heart of an election campaign and that widespread communication has become very expensive. There are, however, many expensive campaign activities that are not themselves communicative or remotely related to speech. Furthermore, campaigns differ among themselves. Some seem to spend much less money than others and yet communicate as much as or more than those supported by enormous bureaucracies with unlimited financing. (p. 263)

Just as important was the governmental interest the Court chose to ignore: the legislative interest in preserving the integrity of the electoral process. It has an honorable history, one dating back in fact to the Supreme Court's first decision on the regulation of campaign finance. In upholding the Congress's requirement in the Federal Corrupt Practices Act of 1925 that certain committees in presidential campaigns report publicly the names and addresses of their contributors and the sums of their contributions, Justice Sutherland's opinion for the majority is sprinkled with references to Congress's interest in protecting the integrity of the presidential election. For example:

> To say that Congress is without power to pass appropriate legislation to safeguard such an election from the improper use of money to influence the result is to deny the nation in a vital particular the power of self protection.[30]

Moreover, it is clear that the Court in 1934 had in mind not the corrupting or even the swaying of later decisions of public officials when it referred to corruption, but the corrupting of *elections* — the buying of voters' votes, the casting of votes from the graveyard, the rigging of electoral counts.

Congress reached the conclusion that public disclosure of political contributions, together with the names of contributors and other details, would tend to prevent the corrupt use of money to affect elections.[31]

In the more than 40 years between *Burroughs* and *Buckley*, the Court frequently returned to the interest of legislatures in protecting the integrity of elections (or of the "electoral process"), using it to justify even limits to First Amendment political freedoms. Just three years before *Buckley*, in fact, the Court noted in upholding New York's requirement that voters register at least 30 days before the primary election: "It is clear that preservation of the integrity of the electoral process is a legitimate and valid state goal."[32] Not at all unexpectedly, then, the Court of Appeals hearing *Buckley* relied heavily on the protection of elections as a recognized and legitimate legislative interest.[33]

So, the Supreme Court has locked itself and all of constitutional jurisprudence into a single, narrowly defined ground on which legislatures may limit campaign finance. It is, moreover, a ground or interest that is largely irrelevant to the issues that American campaigning raises in the 1980s. By focusing on the "corruption" of legislatures and other policy-making bodies, the

---

[30]*Burroughs v. U.S.*, 290 U.S. 534 (1934), 545.
[31]Ibid, 548.
[32]*Rosario v. Rockefeller*, 410 U.S. 752, 761 (1973).
[33]*Buckley v. Valeo*, 519 F.2d 821 (D.C. Cir. 1975).

Court ignores the entire set of issues involving the effect of money on the campaign itself and on the electoral outcome — the issue that in the vernacular is the one about money "buying" elections. And more, the framing of the "legislative" issue in terms of corruption ignores the fact that in the real world the issue is not primarily one of "quid pro quo," of money for promises of performance; it is rather the broader question of access, of influence, of a more sophisticated form of lobbying, of the ability to keep sympathetic incumbents in office and in positions of power.

Pressed to relate its concept of corruption to the issues of the real political world, the Court said in *Buckley*,

> Although the scope of such pernicious practices can never be reliably ascertained, the deeply disturbing examples surfacing after the 1972 election demonstrate that the problem is not an illusory one.[34]

As for specifics, the Court noted two pages in the opinion of the Court of Appeals in *Buckley*. But those pages mention only "huge contributions from the dairy industry," illegal corporate contributions, and contributions from people who wanted ambassadorships.[35] The truth of the matter is quite simply that for all of their shocking betrayals of public trust and ethics, the Watergate revelations did not include "corruption" of the kind the Court seems to have in mind.

Finally, the Court has injected one tantalizing word — "appearance" — into its formulation of the one legitimate interest: "corruption and the appearance of corruption." Appearance to whom? Apparently to the public in general — all citizens, voters, adults. Even if appearances are deceiving? That's the great uncertainty. Is the Court prepared to permit legislative limits on this First Amendment freedom solely on a widespread belief that genuine, "hard core" corruption is rampant, even if there is no empirical evidence or proof that such is the case? And if so, what evidence does it demand of "appearance"? In 1983 the trial court hearing the belated challenge to the limitation on independent expenditures in publicly funded presidential campaigns

[34]*Buckley v. Valeo*, 424 U.S. 1, 28.
[35]Ibid.

dismissed an array of survey data from Roper and Louis Harris polls. The polls dealt too generally with campaign finance, the Court thought.

> Only distrust in the integrity of government engendered by the conduct proscribed by section 9012(f)'s prohibitions can save the statute.[36]

In this case, that is, it was not enough that the public reacted negatively to such independent expenditures; there apparently also had to be evidence that the opinion was related specifically to independent spending in the particular case of a publicly funded presidential campaign. But public opinion is diffuse and general. The public is neither informed enough nor inclined to have an opinion about the consequences of one discrete aspect of the system of campaign finance. The public will see and judge it as a whole. As of 1987, however, no statute has been upheld in an American court on the basis of "appearances."

Once the Court had set down such a sweeping interpretation of the First Amendment rights of campaign spenders and once it had so narrowly defined the legitimate interest of legislatures in regulating them, the results were predictable. Substantial parts of the FECA fell — especially the limits on campaign expenditures, on independent spending, and on candidates' use of their personal resources — and what remained was very imperfectly calculated to achieve Congress's goals in restructuring the system of campaign finance. Similar sections in the legislation of a majority of states also fell, leaving their legislation in tatters, too.

In some instances, indeed, the logic and rules of *Buckley* have led the Court ineluctably to conclusions in cases raising new issues. The elections and campaigns without candidates in the states — those involving initiatives and referenda — are in many ways different from the campaign politics the FECA confronted. Two years after *Buckley*, the Supreme Court heard a case from Massachusetts challenging that state's law forbidding expenditures by banks and corporations in campaigns on all referenda except those directly touching their property or business interests. The highest court of the state upheld the statute, but the

---

[36]*FEC v. NCPAC*, 578 F. Supp. 797, 825 (E.D. Pa 1983).

Supreme Court struck it down as a violation of the First Amendment rights of the banks and corporations (*First National Bank of Boston v. Bellotti*).[37] On the application of its "corruption" standard, the Court was brief.

> Referenda are held on issues, not candidates for public office. The risk of corruption perceived in cases involving candidate elections . . . simply is not present in a popular vote on a public issue.[38]

Since it is the corruption of "quids pro quo" the Court has in mind and since there is no potential officeholder to enter into the exchange of favors in a campaign over an issue, by definition there can be no corruption.[39]

But the line of logic and deduction is not always clear. In that same *Bellotti* case, the Court upheld the rights of political speech and political association of banks and corporations.

> If the speakers here were not corporations, no one would suggest that the State could silence their proposed speech. It is the type of speech indispensable to decisionmaking in a democracy, and this is no less true because the speech comes from a corporation rather than an individual. The inherent worth of the speech in terms of its capacity for informing the public does not depend upon the identity of its source, whether corporation, association, union, or individual.[40]

The Massachusetts statute, in the opinion of the Court,

> amounts to an impermissible legislative prohibition of speech based on the identity of the interests that spokesmen may represent in public debate over controversial issues and a requirement that the speaker have a sufficiently great interest in the subject to justify communication.[41]

Although the majority noted that it was not addressing "the

---

[37]435 U.S. 765 (1978).

[38]Ibid., 790.

[39]See also *Citizens Against Rent Control v. City of Berkeley,* 454 U.S. 290 (1981) in which the Court struck down an ordinance (adopted in 1974 by the initiative process) that limited contributions to campaign committees involved in ballot issues to $250.

[40]Bellotti, 777.

[41]Ibid., 784.

abstract question whether corporations have the full measure of rights that individuals enjoy under the First Amendment,"[42] it could not prevent others from speculating on the implications of its rhetoric. *Bellotti* clearly seemed to throw into question the federal law that prevented direct political contributions by corporations and unions. But then without mentioning *Bellotti*, the majority of justices in 1986 tacitly approved the ban on direct corporate activities when it held unconstitutional those provisions of the U.S. code as they applied to a nonstock corporation formed entirely for issue and ideological goals. In separating that kind of corporation — the Massachusetts Citizens for Life in the case — from the usual business corporation, the Court, while protecting the former, made clear it accepted the case for limiting the latter.[43]

In so exercising its power to define the meaning of the First Amendment, the Supreme Court has become one of the prime architects of the new system of campaign finance. It has to all intents and purposes ruled out statutory limitations on candidates' campaign expenditures, on candidates' use of their personal funds, on anyone's independent spending in campaigns, and on all contributions to "ballot issue" campaigns. The only option that remains for legislatures who want to curb the resulting rise in political spending is voluntary public funding, with limits on candidate spending and/or candidate use of personal resources as a condition for receiving the money. That option, of course, poses a major policy dilemma. Spending limits unquestionably have more political support than does public funding; are legislatures and their publics willing to swallow the latter to gain the former?

Surprisingly, other regulatory possibilities remain untested in the Supreme Court. Ordinarily a denial of legislative authority is followed by policy innovations as legislatures search for alternatives that meet the tests of the Constitution. The invalidation of spoken prayer in public schools, for instance, was followed by the inauguration of silent prayer or meditation, by the saying of the Ten Commandments, and ultimately by silence itself. In campaign finance there has been virtually no legislative response,

[42]Ibid., 777.
[43]*Federal Election Commission v. Massachusetts Citizens for Life*, 107 S.Ct. 616 (1986).

largely because of the loss of the post-Watergate zeal for reform. Thus we do not know how the Court would view the lowering of contribution limits below the 1974 levels — the cutting of the limits on PAC contributions, say, to $3000 or $2000. Nor have we any ruling on new ideas, the liveliest of which would seem to be limits on the total sums candidates may accept from PACs generally. Amid the paucity of regulatory innovations, a Florida appellate court has upheld the statutory provision of that state forbidding the acceptance of contributions after the election; and the California Supreme Court has invalidated that state's attempt to forbid lobbyists from contributing to campaigns or arranging or brokering contributions.[44] Otherwise, there is little else.[45]

Looked at more generally, the Supreme Court's holdings in the campaign finance cases are a part of its extension of First Amendment freedoms in cases involving parties and elections. In historic decisions after 1960, the Court began to put limits on the power of state legislatures, inter alia, to restrict the access of minor parties to the ballot, to set year-long residency requirements for eligible voters, to force state parties to choose delegates to their national party conventions in uncongenial ways, to prevent parties from including independents in their primary election electorates, and to draw legislative districts that worked to the long-run advantage of one party (i.e., were "gerrymanders"). In all of these cases, as in the campaign finance cases, the Court acted to protect First Amendment rights of political speech or association.[46] In the name of the First

[44]*Ferre v. State ex rel. Reno*, 478 So.2d 1077 (1985), and *Fair Political Practices Commission v. Superior Court of Los Angeles County*, 599 P.2d 46 (1979), certiorari denied by the U. S. Supreme Court at 444 U.S. 1049 (1980), with Justices White and Blackmun noting that they would have granted certiorari.

[45]There is a case from Puerto Rico in which a three-judge panel of the U.S. District Court for the Commonwealth struck down a statute providing for governmental inspectors at "mass" fund-raising events to encourage their operating within the law of the Commonwealth. See *Partido Nuevo Progresista v. Hernandez Colon*, 415 F.Supp. 475 (1976).

[46]The citations to Supreme Court cases are, in the order in which they are referred to: *Williams v. Rhodes*, 393 U.S. 23 (1968); *Dunn v. Blumstein*, 405 U.S. 330 (1972); *Democratic Party of the U.S. v. La Follette*, 450 U.S. 107 (1981); *Tashjian v. Republican Party of Connecticut*, 107 S.Ct. 544 (1986); *Davis v. Bandemer*, 106 S.Ct. 2797 (1986). For a fuller treatment of the trend, see Leon D. Epstein, *Political Parties in the American Mold* (Madison: University of Wisconsin Press, 1986), chap. 6.

Amendment, that is, the Court challenged for the first time the power of American legislatures to regulate and shape electoral politics in the United States.

Whatever the merits of its celebration of First Amendment freedoms in these cases, the Court's constitutional jurisprudence on the financing of campaigns fits the structure of the policy debate very badly. Two issues dominate the public debate over campaign finance: the influence of contributors over legislators and other policy-makers, and the influence of money on the outcome of elections. The Court's concession of a legislative interest in preventing "corruption and the appearance of corruption" addresses the first, but its formulation misses the point on influence in the legislative process with an almost quaint irrelevance. As for the second issue, the Court does not address it, even though it had a tool at hand with which to do so — a restatement of the legislature's power to protect the "integrity" of elections. That doctrine remains, however, in the Court's jurisprudence; and the Court may yet turn to it.

For many Americans the realities of campaign finance raise issues bearing directly on the state of the American democracy. The first of their concerns touches on the very process of representation, the process by which the views and preferences of the electorate are represented in the policy-making of government. The concern, of course, is that the influence of contributors, especially the PACs that link money to the power of organized lobbying, is increasing to the disadvantage of party and constituency influence. The second concern centers on the pivotal role of elections in a representative democracy and especially the availability of viable, credible alternatives in competitive elections. And that concern comes exactly at the time at which incumbents are drawing on all manner of advantages to reduce the effective competitiveness of those elections.[47]

In a curious way, the Supreme Court sidled up to the issue of the health of democratic processes when it rejected out of hand any legislative interest in "equalizing the relative ability of individuals and groups to influence the outcomes of elections."[48] But the Court misframed the issue when it spoke in terms of Con-

[47]Some of the concerns about democratic politics will reappear in chap. 11.
[48]*Buckley v. Valeo*, 48.

gress's power "to restrict the speech of some elements of our society in order to enhance the relative voice of others."[49] The purpose is rather to define and protect some fundamental democratic equality in the quest for public office — and to do so in order to protect democratic processes and public confidence in them. In the Court's own word, the Congress must assure the "appearance" of democracy as well as its substance; and in doing so it may choose to promote evenly matched political debate, the full and broad recruitment of candidates, responsible campaigning, and the presence of viable alternatives for voters. In the long run, it is hard to imagine that the Court will cling to an absolute denial of Congress's interest in protecting those ingredients of the democratic process.

III. The Federal Election Commission

The FEC has not lived a charmed life. It was created hastily in 1974 with virtually no precedent; and when its first incarnation was declared unconstitutional, it went out of business right in the middle of the first campaign it tried to cope with: the presidential campaign of 1976. Hastily reconstituted, it resumed its operations in the second half of 1976. Underfunded at the beginning, it was repeatedly impoverished by Congress as its regulatory burdens grew. And in the mere decade of its life, it has been the vortex of pressures and criticisms from the Congress, the reformers of campaign finance, and the getters and spenders in electoral politics. In the Victorian words of W. S. Gilbert, "the policeman's lot is not a happy one."[50] Especially when the policeman's beat is city hall.

The time of troubles began immediately. The original FECA of 1971 dispersed compliance and enforcement authority to the Clerk of the House, the Secretary of the Senate, and the General Accounting Office (GAO). None of these three offices had authority to prosecute violators; they could only refer cases to the Justice Department. It was, with a few changes, the administrative apparatus that had carried out earlier legislation and that had

---

[49]Ibid., 48–49.
[50]W. S. Gilbert and Arthur Sullivan, *The Pirates of Penzance* (1879), Act II.

resulted in boxes full of yellowed reports stored in remote closets. Attempts to enforce the law in the 1972 elections resulted in more of the familiar problems, not the least of which was the hesitance of Justice to pursue cases referred to it. The problem was fundamental: No one given the task of administering the FECA had the resources, facilities, commitment, or expertise with which to do so. Indeed, all of that was behind the recommendation of the special Senate committee investigating the Watergate scandals that a powerful agency be created to oversee and regulate federal elections.

When in 1974 the Congress framed its massive amendments to the FECA, it created for the first time a special agency, the Federal Election Commission, to carry out its plans. The authority of the Clerk, the Secretary, and the GAO was transferred to it; and it was also vested with powers of civil enforcement. Neither the Congress nor the states had any experience in creating a full-blown regulatory agency for matters of campaign finance; and so the model in the minds of the Congress was, apparently, the conventional regulatory agency. The FEC was to look and operate something like the SEC, the FCC, and the FTC. There was, however, one chief difference: the president would appoint two of the six commissioners, but the Speaker of the House and the President Pro Tempore of the Senate each would also appoint two. It was an arrangement that led to the FEC's demise in early 1976 — right in midcampaign — with the Supreme Court's decision in *Buckley v. Valeo.*

In *Buckley* the Court ruled that the role of the House and the Senate in appointing two-thirds of the membership of the FEC violated the Constitution's separation of powers. A commission with such wide rule-making and enforcement powers is an executive agency, ruled the Court, and its commissioners must be appointed by the executive. More specifically the Congress had violated the Appointments clause of the Constitution (Article II, section 2) providing that appointments of "Officers of the United States" be made by the president with the advice and consent of the Senate.[51] The Court granted a 30-day stay of its decision to give Congress time to reconstitute the Commission; it then extended the stay for an additional month. When that extension ran

[51] See *Buckley v. Valeo,* 424 U.S. 1 (1976), 109–143.

out, the FEC folded its tents on March 22, 1976 — squarely in the middle of its first attempt to administer the public funding of the presidential primary period.[52]

Congress resurrected the FEC by giving the president the power to appoint all six commissioners with the advice and consent of the Senate. The Clerk of the House and the Secretary of the Senate were retained as nonvoting ex officio members; Congress also retained the requirement that the six appointments go in equal numbers to Democrats and Republicans. After the six appointments were made and confirmed, the FEC resumed operations on May 21, 1976. The combination of inexperience and interruption plagued its attempts to monitor reports and collect data on the 1976 elections. Understandably, it was not a particularly auspicious beginning.

Nor had it been an auspicious beginning from the Congress's point of view. The Federal Election Commission was not just another regulatory commission; it was the commission regulating the campaigns of the members of Congress and their opponents. It was the policeman at city hall. Full of uneasiness about the FEC's future course, Congress first saw its attempt to control the appointment of FEC members under attack in the courts. Then in December 1975, some of its members — the Democrats in particular — were stunned by the FEC's "advisory opinion" on a matter brought by Sun Oil's PAC.[53] By a vote of 4–2 (with two of the three Democrats in the minority), the Commission held that the FECA permitted a corporation to use its corporate funds to pay the administrative and overhead costs of establishing and maintaining a PAC. The FEC had flashed a green light for the corporate PAC movement and confirmed some of the worst fears in Congress. The FEC's subsequent relationships with Congress were never to be happy or comfortable.

In its decade or so of existence, the FEC has settled into a reg-

---

[52]The temporary demise of the FEC undoubtedly had an effect on the 1976 presidential election. Writes John H. Aldrich in *Before the Convention* (Chicago: University of Chicago Press, 1980), 52:

> During this period [of the FEC's suspension], candidates had to rely on their own sources of money. [Henry] Jackson and [Fred] Harris stated that this change of rules in mid-campaign was a major reason for their dropping out of the campaign.

[53]Advisory Opinion 1975-23 of the FEC (Dec. 3, 1975).

ular and stable pattern of activities. They can be summarized quickly and seriatim:[54]

1. *Disclosure.* The FEC makes available to the public both the full reports of committees and candidates and its own summaries and aggregates of data. The data come in all forms: from photocopies and computer-based summaries of specific reports to lengthy files on computer tapes (e.g., the total number of all contributions to all congressional candidates from all PACs is now beyond the 100,000 mark). The Public Records Office, responsible for most of the contacts with the public, made public some 7.3 million pages of documents through the end of 1985.

2. *Public Funding.* The FEC oversees both public funding programs for the presidential campaigns. It certifies the eligibility of candidates and the payments they are entitled to receive, and it audits the reports of all recipients.

3. *Information and Advice.* Candidates, PACs, and parties, not to mention interested groups and individuals, besiege the FEC for help, information, and clarification in complying with the FECA. The FEC responds with phone information (a toll-free line), publications, workshops, and seminars. More formal clarifications come via the Advisory Opinion, a binding legal opinion the Commission gives and publishes in response to a formal inquiry. Through the end of 1986, the FEC had issued 844 of them. Finally, the Commission issues rules and regulations to codify its interpretations and practice.

4. *Compliance.* The Commission's responsibility for ensuring compliance with all aspects of campaign finance law begins with its review of all reports and requests for additional information and clarification. It may continue with formal audits of the records of campaigns or committees; through 1986 the FEC conducted 392 of them.[55]

5. *Enforcement.* The FEC deals with what it or some complain-

---

[54]Much of what follows comes from the Commission's own glossy report on the occasion of its 10th birthday: *The First Ten Years* (Washington, D.C.: Federal Election Commission, 1985). Data after 1984 come from the Commission's annual reports.

[55]The total includes the statutorily required audits of all presidential candidates receiving public funds.

ant thinks is a violation of the law. Once a complaint is filed or referred to it, the Commission proceeds with what it calls a Matter Under Review (MUR); the process includes a confidential investigation and hearing. If attempts at informal conciliation and settlement fail, the FEC has the power to levy civil penalties and, finally, to seek enforcement in the federal courts. Other parties than the FEC — both complainants and defendants — also have the power to appeal the FEC action to the courts. Through calendar year 1986, the Commission had closed the file on 2,177 such matters.

Finally, the FEC has also taken over a responsibility beyond its regulatory role over campaign finance. In 1974 a small clearinghouse on election administration was transferred to it from the GAO. It has published reports on topics such as state campaign finance laws, voter registration systems, and voting machines.

To carry out these responsibilities, the Federal Election Commission has what are by Washington standards a very modest staff and budget. For fiscal 1986 the Commission had a total budget of $11.9 million and a staff of 229.4 full-time equivalent employees. Some 28 percent of that staff, the largest allocation, was in the Office of General Counsel; 16 percent was allocated to the analysis of the various reports made to the FEC. More telling, these figures represent very little growth from the early years of the agency's existence. The budget increased from $6.2 million in fiscal year 1977 to the $11.9 million for FY 1986, an increase of 92 percent. The rise in the Consumer Price Index alone was 81 percent in that decade. That relative stability of funding, of course, came at a time when the regulatory task of the FEC exploded. In 1976, for example, there were 1146 PACs making a total of $22.6 million in contributions to congressional candidates; in 1986 there were 4157 making a total of $132.2 million in contributions.

Like all other federal regulatory agencies, the FEC "enjoys" the attention of a wide and varied circle of observers and critics. Judgments on its work are not hard to find. Undoubtedly the highest marks go to the Commission's performance in information and disclosure. Its Office of Public Disclosure and its Press Office have combined competence with a helpfulness to the interested public that win all-around applause. Even a brief setback in 1986 with a Gramm-Rudman cut in funds has not tarnished the Commission's record for making reports and data easily available to candidates, journalists, scholars, interested groups, and the public. The Commission has also developed new and innovative ways of making its data public; in 1985, for instance, it made much of its computer-based data available over telephone lines. It takes nothing away from the offices and personnel carrying out the agency's mission of disclosure, however, to say that their's is the Commission's least controversial and most popular service.

Much more apt to breed controversy are the audits, the negotiations, the writing of regulations, the framing of rules, and the ultimate resort to formal enforcement action. Most of these actions are adversarial, and in most of them there are winners and losers — more significantly, perhaps, there are winning and losing *interests* behind the specific parties winning and losing. Many of the issues they raise are hard and perplexing, a veritable political and legal minefield.

● Was a speech by President Reagan to a national convention of the Veterans of Foreign Wars in August 1984 a campaign speech or not? If it was, his campaign committee would have to pay for the trip; if not, the taxpayers would. He did not mention his reelection opponent but criticized some of his positions; he apparently also did not mention his campaign explicitly or seek financial contributions to it. But the speech was just one day after the president had been renominated at the Republican party convention. Rejecting the recommendation of its legal staff, the FEC voted that it was not.[56]

● Should the FEC undertake to regulate the use of "soft money"?[57] Common Cause had petitioned the FEC to do so. The

---

[56]Subsequently, Common Cause brought suit to challenge the ruling, and in its resolution a U.S. district court judge took the FEC's procedures over the proverbial coals. The litigation is recounted by Herbert E. Alexander and Brian A. Haggerty, *Financing the 1984 Election* (Lexington, MA: Lexington, 1987), 66.

[57]The FEC used Common Cause's definition of "soft money": "funds that are raised by presidential campaigns and national and congressional political party organizations purportedly for use by state and local party organizations in nonfederal elections from sources who would be barred from making such contributions in connection with a federal election, e.g., from corporations and labor unions and from individuals who have reached their federal contribution limits." (FEC *Annual Report of 1985*, 10).

issue is in part one of American federalism: campaign money finding the least regulated jurisdiction. But there were charges of an extra twist: that some of the money was being used to support the national campaign and ticket that had channeled the money in the first place. After a good deal of agonizing, the FEC declined to take on the issue. Some members of the Commission thought it lacked the powers to do the job, and others thought the dimensions of the problem exaggerated.

The questions of lesser moment that come to the FEC for resolution are no easier; any dipping into its Advisory Opinions provides a wealth of examples (see box).

The response to the FEC's grappling with such riddles has inevitably been less than enthusiastic. There is one school of critics, typified by Terry Dolan, long NCPAC's executive director and the *enfant terrible* of the PAC movement, that accuses the FEC of bias against the political right. In an opinion piece in the *Washington Times* in late 1985, Dolan charged that the FEC

> is often motivated by an ideological hatred of conservatives, an attitude clearly reflected in FEC rulings, or in some cases, non-rulings. To date, the FEC has a sorry history of singling out conservatives for criticism and penalty, while ignoring conservative complaints filed against the agency's liberal cohorts.[58]

THE TROUBLESOME SMALLER MATTERS

The everyday problems of understanding and complying with the FECA and the regulations promulgated by the FEC are amply illustrated in the questions candidates, PACs, and other committees address to the FEC. The Commission's formal responses are contained in its Advisory Opinions (AOs),

1. Can the PAC of a fast-food chain (McDonald's) solicit contributions from the executive and administrative personnel of its licensees or franchise holders? Yes. (AO 1977-70).

[58]"What 'fairness' means to the FEC," *Washington Times* (Oct. 11, 1985).

2. Would free use of the Kansas City, Kansas, municipal armory for a fund-raising event by a candidate for the Congress constitute an in-kind contribution by the state of Kansas or by the party committee that booked the facility for the candidate? No, if the armory is commonly used for such noncommercial purposes gratis and if it is available for use by candidates without respect to political affiliation. (AO 1979-81).

3. Can a candidate's committee use campaign funds to reward the campaign's faithful contributors with a special reception and with certificates and momentoes? Yes, but the expenditures would have to be reported as a campaign expense. (AO 1983-5).

4. May a PAC accept a bequest of $70,000 to be distributed to it in annual increments? Yes, the funds would be treated as an individual contribution, subject to the annual limit of $5000. (AO 1986-24).

The Fund for a Conservative Majority conveyed a similar message when it sued the FEC in 1984 for harassing it with repeated audits of its reports and records. And Lyndon LaRouche, the author of at least 10 suits against the FEC, has made similar charges of selective enforcement. (The FEC has in turn accused him and his followers of using litigation to frustrate legitimate investigations and to avoid compliance with FEC decisions.) But these are essentially *ex parte* opinions, and they are not widely shared. Indeed, a number of Democratic, liberal, and trade union critics think the FEC has, on the contrary, been too gentle with the political right.

As for charges that the FEC engages in "nitpicking," it is a semantic quagmire. Some of these complaints seem to mean that the FEC is guilty of excessive legalism, of too formal a look at political realities. (In the matter of the Reagan speech to the VFW, for example, critics accused the FEC of ignoring the realities of the campaign in favor of detailed criteria with which to determine when a speech was or was not a campaign speech.) For others nitpicking seems to suggest an excessive attention to little and unimportant matters; one journalistic critic has called the FEC a "dithering nanny," spending too much time on, inter alia, writing regulations and opinions "some of them downright trivial."[59] Some critics are especially eloquent when the FEC's energy has forced substantial costs of reply or compliance on them. For others the word suggests an FEC inclination to pick on "little guys" and other assorted losers — to pursue matters that really don't "matter" in the final reckoning of things. Others seem to mean that the FEC has by their standards been overzealous. (There are critics of the FEC who think it is underzealous as well.)

The FEC and its defenders have two persuasive points on their side. First, in American law and jurisprudence there has never been any correlation between the importance of the facts in a case and the importance of the principles being settled. And second, a regulatory agency is in a legally and politically untenable position when it decides to enforce statutes selectively, even by some distinction involving what it considers to be matters of importance.

There is far greater agreement on two other criticisms of the Commission's work: delay and timidity. "Delay" at least has a fairly clear meaning. According to the 1984 sentiments of Jan W. Baran, then chairman of the American Bar Association's Committee on Election Law, "the biggest criticism of the commission is that it doesn't perform its investigative functions very expeditiously." At the same time, its former general counsel, William Oldaker, found it "far too slow and dilatory."[60] It is a theme that recurs as well in others' writing and talking about the Commission. And indeed formal enforcement actions, especially court cases, do linger from one presidential election to the next, four years later. In part the FEC's difficulty is one imposed on it: the statutory requirements for process generally, for informal conciliation, for formal hearings, and then for the extensive rights of complainants to challenge FEC action or even nonaction in the

[59]Brooks Jackson, "Open Up Federal Campaign Finance," *Wall Street Journal* (July 31, 1984).

[60]Both quoted in the *New York Times* (Sept. 2, 1984) in an article by Robert Pear, "For F.E.C., Justice Delayed Is Routine." Baran later became counsel to Vice President George Bush's campaign for the Republican nomination for 1988. For his part, Oldaker subsequently wrote a measured and balanced review of the FEC's performance and potential; see his "Of Philosophers, Foxes, and Finances: Can the Federal Election Commission Ever Do an Adequate Job?" in Lloyd N. Cutler et al., eds, *Regulating Campaign Finance*, vol. 486 of the Annals of the American Academy of Political and Social Science (Beverly Hills: Sage, 1986), 132–145.

federal courts. In summer 1987 it was still holding hearings on an FEC audit finding that the Reagan-Bush reelection committee had received $244,000 too much from the U.S. Treasury in matching payments in spring 1984. What part of the responsibility for the delays rests with the FEC is not easy to say, but the investigative and complaint-bringing process is largely within FEC control. Stories of 12- to 20-month delays in finding "probable cause" suggest that the FEC's problems cannot all be laid at the feet of procedural requirements.

The charges of timidity are, not surprisingly, a bag of accusations. There are those who charge the FEC with being especially timid before the legislative power of congressional incumbents. They point to the FEC's reluctance to pursue the failings of incumbent campaigns and the relish with which it goes after losers and the politically hapless. A recurrent theme is the inability of the FEC to mete out stiff penalties for transgressions. But the statutes give the FEC no power to fine, penalize, or incarcerate a violator of the FECA. For criminal prosecution it must refer cases to the Justice Department. (No one has apparently gone to jail even for a single day for violating the FECA.) As for civil penalties, the FEC must negotiate agreements on them; if no agreement can be achieved, it must ask a federal court to assess penalties. The fact that the FEC is not anxious to commit resources to lengthy court battles may explain why its record penalty has been the $18,500 levied in 1984 on the Mondale campaign; it also required the Mondale campaign to refund $350,000 of the federal funds it received.[61]

Despite the elements of truth in these judgments, the key to the FEC performance and record in its first decade is in its relationships with the Congress. In the words of Brooks Jackson written in mid-1984,

> Congress keeps tight control of the agency's budget and retaliates when the commission veers toward independence. In 1979, it stripped the commission of the power to conduct random audits because congressmen became irritated at what they considered too-frequent checks. It insists that all enforcement proceedings be conducted in strict secrecy, to guard against election-year em-

[61]See Colleen O'Connor, "Who's Afraid of the FEC?," *Washington Monthly* (Mar. 1986), 22–26.

barrassments. It requires so many procedural safeguards that enforcement cases drag on for years. A probe of Mr. Mondale's
delegate committees isn't expected to be concluded until long
after the election, for example.[62]

The congressional leash has been short in other ways, too. Congress gave itself a veto over FEC rules and regulations, although
it lost it when the Supreme Court held all legislative vetoes unconstitutional in 1983.[63] Not only has the FEC budget not grown
as have the regulatory tasks, but Congress has at least once shown
its capacity for using it as an instrument of its displeasure. After
the FEC had in 1981 cited more than 400 members of Congress
for failing to file the necessary financial reports from the 1980
campaign, the agency's budget for fiscal 1982 was cut by a quarter. Finally, there were attempts led largely by conservative
Republicans in the Senate to abolish the FEC in the early
1980s.[64]

Unlike most of the regulatory commissions, the FEC has no clientele to protect it — nothing like the varied and powerful
support the Federal Reserve Board, for example, can muster for
its most stringent controls of the money supply. And unlike the
other regulatory commissions, it cannot turn to Congress to protect it from the vengeance of its unhappy regulatees. The
members of Congress *are* the regulatees. Nor has it been able to
count on presidential protection; indeed, it met sustained presidential enmity in the 1980s. To understate the matter, the
Federal Election Commission has always been in a very weak political position. It has few friends and no supportive clientele —
except perhaps for Common Cause and a few other sympathetic
groups — and its enemies either vote its budget and statutory authority or have access to those who do.

In such straits it is hardly surprising that the FEC has erred on
the side of caution. Its overriding fault has been a timidity borne
of the need to survive. Much of its slowness and its legalism and
formalism — its playing by the book and the literal letter of the
law — can be explained in terms of that imperative. At least some

---

[62]*Wall Street Journal* (July 31, 1984).

[63]*Immigration and Naturalization Service v. Chadha* , 462 U.S. 919 (1983).

[64]The platform of the Republican party in the 1984 elections declared that
". . . Congress should consider abolishing" the FEC.

of its timidity, moreover, springs from a reluctance to tie up scarce staff and resources in lengthy litigation. The lessons of caution were learned early, too. The SunPAC opinion of 1975 — delivered only a few months after it started to function in its first incarnation — early embroiled the FEC in a massive controversy. It was, ironically, perhaps the most influential decision the FEC has made. Very few subsequent decisions have in any significant way molded the development of the campaign finance system. And that's quite the way the Congress wants it.

Finally, the Commission's uncomfortable place in party politics has also contributed to its apprehensiveness. Its membership is divided by statute into three Democrats and three Republicans, creating a built-in potential for deadlock. Although deadlocks along party lines have not been common in the FEC's history, there are observers who think that it has avoided some divisive issues as a way of avoiding deadlock. But about the partisan nature of the appointment of Commissioners, there can be no doubt. President Jimmy Carter, for example, was forced to withdraw two nominations, one Democrat (whom Speaker Tip O'Neill thought a "do-good Common Cause type") and one Republican (whom Senate Republicans thought too liberal and too closely connected to organized labor.) The second Republican nomination Carter made, incumbent Commissioner Frank Reiche, barely survived a filibuster by Senate Republicans. He was thought by a few Republicans to be a "closet Democrat"; a larger number of them thought him insufficiently protective of Republican interests in his first term on the FEC. In the Reagan years, a deadlock in the Senate (following the administration's refusal to reappoint Democrat Thomas Harris) required the cobbling together of a "package" in which Democrats and Republicans agreed to two appointments, one from each party and each acceptable to his own partisans.

IV. In Conclusion

Seminal legislation like the FECA develops a life of its own. Part of that life reflects the political-legal framework within which it grows and develops. While the media, the courts, and the FEC have all been a part of that environment, their contributions have been of different kinds. The Supreme Court's has chiefly been to modify the regulatory system with its vision of the First Amendment. The FEC's contribution has been less dramatic — largely a conflict-avoiding, somewhat passive, candidate-oriented administration of what survived of the FECA. The media's voice has overwhelmingly been on the side of greater and firmer regulation; more fundamentally, it has pictured a reality of campaign finance that justified expanding the constraints of the FECA. They have been three voices, each expressing a different part of the American political tradition — the Court's political freedom, the FEC's political pragmatism, and the media's latter-day Progressivism.

Contradictions, conflicts, and ironies abound. The Supreme Court's decision in *Buckley* has made difficult, if not impossible, the kinds of reform that the images of the media are making imperative for millions of Americans. And that Progressive world-view of the media, reflected so fully in mass opinion, has been strangely underrepresented in the Court and the FEC. Only small minorities of each — a handful of commissioners and perhaps only Justice Byron White on the Court — reflect them. On the Court those views have yielded to the dominant force of the First Amendment; at the FEC they are scarce at least in part by presidential and congressional design.

The conflict in the environment of the system of campaign finance is surely one reason for the policy stalemate over it. The media and mass opinion push toward greater governmental intervention, and the Court pushes in the other direction toward the First Amendment freedoms. And so in this divided policy environment, what change there has been since 1976 speaks to the needs and problems of parties and candidates and their funders. Above all it responds to the concerns and goals of candidates, especially those in Congress.

So, in a political system ordinarily sensitive to opinion and images, widely held policy preferences have not prevailed. In part this testifies to the power in American politics of the Supreme Court and its interpretation of the Constitution. In part, too, it testifies to the low degree of salience these issues have for most Americans. In part, however, it reflects a parallel deadlock in

Congress and in American politics that results from the sharp division between Democrats and Republicans about how to respond to rising levels of receipts and expenditures. The result is a stalemate born of deadlock both in the immediate politics of campaign finance and in the broader political environment that surrounds them. The result is an extraordinarily complex politics of campaign finance, which we will turn to in Chapter 12.

9

The Fifty States: Unknown Experiences

Because their political institutions, history, traditions, and politics differ greatly, the 50 states are the curse of any commentary about American politics. The many ways in which they raise and use campaign resources are no greater cause for comfort. Legislative races in some states can be run successfully for hundreds of dollars; in California it is not unusual for them to cost hundreds of thousands of dollars. Moreover, no two of the states have the same set of statutory regulations; indeed they differ widely on virtually every possible aspect of regulation. Some states, for example, put contribution limits on corporate PACs, while others do not; two states do not even permit corporations to form PACs. And to complete the frustration, the 50 states differ immensely in the amount of data they collect and make available. The nation's most populous state, California, has one of the most extensive and effective disclosure statutes and publishes some of the most useful data on campaign finance. The nation's second most populous state, New York, issues no aggregate data at all on campaign receipts or expenditures in its campaigns.

When one turns to campaign finance in local elections, discouragement yields to despair. Expenditures in those campaigns are usually unreported and unregulated. Newspapers do carry occasional stories of expenditure levels, but generally only when there is a whiff of scandal or impropriety to spice up the story. We thus have only highly scattered reports about very atypical activities from the cities and counties of the country. It is a circumstance that thwarts even modest description and puts analysis out of the question.

In making the analytical leap from congressional-presidential finance to that of the states, there is another danger: the false assumption that state and local finance is set in the same kind of campaign environment. But all of the revolutions in campaigning, in campaign technology, and in campaign management have filtered down to local elections very unevenly. Most candidates for state legislatures do not take polls and do not hire campaign consultants; moreover, they cannot efficiently use the mass media in legislative districts that are only slivers of radio and TV markets. Old-fashioned door-to-door canvasing and "literature drops," even local meetings and rallies, are much more typical of their campaigns. Moreover, their limited visibility and name recognition make it hard for them to raise money in the new ways. In short, the older modes of campaigning often result in older and more modest systems of finance.

There are also important *governmental* differences among the states and between the national government and the states. There is, for example, a special campaign finance in some states associated with popular votes on initiatives, referenda, and recalls. There are also elections in the states for judges and administrative department heads — attorneys general and state treasurers, for instance — that breed (perhaps) their own patterns of getting and spending. Campaign finance in the states also varies with the role of particular public officials in the making of important public policy. Some commentators have suggested that the diminution of congressional responsibility in areas such as social welfare during the Reagan years — the "new" new federalism — may raise the stakes in state legislative politics. If policy-making power flows to the states, so will money seeking to pick candidates with congenial policy goals.

I. The Contours of State Campaign Finance

Since the middle 1970s, the curve of state electoral spending has matched the growth of spending in congressional campaigns. Herbert Alexander estimates that spending for campaigns for statewide office and state legislative seats in the 50 states rose from $120 million in 1976 to $325 million in 1984.[1] The comparison of these totals with the rising curve of congressional campaign costs reveals a striking similarity (Figure 9-1). The sums are similar, and so, roughly, are the slopes of the curves. If one adds the congressional data for 1978 and 1982 ($195 million and $342 millions), there will be slight off-year bulges in it. To look at the comparison another way, in 1984 the cost of the campaigns of 2036 assorted candidates for Congress amounted to almost $50 million more than the sums spent on the many thousands of races for executive and legislative office in the 50 states that year. But the most important point remains the similar lines of growth, offering at least one piece of evidence for a single growth dynamic in both instances.

These are aggregate totals, though, and they conceal enormous diversity among the 50 states. What evidence we have strongly suggests that expenditure levels are higher in California than in any of the other states. In 1986, for example, all of the candidates for the two houses of the state legislature spent $56.3 million in primary and general election campaigns; that total was more than one-eighth the cost of all congressional elections in the same year ($450 million). The cost per vote cast for the seats in the California Assembly was $3.20 in 1986; for the U.S. House of Representatives in the same year it was $4.59. Indeed, levels of spending in California legislative races are so high that a private commission investigating California campaign finance in 1985 proposed a spending limit (attached to partial public funding) of $375,000 for the Assembly, a figure well above the average for a seat in the U.S. House of Representatives.[2]

[1]Herbert E. Alexander, *Financing the 1976 Election* (Washington, D.C.: CQ Press, 1979), 167; and Herbert E. Alexander and Brian A. Haggerty, *Financing the 1984 Election* (Lexington, Mass.: Lexington, 1987), 83. Alexander's estimate for 1980 is $265 million; *Financing the 1980 Election* (Lexington, Mass.: Lexington, 1983), 104.

[2]California Commission on Campaign Financing, *The New Gold Rush: Financing California's Legislative Campaigns* (Los Angeles: Center for Responsive

FIGURE 9-1
The Rise of Spending in Congressional Campaigns and in Campaigns for State Offices, 1976–1986

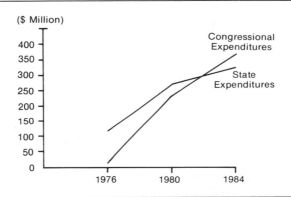

Sources: The sources of the estimates of state campaign spending are recorded in footnote 1.

Since California is the most populous of the 50 states (1980 census: 23,668,049, or more than 10 percent of the nation's population) and the third largest state (after Alaska and Texas), it is not surprising that it leads in campaign spending.[3] But size and population by themselves do not fully explain the sheer magnitude of the California totals. Perhaps one needs to look at levels of affluence and political traditions and cultures. The California Commission on Campaign Financing — the private commission referred to previously — attributes the sharp rise in new spending levels primarily to the use of sophisticated direct-mail campaigns organized by political consultants and supported by the usual apparatus of polls, computers, and message strategists. It may well be the case that California candidates are much further into a form of the new campaigning than are those of the

Government, 1985). It is one of the most comprehensive surveys of a single state's campaign finance available. The Commission is described in the foreword to its report as a "bipartisan, non-profit, private organization funded by the Weingart Foundation of Los Angeles."

[3]To look at the matter another way, the 80 seats in the California Assembly represent an average of 296,101 people; the 435 members of the U.S. House represent an average of 520,803.

TABLE 9-1
Expenditures of Candidates for Lower Houses of Six State Legislatures, 1978–1984°

	1978–80			1982–1984		
	Expenditures	Cost/ Seat	Expends/ Resident	Expenditures	Cost/ Seat	Expends/ Resident
California	$24,845,619	$310,570	$1.05	$30,752,440	$384,406	$1.20
Florida	4,336,209	36,150	.44	7,634,878	63,624	.70
Minnesota	1,818,225	13,569	.45	3,104,182	23,166	.75
Missouri	1,479,406	9,076	.30	1,707,016	10,472	.34
New Jersey	2,532,268	63,307	.34	2,671,499	66,787	.36
Wisconsin	1,307,570	13,208	.28	2,178,591	22,006	.46

°The data are inevitably not fully comparable. The problems are these: All of the totals are for 1980 and 1984 with two exceptions; those from Florida are for 1978 and 1982, and those from New Jersey are from 1979 and 1983. All of the totals with one exception are for the primary and general election; the data from New Jersey are for general election only. The Wisconsin data are for major party, general election candidates only.

other states, but this explanation still begs the question of how they get the money for it in the first place. And that brings one back to hunches about affluence; a voluntaristic fund-raising culture; a communication-centered political culture; and a tolerance, if not expectation, of long and lavish campaigning.

A comparison of legislative campaign costs in six different states suggests the range of those costs, even after one has controlled for the size of the legislature and for the population of the state (Table 9-1) — and even after one makes allowances for the different ways in which the states define and aggregate their data. California is clearly the outlier, although a simple control for population reduces the differences sharply. Most important, there is a comforting similarity, California aside, to the figures of expenditure per resident for the other states; and that similarity would be even greater if primary data for New Jersey were included.[4]

[4]That "anomaly" in the data (and others) is explained in the long footnote in Table 9-1. There is also a structural reason for the jump in Minnesota totals between 1980 and 1984; the state legislature raised the expenditure limits that are a part of the state's public funding program.

As in the campaigns for Congress, incumbent members of the state legislatures enjoy tremendous and growing advantages. Again, one begins with the case of California — where incumbents running for reelection in 1984 won 98 percent of the time. In that same election, incumbents in the aggregate had a 14 to 1 funding advantage over challengers. (In the same year the advantage was only a bit more than 2 to 1 among major party general election candidates for the U.S. House of Representatives.) The ad hoc California Commission reports

> In 1976 the median Assembly incumbent spent about $25,000 in the general election, while the median challenger spent $9,400, a differential ratio of nearly 3-to-1. This ratio increased to 5-to-1 in 1978, 8-to-1 in 1980, 9-to-1 in 1982, and 14-to-1 in 1984. While incumbents' expenditures jumped four-fold from $25,000 to $115,000, challengers' expenditures actually decreased — from $9,400 in 1976 to $8,500 in 1984 . . .[5]

(These totals do not include expenditures in the primaries, that is in the first 18 months of the two-year election cycle; if they did, the margin would be greater than 14 to 1!) It is an incumbency advantage that results at least in part from some skillful districting that has created a great number of safe districts for one party or the other.

That dominance of the incumbents in California is related very directly to PAC expenditures in the state. PACs and businesses account for the great majority of the receipts of legislative candidates; in 1986, for instance, they accounted for more than 80 percent of the receipts of incumbents in the Assembly and about a third of the much, much smaller sums their challengers raised.[6] The nexus of PAC giving and incumbent strength, already apparent in the U.S. House, is far closer in California. It invites speculation whether once again today's reality in California will be the nation's future.

With the success of incumbent candidates so absolute, competitiveness in California legislative politics — at least in

---

[5] *The New Gold Rush*, 31.
[6] Since corporations and businesses can give directly to candidates — and do so — in California, the total here includes them as well as the state's definition of PACs.

Assembly elections — centers very heavily on the open seats. It is in the open seat campaigns, therefore, that one sees the greatest flows of money. The record for the California Assembly was set in 1986 in an open seat race in Sacramento in which the candidates in the primary and the general election spent a total of $2.4 million. The Democratic loser was assisted by total contributions and transfers of $725,000 from the Speaker of the Assembly, Willie Brown.

While incumbent superiority may not be so dramatic elsewhere, it is unmistakable. Edward Olson reports that incumbents running for reelection to the Texas House in 1980 spent an average of $31,000 while their challengers on the average spent $10,000 less.[7] In the same year in Florida, Giles and Pritchard report these averages for candidates for the lower house:[8]

- Democratic incumbents: $41,595
- Republican incumbents: $38,958
- Democratic challengers: $19,055
- Republican challengers: $18,994
- Democratic open seat: $30,994
- Republican open seat: $23,389

In the state of Washington in 1982, incumbents in the House on the average outspent their challengers $22,286 to $12,972.

In other states, too, PACs demonstrate their preference for incumbents. It is apparently one of the great constants in PAC behavior. Eisenstein reports that PACs gave 75 percent of their money in Pennsylvania to incumbents in the 1982 campaigns.[9] Ruth Jones confirms the disproportionate PAC support of incumbents in a number of other states and adds a refinement to the point. In the states PACs are especially generous with the legisla-

---

[7]"Campaign Spending in Texas Legislative Elections," *Texas Journal of Political Studies*, vol. 6 (Winter 1983–84), 40–53.

[8]Micheal W. Giles and Anita Pritchard, "Campaign Expenditures and Legislative Elections in Florida," *Legislative Studies Quarterly*, vol. 10 (Feb. 1985), 71–88.

[9]James Eisenstein, "Patterns of Campaign Finance in Pennsylvania's 1982 Legislative Elections," paper delivered at the annual meeting of the Pennsylvania Political Science Association (Mar. 31, 1984).

tive leadership.[10] That inclination doubtless reflects the fact that in many state legislatures the leadership is more powerful than it is the Congress.

The flow of PAC contributions to incumbents leads logically to the question of the full pattern of candidate receipts in the states. Again, for comparability among the states and with congressional finance, data on state legislative campaigns are the most appropriate. California is again the special case. In 1986, for example, the election receipts (in sums larger than $250) of all California legislative candidates for the two-year cycle came in these ways:

- 11.6 percent from individual contributors
- 62.6 percent from PACs and businesses
- 1.5 percent from the political parties
- 24.3 percent from other candidates and officeholders[11]

Since California permits businesses and corporations to make contributions directly without setting up PACs, that 62.6 percent figure is the best approximation of the federal definition of a PAC one can construct from California data. The enormous role that fund-raising by legislative leadership and caucuses plays is perhaps the most distinctive characteristic of legislative finance in California. It is reflected in the 24.3 percent above from other candidates and officeholders. While it is true that these figures record only the sources of contributions of $250 and above, it appears that six-sevenths of the candidates' receipts come in sums (or aggregates from the same source) of $250 or more; even if the missing seventh came heavily from individuals, the percentages would not be greatly changed.

The role of the many-faceted political parties in California legislative campaigns is best assessed by going back to the fuller data

[10]Ruth S. Jones, "Financing State Elections," in Michael J. Malbin, ed., *Money and Politics in the United States* (Chatham, N.J.: Chatham House, 1984), 189–190.

[11]The categories that the California Fair Political Practices Commission uses need some explanation. The "individual" category includes (as did FEC data until 1984) the contributions of the candidates. Money raised by legislative leaders and caucuses are included in the "candidates and officeholders" categories; thus the "party" category includes only the traditional state, county, and local party organizations.

for 1984. In that year the transfers from party leaders and caucuses within the legislature — led by Speaker Willie Brown's $1.4 million given to 17 candidates[12] — accounted for $4.4 million. These figures dwarf the sums the candidates receive from conventional party organization. In fact, the more traditional party committees outside the legislature contributed only $1.1 million in 1984.[13]

California legislative campaign finance is, therefore, largely an extension of incumbent legislative power and legislative party politics. It is a major instance of the triumph of the legislative party in American politics. Incumbents raise their own funds and those of their fellow partisans, much from PACs and much during the legislative session (and much in the first 18 months of the legislative cycle, the California "primary" period). There are few productive sources of funds outside of PACs and the legislative party. Individuals contribute relatively little, state legislative politics attracts few millionaires who will fund their own campaigns, and traditional party committees are not a major factor. Moreover, it is intrinsically a centralized system of finance; the 1985 study of the Commission on Campaign Financing calculates that in 1982 average winning candidates for the Assembly got 92 percent of their receipts over $100 from outside the legislative district.[14]

The patterns of receipts in the more populous states in the northeast quarter of the country, on the other hand, closely approximate those for congressional campaigns. In fact, they are uncannily similar. Eisenstein reports that in 1982 Pennsylvania legislative candidates received 47 percent of their receipts from individual contributions, 27 percent from PACs, 9 percent from the parties, 12 percent from candidates and their families, and the remaining 5 percent from miscellaneous sources.[15] Klemanski, reporting on a sample of Michigan legislative *winners*, describes a receipt pattern not unlike that for U.S. House winners. Over four election cycles (1978 through 1984), the winners received 51

[12]Speaker Brown gave $2.3 million to 41 candidates in 1982.
[13]*The New Gold Rush*, chap. 5.
[14]*The New Gold Rush*, 55.
[15]Eisenstein, "Patterns of Campaign Finance in Pennsylvania's 1982 Legislative Elections." The miscellaneous category includes interest earned, contributions from law firms, and transfers from other candidates.

percent of their money from PACs. (The 56 percent in 1984 compares with the 41 percent for the House winners in the same year.) Party sources contributed 6 percent over the same four cycles, and individual contributions the remaining 43 percent.[16] In 1983's elections in New Jersey, all of the legislative candidates took 27.4 percent of their receipts from PACs.[17] Finally, one should note that Pennsylvania and New Jersey place no statutory limit on any contributions to legislative candidates; Michigan on the other hand places limits on all, including a very restrictive limit of $250 and $450 on all contributions to candidates for the state House and Senate.

There are also abundant signs that PACs have increased their numbers and their influence in state legislative campaigns since the late 1970s. Klemanski finds that winners of seats in the Michigan House in 1978 got 41 percent of their campaign funds from PACs; by 1984 the PAC percentage had risen to 56 percent. In Missouri PACs accounted for 15.7 percent of all receipts of all legislative candidates in 1980; the percentage rose to 23.9 by 1984. Similarly, the number of PACs active in the states has grown sharply. Jones reports that the number of registered PACs jumped from 84 to 325 in New York between 1978 and 1984, more than quintupled in Arizona between 1974 and 1982, and increased by 400 percent in Louisiana from 1980 to 1983.[18] Official data mark the rise in Wisconsin from 217 in 1976 to 441 in 1982.

Finally, legislative campaign finance in the states has one characteristic that sets it apart from finance in congressional elections: the importance of the primaries in some states. Especially in the one-party dominant states, the effective competition takes place in the primaries, whether as a reflection of factionalism in the dominant party or of a free-wheeling candidate-centered

[16]John S. Klemanski, "PACs, Parties, and Individuals: Direct Contributions to Michigan Legislators, 1978–1984," a paper given at the annual meeting of the Midwest Political Science Association (Apr. 10–12, 1986). Klemanski's percentages for PAC, party, and individual contributions add to 100 percent; he has eliminated other sources of receipts (e.g., transfers and interest income), but candidates' use of their own funds is apparently included with individual contributions.

[17]Data from official state sources; data also limited to general election candidates and to receipts of $100 and more.

[18]Ruth S. Jones, "State and Federal Legislative Campaigns: Same Song, Different Verse," *Election Politics*, vol. 3 (Summer 1986), 8–12.

politics. Understandably, money flows fast and deep in the primaries in such states. In Missouri, for example, 58.7 percent of all legislative candidate receipts were in the campaign treasuries before the date of the primary in 1980. In 1984 the same percentage was 54.9.[19]

II. Money in the Nonlegislative Campaigns

Among the rest of the state campaigns, only those for governorships offer much of a basis for comparison. Spending by all gubernatorial candidates in a number of states in the 1980s is roughly comparable to spending for Senate seats (Table 9-2), and appropriately so, since the constituencies are the same. The gubernatorial totals are higher in most cases, but that can be attributed to the greater primary activity in the races for governor. In Missouri, for example, 10 candidates spent $4,413,750 in the 1984 primaries, while the two major party candidates spent only $2,600,942 in the general election campaign.

At the level of individual campaigns (including both primary and general election campaigns), Mario Cuomo spent approximately $5.3 million winning the governorship of New York in 1982. As it turns out, however, he was a long way from setting records. According to Thad Beyle, the most expensive individual campaign for a governorship between 1977 and 1985 was waged by the man Cuomo beat: Republican Lewis Lehrman who spent $14 million. John D. Rockefeller IV, a Democrat, placed second by spending $11.6 million in 1980 to win in far less populous West Virginia. The third most expensive candidacy was that of Democrat Edwin Edwards who won in Louisiana in 1983 with a campaign costing $10.2 million. In the eight years under study,

[19]The entire issue is, of course, primarily one of understanding the reasons for more effective primary challengers in state legislative races, for on the face of it one would expect the ability of incumbents to raise money to diminish primary competition. As the old saying goes, we need more research on the problem. For a comment on it and more data, see Ruth S. Jones's article in Malbin, ed., *Money and Politics in the United States*, 177–178. Finally, in the period from the general election campaign, there is fundamental ambiguity; receipts and expenditures are simply "early" funds, whether or not they have been raised and spent explicitly in a primary battle.

Beyle identified 37 gubernatorial campaigns costing more than $4 million in constant 1985 dollars. For 1986 he calculated an average major party candidacy as costing about $7 million.[20]

TABLE 9-2
Total Expenditures of Gubernatorial Candidates in Selected States in the 1980s

State	Year	Total Spent
Arkansas	1984	$1,944,113
California	1986	22,464,657
Florida	1982	4,222,742
Massachusetts	1982	7,718,062
Missouri	1984	7,014,692
New Jersey	1985	10,459,473
New York	1982	23,558,518
Oregon	1982	1,933,604
Wyoming	1982	825,770

Source: Data for California, Missouri, and New Jersey from official state reports; others from Thad L. Beyle, "Governor's Chair now costs $7 million," *State Government News,* vol. 29 (Oct. 1986), 21–23.

Beyond the data on expenditures in gubernatorial campaigns, one would like to know something about the sources of receipts. Unfortunately, data on receipts are harder to come by; many states do not, apparently, aggregate and publish such data. Missouri reports that individual contributors accounted for 44 percent of the receipts of major party general election candidates for the governorship in both 1980 and 1984; PAC contributions, plus those directly from corporations, unions, and associations, accounted for 33 percent in 1980 and 39 percent in 1984. Wisconsin reports individual contributions around the 50 percent mark, too, in the 1980s; but its matching requirement for public funding provides an extra incentive for them. In both states the contributions of party committees have been well under the 5 percent mark. Of the methods and devices of fundraising, we know even less (but for an exception, see box.)

[20]Thad Beyle, "Governor's chair now costs $7 million," *State Government News,* vol. 29 (Oct. 1986), 21–23.

RAISING MONEY IN MASSACHUSETTS

In focusing on national politics and national campaign finance, it is too easy to overlook the fascinating local variations and innovations in American politics. A 1986 report from Boston describes the very individual way in which the governor of Massachusetts, Michael Dukakis, raises money for his campaigns.

> On a warm Monday last July, the carpenters' union organized a fund-raiser for Gov. Dukakis at the IBEW union hall in Dorchester. Some 600 carpenters from several union locals paid $10 each to hear the governor, in splendid contrast to the way labor usually helps finance its friends. . . .
>
> In Massachusetts, Dukakis won't take PAC money. But by distaining PACs, he also converts good government into smart politics. Dukakis is happy to take campaign money from unions — or human service workers, or other interest groups — he just insists that the money involve voters directly. "We're not running away from unions," says a Dukakis strategist. "Far from it. We are running away from money that doesn't have personal commitment behind it." . . .
>
> Instead of identifying potential contributors through mass mailings, Dukakis uses small fund-raising events, slowly building up a base of small donors. At the state level, most candidates do not bother with $10 and $20 fund-raisers, but Dukakis has adroitly used them to build a computer bank of 40,000 proven backers, 7,000 of whom were newly recruited in 1986. About half of them have personally attended some campaign event. Most of them donate more than once.
>
> —*Bob Kuttner, "The Dukakis money-raising machine,"* Boston Globe *(Sept. 15, 1986).*

Among campaigns for other state offices, we know the most about those of judges, largely because the business of campaigning and financing campaigns for elections raises serious issues of judicial ethics for the bar and legal scholars. To begin, all evidence we have points to levels of campaign expenditures by judges and their challengers that are below those of other campaigns; in most instances they are in five figures, although campaigns for state supreme courts do get into six. (There are exceptions, of course; the campaigns "pro" and "con" the attempt to remove Chief Justice Rose Bird and two other justices from the California Supreme Court in 1986 spent a total of $6.6 million.[21]) The funds tend to come primarily from two sources: the candidate and other attorneys and law firms. Individual contributors (who are not lawyers) would appear to be the third most important source. In these campaigns one also sees the major attempt at nonpublic regulation of campaign finance. In Dade County, Florida, for example, the Bar Association solicits contributions to a single fund — and discourages direct lawyerly contributions to individual candidates; the fund is then allocated to county judicial candidates in differing sums that reflect the Association's assessment of their qualifications.[22]

The rest is virtually unknown. Few scholars seem determined to document the campaigns of the attorneys general, public utilities commissioners, and state auditors around the country.[23] Ballot measures — initiative, referenda, and recall elections — do get some attention. And those campaigns are very likely most expensive in California, both by reason of its population and its tradition of direct democracy. In 1984, for instance, Californians found six initiatives on the ballot; the campaigns on all sides of all

[21]One committee alone, Californians to Defeat Rose Bird, reported spending $4.2 million. But *caveat lector!* Many of these committees raised their money by direct-mail appeals, and they show a major part of their spending for marketing advice, list rental, printing, postage, direct-mail management, and computer rentals. They would appear, in other words, to operate and spend in ways similar to those of the conservative nonconnected PACs that report large independent expenditures to the FEC.

[22]All of the data in this paragraph, with the exception of the totals on the Bird campaign, come from Roy A. Schotland, "Elective Judges' Campaign Financing: Are State Judges' Robes the Emperor's Clothes of American Democracy?," *Journal of Law and Politics*, vol. 2 (Spring 1985), 57–167. Any serious inquiry into judicial campaign finance begins with Schotland's long article. See also Marlene A. Nicholson and Bradley S. Weiss, "Funding judicial campaigns in the Circuit Court of Cook County," *Judicature*, vol. 70 (June–July 1986), 17–25.

[23]One exception: James Eisenstein and Susan J. Pappalardo, "Patterns of Campaign Finance in Pennsylvania's 1984 Statewide General Elections," paper delivered at the annual meeting of the Pennsylvania Political Science Association (Apr. 20, 1985).

six cost an aggregate $32.2 million.[24] Campaigns on five measures in 1986 cost a grand total of $22.5 million.

Finally, it is probably worth considering a campaign expenditure one does *not* find very often in the states: independent spending either by individuals or groups. Their low levels or virtual absence is not surprising in a state such as California, since corporations and labor unions may contribute directly and since there is no monetary limit on any contributions to candidates.[25] But why are there none in the states in which campaign finance is heavily regulated? In truth we don't know that there are none; one can only say that we are not aware of any. In some states independent expenditures need not be reported; in other states (Minnesota is one) they are reported by individuals and groups making them, but those individual reports are nowhere brought together in aggregate totals or reports. So, whatever the reason, independent spending in the states remains a great unknown.

III. Public Funding in the States

Like many other terms of ordinary political use, "public funding" has a spurious specificity. It is, unfortunately, not like measles or the chicken pox — not a simple case of whether one has it or doesn't have it. Almost half of the American states have some way of using the authority of the state to channel money, directly or indirectly, into the waging of campaigns for public office. They differ very much, however, in the ways and directness with which they do so — all the way from direct campaign subsidies to indirect forms of aid such as tax deductions for contributions to candidates. Conventional political semantics, arbitrary though they may be, generally limits phrases such as "public funding" or "public financing" to the direct forms of aid.

In other words, one can arrange state programs along a continuum from the greatest degree of state aid to campaigns to the

---

[24]For additional data on the campaigns surrounding direct democracy, see Ruth S. Jones in Malbin's, *Money and Politics in the United States*, 204–208. See Betty H. Zisk, *Money, Media, and the Grass Roots* (Beverly Hills, Cal.: Sage, 1987) for a study of the politics of ballot campaigns and their financing in four states.

[25]On independent spending in California legislative races, see *The New Gold Rush*, 157.

least. In considerable part that grading reflects the size and the directness of the subvention. While no state program funds a campaign to the full expenditure limit — as does the federal program for the presidential candidates of the major parties after the conventions — at least two come close: Michigan and New Jersey give major party candidates in the gubernatorial elections sums that approximate 60 percent of their general election receipts. On the other hand, the state "benefit" is far less substantial when it is a tax deduction and thus an "incentive" to contributors who may or may not have given money to a candidate without it or when it is merely an opportunity to pay an extra dollar in taxes for the party of one's choice.

We turn first, then, to those programs that are conventionally thought of as "public funding" for campaigns and campaigners. They fall into two groups:

● Three states fund both legislative races and some statewide executive campaigns (always including the governor): Hawaii, Minnesota, and Wisconsin.

● Five additional states fund only races for statewide executive office (again, always including governor): Florida, Massachusetts, Michigan, Montana, and New Jersey. Florida's funding will not begin until the campaigns for election in 1990.[26]

In seven of these states — Montana is the exception — the acceptance of public funding brings with it the obligation to observe statutory expenditure limits in the campaign. In Montana and Massachusetts, the funding program is financed by an "add-on" to the state income tax; sums available are, therefore, relatively small. The other six states fund theirs by an income tax checkoff (in which the taxpayer does not pay any additional tax),

---

[26]These categorizations of state programs and the ones that follow rely on the following sources: Herbert E. Alexander and Mike Eberts, *Public Financing of State Elections: A Data Book on Tax-Assisted Funding of Political Parties and Candidates in Twenty States* (Los Angeles: Citizens' Research Foundation: 1986); California Commission on Campaign Financing, *The New Gold Rush: Financing California's Legislative Campaigns* (Los Angeles: Center for Responsive Government, 1985), chap. 10; James A. Palmer and Edward D. Feigenbaum, *Campaign Finance Law 86* (Washington, D.C.: National Clearinghouse on Election Administration, 1986); and Sandra K. Schneider, ed., *Campaign Finance, Ethics & Lobby Law Blue Book 1986–87* (Lexington, Ky.: Council of State Governments, 1986).

direct state appropriation, or a combination of the two. Florida alone of these states has no income tax and will therefore rely solely on appropriations from general state funds. Beyond those two main areas of relative agreement among the eight programs, the differences among them are rampant.[27]

For example:

● Some states, but only some, require the candidates to raise certain amounts of money in certain ways before they become eligible for public funding — in the same general way that presidential candidates do before the conventions.

● Some states fund primary campaigns; others do not. The funding of them is widely believed to lead to an increase in the number of primary candidates; Michigan funded a total of 10 Democrats and Republicans in its gubernatorial primary in 1982, and in 1986 four Democratic contestants each received between $440,000 and $650,000 for the primary race for the Democratic gubernatorial nomination in New Jersey.

● Some states give substantial sums of money; others do not; Hawaii's grants of $50 to legislative candidates contrasts sharply with averages more than 60 times that figure in Minnesota ($3245 in 1984 for campaigns for the state's lower house).

● Some states make grants of fixed sums, while others disperse according to long and arcane formulae. And while most states fund only races at the state level, Hawaii's program channels money to local elections as well.

Ten additional states — Alabama, California, Idaho, Iowa,

---

[27]Two other states have had a brief history of public financing of campaigns in the aftermath of Watergate and the wave of reform it ignited. Oklahoma enacted a program of financing of both parties and campaigns from a tax checkoff fund in 1978; it was never put into operation because of an inconclusive constitutional impasse; see *Democratic Party v. Estep*, 652 P.2d 271 (1982). Maryland had a small program of aiding candidates based on a state income tax add-on, but Maryland ended it in 1982 because the fund was too small to finance the program. It has since revived the program for the 1990 gubernatorial election as a one-time way of spending the $1.6 million that has accumulated in the fund over the years. Finally, another state, Rhode Island, will apparently make its debut in public funding of candidates; in 1986 the voters of the state approved a constitutional amendment directing the general assembly to provide a program of public funding for "campaigns for governor and such other general officers as the general assembly shall specify."

Kentucky, Maine, North Carolina, Rhode Island, Utah, and Virginia — have programs of public funding for the political parties. They, too, vary in generosity, depending primarily on whether they are funded by income tax checkoffs or add-ons and on the sums that can be designated.[28] The particular amounts that a party receives may also be affected by the party preferences of the participating taxpayers and/or by state distribution formulas. North Carolina divides its funds by the ratio of party registrations; the Democrats get about 70 percent. The other states permit taxpayers to channel money into the party of their choice; and as of late 1985 Republicans were leading only in Idaho, Iowa, and Utah.[29]

Public funding for the parties, however, is not necessarily public funding for the candidates and campaigns. None of the states mandate that the funds be spent on candidates or campaigns, even though several set up intraparty procedures for doing so. While the states permit the spending of public funds directly on campaigns, there may be statutory restrictions on doing so, the most common being a prohibition against supporting any candidate in a primary battle. In general, we really have no idea how much of these funds go to fund campaigning, either directly or indirectly. And when it does eventuate in party contributions to candidates, we do not know the extent to which it replaces other monies the parties might have given. To put the point another way, we know that some of these funds go to support party organization activities and administrative costs; we do not know how much does not.[30]

Finally, 18 states also grant either tax deductions or tax credits (or a choice between the two) for certain contributions given to candidates or parties. The size of the deduction or credit varies, but in 10 states it is $100. (Twelve of those 18 states are states that already have public funding either of candidates or parties.) These tax provisions provide incentives for individuals to make campaign contributions, but as a public benefit they fall outside

---

[28]California provides for a surcharge of up to $25 per taxpayer; the other states limit generosity to one or two dollars.

[29]Alexander and Eberts, *Public Financing of State Elections*, 8.

[30]On state funding of the parties, see Ruth S. Jones, "State Public Campaign Finance: Implications for Partisan Politics," *American Journal of Political Science*, vol. 25 (May 1981), 342–361.

of usual definitions of public funding. For awhile, the most generous of all the state incentives was that of Alaska. Not having an income tax to which to attach a deduction or credit, the state embarked in the 1980s on a program of making direct refunds of up to $100 to contributors to candidates for national, state, or local office. In 1982 Alaska returned $1.3 million to political contributors; fiscal problems forced the state to abandon the plan shortly thereafter.

Two points about such state incentives to contribute are worth noting, however. First, pressure may build over the next few years to repeal those credits and deductions as the states try to bring their income tax laws (and tax return forms) into agreement with the new federal law. Second, at least two of these states — Hawaii and Minnesota — require candidates to agree to expenditure limits before contributions made to them are deductible or creditable. It is an avenue to expenditure limits that does not necessarily involve direct public funding; so far its constitutionality remains untested.

It is the direct funding of candidates, however, that has the most important and visible impact on the system of campaign finance. And to assess that impact it is important to consider two fundamental aspects of the operation: the size of the subentions and the percentage of candidates choosing to accept them.

The amounts of aid to candidates depend both on the amounts of money raised for the special funds and the statutory formulas for dispersing them. States that raise funds by income tax checkoff average a participation around 20 percent; those that depend on add-ons (i.e., surcharges) average between one percent and two percent participation.[31] (Obviously, too, there are funding implications in the legislative decision to permit checkoffs of two rather than a single dollar.) One add-on state (Maryland) has already abandoned its public funding as a result of failure to raise the necessary sums, and two others (Massachusetts and Montana) make payments to candidates that can only be described as modest. Massachusetts in 1982 offered a maximum

---

[31]The state funds and differences in citizen participation in them are explored by Jack L. Noragon, "Political Finance and Political Reform: The Experience with State Income Tax Checkoffs," *American Political Science Review*, vol. 75 (September 1981), 667–687.

of $250,000 to gubernatorial candidates, in contrast to the New Jersey maximum of $1.2 million in the year before.

Montana in fact provides something of a "natural experiment" on the different revenue implications of the fund-raising alternatives, having shifted from checkoff to add-on. The participation rate on its last year of checkoff in 1978 was 16.4 percent; and in 1979, the first year of the add-on option, the percent was 1.5. The new Florida program, the first in a state without an income tax, will of necessity be funded entirely by legislative appropriations.[32]

Since public funding must be voluntarily chosen, the art of drafting a state program lies in part in providing incentives for acceptance. The trick is in making sure than the subsidy is not too low and that the spending limit is not too high. Certainly the $50 subvention of Hawaii is not large enough to convince many candidates to accept spending limits, and one can only suppose that the legislators who passed the legislation knew that. In 1982 only 16 legislative candidates accepted public funds, and in 1984 only two.

Before the 1982 elections, Minnesota conducted *its* little experiment in increasing acceptance rates. After it raised the size of the public subsidies and doubled the attendant expenditure limits, the acceptance rate among legislative candidates climbed sharply (Table 9-3). The Minnesota experience also offers some evidence on the frequent assertion that philosophical convictions about the proper role of government prevent Republican candidates from accepting public funding. In the period before the raising of the spending limits, Democrats did accept public funding at a rate significantly higher than did Republicans. In the surge of participation in 1982, Republicans began to accept public funds in about the same proportion as Democrats. In 1984, however, participation dropped back somewhat in Minnesota, suggesting that rising levels of receipts and expenditures made the constraints of the system less attractive.

Just as interesting is a comparison of legislative acceptances between legislative candidates in Wisconsin and Minnesota in

---

[32]The data of this and the following paragraph come from Alexander and Eberts, *Public Financing of State Elections.*

TABLE 9-3
Candidate Acceptance of Public Funds by Major Party Candidates: Minnesota House, 1980–1984°

	1980	1982	1984
I. Democrats			
% Accepting public funds	83.7%	96.9%	84.3%
Avg. amount received	$2,190	$3,168	$3,271
Avg. total expenditure	5,825	8,834	11,181
Avg. total expenditure of			
nonfunded cands.	12,338	21,144	12,926
II. Republicans			
% Accepting public funds	50.4%	83.2%	75.2%
Avg. amount received	$1,630	$2,021	$3,296
Avg. total expenditure	5,540	9,669	9,754
Avg. total expenditure of			
nonfunded cands.	9,005	17,099	18,844

°Includes only candidates for the general election.

the same years. The two states share similar post-Progressive political traditions as well as similar populations and square mileage. Yet their participation rates differ; in 1982 only 61 percent of Wisconsin's legislative candidates opted for public funds against the much higher rates in Minnesota. Two scholars of that difference report that there are explanations beyond the higher expenditure limits in Minnesota; they single out three other provisions in the Wisconsin program that distinguish it from Minnesota's:

● The requirement that candidates raise a certain sum in individual contributions in order to be eligible for public funds.
● The provision that reduces the public funds candidates are eligible to receive by the sum of any PAC money they accept.
● The prohibition against paying public sums to candidates without major party competition.[33]

[33]Elizabeth King and David Wegge, *The Rules Are Never Neutral: Public Funds in Minnesota and Wisconsin Legislative Elections,* paper delivered at the annual meetings of the Midwest Political Science Association (Chicago: Apr. 12–14, 1984), as summarized in *New Gold Rush,* 184.

TABLE 9-4
Candidates Receiving Public Funds in Gubernatorial Campaigns in Michigan
(1986) and New Jersey (1985)

	Michigan	New Jersey
I. Primary		
# Democratic candidates	1	4
# Republican candidates	3	1
Avg. public money/candidate	$366,462	$594,511
% Receipts from public $$	39.5%	58.7%
II. General Election		
Public $$/major party cand.	$750,000	$1,285,000°
% Receipts from public $$	59.6%	60.3%

°The candidates received slightly different sums; Kean, the Republican incumbent, received $1,287,145; Shapiro, the Democrat, received $1,281,083.

One can perhaps put the matter another way. The Wisconsin public funding statutes aim more than Minnesota's to affect the nature of nonpublic campaign funding and, in doing so, sacrifice some degree of candidate acceptance.

Only in campaigns for the governorship in two states, Michigan and New Jersey, does public funding in the states become the dominant source of campaign receipts (Table 9-4), both in the primary and the general election campaigns. In Michigan in 1986, one should note, one losing Republican candidate in the primary (Chrysler by name!) did not accept public funding and reported receipts of $3.3 million. If one includes him in the total primary receipts, then Michigan funding accounts only for 21 percent of all candidates' primary intake. Neither Minnesota nor Wisconsin fund primary campaigns for gubernatorial aspirants, and their level of support in the general election falls far short of that in Michigan and New Jersey. In 1982, for example, public money — $241,551 apiece — accounted for 26.5 percent of the receipts of the major party candidates in Wisconsin. In 1986 payments from public monies ($758,625) accounted for 22 percent of the receipts of the Democratic and Republican general election candidates in Minnesota.

As one might expect, gubernatorial candidates are less likely to accept smaller grants of public money. In the general elections of 1978, 1982, and 1986 in Minnesota, the Democratic candidate (Rudy Perpich in all three elections) accepted public money; Republicans declined in 1978 and 1982. (Failure to accept it and the spending limits did not prevent Republican Al Quie from winning in 1978.) In Wisconsin both candidates declined in 1978, but both accepted in 1982 and 1986. In Michigan, on the other hand, both candidates took public funds in the same three years; and in New Jersey candidates of both major parties accepted public financing in 1977, 1981, and 1985.

Naturally, too, Michigan, Minnesota, New Jersey, and Wisconsin offer the best evidence of the impact public funding has had. Some of the consequences seem to affirm the goals of the reformers; others, in effect, confirm the fears and objections of their opponents. Unhappily, one can offer only snippets of data and impression; extensive scholarship seems to have bypassed the public funding experiments in the states.

Altering Patterns of Receipts. When public funding assumes a major part of receipts and expenditures — such as it does in gubernatorial elections in New Jersey and Michigan — the effect on patterns of receipts needs little comment. If the goal has been to free candidates and public officials from the importunings of private contributors, the goal perforce has been substantially reached. When the public funds amount to only 20 or 30 percent of candidate receipts — as they do in Minnesota and Wisconsin's legislative and gubernatorial campaigns — the effect is less clear. In Wisconsin, for example, the pattern of receipts remains not unlike the pattern of receipts we see in congressional funding. In 1984 the receipts of all Wisconsin legislative candidates came from these sources: 50 percent from individual contributors, 23 percent from public funds, 17 percent from PACs, 8 percent from party committees, and 2 percent from other miscellaneous sources. Aside from the effect of public funding, the percentage of receipts coming from PACs obviously has been depressed by Wisconsin's plan that discounts the size of public grants to "offset" receipts from PACs.

Depressing the Rising Curve of Campaign Spending. There can be little doubt that well-crafted expenditure limits can depress the growth of campaign spending, just as they have in the case of American presidential campaigns. The secret is in finding a spending limit that will "depress" without frightening away candidates willing to choose public funds. One accomplishes little with a program in which only the hopeless cases among the challengers opt for the funds and the spending limits. It is not obvious, however, that such a restraining formula is easy to find; between 1980 and 1984 campaigns for both the Minnesota House and the U.S. House increased in cost by an identical 74 percent.

Fostering Competition. Arguments for and against public funding are most often joined on this issue: the proponents hope that public funding will open the way for new candidates, while the opponents argue that it will further advantage the already advantaged incumbents. The evidence, too, is divided. The availability of public money in the primaries apparently has increased competition; not only do the numbers from Michigan and New Jersey's gubernatorial politics suggest so, but so do close political observers in those states. But on the other hand, the spending limits in general elections may very well protect incumbents and deny their opponents the funds needed to overcome incumbency. That case has been made, for instance, in New Jersey's gubernatorial elections.[34] The conclusion may very well be that public funding both fosters *and* inhibits competition — the availability of new money encourages new candidates, while the spending limits make it harder for them to defeat incumbents. Like so many conclusions about state campaign finance, it will have to do until scholars address the problem.

[34]Both the New Jersey Election Law Enforcement Commission and the New Jersey legislature have sought to remove spending limits in campaigns for the governorship in view of public funding and the limits on contributions. In 1980 Governor Brenden Byrne vetoed a bill that would have done just that. For a fuller discussion of these events and the question of the impact of spending limits on general election competitiveness, see Alexander and Eberts, *Public Financing of State Elections*, 8–9.

Assisting One Party or the Other. Legislative majorities have been accused of assisting their own party by creating programs in which the taxpayers designate funds for one party or the other. The majority party usually ends up with larger checks. But in the states that fund candidates rather than parties, only Minnesota draws from party designated funds.[35] Given the distribution of party loyalties in the state, there is more money available to Democratic (i.e., Democratic-Farmer-Labor) candidates. In recent years the Democratic designations have been between 15 and 33 percent above those of the Republicans. The other states draw from a single general fund and make no distinction between Democratic and Republican candidates.

Candidate choice of public funds has been clearly Democratic. That is, state upon state records a higher percentage of Democrats than Republicans opting for public funds. Thus, in the aggregate more Democrats see public funding, even with the accompanying spending restrictions, to their strategic advantage. Republicans, on the other hand, are either philosophically less comfortable with public subsidies or less willing to accept the spending restrictions that come with public funding.[36]

IV. The Web of Regulation in the States

Since the Supreme Court's rulings apply to the states via the Fourteenth Amendment, the limits on campaign expenditures that the majority of states passed after Watergate fell within the effect of the *Buckley* decision in 1976. Only those spending limits attached as a condition to the voluntary acceptance of public funding could survive. "Regulation" in the states as in the

---

[35]Minnesota taxpayers, in fact, can check off funds to *either* a general fund or to one of the two partisan funds. To cope with distributing funds to candidates from such a complicated set of funds, the state's legislature devised a devilishly complicated disbursement formula that takes into account (inter alia) the dollars checked off in the candidate's district, the partisan preferences of those checking off, and the size of the vote cast for it in the last legislative election.

[36]On the general treatment of party advantage in the various kinds of public funding, both of candidates and parties, see Jones, "State Public Campaign Finance: Implications for Partisan Politics."

nation, therefore, became largely regulation of campaign contributions.[37]

Depending on how and what one counts, only about half of the states place limitations on some or all campaign contributions. Generalizations about them do not come easily, but a few are possible:

- All of the eight states with public funding of candidates have limits on contributions, and they tend to be among the most comprehensive and detailed of those limitations. (All but Montana, as I noted earlier, also have limits on expenditures which are a condition of getting public funds.)

- The 25 states with some limits on contributions are spread fairly evenly across the United States with one exception: there are no contribution limits in any of the seven Southwestern states (Arizona, California, Colorado, Nevada, New Mexico, Texas, and Utah). If one considers Oklahoma in the Southwest, there are limits in one of eight.

- When the state limits are fixed simply for campaigns for all offices, the limits tend to be set between $1000 and $5000 for individual, PAC, and party contributions. When they are specific to campaigns for various offices, the limits for legislative candidates tend to fall below $1000.

- Most of the states with limits on contributions enact a comprehensive set of limits that restrict most or all kinds of contributors. A few states limit only one kind; six, in fact, apparently limit only the size of contributions from individuals (Kentucky, Maryland, Massachusetts, New Hampshire, South Dakota, and Wyoming).

Most states treat loans as contributions; a few states with limits on contributions place none on loans; and a few distinguish between loans from financial institutions and loans from other sources. (See Table 9-5 for a summary listing of states with or without limits on contributions generally.)

[37]The following paragraphs rely on the summaries in Schneider, *Campaign Finance, Ethics and Lobby Law Blue Book 1986–87.*

TABLE 9-5

Degree of Regulation of Campaign Finance in the American States: Three Indicators*

	Limits on Contributions[1]	Public Funding[2]	Publishes Data[3]
Alabama	no	parties	no
Alaska	yes	no	yes
Arizona	no	no	no
Arkansas	yes	no	no
California	no	parties	yes
Colorado	no	no	yes
Connecticut	yes	no	no
Delaware	yes	no	no
Florida	yes	[4]	yes
Georgia	no	no	no
Hawaii	yes	candidates	yes
Idaho	no	parties	yes
Illinois	no	no	no
Indiana	no	no	yes
Iowa	no	parties	yes
Kansas	yes	no	yes
Kentucky	no	parties	yes
Louisiana	no	no	no
Maine	yes	parties	no
Maryland	no	no	no
Massachusetts	no	candidates	no
Michigan	yes	candidates	yes
Minnesota	yes	candidates	yes
Mississippi	no	no	no
Missouri	no	no	yes
Montana	yes	candidates	yes
Nebraska	no	no	yes
Nevada	no	no	yes
New Hampshire	no	no	no
New Jersey	yes	candidates	yes
New Mexico	no	no	no
New York	yes	no	no
North Carolina	yes	parties	no
North Dakota	no	no	no
Ohio	no	no	no
Oklahoma	yes	no	no
Oregon	no	no	yes
Pennsylvania	no	no	no
Rhode Island	no	[5]	yes

South Carolina	no	no	no
South Dakota	no	no	no
Tennessee	no	no	no
Texas	no	no	no
Utah	no	parties	no
Vermont	yes	no	yes
Virginia	no	parties	no
Washington	no	no	yes
West Virginia	yes	no	no
Wisconsin	yes	candidates	yes
Wyoming	no	no	no

[1]"Yes" indicates broad limits on the size of contributions; "no" indicates none or limit on a single source.

[2]The programs of aid to parties and candidates may be funded by income tax checkoff or add-on or by direct appropriation.

[3]"Yes" indicates that the state aggregates and publishes data from the reports of individual candidates, committees, etc.

[4]Begins in the 1990 elections.

[5]Mandated by 1986 constitutional amendment.

Source: With the exception of a few modifications to reflect later events, the data come from Sandra K. Schneider, ed., *Campaign Finance, Ethics and Lobby Law Blue Book 1986–87* (Lexington, Ky.: Council of State Governments, 1986).

Beyond limits on the size of contributions, most states also prohibit contributions from certain sources.

- 36 have absolute prohibitions against anonymous donations; three more prohibit them above a stated sum.
- 20 prohibit contributions by corporations (two of the 20 limit the prohibition to contributions to candidates).
- 10 prohibit contributions by labor unions.
- 27 forbid contributions by any utility or business regulated by the state.

There are also widespread prohibitions against contributions made in the name of another person.

Many of the states with prohibitions are also the states with substantial limits on the size of contributions. Indeed, if one considers prohibitions the ultimate regulation of contributions and adds them to state contribution limits, one comes up with a rough but useful separation of "high" and "low" regulation states. Using that measure, there were 13 states (as of the beginning of 1986) that had no contribution limits and no prohibition against contributions by corporations, unions, or regulated industries: California, Idaho, Illinois, Indiana, Louisiana, Missouri, Nebraska, Nevada, New Mexico, Rhode Island, Utah, Virginia, and Washington. Another five limited nothing and prohibited only contributions by regulated industries: Alabama, Colorado, Georgia, Oregon, and South Carolina. Ohio limited nothing and prohibited only corporate contributions.[38]

At a less exigent level of regulation, every state requires some kind of reporting of campaign finance from at least some candidates and party committees. Reporting requirements vary greatly, especially in the frequency of reporting and the deadlines for it; but in the long run the major test of any reporting law is the availability of the data the candidates and committees report. Despite the universality of reporting, only 22 states publish aggregate data on receipts and expenditures (Table 9-5). Fourteen of those 22 — Alaska, California, Colorado, Hawaii, Idaho, Iowa, Kansas, Minnesota, Montana, Nebraska, Nevada, Oregon, Washington, and Wisconsin — come from the Northwest quadrant of the United States, the region of the country most affected by turn-of-the-century populism and Progressivism. It may very well be that they still reflect the old Progressive confidence in the power of information and disclosure and, ultimately, in the importance and power of an informed electorate.

In fact, the main generalizations one can make about the extent of regulation among the 50 states are regional. There is a reluctance to limit the size of contributions in the Southwest. Reliance on the effects of publishing data is greatest in the old areas of Progressive power. And an aggregate view of commitment to regulation, such as that reflected in Table 9-5, makes clear another regional fact. Six of the 10 states of the Confederacy (60 percent of them) have none of the three regulations detailed there; among the other 40 states there are only 10 more (25 percent). Beyond these observations one comes down to state political traditions. If one asked a group of reasonably well-informed observers to pick from among Illinois, Minnesota, Pennsylvania, and Wisconsin the two states that had no substan-

---

[38]Almost all of these states do, of course, have prohibitions against contributions of other "less controversial" kinds: against anonymous contributions or contributions made in the name of another person, especially.

tial limits on contributions, no programs of public funding, and no program of data publication, one suspects that the "guesses" would focus on Illinois and Pennsylvania.

Beyond these broad categories of state policy, there are the fascinating little idiosyncrasies in state regulation, the instances in which one or a few states have innovated in dealing with campaign finance. Among them:[39]

- Montana, alone among the states, has placed a limit on *receipts*; candidates for the two houses of the legislature are limited to $600 (the House) and $1000 (the Senate) in receipts from PACs (political committees). It is, of course, the kind of limit that the U.S. Congress has debated from the Obey-Railsback proposal of the late 1970s to the proposals of Sen. David Boren in 1986 and 1987. There has apparently been no test of the constitutionality of the law in either a state or federal court.
- A number of states (17) limit transfers of funds from one candidate to another by treating them as individual contributions, but three states (Connecticut, Hawaii, and Michigan) have banned them altogether.
- Two states have sharply regulated the contribution of money in the odd-numbered year of the political cycle. Minnesota places more stringent limits on contributors, and Texas bars contributions in a period from 30 days before a legislative session to its adjournment.

Almost as fascinating are the proposals that "almost" made it into law. Democratic majorities in both the California and Illinois legislatures passed public funding bills, only to have them vetoed by Republican governors — Illinois in 1984 and 1985 and California in 1984. In 1984 California voters also rejected an initiative measure that would have introduced very limited public funding and severe spending limits. In the 1980s Minnesota flirted with public funding for candidates for its eight seats in the U.S. House of Representatives. Bills passed in both houses of the state legis-

---

[39]For fuller citations to statutes, see Schneider, *Campaign Finance, Ethics and Lobby Law Blue Book 1986–87* and *The New Gold Rush*, chap. 10.

lature in one year, but a conference committee at the end of the session was unable to reconcile differences between them.

The effectiveness of state regulation — at whatever level the state sets it — depends ultimately on the will and authority of an administrative agency. In his recent survey of state regulatory administration, Robert Huckshorn finds that 24 of the 50 states have merely designated an existing state officer, usually the secretary of state. These are normally the states of the least demanding regulations, and their enforcement demands little, too. The remaining 26 states have created special commissions or boards to administer the campaign finance statutes; but only 16 of them, Huckshorn concludes, meet a minimum criterion for administrative effectiveness: the ability to levy fines. Of the 16, 12 are "limited either by restrictive statutory provisions or self-imposed limits that cast their application of civil penalties into the nuisance mold of traffic tickets."[40] Four state bodies have "strong" enforcement records: those of California, Connecticut, Florida, and New Jersey. Other scholars might come up with a somewhat different honor roll, but only the foolhardy would deny that the list is small. If it is the case that the effectiveness of the FEC is hampered primarily by its relationships with the Congress, it is even truer that state legislators have hesitated to create strong and effective agencies for regulating their own campaign finance.

V. Campaign Money in the Localities

Of local campaign finance and its regulation, we know least of all. What indications we have of the costs of campaigning come almost entirely from newspaper reports and primarily of big city mayoral races. Mayor Edward Koch alone spent about $7 million in his successful reelection campaign in New York in 1985. The mayor reported that he raised that sum from 18,000 contributors, more than 12,000 of whom contributed less than $100. Mayor Tom Bradley of Los Angeles spent more than $1.5 million

---

[40]Robert J. Huckshorn, "Who Gave It? Who Got It?: The Enforcement of Campaign Finance Laws in the States," *Journal of Politics*, vol. 47 (Aug. 1985), 787. Huckshorn names no names; therefore, we do not know the identities of the 16 or the 12.

in defeating unimpressive opposition in 1985. The mayor of St. Paul, George Latimer, on the other hand, spent $223,000 in his five successful campaigns in that city; the average cost per campaign thus was $44,600. (The Koch campaign cost 99 cents per resident of New York, according to 1980 census figures; Latimer's average came to 17 cents per resident.) In more general terms, campaign budgets can easily hit the $500,000 to $1 million mark in the nation's 30 largest cities.[41]

Herbert Alexander's estimates for the total cost of local campaigns in presidential years climbs from $120 million in 1976 to $200 million in 1984. That is only a 67 percent increase, less even than the 82 percent rise in the Consumer Price Index over the same period.[42] Can it be that the explosion of campaign costs has passed by the local campaign? Yes, because the revolution in styles and techologies has probably passed by the localities. That would mean that the noncash component of campaigning has remained highest in these local campaigns and that the most expensive media and specialties, except for the largest cities in the country, are the least employed in them.

As for public funding in local elections, there are at least three cases. The Hawaii law that provides funding for state executive and legislative races also provides up to $15,000 for mayoral races in the large counties and $2000 for those in the less populous counties; it provides $500 for all other campaigns. In reality, only one mayoral candidate claimed funds in 1982 and 1984; in the same two elections combined, only three candidates for city council received funds.[43] Seattle has a comprehensive program that provides matching funds for contributions of $50 or less, limits on contributions, and spending limits of $250,000 on mayoral campaigns and $75,000 on races for other city offices. Finally, the voters of Tucson in 1985 voted to write a public funding program similar to Seattle's into the city's charter. (For a report on a city that almost had public funding, see box.)

---

[41] Jerry Hagstrom and Robert Guskind, "Mayoral Candidates Enter the Big Time Using Costly TV Ads and Consultants," *National Journal* (Apr. 6, 1985), 737–742.

[42] See footnote 1.

[43] Alexander and Eberts, *Public Financing of State Elections*, 29–38.

"CLOSE BUT NO CIGAR"

In the state of New York, local municipalities apparently have limited control over local public finances. So, in 1987 the state legislature found itself debating a plan of public funding for the city of New York. The proposal failed finally; according to a newspaper report,

> It died, most people involved in the negotiations agree, because Republican State Senators, who control their house, could not overcome their philosophical opposition to public campaign financing — even when it was limited to candidates for heavily Democratic New York City offices. . . .
>
> While the final draft would have provided public campaign funds only for candidates for the eight positions on the Board of Estimate — the Mayor, the Comptroller, the President of the City Council and the five Borough Presidents — proponents say it would have been the Legislature's first major step toward addressing one of the most significant sources of political corruption. Mayor Koch had lobbied vigorously for the bill, and the State-City Commission on Integrity in Government, created last year to explore ways to combat corruption, listed public campaign financing as essential. . . .
>
> With the matching funds would have come contribution limits, $3,750 in the case of mayoral candidates, and the city's first campaign spending limits: a $5.2 million maximum for Democratic mayoral candidates, as compared with the nearly $7 million Mr. Koch spent on his last election.
>
> — *Elizabeth Kolbert, "Public Campaign Financing: Close but No Cigar,"* New York Times *(July 12, 1987).*

Much of the regulation of local finance is embedded in statewide legislation. The overwhelming majority of the states require reporting by local candidates and party committees; and the state's categories of prohibited sources apply to localities, too. Moreover, the more extensive state regulations of the sums of contributions sometimes specify limits for local campaigns. To all of these extents, the localities are woven into the statewide web of regulation.

Of local legislation on campaign finance, we know even less. California law requires that cities and counties inform the California Fair Political Practices Commission of ordinances regulating campaign finance. Compliance with that requirement has, apparently, been spotty. After prompting and chivying the localities, the Commission gathered what data it could and reported the results in 1980. It could identify 21 cities and six counties in the state with regulations. The most common form was a limit on contributions; 24 localities had adopted one kind or another. Nine jurisdictions set up more stringent reporting requirements than those of state law. Perhaps the most experimental ordinances were those (three) publishing campaign statements by candidates in the local newspapers and two banning personal use of campaign funds. Berkeley, Fresno, San Diego, San Francisco, and San Jose were the largest cities in the group reporting ordinances.[44] If there are other reports on local regulation, they have escaped my notice.

Without having very much evidence, it seems logical to conclude that two factors affect the amount of regulating that localities will do in a state. First, regulation depends, obviously, on how much freedom (autonomy) the state gives its municipalities to act on matters such as this. Second, it depends on the nature of the regulations the state itself has adopted. Certainly the unwillingness of the California legislature to limit contributions to campaigns in any way explains, at least in part, why 24 localities should want to do so. All other things being equal, one expects to find less local regulation where the state legislatures have taken comprehensive action.

Without very much specific regulation, attention to enforcement, or even ordinary media publicity, campaign finance in the localities probably relies to an unusual extent on very interested money. All observers seem agreed on that point. Real estate owners and developers, contractors with the city or county, downtown commercial interests, and organized labor (especially unions of teachers and public employees) have become the clas-

---

[44]California Fair Political Practices Commission, *Summary of Local Campaign Disclosure and Contribution Limitation Ordinances* (Sacramento: CFPPC, n.d.).

sic municipal "fat cats." A study of donors to mayoral campaigns in Los Angeles finds, for example, that 42 percent of the contributors "either do business with the city or need the city's approval for work that they or their clients want to undertake"; 25 percent of the contributors, in fact, had occupations in real estate.[45] It is important to keep in mind, though, that campaign finance in the cities is, as it is in the Congress, a two-way relationship. Many of those contributors were "invited" to fund-raising events or were otherwise solicited by incumbent candidates.

VI. The Lost World of Campaign Finance

In the experience of the 50 states, we ought to have the materials for a deeper understanding of American campaign finance. It is not only that the states offer differences of size, population, parties, and political traditions, but they have also embarked on greatly differing attempts to influence the funding of their campaigns. It would, in fact, be hard to find many other policy domains in which official state reactions have differed so widely, from virtual "hands off" policies to intense regulation combined with public funding. Some of that regulation is prime evidence that the states, as Justice Holmes once said, function as "insulated chambers" for experimentation.

Unfortunately, when "experiments" in public policy are undertaken, however unconsciously, they rarely seem to be observed. Montana's singular regulation of campaign receipts (as opposed to contributions) has gone unchallenged in the courts, and its consequences go unreported in the press or scholarly literature. We might have found in Montana some useful information about the application of *Buckley* to the untested limit on receipts or about the impact of such limitations on candidates' searches for funds and the PAC strategies of contribution. But we haven't. The sad truth is that state and local experience remains the "lost world" of American campaign finance. In part the problem results from the paucity of systematic data in the majority of states, and in part it results from the unwillingness of journalists and scholars to turn from the flashier events of congressional and

[45]Frank Clifford, "Political Donors Seeking an Ear," *Los Angeles Times* (Mar. 11, 1985).

presidential campaign finance.[46] But whatever the reason, our collective understanding of American campaign finance is the loser.

It is not difficult to frame the questions that the states' experience ought to help us address. Perhaps the most basic of them all concerns the determinants of the levels of campaign getting and spending. Obviously the number of people in the constituency or the entire state makes a difference; running for mayor of New York is not the same as running for mayor of Natchez or Des Moines. And yet there are enormous differences even when one calculates the ratio of money spent to number of people, voters, or votes cast. Perhaps different political cultures and traditions matter or different political institutions or patterns of two-party competitiveness or interest group politics. And what of different levels of education and income? To put the question a little differently, do the elites of campaign finance — the candidates, the brokers, the contributors, the parties — behave in the states as they do in congressional campaign finance? And if not, why not?

Ultimately, one also wants to know why some states turn to public funding and systematic regulation while others do not. Do those decisions reflect the strength and weakness of participants in an existing system of campaign finance; or do they reflect instead a more fundamental political culture, ideology, or tradition? Has California resisted regulation and public funding precisely because of its extravagant campaign finance — a kind of finance that would ironically lead one to expect regulation? Or indeed, do the events post-Watergate suggest that regulation and reform is related to a specific occasion or crisis, that it depends on the catalytic event to mobilize latent, widespread, but not very intense mass opinion? Certainly the relative absence of regulatory legislation in the states since 1976 lends credence to that hypothesis.

As profitable as comparisons among the 50 states would be, we already have at hand materials for a very useful comparison between congressional campaign finance and that of the nation's most populous state. It is almost as if one is comparing two American nations, for California's population (in 1980) of almost 24

---

[46]This is certainly not to denigrate the work of the scholars who have already turned to state campaign finance, especially Ruth S. Jones. It is only to say that the scholarly enterprise needs more scholars like them working in the states.

million puts it among some of the more populous democracies of the world.[47]

Much of the experience of the states, except for California, fits comfortably with the congressional experience. Candidates in the state legislatures we know about seem to get their funds from the same sources as do congressional candidates and in about the same proportions. Incumbent-challenger imbalances are of about the same magnitude. And the growth of expenditures in most states follows the congressional curve. In California, however, the dominance of PAC contributions, the enormous incumbent advantage, the sheer size of the sums spent, and the fund-raising role of the legislative party and leadership bespeak another kind of campaign finance altogether.

And why is California a special case? Perhaps it is the combination of wealth and intense political involvement. The reliance of senatorial and presidential candidates on fund-raising trips to Los Angeles and San Francisco supports that explanation. Moreover, fund-raising goes on in California with a scope and panache almost unknown in the other states. The organizations fighting the ballot issues raise money like the big national ideological PACs — with aggressive direct-mail and media-based campaigns. And legislative incumbents raise it even more effectively than the experienced members of the U.S. House. They also survive reelection campaigns with comparative ease; only one member of the Assembly was defeated in 1986, and almost half of the winners won with 70 percent or more of the vote. All of this takes place, of course, without much interference from a chronically weak set of state and local party organizations. In short, the California picture is one of organized giving, of organized taking, and of the dominance of legislative incumbents and leadership — a picture, that is, of the ultimate alliance of organized campaign money and organized legislative power. For the moment it is a matter of speculation whether California's traditions are an alternative route or a glimpse of the American future.

---

[47]Just among the democracies of continental Europe, California has more residents than Austria, Belgium, Denmark, Finland, Greece, the Netherlands, Norway, Portugal, Sweden, and Switzerland — not to mention Luxembourg, Monaco, and San Marino. It also has about half the population of either France or Italy.

10
Consequences and Impacts: The Policy Concerns

Concern about campaign finance far outstrips knowledge about it. Americans who have no idea what campaigns for the House or Senate cost or who cannot distinguish between contributions and independent spending tend to be very sure of the effects of "all that money" moving in the system. Since those concerns are widely shared, they become policy issues. The resulting debate, even if poorly defined, is ultimately about the impact of campaign finance on American politics and the American democracy.

From the welter of popular concerns, it is not hard to identify the major questions. Journalists, scholars, and the mass public tend to agree on them, even if they do not agree on the answers. Heading any list are the two that have had the greatest media coverage since 1974: the impact of campaign spending on elections and its impact on policy-making, especially in legislatures. In the tendentious phrasing of reform rhetoric, do greater levels of campaign spending "buy" election victory, and do they subsequently "buy" legislative votes? The importance of such questions is self-evident — they ask whether the getting and spending of campaign resources affects the processes of representative government at the two key points: the selecting of public officials and the making of public policy. In a less direct

297

way, they also address the question of the impact of the new cash resources on American politics itself — whether the providers of the new campaign resources have reduced the political role and influence of other more traditional actors in elections and legislatures: parties, voters, and interest groups, especially.

A third and final major question emerges from the intersection of money and regulation: the question or questions of avoidance, evasion, noncompliance, and violation of the statutory attempts to regulate the new campaign finance. At the national level, at least, few accusations of intentional violation stick. Clear violations of federal law and the rules of the FEC are not substantial and, in any event, almost entirely a result of ignorance and inefficiency. Whatever the mass public may imagine, close observers of campaign finance frame the issue as one of evasion and/or avoidance. If these words are not used with great care or precision, neither are the more colloquial ones: "loopholes" and "underground money." Part of the trouble is that those words are intended to convey both meaning and judgment. Understanding this issue is in good part one of defining with some precision the legalities and moralities of living inventively in and around the structure of regulation.

I. The "Buying" of Election Victory

There was a time, not too long ago, when accusations of "buying" American elections did not have to be put in quotation marks. Elections were quite literally bought and sold in the United States throughout the 19th century and well into the 20th. Payments to voters for their votes, indeed, prompted the states to adopt the Australian ballot. When parties distributed their own ballots of different sizes and colors, party poll watchers could see if voters cast the votes they had sold. The marking in secrecy of a uniform, government-provided ballot, the reformers hoped, prevented any enforcement of the bribe and thus would end the bribery itself. Similarly the widespread closing of bars and taverns on election day was intended to foreclose that particularly liquid way of purchasing votes.[1]

---

[1] On that earlier, less innocent time, see Earl R. Sikes, *State and Federal Corrupt-Practices Legislation* (Durham: Duke University Press, 1928).

"Buying" in the purely figurative sense has always been an issue, too, even back to the last century. It does not generally grow out of a rise in spending levels but out of gross inequalities of candidate spending at any general level of spending. It was therefore an issue throughout the long reign of the "fat cats." Mark Hanna's ability to raise large sums of money from the new industrial giants for William McKinley's presidential campaign became a point of contention in the 1896 campaign. And it was rarely out of sight after that in American presidential campaigns. Thayer, in fact, refers to the period between the Civil War and the depression of the 1930s as "The Golden Age of Boodle,"[2] and Richard Nixon's spending in 1968 did as much to spur reform legislation as the transgressions of Watergate four years later.

The entire issue of money's impact on outcomes rests on the assumption that money is a potent, perhaps the most potent, campaign resource because of its ability to purchase the instruments of political persuasion. The "persuader" may have been a glass of whiskey 100 years ago; today it is the 30-second spot on television. The issue is that money buys it, and "it" persuades voters and so determines the outcome of the election. The logic of the argument at times seems to ignore all of the other determinants of voting decisions, and the mass public finds it easy to conclude that spending itself is the main or only instrument of influence. Then, one is but a very short leap to the conclusion that the candidate spending the greater sum will win the election.

It does not always turn out that way, of course. Every election produces its own breathless discoveries that a good many winners in the cash column lost in the vote column. The graveyards of political ambition are in fact filled with bodies of losing candidates who outspent their opponents. Two newspaper reports from 1986 illustrate the rediscovery of that truth:

> Although there is a common political assumption that campaign dollars are almost as good as votes, all but one of the nine Democrats who captured Republican-held U. S. Senate seats Tuesday raised substantially less campaign money than their opponents . . .[3]

[2]George Thayer, *Who Shakes the Money Tree?* (New York: Simon and Schuster, 1973), chap. 3.

[3]Paul Houston, "Outspent Senate Candidates Still Winners," *Los Angeles Times* (Nov. 6, 1986).

The National Republican Senatorial Committee raised nearly 8 times more than its Democratic counterpart in this election cycle — $77.7 million against $9.9 million — but money failed to be a decisive factor in an election in which Democrats won back control of the Senate. . .

In the 16 competitive Senate races, the Republican candidates each raised an average of $3.81 million, a million dollars more than the $2.8 million Democratic average. The GOP, however, lost 11 of those 16 contests.[4]

So, in politics as in life, money doesn't buy everything. The real question, though, is whether it buys something.

The myths of the power of spending die slowly. It is not only the media that cling to them; contributors and politicians do, too. Contributors to well-financed candidates who nonetheless lose the election do not hesitate to complain that "their" money was not well used. Even activists in the parties are hostage to the myths. After the same Republican losses in the 1986 Senate elections, Roland Evans and Robert Novak quoted the unwillingness of a Republican county chairman in Illinois to give money to the National Republican Senatorial Committee. The point of the report was that the chairman considered the NRSC an "unmitigated disaster" because it had, in the words of the columnists, "outspent Democrats but lost eight Senate seats."[5]

At bottom the question is really why cash superiority does not always translate into electoral victory. Looking at the common sense of it helps. Intuition and experience suggest, first, that in most elections money is a necessary but not sufficient condition for winning. Moreover, while money does translate into persuasion, it does so at a diminishing return. A hundred dollars on top of a thousand does more than a hundred after a million has been spent. Second, we also know that money is not the only campaign resource; in any electoral district or any state, the distribution of party loyalties, volunteer campaign workers, candidate name recognition, and campaign skills will favor some candidates over others. That maldistribution may in fact create an electoral advantage so great for a candidate that no amount of spending or

[4]Thomas B. Edsall, "GOP's Cash Advantage Failed to Assure Victory in Close Senate Contests," *Washington Post* (Nov. 6, 1986).
[5]"Dunning the GOP," *Washington Post* (Jan. 7, 1987).

campaigning by another candidate can overcome it. Third, it is conventional political knowledge that campaigns also reflect more distant influences — the popularity of a president, for example, or the rate of inflation in the economy, or an unpopular war. In sum, the amount of money needed for victory in a campaign depends on the way the other factors in the campaign are shaping the outcome. It is not a question of "more" money; it is rather a question of "enough." "Enough" is defined by the distribution of other resources and influences in the campaign. Money will not translate into enough votes if the persuasion it buys cannot overcome the opposing means and resources of persuasion.

All of that seems clear now, thanks largely to Gary Jacobson's demonstration that money spent by challengers produces increased votes, while money spent by incumbents does so only very marginally. In Jacobson's words,

> . . . campaign spending does have a strong effect on congressional election outcomes and . . . money is a particularly important campaign resource for nonincumbent candidates. Incumbents do not seem to benefit from campaign spending to anywhere near the same degree. The more they spend, the worse they do; with challenger spending controlled, their spending has little apparent effect on the vote.[6]

Incumbent spending, that is, is primarily a reaction to the severity of the challenge in the campaign — including the challenger's level of spending — and it will rise as the danger of a close or even lost election rises. But the central fact is that incumbents generally hold the major political advantages in the campaign (e.g., name recognition), and the challenger must spend heavily to overcome those advantages. In a very real way the campaign per se is more important for the challenger, and, therefore, so is the money that buys the campaign.

There is, however, one major problem in understanding the direct relationship between challenger spending and challenger

[6]Gary C. Jacobson, *Money in Congressional Elections* (New Haven: Yale University Press, 1980), pp. 48–49. For early findings that predate and presage Jacobson, see Stanton A. Glantz, Alan I. Abramowitz, and Michael P. Burkart, "Election Outcomes: Whose Money Matters?" *Journal of Politics*, vol. 38 (Nov. 1976), 1033–1038.

share of the vote. Does challenger spending in the campaign produce more votes, or does money flow to a challenger because it is
clear that for other reasons — party fortunes, the nature of the
district, or the candidate's attractive personality, for instance —
the challenger has a chance of winning the election? Or is it possible that "cause" moves in both directions, that the relationship
is reciprocal and interactive? Is it possible, that is, that campaign
spending increases voter support, which increases the prospect
of victory, which in turn brings in more money — the spending of
which increases voter support another notch, which brings in
more money, and so on? Jacobson tackles this riddle by examin-
ing the effects of spending on candidate visibility (i.e., name
recognition). Poll data show that spending affects that visibility;
so spending does seem to have some effect of its own on the outcome of the election. He concludes, therefore, that

> candidates are given money according to how well they are ex-
> pected to do, but campaign expenditures have an independent
> effect on how well they actually do, because without them, the ex-
> pectation would not be realized. The process is largely recursive
> because elite perceptions and strategies determine how much is
> spent in campaigns, and the level of campaign spending in turn de-
> termines how much is known about candidates and therefore how
> much support they actually receive from voters. Elite expecta-
> tions about how the vote will go are only fulfilled if they do, in fact,
> supply enough money to the candidate.[7]

That is, the decision to contribute money to a promising candidate initiates the confirmation of the optimistic prophecy.

While challengers may spend and increase their share of the
vote, however, the truth is that they don't often get enough votes
to win, especially in elections to the House of Representatives. In
recent years incumbent members of the House seeking reelection have been winning more than 90 percent of the time; in
1986 incumbent candidates set a record by winning more than
98 percent of their races. The success ratio of Senate incumbents

[7]Jacobson, *Money in Congressional Elections*, 162. Jacobson and William
Welch have had a debate on this issue of simultaneity in the pages of *Public
Choice*. See Welch, "Money and Votes: A Simultaneous Equation Model," vol. 36
(1981), 209–234; and Jacobson, "Money and Votes Reconsidered: Congressional
Elections, 1972–1982," vol. 47 (1985), 7–62.

fluctuates more, a reflection perhaps of the different set of races each two years. Recently, however, they have won reelection between 60 and 80 percent of the time; the exact figure in 1986 was 75 percent. In view of their security, one may well wonder why incumbents, especially those in the House, work so hard to raise and spend as much as they do. Aren't they aware of the advantages of incumbency? While they will spend heavily in reaction to a serious and threatening challenge, don't they also "overspend" in the absence of one?

There are really two answers to that question. The first is that incumbents, like other candidates, are not really sure of the effects of the campaign and thus of the money spent on it. Especially when they find themselves in a potentially close campaign, they will spend as much money as they can raise in the hope that "something will work." In the words of Jacobson again, "it may take a great deal of money to buy very few additional votes, but if the election is close enough, those few votes may make all the difference. If this is true, then spending by incumbents might influence the chances of winning or losing, even though its influence on the vote is statistically negligible."[8] At the same time they understand the hard truth that "a wide margin of victory in one election does little to improve chances against a well-funded challenger riding a favorable partisan tide in the next election."[9] So, while incumbents may appear to have been electorally secure after the votes have been counted, the outcome often looks less secure months earlier.

The second answer is that incumbents make fund-raising and spending decisions early in the two-year election cycle, and they make them for reasons that relate only indirectly to the approaching campaign. They may raise money simply to frighten off potential challengers either in their own party or in the other party. They may want to build their margin of victory or their name recognition for a step up on the political career ladder — for a race for the Senate or statewide office, perhaps. They may spend money simply because they raise it, and they raise substantial sums from contributors who give it to them for reasons that have everything to do with access to incumbents and nothing

[8]Gary C. Jacobson, "Enough Is Too Much: Money and Competition in House Elections, 1972–1984," in Kay L. Schlozman, ed., *Elections in America*, 181.
[9]Ibid., 185.

to do with any danger the incumbent may face in the approaching election. In sum, since incumbents have reason not to be completely sure of victory and since they raise and spend money for reasons not related to the anticipated closeness of the election, their spending is much less closely related to the election vote than is challenger spending.[10]

It is dangerous to extend these or any other generalizations about congressional campaigns to those for state legislatures. Indeed, one of the findings of Giles and Pritchard about Florida reinforces that point emphatically. In the 1980 elections to the Florida House, the effects of candidate spending were "negligible," suggesting that in that year at least "most candidates in Florida House elections will not enjoy an expenditure advantage sufficient to offset an incumbency or party advantage of their opponent." The expenditures necessary to offset the effects of party and incumbency would be "astronomical."[11] These conclusions, limited though they may be, suggest that in less visible campaigns the effect of the campaign on the voting decision is less than in congressional campaigns and that the power of longer term forces such as incumbency advantages and residual party loyalties are greater. If the campaign is less crucial to the outcome, so, too, is money spent in the campaign.

In assessing the tie between spending and election outcomes, we appear to be at the intersection of three great determinants of election outcomes: party loyalties, incumbency advantages, and the campaigns themselves. In the case of elections to the House, incumbency dominates and only substantial challenger spending can usually overcome it. In at least some state legislative elections, the strength and concentration of party loyalties added to the incumbency advantage overpower the efficacy of campaign spending. In some gubernatorial campaigns, the power of incumbency is weaker and the superiority of Democratic party loyalties takes its place of dominance. Republicans thus must spend heav-

---

[10]The studies of the relationship between money spent and votes won do not control for primary competition. If one factored in the competition that incumbents face, one *might* find a closer relationship between incumbent spending and vote outcome (since they all won any contested primaries in these studies in order to become general election candidates).

[11]Micheal W. Giles and Anita Pritchard, "Campaign Expenditures and Legislative Elections in Florida," *Legislative Studies Quarterly,* vol. 10 (Feb. 1985), 83.

ily to overcome that Democratic advantage.[12] Open seat races for the U.S. House show a similar power of party loyalties in the district in the absence of the influence of incumbency; the candidate running against the party majority, Democratic or Republican, must spend more heavily to overcome that advantage with the other candidate.[13]

One study of local campaign finance, on the other hand, reports that incumbency, party, and campaign spending in the locality explain considerably less of the election outcome than they do in other cases.[14] The effect of campaign finance certainly varies with the nature of campaigns, and local campaigns are perhaps fundamentally different. Noncash contributions, especially in volunteer labor, are more important. Personalism and face-to-face campaigns are the norm, and incumbency and party loyalties often carry a good deal less weight. Candidate visibility and communication in them can be achieved without the spending of much money.

If measuring the effect of money on electoral outcomes has preoccupied academic scholarship, Democratic-Republican differences in spending and winning have absorbed the media. Following the 1982 campaigns and elections, for instance, the *New York Times* twice addressed those differences:

- Patrick Caddell, in a piece on the Op-Ed page, reported that Democrats won 78 of the close House elections (totals of 52 percent or less of the vote) when spending was "comparable" and only 29 percent when they were outspent by two to one or more.[15]
- A *Times* analysis of the same campaigns, written by Adam Clymer, found that the Republicans won 42 and the Democrats 41 of the races in which the victors won by 55 percent or less. But 69 percent of these Republican winners spent at least $50,000

[12]Samuel C. Patterson, "Campaign Spending in Contests for Governor," *Western Political Quarterly*, vol. 35 (Dec. 1982), 457–477.

[13]David C. Linder, *Money and Competition in House Open Seat Elections*, thesis for the baccalaureate degree summa cum laude in political science at the University of Minnesota (Spring 1986).

[14]Theodore S. Arrington and Gerald L. Ingalls, "Effects of Campaign Spending on Local Elections: The Charlotte Case," *American Politics Quarterly*, vol. 12 (Jan. 1984), 117–127.

[15]"A Lens on the Election," *New York Times* (Nov. 14, 1982).

more than their opponents while only 15 percent of the Democrats did.[16]

These reports and others like them fail to control for the effect of incumbency. When Jacobson did, he found that Republican expenditures for both incumbents and challengers were more effective in two elections (1974 and 1976). The explanation begins with the fact that Republican candidates

> are at a general disadvantage (one that was severely exacerbated in 1974). Certainly the figures on party identification — and the ratio of Republican to Democratic officeholders at all levels — are strong reasons for assuming that this is indeed the case. With far fewer partisan supporters in the electorate, Republicans rely more heavily on campaigning — and thus campaign spending — to win votes. Transmitting campaign information beyond the party label is essential.[17]

So, one comes back to the main theme again: campaign spending is more important for disadvantaged candidates, whatever the source or nature of the disadvantage. The campaign per se is the final, crucial time for reversing the odds; and to the extent that cash is necessary for sustaining an effective campaign, it is a major "equalizer" in campaign politics.

Finally, there are genuine limits to what money can accomplish in a campaign. There is no guarantee that the money will be used well, that funds will be distributed in strategically rational ways, or that the candidate and the message will be presented in the most effective ways. Nor does money determine the content of the campaign — the issues or the focus of the campaign, for example. Money, in short, is no guarantee of the effectiveness, the persuasiveness, the quality of the campaign. Ultimately it is the impact of the campaign that counts, and some campaigns get considerably more impact out of $300,000 than others do.

In relating the issues of finance and quality in campaigns, Jacobson has suggested a concept of threshold. Spending is necessary up to that level (at least in cash-based campaigns) to

---

[16]"Campaign Funds Called a Key To Outcome of House Races," *New York Times* (Nov. 5, 1982).

[17]Jacobson, *Money in Congressional Elections*, 48.

achieve the volume or extent that offers the possibility of competitiveness. Beyond that threshold, content matters more and more. And so do the experts in campaign strategy and effectiveness — the pollers and consultants, the large PACs giving in-kind contributions of campaign professionalism, and the increasingly sophisticated party committees. To put the point in terms of the parties, it is not only that Republican committees spend more money, but that they spend it effectively. Their skillful last minute spending in the House elections of 1982 that the *New York Times* commented on may very well have reduced the party's losses in a very unpromising election year.[18]

To summarize, cash superiority won't win all or even most elections. The question, however, is not really one of superiority — who wins the spending race — but rather one of spending sufficiency. And what is sufficient depends on the balance of the precampaign strengths and weaknesses of the candidates, whether they are of party, incumbency, or other political forces or considerations. If a campaign faces a deficit in the reckoning of assets, the campaign will have to achieve a persuasive superiority in order to turn the tables. If the campaign is of a new style cash-driven type, the resources needed to overcome the disadvantage will be primarily those of money. If it is an old-fashioned local campaign, cash may be one of its lesser needs. So, money can determine election outcomes, but it cannot if the campaign starts at a disabling disadvantage. It all depends, and the trick is in establishing on what it does or does not depend. Usually the question is one of the extent to which campaign funds weigh on the side of already substantial candidate advantages.

II. The "Buying" of Public Policy

The fear that contributors to campaigns, especially the contributors of large sums, will "purchase" leverage over public policy pervades Americans' views of their campaign finance. The issue centers very much on PAC contributions and on recipients who are legislative candidates — hence the cliche about "the

[18]Jacobson, "Money and Votes Reconsidered: Congresssional Elections, 1972–1982," 43.

best Congress money can buy." There is, however, no logical reason to limit the issue that way. Contributors other than PACs, individuals especially, may want to affect specific public policies. (Ironically, the strengthened political parties that many Americans advocate would have exactly that ability to impose their policy programs; very few Americans accuse them of doing so, however.[19]) Nor are legislatures the only elected policy-makers; voters in the states select a wide range of executive, administrative, and judicial officials after campaigns of varying extensiveness. Yet whatever the scope of the issue, central to it is the link between campaign money and policy outcomes.

Common Cause and the mass media have popularized the issue in a predictable form: the case study of a link between PAC contributions and a congressional decision. Examples abound. Over the years the best publicized have involved the contributions of doctors, dairy farmers, realtors, used car dealers, bankers, and gun owners.[20] For the limited space of this book, the events surrounding the 1986 success of the National Rifle Association (NRA) in loosening the federal control of interstate gun transactions will have to suffice.

In March and April of 1986, the House of Representatives voted to weaken the Gun Control Act of 1968 to permit interstate sales of rifles and shotguns and to ease the record-keeping in commercial gun transactions. (The Senate had earlier passed similar but not identical legislation.) It was a major legislative victory for the National Rifle Association, an association of about 3 million gun owners. In the defeated opposition were law enforcement officials and their much smaller and less well-funded organizations. The NRA, of course, was a major spender in congressional campaigns in 1984 ($700,324 in contributions and $785,516 in independent expenditures.)

NRA campaign spending did not go unnoticed in the press, and at the time of a crucial petition to force the bill out of committee, the *Washington Post* wrote that at least 129 of 156 (84 percent) of

[19]Such hopes for the parties have been most often identified within academic political science with the proponents of "party responsibility."

[20]See, for example, the reports of Common Cause, *Looking to Purchase or Rent* (late 1984) and *Financing the Finance Committee* (Mar., 1986). These (and other similar Common Cause case studies) were widely reported in the newspapers of the country.

the signers of the discharge petition had received NRA money in 1984 or 1986. The next day a *Post* editorial proclaimed that the NRA "has done a bang-up job of buying support in Congress."[21] But while some of the press assumed the PAC-policy connection, there were intimations in some of the nation's newspapers that the connection was not quite that simple. Sources of influence beyond the PAC and campaign finance seemed to be at work (see box).

THE SEARCH FOR THE SMOKING GUN

In various ways the nation's press provided a number of hints that the National Rifle Association's success in weakening the Gun Control Act of 1968 had roots in sources of influence other than money. From Minneapolis, New York, and Washington:

- The *Minneapolis Star-Tribune* quoted an anonymous Western Democrat as saying "It's the kind of an issue that could defeat me when nothing else could. In a typical year, this is an issue in a Rocky Mountain district that could move 4 to 5 percent of the people to vote the other way . . ."[22]
- The *New York Times*'s Linda Greenhouse attributed the outcome to "the power of the National Rifle Association, one of the best organized and most feared lobbies in Washington," noting in conclusion that the NRA had "dedicated $1.6 million of its $5 million annual legislative budget to the bill."[23]
- Somewhat later the *Washington Post* printed a four-paragraph opinion piece by Rep. David S. Monson, a Republican from Utah, challenging its interpretation of the vote on the bill. Wrote Representative Monson: "As a recipient of NRA contributions, I can unequivocally assure voters that my votes would have been the same without one dime of support from the NRA.

---

[21]Howard Kurtz, "House Speeds Timetable For Gun Decontrol Bills" (Mar. 3, 1986), and "NRA: More Bang for the Buck" (Mar. 4, 1986).
[22]"House votes to weaken gun act" (Apr. 11, 1986).
[23]"The N.R.A.'s Lobbying Is as Effective as Ever" (Apr. 13, 1986).

That is because my constituents and I believe that the current enforcement of gun control legislation is a disgrace."[24]

Case studies such as this one raise all manner of questions. To begin, the direction of the cause is easily inferred, but less easily proven. Do the votes follow the money, or does the money follow the votes? While the votes in Congress may be influenced by the contributed money, it is more likely that the contributions result from the contributors' approval of the values and/or voting record of the candidate. PACs do give the greatest share of their money to incumbent candidates with well-established voting records; for candidates without a record of legislative voting, they usually try to discover basic values in interviews or questionnaires. PACs do not contribute at random; just as individual contributors do, they support candidates whose ideas and values they like. The key question — and a very difficult one it is — is not whether legislators vote in ways that please their contributors, but whether they would have done so in the absence of a contribution.

It is, moreover, very hard to separate the effects of lobbying and of constituency pressures from the effects of a campaign contribution. The NRA has three million loyal members who respond with considerable intensity to the alarms of the organization, either in grass-roots pressure or in voting. Its Capitol Hill lobbyists are experienced and well financed. To speak of the NRA is to speak simultaneously of a powerful lobby, an affluent PAC, and a potent grass-roots organization. It is also to speak of a group of voters with such intense feelings about gun control that they are the prototypical "single issue" voters — voters for whom a single issue overrides all others.

Even if we can show that it was money that made the difference and that the votes did in fact follow the money, we have only explained a single case or instance. We have not even examined PAC

---

[24]"It Was Conscience, Not NRA Money" (May 10, 1986).

activity on other sides of that issue. We have counted the winners, but not the losers. Nor do we know how typical our single case is of the whole business of a legislative session. To show the impact of campaign contributions on the legislative process, one would have to understand at least a good sample of roll calls and a map of PAC losses as well as victories. In recent years, indeed, it has been clear that some of the heaviest spenders in the PAC movement have been among the biggest losers in the Congress. One need only mention the American Medical Association's losses on Medicare cost containment and the National Realtors Association loss of real estate tax shelters in the income tax revision of 1985–86.

Finally, most of the journalistic reports of PAC influence in legislatures suffer fatally from too simple a model of legislative decision-making. What of the role of constituency pressures; of legislative party; of the personal outlook and information of the legislator; of general public opinion; of the legislative peers and leaders; of groups and their lobbying; and, for at least some members, the programs and promptings of the president?[25] One can hardly assume that the search for campaign contributions overrides all or even some of these imperatives. Any serious attempt to establish the independent effect of contributions must control for them, and many of the scholarly studies attempt to do so. Often, in fact, the argument shifts to the adequacy of the controls. Is a congressperson's previous record of liberal or conservative voting, for example, an adequate control for the aggregate effect of those external influences? That's a far tougher issue, of course, but at least all parties arguing it have rejected the simple correlation of PAC contributions and roll call votes.

Scholars working on the problem have begun to approach it with strategies more complex and sophisticated than the usual journalistic treatment. In some instances they have expanded the relationship to more PACs and a broader set of roll call votes. In some they have attempted to control for other factors such as party and constituency pressures. Yet others have extended the analysis over time, hoping to relate changes in contribution patterns with changes in votes. The results have been disappoint-

---

[25]For example, John W. Kingdon, *Congressmen's Voting Decisions* (New York: Harper and Row, 1973).

ingly mixed and ambiguous. Some studies find modest relationships and an independent effect of contributions, but others do not — an outcome probably the result of the different methodologies and the different groups and votes in the various projects.[26]

From that diverse body of scholarship and its diverse conclusions, three conclusions seem warranted. First, and most important, there simply are no data in the systematic studies that would support the popular assertions about the "buying" of the Congress or about any other massive influence of money on the legislative process. Second, even taking the evidence selectively, there is at best a case for a modest influence of money, a degree of influence that puts it well behind the other major influences on congressional behavior. Third, in some of the studies with a time dimension, there is evidence that vote support for the PAC's legislative position leads to greater campaign contributions. They do not, however, answer the question whether the legislative votes changed in order to "earn" the reward of increased contributions.

Recent work has also begun to factor into the explanations the nature of PAC decision-making, the sources of PAC and group power, and the expectations of the contributors. They have, in other words, put the PACs into the equation! John Wright, for example, considers the way a group of large, often federated, PACs conduct their business:

> Because money must be raised at a local, grassroots level, local PAC officials, not Washington lobbyists, are primarily responsible for making allocation decisions. Consequently, congressmen who desire contributions must cultivate favorable relationships with

[26]See, for example, Kirk F. Brown, "Campaign Contributions and Congressional Voting," paper presented at the annual meeting of the American Political Science Association (Sept. 1–4, 1983); Janet M. Grenzke, "Shopping in the Congressional Supermarket: The Currency is Complex," *American Journal of Political Science*, vol. 33 (forthcoming); Benjamin Ginsberg and John C. Green, "The Best Congress Money Can Buy: Campaign Contributions and Congressional Behavior," in Ginsberg and Alan Stone, eds., *Do Elections Matter?* (Armonk, N.Y.: Sharp, 1986), 75–89; John E. Owens, "The Impact of Campaign Contributions on Legislative Outcomes in Congress: Evidence from a House Committee," *Political Studies*, vol. 34 (June 1986), 285–295; William P. Welch, "Campaign Contributions and Congressional Voting: Milk Money and Dairy Price Supports," *Western Political Quarterly*, vol. 35 (Dec. 1982), 478–495; and John R. Wright, "PACs, Contributions, and Roll Calls: An Organizational Perspective," *American Political Science Review*, vol. 79 (June 1985), 400–414.

local officials, and this arrangement tends to undercut the value of contributions as a bargaining tool for professional lobbyists.[27]

Janet Grenzke points to the effect of a different aspect of the PAC's basic organization and structure. Generally when one finds a positive causal relationship between contribution and pro-PAC change in a legislator's vote, she writes,

> the contribution is consistent with and may be considered a measure of the more important endorsement and campaign activities of the organization, which can influence member votes. Eliminating the contribution will not significantly change the organization's power because its power is based primarily on its ability to mobilize votes.[28]

In brief, PACs differ vastly in their organizations, goals, strategies, and decision-making; and those differences affect both their desire and their ability to use contributions to alter legislative votes.

When one considers PAC goals, one can of course take the PACs at their word; and the word has always been "access." Larry Sabato summarizes PAC expectations:

> While some legislators confess that PAC dollars affect their judgment of the issues before them, PAC officials are adamant that all they get for their investment is access to congressmen — a chance to "tell their story." Political analysts have long agreed that access is the principal goal of most interest groups, and lobbyists have always recognized that access is the key to influence . . .
>
> A congressman's time is often as valuable as his vote because, as the Public Affairs Council's Richard Armstrong declares, "except maybe for some guy from Idaho . . . they haven't got time to see everybody. Some congressmen *say* they see everyone, but that's bullshit."[29]

In the broader world of American politics, "access" has always

[27]Wright, "PACs, Contributions, and Roll Calls: An Organizational Perspective," 411.

[28]Grenzke, "Shopping in the Congressional Supermarket: The Currency is Complex," 12.

[29]Larry J. Sabato, *PAC Power* (New York: Norton, 1984), 127. The ellipses in the Armstrong quote is in the original.

been a slippery word, sometimes serving in fact as a code word for palpable, demonstrated influence. As the PACs use it, however, it most often has a literal meaning: a chance to persuade, an opportunity to make a case or argue a point. If that argument seems self-serving, it is honestly made in the great number of instances. More important, mirabile dictu, it squares with what systematic evidence we have about the money-vote relationship. It fits with the complex variety of PAC organizations and with the diversity of their goals, especially with their disposition to contribute to candidates for all kinds of reasons that have little or only something to do with specific policy goals. The more generalized goals of access simply fit the realities of PACs better than do assumptions of a more purposeful, impact-on-policy strategy.

To be stubbornly skeptical about it, however, we have no systematic evidence that contributions do in fact produce access. The testimony of journalists, members of Congress, and PAC leadership suggests that PACs do enjoy it. The harder question remains unanswered: would that access have been granted in the absence of the contribution? If one concedes the access, it is easy to spin out a broader hypothesis. What appears to be a limited independent influence of PAC contributions is achieved largely through the persuasion afforded or facilitated by access. Access thus converts to an edge in influencing the decisions of members of Congress. Moreover, persuasion is easier when other players in the legislative process are less exigent. Thus the influence of the contributors varies with the nature of the policy at stake; it is greater in the narrower, less salient issues that escape party, presidential, or popular attention.[30]

Alternatively, one can recast the problem of money's influence on legislation in terms of pluralism — the struggle of competing interests and their PACs for access or influence in a diverse and many-sided legislative contest. It is a view of intricately divided and opposing influence, one in which countervailing interests check and offset each other.[31] Such an argument about counter-

[30]For a similar conclusion, see Sabato, *PAC Power*, 135–140.
[31]I hope it is clear that I am not suggesting that all interests are represented or represented fully in this pluralist struggle. The argument here is simply that for the purposes of limiting group power in this countervailing system that "more is better," that the more interests that are active, the more likely the system is to be self-limiting.

vailing group power often stuns the ordinary citizen, for it leads to a conclusion that, all other things being equal, more PACs are "better" than fewer PACs. The view, moreover, is more than hypothetical; there are pieces of evidence that groups consciously attempt to offset the influence of their opponents. Certainly the success of conservative PACs in the late 1970s and early 1980s stimulated the formation of liberal PACs. And one scholarly study has found evidence of corporate PACs making contributions to members of the House Education and Labor Committee about two months after labor PACs had done so.[32] The resulting system of countervailing pressures thus liberates the legislator from the agonies of choice and gratitude. In the words of Rep. Barney Frank, a Democrat from Massachusetts,

> Business PACs invest in incumbents. It's the banks against the thrifts, the insurance companies against the banks, the Wall Street investment banks against the money center commercial banks. There's money any way you vote.[33]

The recipient may therefore be in a stronger bargaining position than the contributor.

The other side of the pluralist argument is that as PACs proliferate, the contribution of any one accounts for fewer and fewer of the receipts of the average candidate and, therefore, the political influence or leverage attached to it diminishes. The growing dispersal of PAC contributions and the diminishing dependence of a member of Congress on any one of them is apparent (Table 10-1). In fact, the dispersal is even greater than one might have expected because there are two trends at work: the number of PACs is increasing *and* the "average" PAC is spreading its contributions to more candidates rather than sharply increasing the sums of money it gives to each. The bottom line, then, is that the share of the total receipts that the average PAC contribution represents is well under one percent; for incumbents it is less than a

---

[32]Dickinson McGaw and Richard McCleary, "PAC Spending, Electioneering & Lobbying: A Vector ARIMA Time Series Analysis," *Polity*, vol. 17 (Spring 1985), 574–585.
[33]Quoted in Robert Kuttner, "Ass Backward," *The New Republic* (Apr. 22, 1985), 22.

third of one percent. If money is leverage, the leverage is not very substantial.[34]

TABLE 10-1
Dispersal of PAC Contributions to Major Party Candidates for the House of Representatives, 1982–1984

	1982	1984
Number of PACs contributing to average candidate	46	54
Number of PACs contributing to average incumbent	140	160
Average PAC contribution to average candidate	$816	$960
Average PAC contribution to average incumbent	$741	$890
Average total receipts from PACs (all candidates)	$37,904	$52,230
Average total receipts from PACs (incumbents)	$128,795	$142,352
Average PAC contribution as % of average candidate receipts	0.63%	0.76%
Average PAC contribution as % of average incumbent receipts	0.27%	0.28%

To summarize once again, the evidence simply does not support the more extravagant claims about the "buying" of the Congress. Systematic studies indicate at most a modest influence for PAC contributors, a degree of influence usually far less important than the voting constituency, the party, or the values the legislator. Moreover, several other studies suggest that the goals and capacities of most PACs are not congruent with assumptions that they set out to change congressional votes. In fact, both the extent of their influence and the nature of their operations fit much better their own stated goal of access. Finally, the development of PAC pluralism — both in the increase of countervailing PACs and in the wide dispersion of their contributions in small sums — also leads one to a more modest assessment of PAC influence. Such conclusions may serve few demonologies, but they are the only ones that serve the facts as we know them.

One last matter remains on the money-policy agenda. Several journalists have proposed a different and more basic link between money and legislative votes, one involving not individual

[34]For a similar argument, see John E. Owens, "The Impact of Campaign Contributions on Legislative Outcomes in Congress: Evidence from a House Committee," *Political Studies*, vol. 34 (June 1986), 285–295.

members of Congress but an entire legislative party. They argue that the Democrats in Congress, in order to compete with Republican fund-raising, have moved the party's ideological weight closer to the political center. The claims always refer to Rep. Tony Coelho's chairmanship of the Democratic Congressional Campaign Committee and, more generally, the party's Washington money-raisers. Among the latter, the "most corrosive of the party's identity" are said to be

> the rising Washington-based lawyers who can invest a few years laboring for the party, making contacts, and distributing funds — and then cash in handsomely in an enlarged law/lobby practice that serves mostly Republican-oriented business interests.[35]

It is not easy to assess the charge. The Democrats are certainly raising more corporate and business PAC money than they earlier did, and voices within the party urging a move to the ideological center are now louder than they were in the 1970s. But the argument rests on the proposition that individual members of Congress have altered their voting positions in order to facilitate collective party fund-raising. That proposition does not easily square with the weakness of party caucuses and steering committees in Congress, nor does it square with the fact that incumbent members of Congress raise their own reelection campaign funds — and raise them very well, too.

III. The Money Outside of the System

If we were talking about obviously illegal money, distinctions and judgments would come easily. But we are not. The issues of money unaccounted for are ones of the gray and murky areas in the law governing campaign finance. In everyday parlance they are issues of the "loophole," with all the imprecision that afflicts that word. It is a word that conjures up both legal and moral concerns — legal because some of the practices are in the ill-defined border country between legality and illegality, and moral because even when the loopholes are clearly legal we are

---

[35]Kuttner, "Ass Backward," 19.

disturbed that someone should have been shrewd enough to use them advantageously.[36]

The distinctions and ambiguities remind one of those surrounding American income tax law. There is the same distinction, however imperfectly observed, between the legal "avoidance" and the illegal "evasion." There is the same disapproval of the successful "avoiders" — no matter how clearly legal they are. There is the same frenzied attempt by lawyers and accountants to find the avenues of freer action, the regulatory loopholes or the shelters from taxation. And there is the same endless probing and litigating in the gray areas of the law, the same search for favorable rulings by the FEC or by the Internal Revenue Service.

For more than a decade, the most commented upon loophole in American campaign finance has been the one permitting independent spending. Congress had tried to restrict it in both congressional and publicly funded presidential elections, but the Supreme Court held those restrictions to be unconstitutional limitations on First Amendment rights. Whether one agrees with the Court or not, independent expenditures are now not only unambiguously legal, they are expressions of very important First Amendment freedoms. One would hardly think so, however, from much of the reporting on them.

On independent spending note, for example, the following sentence from one of campaign finance's best reporters in one of the most serious periodicals devoted to American politics:

> The tool the PACs used was independent expenditures — a controversial device, sanctioned by the Supreme Court in a landmark 1976 case, that allows individuals and PACs to skirt federal campaign contribution limits.[37]

---

[36]Not every issue these days is one of border-line legality. In late 1986 a grand jury accused three campaign committees associated with Lyndon LaRouche, seeker after the Democratic presidential nomination, with fraudulently "taking" political contributions. The indictments alleged that solicitors accepted political donations from individuals by credit card and then used the credit card numbers to "obtain" additional contributions without the cardholders' consent.

[37]Richard E. Cohen, "Spending Independently," *National Journal* (Dec. 6, 1986), 2932.

Or take the following long sentence from the *Wall Street Journal*:

> Creative accounting and "independent spending" on behalf of favored candidates are being used by special-interest groups to skirt the $5,000 limit on what their political-action committees can give directly to federal candidates.[38]

First, these sentences gratuitously impute a motivation to independent spenders. As a matter of fact, most of them have approached contribution ceilings in only a minority of their contributions to congressional campaigns; there are other strategic reasons for which they make independent expenditures. Both writers, too, use the same pejorative verb: "skirt." (Thus are political cliches born.) That is not to say that there are no reasons for concern about independent spending; it does indeed raise significant issues of responsibility. Recently there have been challenges to the genuine "independence" of some of those expenditures. There is indeed reason to ask whether in the closed world of campaign finance and campaign expertise independence can be sustained even with the best will and effort.[39]

The concerns over independent spending are constant, but other issues come and go as new loopholes come to the public's attention. When labor waxed in the late 1970s the statutory provision exempting voter mobilization programs from reporting and spending limits was widely regarded as the major one. In the late 1980s concern centers on two somewhat infelicitously named practices: "soft money" and "bundling." Soft money in campaign finance means something quite different than it does to accountants, and bundling clearly has nothing to do with the strange courtship practices of the 17th century Puritans. Both are also more interesting cases in "loopholing" than independent spending because their legality is both by law and logic less clearly settled.

Bundling is action by a PAC or party committee to assist con-

[38]Brooks Jackson, "Loopholes Allow Flood Of Campaign Giving By Business, Fat Cats," *Wall Street Journal* (July 5, 1984).

[39]On the issue of responsibility, see chap. 5. On the problem of independence of spender from the management of the campaign, one illustration will have to do. If a PAC has made contributions to a candidate and communicated with the candidate or the candidate's managers in doing so, can it then make a genuinely independent expenditure in that campaign? Can it by separating contribution managers from independent spending managers within the PAC?

tributors in making their contributions to candidates rather than to the party or PAC. At least one PAC, that of the Council for a Livable World (CLW), makes it a way of political life. The CLW prepares a list of candidates it is supporting and requests its adherents to make contributions directly to one or more of them. The Council collects and transmits the contributions; hence the term "bundling," apparently. In other instances the PAC or party committee may, when it has reached the statutory limits of its own ability to spend, turn subsequent would-be contributions into direct contributions to a chosen candidate. The National Republican Senatorial Committee (NRSC) did exactly that in 1986; having spent to the limit on endangered Republican incumbents, it then channeled an additional $6 million directly to Republican candidates. Those contributions will appear on the FEC record, both as receipts and as contributions, but not as the contributions of the NRSC.

As for "soft money," the phrase was popularized by Elizabeth Drew, the Washington columnist, in her book *Politics and Money*.[40] Although the term takes on amoebic contours in other hands, for Drew and Common Cause it refers to contributions that would be illegal under federal law (e.g., they come from illegal union or corporate sources or they would exceed a statutory limit) but that are diverted to safe financial havens in the states. Those "havens" may, too, be safe for a number of reasons. They may be candidates in states permitting contributions directly from corporate or union treasuries or having no limits on the size of contributions. Or they may be state party committees engaged in voter registration and turnout activities or other "party-building" activities excluded from the limitations of the FECA by a specific 1979 amendment to the law. Commenting on that 1979 exclusion, Drew writes,

> The theory was that the state parties should be able to participate in the publicly financed Presidential campaign. In many states, including some of the most populous ones, the laws allow union and corporate-treasury money, plus unlimited individual expenditures, to be used for political activities. But in 1980 the national parties assumed the role of raising and distributing such funds —

[40](New York: Macmillan, 1983), especially p. 15. The book's subtitle, which is more than usually revealing, is: *The New Road to Corruption.*

which was not the intent of the law — and have significantly expanded their use. Through an imaginative and questionable interpretation of the law, both parties now use soft money for congressional as well as Presidential campaigns. . . . Their rationale is that they are using soft money for non-federal elections — for governorships, state legislatures, and so on. (The only federal election mentioned in the 1979 change in the law was the one for President.) But, obviously, efforts to motivate people to vote for a party ticket at the state level are likely to benefit the candidates for federal office as well.[41]

Other commentators have broadened the concept of soft money to include the diversion of funds by national committees directly to the committees of congressional or state candidates. But whatever, soft money is directed by knowledgeable committees (almost always a party committee, it seems) from the national level to some appropriate state or local candidate or party committee. Officials for the two national committees and presidential campaigns have given estimates of the sums involved in the 1984 elections: $5.6 million for the Republicans and $6 million for the Democrats.[42]

THE CASE AGAINST SOFT MONEY

One of the most articulate voices on the side of strict enforcement of the FECA has been the Center for Responsive Politics, a Washington public policy organization. Its publications make a focused case against the use of soft money, in considerable part because it limits its use of the term to monies flowing to state and local party organizations as a result of the 1979 amendment to the FECA intended to stimulate party building in the states. In the Center's words,

> While rebuilding parties at the grass roots level is a legitimate and laudable goal, today's soft money is designed to benefit federal, not non-federal entities. Soft money supporters who argue the opposite ignore several facts. First, the national parties receive huge

[41]Ibid., 15.
[42]Herbert E. Alexander, 'Soft Money' and Campaign Financing (Washington: Public Affairs Council, 1986), 17–25.

sums of money from national donors; then they use national criteria to decide which state and local organizations get the money.
Quite often the money goes only to those regions with important
federal [i.e., Congressional] contests . . .

Second, though the operators of one or two accounts have voluntarily disclosed their funds, soft money entrepreneurs have
interpreted the law to say that they do not have to disclose any
money collected for "indirect" or "non-federal" purposes. This interpretation has enabled national parties to raise millions of
dollars without telling anyone their financial sources. . . .

Third, the history and current operation of soft money accounts
contradicts any claim that these accounts are "non-federal" in nature. Fundraisers for national parties tell prospective donors the
money will help federal candidates.

> From *Money and Politics: Campaign Spending out of Control*
> *(Washington, D.C.: Center for Responsive Politics, 1985), 23–24.*

Bundling and soft money have a number of characteristics in
common, characteristics that define a major regulatory frontier
for campaign finance in the mid-1980s.

● Both involve a kind of creative brokering, whether one calls it
channeling or funneling. And the exact position and degree of
aggressiveness of the broker is often the issue. No one, probably,
condemns a passive response to a potential contributor's question about legal options. But Common Cause's complaint about
bundling during the 1986 campaign charged more active initiatives. The Senate Republicans, it said, were soliciting funds for
candidates and accepting checks for them, but made out to the
committee. (See box for a similar view.)

● In both instances the Federal Election Commission, despite
pressure from Common Cause and others, declined to deal com-
prehensively with the practices in its formal rules. Whatever may
be its reasons and justifications, its failure to do so provided new
fuel for its critics.

● In both bundling and the raising of soft money, it is committees of the political parties who are the major brokers. That may reflect their greater political sophistication and their broader network of contacts and committees. It may also reflect the parties' greater willingness than the PACs to take political risks. In the case of the Republicans, it probably also reflects the kinds of pressures an actor in the regulatory system will create when its capacity to raise money bumps up against the constraints of the regulatory system.

And in both instances, the attempt to arrange contributions outside of legal constraints has greatly blurred responsibility for them.

Bundling and soft money are by no means the only employable loopholes in the federal regulations, however. Among others of recent celebrity are these:

● A few of the ideological PACs have set up educational foundations. They occasion no raised eyebrows when they use receipts (tax deductible receipts, that is) for educating the world. When they begin to use them to educate campaign managers in the political arts (as NCPAC is said to have done), the eyebrows begin to arch.

● Individuals and banks have in recent elections lent candidates sums of money greater than prospects for repayment seemed to warrant. Stewart Mott, a very substantial contributor to liberal candidates in the days of the old campaign finance, has boasted of lending John Anderson more than $400,000 in 1980 when doubtful prospects of repayment made it look like a very possible "contribution."

● At least in part to avoid the spending limit on the New Hampshire presidential primary campaign, Walter Mondale's organization formed separate committees for the campaigns of delegates pledged to him so that they could receive contributions for their campaigns and thus for the Mondale campaign. Adverse public reaction forced Mondale to end the practice.

Others will certainly appear from election to election, for if the media has any overriding goal in the reporting of American campaign finance, it is the spotting of candidates and committees in the regulatory no man's land.

That investigative zeal has its troublesome side. It is the tendency for the meaning of "loophole" to expand to include all money in federal campaigns outside of the scope of the FECA.[43] As the definition expands, so does the implication of financial finagling. And when pieces of reporting are furthermore given titles such as "Money in the Shadows,"[44] readers must certainly get the impression that "politicians" are once again "getting away with something." Behind such definitions of the loopholes lies an inarticulate major premise: that all contributions and all expenditures to influence federal elections ought to be limited and/or reported. That might very well be wise public policy, but Congress did not adopt it in the FECA. It chose for various reasons to exempt some flows of money, in part for practical reasons and in part for political reasons. So, spending for voter mobilization, the overhead costs of connected PACs, and local party building, for example, are outside of the reporting and control of the FECA.

To summarize once again, debate and consternation over loopholes raises both judgmental and empirical questions. As for matters of judgment, a good many distinctions are necessary. Some of the so-called loopholes involve spending that is unmistakably legal by reason of statute, administrative rule, or court decision. Independent spending, spending on voter mobilization, and spending on local party building afford but three examples. One may argue that such spending ought not to be legal, but that is an argument for new public policy. In some instances those legal and proper channels of spending have been abused in practice — by independent spending that is collusive, for instance — but that, too, is a separate issue. Some of these practices, finally, are less clearly legal. Bundling, for example, does not enjoy an explicit protection in the law; and some of its

---

[43]See, for example, Ronald Brownstein and Maxwell Glen, "Money in the Shadows," *National Journal* (Mar. 15, 1986), 632–637. Herbert Alexander also accepts that definition and even expands it a bit in *'Soft Money' and Campaign Financing.*

[44]Ibid., Brownstein and Glen.

forms, at least, appear to violate the logic and intent of the law (i.e., the FECA). In short, there are loopholes and loopholes, and they raise different kinds of judgmental issues.

As for the empirical matters, four somewhat distinct points seem appropriate and useful.

1. Political money not only flows to an open outlet, but it seeks as well to make an opening in the weakest points of the wall that contains it. The important compliance and enforcement issues in campaign finance today cluster in the gray areas, the legal uncertainties, the regulatory borderlines — whatever one prefers to call them. The controversy is at the margins.

2. Party committees and nonconnected PACs seem more inventive and persistent than other PACs and individuals in seeking the greatest freedom to spend. In part that aggressiveness results from their politicality and political expertise; but in part, too, it results from the absence of the kinds of organizational constraints that limit the connected PACs.

3. The prominence of affluent Republican party committees in these allegations suggests what is perhaps obvious: the greater the constraint of the regulatory system on a potential spender, the greater the incentive to probe its outer limits.

4. In the pressure and probing for the limits and the boundaries of regulation, the Federal Election Commission "pushes back" less firmly than spenders push forward. To be sure, its powers are limited and it constantly confronts a series of hard cases, but it is the hard cases that define the limits or weakness of a regulator.

To return to the income tax analogy, the danger to the FECA's regulatory system is not evasion or blatant illegality. It is that avoidance — however legal or, at least, "not illegal" — compromises the perceived fairness and equity of the system. Even without media overreporting, it creates a cynicism built on the assumption that the clever and powerful, armed with clever advice, can escape the restrictions of the law and, more than that, even turn them to their advantage.

IV. In Conclusion

These are three serious issues in campaign finance, and ultimately in the viability of democratic politics. They are not illusory issues, no matter how exaggerated they may be. Money does affect the outcome of elections, money does provide some basis for legislative influence, and money does sometimes try to escape the structures of regulation. It does not, however, rule American politics with the power so many Americans imagine. Whether their fears and images are susceptible to counter arguments is by no means clear. Part of the problem is that the burden of proof has shifted. One apparently doesn't have to prove that money "buys" an election or a Congress. Since common sense and conventional wisdom do not yield, one is expected to prove that it does *not*. That shift of presumption is perhaps the best indication of the strength and direction of pervasive public attitudes about money in American campaigns.

So, all three of these issues share one very important characteristic: they all reflect a set of beliefs about the harmful ways of campaign money. They reflect, that is, one very important level of reality about American campaign finance. That these attitudes and perceptions do not meet the usual scholarly standards of evidence or conceptual clarity is neither here nor there. They answer to their own system of authority — one in which the mass media play a major role. It is a system by which current anecdotes authenticate the truths and explanations of the political worldview of the Progressives. To an extraordinary degree, reporting of campaign finance is "investigative" in the best traditions of the Progressives, which is to say that its judgmental agenda is very close to the surface. So, the real events of campaign finance come to the public thoroughly intermixed with negative words, symbols, and judgments. The crediting of those reports is facilitated, of course, by the disposition of the perceiving public to share the neo-Progressive agenda.

Standards of evidence aside, it is the Progressive view of reality that animates the policy debates over campaign finance. It is certainly the view of those who would reform it. And, indeed, much of the debate over specific reform proposals is a debate over which version of reality, which picture of the nature and consequences of the new campaign finance, is the more credible. We will examine that policy debate and its attendant debate over reality in the final chapter.

11

The Campaign Finance System

Like other systems of campaign finance — those in the American past and those in other democracies — the system of today reflects with uncanny accuracy the outlines of the broader political system. Its qualities are a catalog of the special qualities of American government and politics — separate elections to separate branches, many elections to offices with fixed terms, media-based and candidate-centered campaigns, weakened political parties, constitutional limits on regulations of politics, and plurality elections in single-member districts. Where few or none of these conditions prevail — in today's European democracies, for example — campaign finance is inevitably very different.

The special nature of the new American campaign finance, however, has roots in American practices beyond the political. The raising of funds from millions of individuals reflects a uniquely American way of fund-raising, one central also to funding much of religion, charity, social services, and the performing arts in American society. It is literally unimaginable that the sums of money raised by direct-mail or media appeals in the United States could be duplicated — even with allowances for population and standard of living — in any other society in the world. Nor could one duplicate the rich and varied organizational life of the American society that underlies the substantial role of inter-

328

est groups and PACs in campaign finance. The profusion of interests reflected just in the 4,200 PACs registered with the FEC makes a peculiarly American statement.

A special political and social environment thus has produced a very characteristically American system of campaign funding. Its most salient features effectively set it apart from other nations' ways of funding campaigns.

- It is based on mass voluntary contributions, contributions from as many as 10 or 15 percent of the adults in the United States.
- It relies to a relatively small degree on public treasuries, either in direct cash payments or in "in-kind" contributions (e.g., free postage or media time).
- To an extraordinary degree, it is candidate centered and candidate controlled, both in the raising and the spending of funds.
- It raises and spends sums of money that are by the standards of European democracies, at least, very great.[1]
- Finally, it has only a relatively small role for the political parties qua parties, even taking into account their recent revival as fund-raisers.

To describe the system, however, is only to say what it is and how it compares with other nations' systems. It is not to explain how it came to be, how it operates, and how it affects the rest of American politics. These questions, in turn, form the agenda of this chapter.

The chapter begins with a look at the micropolitics of campaign finance, especially the pursuit of goals and benefits by contributors and candidates. The second section deals with the political environment or context of campaign finance and with the nature of money as a resource base. Next, we examine the growth dynamics of the system, especially the role of incumbent candidates in those dynamics. Finally, the chapter concludes with a discussion of the impact of campaign finance on representative democracy in the American political system.

---

[1]When one controls for number of voters or residents, however, campaign spending in the United States sets no international records. By such reckonings West Germany, Ireland, and Israel all outspend the United States. See Howard R. Penniman, "U.S. Elections: Really a Bargain!," *Public Opinion* (June/July 1984), 51–53.

I. Goals, Benefits, and Bargaining Power

The argument of the last chapter — that money "buys" some political influence, but not as much as conventional wisdom has it — will certainly raise a number of skeptical questions. If that's all contributors "get" for their money, why do they continue to give? Why do they settle for so little? Since money is by definition "smart," why do its contributors repeatedly give even when they seem not to get their money's worth? Why don't they put their money into more rewarding political activities? Such questions, of course, suggest very strongly that the initial conclusion about the influence of money is in error; they are, therefore, often rhetorical questions. But they are appropriate, and they lead easily to some useful conclusions about the use and value of political money.[2]

What *do* contributors get for their money? To begin, they get a good many hard-to-specify nonpolitical benefits — perhaps a nice party, the approval of superiors, proximity to the famous, friendship or a business contact, the benefits of organizational loyalty, perhaps just relief that a solicitor has gone away. Even the more political and more rational PACs have nonpolitical goals. PACs collect and contribute money just to survive, to pay or justify administrative and entrepreneurial salaries, to please the leadership of the parent organization, to maintain donor satisfaction, perhaps just to build stature and esteem for themselves or a parent. There are other reasons, too, but whoever neglects the nonpolitical rewards for funding candidates does so at considerable peril.

Nonetheless, the political goals and benefits are more important. Most of them can be divided into the electoral and the legislative. Individuals, PACs, and parties give money above all to influence the outcome of elections — that is, to elect and main-

---

[2]One can also approach the questions by arguing that the magnitudes of the sums contributed are insufficiently large to serve as a base for the generation of more political influence. I have in several places earlier in the book raised the issue, and it is worth noting again that the sums are small except by the standards of personal finance. The sums spent on all campaigns for the Congress, for example, are less than one-third the total advertising budgets of the Big Three American automobile makers. The difficulty with the "too little" argument is that one too easily slips into the circularity of supporting the argument by showing how little it "buys."

tain in office like-minded men and women. And in the aggregate they doubtless do, funding being a necessary resource for most candidacies. The problem is in telling whether a specific contribution or contributory strategy has done so, either for a candidate or a legislative party. Many PACs achieve a pseudo-certainty about electoral impact by giving heavily to incumbents and then proudly displaying a winning record to donors. For many other contributors it is an impact they take on faith, as a part of the good fight fought or the civic duty done, much as they might reckon the efficacy of a vote in an election.

The legislative benefit (or "payoff") is primarily one of access. That access converts by some mechanism — persuasion, gratitude, or whatever — to some modest degree of influence over votes cast in the chambers and the committees of Congress. Often it does so as a part of a strategy that links campaign finance to lobbying, grass-roots mobilization, and other techniques of influencing policy. There also may be additional legislative benefits: the attention of the powerful and important, the introduction of favorite bills, speeches and other overt support for policy positions, case work for the individual or group contributor, for instance. Again, the identification of the benefits is not certain, but it is easier than the identification of electoral benefits. Access can be measured in terms of appointments granted and phone calls returned; and case work, bill introductions, and the votes of members of Congress can easily be toted up. Determining who deserves credit for a "right" vote on the floor may be chancier, but the combination of the will to believe and cues from the member of Congress casting the vote make it hard to resist a self-pleasing conclusion.

Whether those benefits or accomplishments are "enough" only the contributors can say. But they are not so little as to turn most of them away from campaign finance. The question might better be put in other ways: why don't contributors ask for more than they do, or why don't they set their political sights somewhat higher? To some extent they are constrained by their political position. There is no doubt that all of the negative publicity and popular suspicions have put contributors, especially PACs, on the defensive. Whether the publicity is fair or accurate is somewhat beside the point; it is there, and it finds supporting

resonances and credibility in the mass public. It is understandably intimidating; and what is intimidating is limiting, especially
for the PACs with parent organizations concerned about public
images.

Uncertainty and misinformation also confuse the contributors'
assessments of benefits. It is not easy to assess the impact of a contribution on a campaign or an election; nor is it always easy to
gauge the outcome of access. But in such a setting of uncertainty,
contributors are being assured by their critics that they have the
ability to buy elections, buy members of Congress, buy the Congress itself. The more sophisticated among PAC managers may
come to their own more realistic estimates; but the extravagant
assessments weigh more heavily with the less sophisticated, all
the way from corporate CEOs to donors to the PAC. When the
bullish claims for PAC influence come from members of the Congress itself, the claims are all the more credible. Even for those
contributors who see the mixed signals, the uncertainty over who
to believe promotes more contributions. Groups especially hesitate to bypass a route of possible influence that competing or
opposing interests are taking. It is not that they always seek advantage; they may only seek not to be at a disadvantage.

Finally, contributors are constrained by an ample supply of
campaign money. It is a supply shaped by American voluntarism,
mass political participation, and group pluralism. The sums of
money are substantial; there has been, that is, no great shortage
of it. It has increased by more than threefold between 1976 and
1986. Moreover, it comes from a large number of different
sources — diverse PACs, individuals, party committees, and
public treasuries. Very few contributions are indispensable to a
single candidate. Not many of them account for more than a few
percent of a candidate's receipts, and the average is far below
that. Moreover, no group of contributors can greatly affect the
supply of campaign money. And most of them are, from the point
of view of many candidates, easily replaced.

Take the expansion of campaign money in the 1970s and 1980s
as a case in point. As the supply of campaign money grew, contributors continued to adhere to a low-risk and low-benefit
strategy — to a strategy of modest expectations. They continued
to give to incumbents, and they continued to spread their contri-

butions widely in relatively small sums. While the myth-makers talked about PACs "maxing" out, the average PAC contribution was only a little more than one-tenth the combined PAC contribution limits for the primary and general election ($10,000). To be sure, some of that dispersion resulted from the unwillingness of some candidates to explain large contributions from PACs. But that point in turn only illustrates both the power of the contributors' critics and the easy availability to candidates of alternative sources of money.

Conversely, candidates, especially incumbent candidates, are in a particularly strong position in the exchange. They complain about the rigors and embarrassments of fund-raising, and certainly not every candidate finds it easy to tap the pool of available money. Contributors do not squander it on improbable causes, and even the competitive challenger does not easily find the risk-takers among the contributors. But once the candidate finds it, it comes with expectations that are not hard to meet. Access is a powerful and benign incentive for incumbents to use and for other candidates to promise. It can be spread as widely as time and energy permit. Unlike ideology or issue support — likemindedness, that is — it can be offered to all contributors regardless of issue commitments. Case work, the introduction of bills, the supporting floor speech — all of these costs are usual political services that most congressional offices are staffed to provide. Even influence over the member's vote may come easily, especially if it is on a "free vote" — a vote on a detailed and less visible matter in which no other claimants (party, constituency, leadership, strong personal convictions) are alert and demanding.

To be sure, fund-raising takes a toll of the time, energy, and attention of legislators. The raising of money for the next campaign follows hard on the heels of the previous one, and there is little relief or surcease. It is a task that tires even the most enthusiastic fund-raisers, and it depresses those incumbents who find it distasteful. It is a task that is bound, in the nature of it, to complicate the relationship of legislators and lobbyists; and especially with the holding of fund-raising events during legislative sessions, it risks the semblance of impropriety. To reduce the costs, candidates have several options. They, especially incumbents, may begin to raise money in bigger and "more efficient" chunks — from PACs primarily. Or they may legislate to modify the system itself; at least some of the reformist zeal in Congress in 1986 and 1987 resulted from that spur.

The benefits of the system for the candidate are nonetheless substantial. Money buys freedom — freedom for candidates to run their own campaigns, freedom from the limitations of the party, freedom to plot a future political career. Even money from party committees tends to come without strings; the one source of money with a legitimate claim to demand candidate loyalty in return for it, ironically, rarely makes that claim.[3] For the incumbent candidate, the easy availability of money opens even greater career opportunities. Early money frightens away able challengers, both in their own and in the other party, and the ability to raise money opens the way to other and higher public offices. Money organized through personal PACs may even open the way to positions of legislative leadership. The effect is certainly to reduce electoral competitiveness; but that is, after all, the purpose of it.

So, the demands attaching to political money are moderated both by limitations on the goals and expectations of contributors and by the bargaining strength of candidates in the transactional exchange. Money, therefore, seems not to purchase — or be capable of purchasing — what political mythology says it can. In addition, the argument so far leads to two surprising conclusions about money in the American political context. First, it suggests that money works poorly as a separate and independent base of political influence and that its effectiveness is limited by other structures and influences in the political system. Second, and even more contrary to conventional views, it suggests that the efficacy of money is related inversely to its supply and to the breadth of the distribution of that supply — and that the expanding supply of campaign money actually diminishes the leverage that attaches to it. Before we accept these conclusions, however,

---

[3]It has long been the hope of advocates of "party responsibility" that by recapturing control of the necessary resources of campaigns the party would develop the sanctions and capacity with which to assure candidate loyalty to the party program and thus establish the capacity of the party to govern. There are as yet no signs that things are working out that way for the parties.

an excursion into the political context or environment of campaign money will help to clarify things.

II. Money as a Political Resource

Two great changes in the environment of American campaign finance after World War II have governed its major contours in the era of the 1970s and after. First, there are the myriad changes in American electoral politics — the use of mass media, the rise of new campaign technologies and technocrats, the decline of parties and party loyalties, more selective and more volatile patterns of voting behavior, and the emergence of the candidate as both the focus and the planner of the campaign. Those changes demanded a new cash economy for the new campaigning. Money bought or rented almost everything, while voluntary labor and party-based skills counted for much less.

AN EXPLOSION OF ORGANIZED INTEREST: SOME INDICATORS

The changes in the country's interest group system in the 1960s and 1970s reflected itself in a number of very concrete ways in the nation's capital. One certainly could have found similar indicators in the states and localties.

Fully 40 percent of the organizations having offices in Washington have been founded since 1960 and 25 percent since 1970. Equally striking is the distribution for the various categories. Seventy-six percent of the citizens' groups, 56 percent of the civil rights groups, and 79 percent of the social welfare and poor people's organizations but only 38 percent of the trade associations and 14 percent of the corporations were founded since 1960.[4]

[4]Kay L. Schlozman and John T. Tierney, *Organized Interests and American Democracy* (New York: Harper and Row, 1986), 75.

Lobbyists registered with Congress increased from 1317 in 1974 to 2335 in 1984.[5] Interest mobilization blossomed even within Congress; interest caucuses began to multiply rapidly in the 1970s. The first of the congressional caucuses, the Democratic Study Group, came on the scene in 1959. The Congressional Black Caucus, founded in 1971, was only the fourth. None were added in 1972, and then the growth escalated.

Year	Number Begun	Example from the Year
1973	6	New England Congressional Caucus
1975	4	Congressional Mushroom Caucus
1977	12	Blue Collar Caucus
1979	14	Senate Coal Caucus
1981	19	Congressional Arts Caucus
1983	16	Local Government Caucus
1985	19	Senate Anti-Terrorism Caucus

(By 1987 there were 105 caucuses in operation.)

Source: The Congressional Research Service of the Library of Congress, published in the newspaper of Capitol Hill, Roll Call, on Mar. 16, 1987.

A little later than these changes in electoral politics and a little before the new era in campaign finance, American politics also experienced an explosion of organized political activity. By any number of indicators the number and activity of organizations reached new dimensions in the 1970s (see box). From Washington down to the neighborhood level, increasing numbers of Americans began to ally themselves politically not with a large and omnibus political party, but with a narrower, more focused group that expressed their particular, even isolated, interests and commitments. Deriving from the expansion of group resources and activity was a new attention to matters of policy in the nation's politics. That attention was perhaps symbolized by the

---

[5]There were only 603 registered in 1972. Data come from the annual volumes of the Congressional Quarterly Almanac and include both individual and group registrations. Similarly, Washington Representatives (Washington, D.C.: Columbia, 1979) listed 5570 organizations with representatives in its 3d ed.; by the time of the 1982 ed., the number had jumped to 7763, an increase of 39 percent in three years.

single issue voter, the one so narrow and dedicated in a political focus that nothing else mattered but that one issue.

Integral to the new mobilization of interests was an expansion of the nation's political agenda after World War II. Groups multiplied and became more important simply because there were more policy domains about which to be concerned. One need note only the addition of issues such as race and gender, worldwide foreign policies, defense and disarmament, energy and conservation, the environment, lifestyle and morality, consumerism, and sexual and reproductive freedom. The scope and range of government interventions grew, and more and more people had greater and greater stakes in what it was doing.

The explosion of organized activity, of course, had its impact on American campaign finance. The number of PACs registered with the FEC grew from 608 at the end of 1974 to 4157 just 12 years later. More important, the sum of money they contributed to congressional campaigns increased from $12.5 million in 1974 to $132.2 million in 1986. Organized groups and interests had always participated in American electoral politics — organized labor being a good example — but until the 1970s it was at least roughly true that groups largely left electoral politics to the political parties. It is no longer the case. At least in the provision of cash resources for campaigning, groups and their instruments eclipsed the parties. Nor were individual contributors untouched by group loyalties. Much of the fund-raising in the major urban centers of the country drew on the group loyalties of, for example, women, industry groups, and ethnic and religious communities.

These two great changes created a politics of money and organization. Money certainly assumed a new importance, a new centrality, in the country's electoral and legislative politics. The developments that raised money to new importance also created new elites in campaign finance. Parties and wealthy individuals were the royalty of the old way; candidates and organizations inherited their positions in the new one. But it was not money that made the candidates and groups into the chief actors in the campaign finance system. Their position was established by more fundamental changes in American society and politics. Money flowed to them as a result of their enhanced position.

Perhaps nothing illustrates that point more clearly than the struggle of the political parties to redeem themselves through money. Nationally at least, they raise and spend more money now than at any time in the last generation. From 1976 to 1986, for example, party spending on behalf of congressional candidates increased by more than four times from $4.9 million to $20.3 million. They also have armed themselves with expertise of all kinds for recruiting party candidates, for rebuilding state and local party organizations, and for staging effective campaigns. Money, not volunteered effort, was the resource of choice. But the parties have been unable to use their spending for very much beyond the electoral goals of their candidates. Much of the money they raise, in fact, has been raised by the legislative parties, whether one thinks of the Hill committees in Washington or legislative caucuses in many states. Looked at generally, the parties have not been able to regain control of the campaigns of their candidates, and they certainly have not been able to promote support for any platform or policy goals with their campaign money. Their position in American politics simply provides little on which to build, and money alone hasn't provided the foundation of new party power.

The uses of political money, that is, grow out of and reflect the configurations of influence in American politics. There were initially both fears and hopes that it might be otherwise — that, for instance, broad coalitions of business and corporate PACs would form. Just as their parents are fragmented and slow to form coalitions or even communication networks, PACs also pursue relatively individualistic and separate goals and strategies. It is a separatism borne of a lack of internal cohesion and of their external conflicts over policy and their different contribution strategies. Nothing better underscores the individualism of PACs than their self-professed goal of legislative access, for access, unlike ideology, is a very individual and particularistic goal. Their low-risk, low-benefit, incumbent supporting strategies are extensions of the kinds of strategies organized interests pursue in legislative politics or grass-roots voter mobilization.

American campaign finance can best be understood, therefore, as an extension of deeply set patterns of interests and influence in American politics. Contributors do not easily subordinate individual goals or interests for the collective, whether it is a collective of party, ideology, or overarching interests (e.g., "business"). They fight constantly for political advantage or survival in an extraordinarily dense and complex array of groups and individuals who also pursue varied, limited, and specific goals. The nonpolitical and the political goals of contributors are amazingly diverse, and they pursue contributory strategies that range from the simple and unsophisticated to extensive ones that combine contribution with lobbying or voter mobilization.

To summarize: money seeks electoral and legislative influence, but it does so in a limited and derivative way. While money is a useful resource for achieving electoral victory and even shaping legislative policy, it is not by itself sufficient. And it will not be in a healthy, plural democracy in which a large number of organized interests contest for influence and in which the power of local electorates remains the determiner of who wins and who loses elections. A paradigm of congressional decision-making sums up the reasons why it is not sufficient. Money shares influence with the presidency, with legislative peers and leadership, with the parties, with groups and lobbyists, and with the electorates back in the constituencies — whether the sharing results from conflict over specific policies or from separate hegemonies over specific policy domains. (For a similar view, see box.) In pursuing strategies that link the use of campaign money to other forms of political influence and political mobilization, many of the most experienced PACs testify to the importance of linking campaign finance to other means and avenues of influence.

THE NATURAL LIMITS TO PAC POWER

Elbows are sharp and abundant in the Washington push for influence over congressional policy-making. Is there a regulatory or limiting mechanism in that pushing and shoving? Traditional pluralist arguments would say yes, and so does a prominent Washington commentator.

. . . there was little doubt in the last Congress that members of the House Commerce Committee could take in more campaign money by supporting the pro-industry position on revision of the Clean Air Act than by opposing it. The number and size of the PACs on the industry side dwarfed what the environmentalists had.

But it did not take many trips home in 1982 to convince uncommited members that siding with industry on clear air was not a very good political vote. For all the recent criticism of environmentalists as being hostile to job and economic growth, members of Congress are notoriously skittish about giving an opponent a chance to portray them as being against clean air or clean water.

How many incumbents feel $50,000 in PAC money is worth the risk of a commercial in the next campaign accusing them of being in bed with polluters? In most parts of the country, not many.

— *Alan Ehrenhalt, "The Natural Limitations of PAC Power,"*
Congressional Quarterly *(Apr. 9, 1983), 723.*

I would not want to argue on the basis of campaign finance in the United States, 1974–1987, that systems of campaign finance are intrinsically derivative or (as the sociologists say) epiphenominal. The evidence is too limited. It may well be the case that money has generated new structures of influence in other places and in other times in American history. At least it seems in retrospect that money was more powerful in America's Gilded Age than it has been recently. But was it? Or was campaign money of that era merely an extension of a system of influence in which a small wealthy elite dominated public discourse and public office in the states and nation?

Perhaps the distinction we seek is a rudimentary one. In political systems in which influence largely reflects wealth, the money of the system of campaign finance merges with and flows from the wealth that organizes influence more generally. Distinctions about what is derivative and what is independent are almost scholastic. But in political systems in which influence reflects bases other than money, that money, especially if its sources are diverse, will reflect the reigning configuration of influence. The "real" question concerns the ability of large amounts of campaign money (especially from limited sources) to work a fundamental change in the existing distribution of influence, perhaps even to convert its diverse base to one of wealth. But that is a "natural experiment" we have not yet conducted.

In understanding the status quo and in working through future scenarios, it seems clear that the supply and distribution of campaign money are matters of the greatest importance. In the new American era of campaign finance, money has been derivative of existing patterns of influence largely because we have achieved a fragmentation of its sources and a limit to their contributing — a greatly broadened base — without at the same time constricting the total supply of campaign money available. That, without any doubt, has been the FECA's finest accomplishment.

That ample supply remains a major constraint on the demands and expectations of contributors. But the exchanges of campaign finance are bilateral, and one may fairly ask whether that supply of campaign money has not shifted the advantage too far to the side of incumbent candidates. Both in the states and the nation they are accused of pursuing it to the neglect of their legislative duties and of using it to diminish the competitiveness of our electoral politics.

III. The Driving Mechanism: Incumbency

A controversy, however poorly joined, has raged since the take-off of campaign expenditure levels over the cause or causes of the sharp increases. Are they the result of more lavish contributions, especially those of PACs, or are they the result of the escalating costs of media advertising? The question is an interesting one on its own terms, but beyond those terms the answers to it also provide further clues to the nature of the campaign finance system. Is the growth dynamic at operation in that system internal or external to it? Does it cast some light on the contributor-candidate relationship?

The central facts behind the rise in spending are beyond dispute. Direct political expenditures in the 1976 congressional elections — all candidate expenditures, all independent spending, and all of the party "on behalf of" spending — totaled

$104,346,477; by 1986 the comparable figure had risen sharply to $478,804,432.[6] That's an increase of 359 percent in a little more than a decade; even if one discounts for the 93 percent rise in the Consumer Price Index, it is an increase of 148 percent, since the 1986 expenditures are "worth" approximately $258.4 million in 1976 dollars.

Conventional wisdom propounds two quite different explanations for the growth. Much of the media and public subscribe to an explanation that attributes the steep rise in spending to the increased availability of money, especially PAC money. Campaign finance insiders, on the other hand, most commonly hold to a "cost-push" explanation. Costs have shot up because the costs of campaign technologies — especially the media and related costs — have shot up well beyond the climb of the CPI.

Neither of the explanations passes muster. PAC contributions have risen at a rate only somewhat greater than the total costs of the congressional campaigns. Candidates still tap individual contributors for more than half of their receipts, and party spending is increasingly important.[7] Furthermore, there is no substantial body of evidence of contributor aggressiveness or competition in setting new funding levels. Most contributors remain relatively passive participants in the transactions of campaign finance. Even as contributions rose sharply, their contributing strategies remained the low-risk and limited-benefit ones of the early years post-FECA.

As for the cost-push explanation — the rising cost of campaigns and their technologies — it suffers too from a faulty major premise. Notwithstanding all the assertions, there are no convincing data to support the argument that media and other costs have in fact risen faster than the CPI. Between 1976 and 1982, the period of the great explosion of campaign expenditures, the McCann-Erickson index to media advertising costs rose 79 percent (Table 11-1) against a rise of 69 percent in the Consumer Price Index. The 10 percentage points difference seem even less

---

[6]The 1976 FEC data, however, understate total candidate expenditures, since they include spending only by the candidates in the general election. Later estimates of total spending in 1976 add $16.5 million to the FEC's original sums. If one adds it here, then the gross percent increase between 1976 and 1986 is 296 percent, which after adjustment for the rise in the CPI is 114 percent.

[7]Supporting data are scattered throughout chaps. 3, 4, and 5.

important if one keeps in mind that the largest jump was registered in the medium (evening network television) that congressional candidates are least likely to use.

TABLE 11-1
McCann-Erickson Index to Media Advertising Costs, 1976–1982

Medium	% Increase
Evening network television	121
Spot television	50
Newspaper	77
Spot radio	98
Direct mail	38
Outdoor	104
Composite advertising index°	79

Source: Robert J. Coen's articles in *Advertising Age,* Sept. 25, 1978, and Nov. 7, 1983; the data measure unit costs (rather than cost per thousand persons reached).

°This apparently is an index of all advertising costs, weighted by relative use; it includes network radio and magazines in addition to the six media listed in the table.

Beyond this issue of fact, there is an especially thorny analytical issue in the cost-push hypothesis. Some observers of American politics would say in reply to the last paragraph that the explanation is not in increased media costs per unit but in the "need" of candidates to buy *more* units to be competitive. Indeed, the argument often extends to the claim that candidates must buy more of most things in the campaign. (No matter that these observers never take account of the instances of decreased costs, technological efficiencies, and eliminated costs in contemporary campaigns.) The "proposition of more" may be a useful statement on the futility of fighting modern campaigns without the best and most varied set of weapons; but as an explanation of the rising costs of campaigns, it will not do. It is substantially a circular argument that higher expenditure levels are caused by greater spending.

In fact, the driving mechanism for the upward spiral in campaign costs appears to be the candidates themselves. Implicitly, at least, they have shared a central assumption with nonpolitical fund-raisers: that money is "out there" for the asking. And it has been — in an ever-expanding pool. One might even argue that it has exerted the force of Say's law: that supply creates its own demand. So, impelled by the interests of their political careers and enabled by the availability of more and more money, candidates have driven up the costs of campaigning. As fund-raising has become more aggressive and more artful, it has furthermore become clear that one subset of candidates, the incumbents, have far outstripped their challengers at it. By the late 1980s one must conclude, I think, that they, the incumbents, are the driving mechanism in rising campaign costs. It is true that open seat candidates, attractive for their competitiveness and electability, match or exceed incumbents in the sums they spend; but their numbers are too small to control the dynamic.

TABLE 11-2
Two Indicators of Increased Incumbent Funding, 1976–1986

	Incumbent Spending as % of Incumbent-Challenger Spending	% PAC Total Contributions Going to Incumbents
1976	61.9%	—
1978	61.1	60.4
1980	59.8	65.8
1982	65.8	66.8
1984	70.8	72.4
1986	71.5	68.9

In fact, one sees the onset of incumbent domination in the funding of their congressional campaigns from 1976 to 1986 (Table 11-2). Incumbent spending has increased at a rate faster than that of their challengers; thus incumbents account for an increasingly larger percentage of incumbent-challenger spending. Their share of the PAC bounty also increased slowly but inexorably — and PAC money is inclined to be valuable early money. The availability of that intimidating early money is, however, best indicated by the sums of cash candidates report having on hand at the beginning of the election cycle. At the beginning of the

1977–78 cycle, House incumbents had $5 million in the bank, and Senate incumbent candidates had $.7 million; by the 1983–84 cycle, the House incumbents had raised the count to $18.6 million and Senate incumbents to $3.1 million. Virtually no other candidates, one should understand, begin cycles with cash on hand; the 1984 House incumbents had 99.4 percent of the beginning cash of all House candidates, and the Senate incumbents had 93.5 percent of the Senate total. So, incumbents, especially those in the House, work themselves into a fundraising–reelection interaction in which greater fund-raising success increases their reelection rate and their reelection rate bolsters their fund-raising successes.

The early affluent funding of incumbents probably also sets the funding norm or target at which other candidates aim. Given incumbent success rates in winning reelection, what incumbents spend is also what winners spend. Those averages or approximations quickly enter the conventional wisdom of politics as one measure of "what you have to raise to have a chance of winning." To a great extent their campaigns also define modernity and professionalism in contemporary campaigning — and so they also set the norm for the activities of a competitive campaign. The norms of funding and the norms of campaigning, in turn, feed on and reinforce each other.

In the arms race of campaign funding, there have been precious few doubts about the availability of resources. The growth dynamic seemed to work in a limitless pool of resources. In the early years of the operation of the FECA, the supply of resources grew out of a contributor confidence that, in some often unspecified way, contributions converted directly into substantial political influence. The growth also reflected contributors' fear of being excluded by their own lack of enterprise from a new and potent political avenue. Behind the confidence of contributors, millions of Americans, for a complex set of reasons, lined up to surrender a small part of their assets to fund campaigns.

By the latter 1980s, however, there were signs that contributor confidence was waning, that experience was leading contributors to have a more modest and more realistic set of expectations. A decade of occasional losses in congressional politics and a more general difficulty in achieving political goals were said to be taking their toll. At the same time aggressive fund-raising, especially by incumbents, began to fuel a reaction. One increasingly heard talk of PACs being exploited and of contributions being "extorted." Reporting on in-depth interviews with 20 managers of corporate PACs, a report of the Conference Board concluded in part

> While the managers recognize the pressure on them to gather large amounts of money, they observe that the role of individual corporate contributors to candidates remains rather small. There is general agreement that the PAC system is beloved by many members of Congress because, the executives reason, the broader the base of support the less accountability there is to individual campaign contributors.[8]

Beneath all of these complaints is one common theme: contributor subjugation by candidates, especially incumbent candidates. Some group contributors even began to have trouble raising money from individuals; the problems of Republican committees and the ideological PACs of the right have already been set out. Even some of the profitable devices of political fund-raising failed; direct-mail solicitations especially no longer seemed able to provide the clutch of golden eggs.

Yet for all the unhappiness and all the portents of contributor resistance, for all of the problems some PACs and party committees have getting the money to give, the aggregate sums of money available to candidates are not diminishing. Contributor resistance, at least in part still at the talking stage, may some day alter that aggregate total, and then contributor-candidate relationships will change drastically. Until then, however, the candidate is king, especially the incumbent candidate. Perhaps the ultimate weapon in the hands of the candidates, the one that gives them a permanent advantage in the money relationship, is their control of public office or the possibility of that control. If it is, we have yet one more indication of the relationship of campaign finance to the broader politics of influence over policy-making.

For now, then, the evidence that it is the incumbents who have led the upward spiral of campaign costs also testifies to their

---

[8]Catherine Morrison, *Managing Corporate Political Action Committees* (New York: Conference Board, 1986), 21.

strong position vis à vis contributors. They thrive in a marketplace in which they negotiate with many diverse and fragmented contributors of relatively small sums. They have many funding alternatives, no one of which can thus exert much leverage on them. Their position is strengthened, moreover, by all of the assets of office they have over their would-be challengers. Individually they pursue their own career goals without great limitation, and collectively they keep the money machine in motion.

Finally, if it is the incumbents rather than the costs of campaigning that explain the growth dynamic within campaign finance, we have one more bit of evidence that the campaign finance system is indeed a system. It is an enclosed mechanism powered by the interactions of its components, one in which the behavior of one set of actors has consequences for the others and for the system as a whole. It is indeed constrained by an external environment, but its basic dimensions and rhythms are driven by relationships contained within it.

IV. Money and Representation

Campaign money does generate some measure of influence over American elections and policy-making. The only argument is over how much. To some debatable extent, then, contributors and spenders become important new participants in the open contesting of American democratic politics. Indeed their activities focus on the two key points in the chain of processes that connects citizens to what popular government does: the election of representatives and the policy-making of those representatives.

The nub of the power of the new campaign money — the campaign resource constituencies — is in their separation from the electoral constituencies. At an earlier time in American politics, resources for campaigning were controlled, as they now are elsewhere, by the political parties. Moreover, cash accounted for a much smaller percentage of those resources than it now does. The parties raised a major part of the cash, and they monopolized the noncash resources: the volunteer campaign labor, the events and media of the campaign, the information about voters (i.e., the fruits of canvassing), even the symbols and slogans of electoral politics. The electoral and resource constituencies were congruent. Both were rooted in the localism of the geographically defined voting constituency and in the matching units of party organization. Legal definitions of the parties by state law made sure that party organizations did in fact match the voting districts.

The new cash politics, however, produced new resource constituencies. Made up of PAC and individual contributors, they are fluid and fragmented, but above all, increasingly regional or national. The people who give the resources for the campaign are, therefore, increasingly different from the people who vote in the election. Money and the disposition to give it to candidates are simply not distributed across the country in the same way as are voting adults. And in view of that fact, therefore, the *more* money campaigns use, the less local will be the resource constituencies. So, nationally organized and managed PACs assume a larger role. The major parties find a new role in cash support of candidates by national committees; in some instances, indeed, state party organizations sign agency agreements ceding their statutory spending authority to national party committees. And candidates troop across the country to raise money from affluent individuals in the country's metropolitan areas.[9]

The divergence of electoral and resource constituencies have enriched and complicated representation in the American democracy. For example,

1. The two constituencies do not always have the same preferences on issues of public policy, a disjuncture more likely for Democratic than Republican candidates. Conflicting pressures both in the campaign and in public office follow. To some extent incumbents can "manage" the cross-pressures by appealing to the electoral constituency with a variety of case

---

[9]Janet Grenzke in a study of 172 House incumbents finds that 52 percent of their individual contributions of $500 or more came from individuals within the district in 1977–78. By 1981–82 that figure had declined to 39 percent. It is difficult to say, however, whether the declining percentage is a result of long-term trends or of the effect of incumbency on fund-raising. *District Contributions and Congressional Voting Behavior: What Is the Connection?* (unpublished manuscript).

work and constituency services that have very little to do with policy questions.[10]

2. The candidate who raises substantial "out of state" (or "out of district") money runs the risk of backlash in the electoral constituency. Local voters resent the intrusion of distant money, and the national cash constituencies enter campaigns precisely because they are unwilling to let local constituencies affect interests they think extend far beyond the local boundaries. The issue is sharply drawn: ought an influential member of Congress, one with important committee or subcommittee responsibilities that can affect the interests of people all across the nation, answer only to a few hundred thousand, or even a few million, folks back home?

3. The increasing amounts of campaign money thus become another influence shaping an extra-legal, informal functional representation. One of the reasons for the decay of party loyalties and straight-ticket party voting, in fact, has been the increasing desire of many better-educated middle-class Americans to identify with and act with others who share well-defined and well-focused interests. In a word, they want to "diversify" their political investments in a way in which loyalty to a party never permits. The result is an uneasy amalgam of party, local, and functional participation in campaigns — and eventually in all of American democracy.

This development of a broader resource constituency has had other ramifications. It has helped to increase the role of policy in electoral politics and, thus, to foster the greater homogeneity and cohesion of the parties in Congress. But above all, the penetration of regional or national interests into local electoral politics is also at the very heart of the insecurity of incumbents. Incumbents can win the loyalties of local political elites and maintain the loyalty of enough constituents with the usual incumbent advantages; the one contingency out of their control is the sudden and substantial support for challengers that outside

---

[10]Morris Fiorina details that form of constituency cultivation in *Congress: Keystone of the Washington Establishment* (New Haven: Yale University Press, 1977).

money can provide. Thus the new resource constituencies have raised the stakes *of* politics while raising the stakes *for* politics.

For all of the diversity of the interests they represent, the new resource constituencies largely share one common characteristic: they reflect a politics of the middle class. To be sure, organized labor was a powerful resource constituency before 1974, and it continues to be. Much of the new growth in national contributors, however, has been in individuals and PACs reflecting the new middle-class agendas, all the way from profession and occupation to conservation, gender, and life-style. The growth of the PAC movement surely reflects the middle class's political loyalties, its sophistication about issues, its organizational skills, its preference for spending money rather than its leisure times, and its increasing rejection of party politics, especially those of party organizations. Above all, the middle-class nature of the new resource constituencies reflects the money's origin: the American tradition of voluntarism that reflects heavily the values and the affluence of the middle class.

The middle-class nature of campaign resources holds true whether one talks of cash or noncash contributions, for middle-class skills and education are just as important in today's volunteer campaigning as is middle-class money on the cash side. Moreover, it holds whether one is talking of national or local sources of cash. Even in discussing cash raised within the electoral constituency, one speaks increasingly of modest contributions by middle-class contributors. To simplify somewhat, the cash of the very wealthy is not as dominant as it once was; and the noncash contributions of unskilled or semiskilled activists are no longer as important as they once were. The contributions of an educated and affluent middle class become central and crucial. It is likely, surely, that their effect will be to strengthen support for the middle-class agenda in the making of public policy.

One cannot forget that the new resource constituencies are very broadly based, for the new era in American campaign finance is probably the most broadly based voluntary system any democracy has achieved. Some 10 to 15 million Americans, at the very least, contribute money each year to candidates, parties, and PACs. Contributing money to electoral politics has become the second most common form of political activity in the

American polity, second only to voting. While many of the contributions result from heightened political awareness, in many instances they actually heighten awareness and political involvement. And so, the sheer numbers of people in these heavily middle-class constituencies give one more push toward a prevailingly middle-class politics in the United States — one protective of middle-class social and economic interests, one centrist and pragmatic by the usual ideological measures, and one more attuned to specific candidate and group appeals than to the all-embracing agendas of political parties.

These are by no means the only impacts of campaign finance on the processes of representative democracy. They are only the ones we know about most or have thought about most. In addition to them, there are a number of significant questions that are, despite their lesser visibility, no less important or worthy of attention. For instance, we ponder very little the impact of the ways of campaign finance on the campaigns and elections themselves. There is reason to think that spending in campaigns boosts turnouts,[11] but very little more. That conclusion supports a straightforward logic: spending increases the quantity of the campaign, which increases its salience for voters, which in turn stimulates them to vote. But we know very little about the effect of new levels of funding on the content, the quality, of campaigns — and of those effects on voters or, just as important, on potential voters.

Within the conventional wisdom — largely in the point-scoring subdivision of it — there are two schools of thought about the effect of the new finance on the electorate. One school argues that the excesses of getting and spending money lead to feelings of disgust or outrage in the electorate, which in turn leads to increased nonvoting. Another school maintains that we need to spend more to bring issues and candidates to the attention of voters and thus spur them to vote. Obviously both sides can't be right; and given the judgmental tone of the debate, it seems unlikely that scholarly evidence will settle it. Nonetheless, there is no evidence on the side of the "disgust and loathing" hypothesis, and there is some on the other side. Perhaps the sur-

[11]Samuel Patterson, and Gregory Caldiera, "Getting Out the Vote: Participation in Gubernatorial Elections," *American Political Science Review*, vol. 77 (Sept. 1983), 684ff.

est conclusion is that such arguments in the end have little to do with evidence and understanding.

There is also the question of campaign funding's impact on the recruitment of candidates themselves — another question to which there is no answer. Do we lose the potential services of talented individuals who shun candidacy because they cannot or will not raise money? Ought that skill at or taste for raising money be permitted to define a pool of talent for elective public office? And does that screen for talent in fact select candidates with characteristics different from those the pool would otherwise have? And what indeed might those different qualities be — apart from the obvious ones in raising campaign resources?

Regardless of how one answers these questions, it seems beyond argument that candidates for Congress are by and large successful fund-raisers and that they have in part been selected for that reason. Many of them are already experienced at it, having previously run for or held office. Their skills are apparent in the high levels of expenditure that characterize open seat races for the House and Senate. One can in fact argue that a process of natural selection is at work and that fund-raising skills are conspicuous among those skills necessary for political survival. We breed, therefore, a class of officeholders who are especially apt in finding campaign resources. That "selection" and its consequences adds one more impetus to the incumbent-driven escalation of the costs of campaigning.

Finally, the uneven distribution of money for American campaigning inevitably affects the nature and extent of competitiveness in American elections. In most instances the effect is to further entrench incumbents in office by enabling them to win by wide margins or even without serious competition. The success of incumbents in reelection campaigns, to be sure, owes to much more than campaign funding. Their staffs and free mail privileges, their access to the media and publicity, and the fruits of case work and services for the constituency all lead to gratitude and name recognition. Additionally, they may be protected by districting intended to extend their political careers. But the ability to raise, even stockpile large sums of campaign money is among those advantages of incumbency that push more and more legislative elections in the United States out of the range of competitiveness and that increasingly limit genuine two-party, ins-versus-outs competition to open seat races. The implications of these trends for democratic representation and the viability of choice in American elections are too obvious to bear any comment.

V. Coda

All of the issues of this and the last chapter are no less than the issue of the health and efficacy of American representative democracy. Campaign finance affects both every aspect of the contesting of elections and the relationships between citizens and the policy-making of their representatives. There is virtually no key step in the chain of assumptions and processes we call democracy that is not in some measure affected by campaign resources. To argue that these effects are not as great as many would have them is not to deny either an effect or its importance.

Yet at every turn the issue is also one of money as a political resource, as a base of political power. Its special qualities give rise to special fears. Unlike social status or esteem, for example, it is almost effortlessly converted into political influence. It is easily observed and easily measured, but because of its easy mobility and easy adaptability to new courses of action, it is regulated and contained with difficulty and often with unanticipated results. And it is unevenly distributed in American society, in very direct and obvious contrast to the equality of the formal power of the ballot. Consequently, it has for a long time symbolized the dark side of American politics — the inequality of political power, the domination of status and privilege, and the power of small but monied minorities.

Such issues and fears produce great issues of public policy. And when those issues divide along party lines, each party supported by separate pictures of reality, the resulting policy debate is one of high tension and daunting complexity. We turn to that debate now in the final chapter.

12

The Politics of American Campaign Finance

We live with a number of realities about campaign finance, each with its believers and advocates for whom it is the only reality. Much of the politics of campaign finance is a struggle among these visions of reality, for all the reports and reporting under the FECA have not made the reality of it much clearer. We can agree on basic data and totals, but there is no agreement on what they mean or what their consequences have been.

Regardless of what may seem to be reality to some experts or practitioners, the mass public, buttressed by the media and much of the Democratic party, largely holds to a set of perceptions and opinions about campaign funding that reflects the neo-Progressive image of reality. It confirms and is confirmed by fundamental beliefs about influence in American politics and the role of money in achieving it. For the politics of the issue, then, it makes not a great deal of difference that on the central issues of impact — money's role in elections and in legislatures — few experts subscribe to the opinions that many Americans hold. Their reality has taken a life of its own, and it dominates the politics of campaign finance at least to the extent that it frames the problems and the agenda.

The Progressive image of contemporary campaign finance invests it with an exceptional immediacy, for it involves a democratic politics that millions of citizens experience very directly. Indeed, if there is a dominant characteristic that sets the politics of campaign finance apart, it is its very politicality. For the members of the mass public, it touches some of the pivotal decisions and processes in their democracy. It affects as well the basic political interests of candidates and officeholders, of the political parties, and of the major nonparty political organizations. It engages the millions of Americans who contribute their resources voluntarily to political combat. It is thus a politics in which virtually none of the activists in the political process are without firsthand experience and involvement and in which it is hard to find a detached or disinterested point of view. It is a policy issue the politics of which are not easy to separate from the politics of democracy itself.

I. The Players and the Interests

Considering the popular uneasiness about the status quo in American campaign finance, it is surprising how relatively low key its politics have been. The issue surfaces in campaigns as one candidate belabors the other with charges of excessive spending and/or compromising sources of contributions. There is, however, little evidence that issues of campaign money materially affect the outcomes of many elections. They appear not to be high-priority issues for many Americans, and the observation that one group made about one state probably holds for many more:

> Although most voters decry the large amounts spent on campaigns, they have not translated their disapproval into votes against high-spending candidates . . . In California, voters react more negatively to "dirty campaigns" than to expensive ones.[1]

For the nature of the campaign to be an issue in itself, the cam-

[1] California Commission on Campaign Financing, *The New Gold Rush: Financing California's Legislative Campaigns* (Los Angeles: Center for Responsive Government, 1985), 51.

paign has to be very visible; and the use of public funds for the presidential campaigns of 1976, 1980, and 1984 has virtually removed money as an issue from that most visible of all campaigns.

THE PARTY PLATFORMS: A SAMPLER

Both of the major political parties grappled with campaign finance in both their 1980 and 1984 national party platforms. The major relevant passages follow, Democrats first and then Republicans.

- *Democratic platform of 1980*: "In the 1980s we need to enact reforms which will: Provide for public financing of Congressional campaigns; Lower contribution limits for political action committees; Close the loophole that allows private spending in Presidential elections contrary to the intent of the election law reforms . . ."
- *Democratic platform of 1984*: "We must work to end political action committee funding of federal political campaigns. To achieve that, we must enact a system of public financing of federal campaigns."
- *Republican platform of 1980*: "We support the repeal of those restrictive campaign spending limitations that tend to create obstacles to local grassroots participation in federal elections. We also oppose the proposed financing of congressional campaigns with taxpayers' dollars as an effort by the Democratic party to protect its incumbent members of Congress with a tax subsidy."
- *Republican platform of 1984*: "Forced taxpayer financing of campaign activities is political tyranny. We oppose it. In light of the inhibiting role federal election laws and regulations have had, Congress should consider abolishing the Federal Election Commission."

While the parties take few formal steps to dramatize the questions of campaign finance, there are unquestionably quite different Democratic and Republican positions on them. Those differences have been regularly reflected in their national platforms (see box). Democrats in Congress have generally favored public funding, Republicans have not; Democrats have generally preferred more regulations, Republicans have preferred fewer. In part these differences reflect more general attitudes about the scope of government and the efficacy of governmental regulation — differences that have for several generations helped define differences between liberalism and conservatism. But in part, too, they reflect the Democrats' historic inability to match Republican fund-raising in an unregulated political environment. These policy differences between the parties were present early in the 1970s as Congress wrote the FECA and its amendments, and they have continued to today. Virtually every roll call vote on an issue of substance in Congress in the 1980s has very markedly divided Democrats and Republicans.

Amid a pervasive but low-level unease about the funding of campaigns, a few groups and individuals have struggled to keep the issue before Congress. The major protagonist has been Common Cause. Founded in 1970 as a "people's lobby" to enter the wars against special interests and their political agendas, it quickly enlisted 200,000 members in the crusade. Reform of campaign finance was from the start a central concern, and its successful suit in 1972 to force the Nixon campaign to disclose the sources of its receipts before the FECA went into effect was one of its earliest victories. It was also a force behind the passage of the 1974 amendments to the FECA, amendments pretty much to its specification except for the absence of public funding for congressional campaigns.

Throughout its first 17 years, Common Cause has kept campaign finance near the top of its program priorities. It remains a strong presence in Congress on behalf of legislated reform, and it has been active in other forums, too. It has gone to the federal courts a number of times to argue the constitutionality of the FECA, and it periodically presses the Federal Election Commission to seize opportunities for reform and change. It has taken it to court, for example, to force it to end the flow of soft money. Common Cause also remains an important source of data, vying with the FEC for the attention of the media and often beating it (and some state regulatory agencies, too) to the media with new totals and its interpretations of them.

If Common Cause has been good for reform of campaign finance, reform of campaign finance has apparently been good for Common Cause. The subject has for some time been a fundraising and membership-boosting theme for Common Cause. Throughout much of the 1980s, it has featured a "People Against PAC$" membership appeal. One piece of literature in the appeal begins: "It's a Disgrace . . . that our United States Congress is on the auction block. UP FOR GRABS to the highest PAC bidders." The persistence of the campaign suggests its success.[2]

Common Cause does not, however, monopolize the reform issue. Project Democracy, has been a persistent voice, as has its director, Mark Green, a product of the Nader movement. The Center for Responsive Politics, under the leadership of Peter Fenn and then Ellen Miller, has been a similar voice for change. It is a private "action-research organization" funded by private foundations and individuals; "money and politics" is one of its four program areas. Both of these groups share Common Cause's neo-Progressivism, and their criticisms of and prescriptions for campaign finance are not greatly different.

Then there are the individual reformers in Congress. From the late 1970s to the late 1980s in the House, they have included the following representatives: Dan Glickman (Democrat from Kansas), Jim Leach (Republican of Iowa), David Obey (Democrat from Wisconsin), Tom Railsback (Republican from Illinois), and Mike Synar (Democrat from Oklahoma). More recently the impetus for reform has shifted to the Senate where David Boren, Democrat from Oklahoma, has made it a personal crusade. This list is by no means exhaustive, but it is probably not without accident that the names on it come from the parts of the country in which the Progressive tradition still lives.

Reform has support, too, from groups whose main concerns are more diffuse. The publishers and editorial writers of the nation's newspapers, even those that proudly wear a conservative

---

[2]The ellipses are in the original. For an extended treatment, see Andrew S. McFarland, *Common Cause: Lobbying in the Public Interest* (Chatham, N.J.: Chatham House, 1984). Chapter 7 details the Common Cause involvement with reform of campaign finance.

label, have weighed in repeatedly in the 1980s.[3] So have traditionally liberal groups and organizations; despite its role in campaign finance, much of organized labor has supported public funding for congressional campaigns. Indeed, the 198th General Assembly of the Presbyterian Church (U.S.A.) resolved in June of 1986 to support bills in the Congress (such as the Boren bill) that would place limits on candidate receipts from PACs, noting that "an overall limit on aggregate PAC receipts would help shift the focus of congressional fundraising away from large PAC contributions and back to small contributions from individual donors, thus bringing our democratic system back to the people."

Finally, the mass public has remained firmly skeptical about money in campaign politics. Interestingly, no published polls seem to ask state or national samples for their views about the status quo in campaign finance; perhaps that would be elaborating the obvious. Their questions, when they do turn to campaign finance, seek opinion about reform options. The results generally are of a single piece; the public is wary of public funding, but it supports limits on contributions and expenditures. When the two issues are combined, the results are closely divided. In July 1984 the Gallup poll asked a national sample the following question:

> It has been suggested that the federal government provide a fixed amount of money for the election campaigns of candidates for Congress and that all private contributions from other sources be prohibited. Do you think this is a good idea or a poor idea?

Although 12 percent of the respondents had no opinion, 52 percent thought it a good idea, 36 percent a poor one.[4]

Perhaps the most extensive and revealing of all the polls on campaign money was the one the Field poll conducted in California in February of 1985. Its statewide sample responded to seven propositions this way:

---

[3]In Feb. of 1986 Sen. David Boren spread on the pages of the *Congressional Record*, pp. S990 and after, editorials supporting reform from 48 daily newspapers from 33 different states; included were pieces from Albuquerque (N. Mex.), Keene (N.H.), Lakeland (Fla.), Hammond (Ind.), Salina (Kans.), Lansing (Mich.), York (Pa.), Holyoke (Mass.), Boulder (Colo.), Mesa (Ariz.), and Newark (Ohio).

[4]Reprinted in *The New Gold Rush*, 341. The Gallup people got a 55–31 approval for the same question in 1982; see *The Gallup Poll Public Opinion 1982* (Wilmington, Del.: Gallup, 1983), 292.

- 76 percent disagreed with the proposition that there should be no limits on contributions to a candidate by an "individual or group."
- 86 percent agreed that there should be limits on PAC contributions.
- 81 percent supported a proposed limit on receipts from PACs.
- 56 percent disagreed with a statement approving transfers of money from one candidate to another.
- 81 percent favored a limit on the sums campaigns can raise and spend.
- 72 percent disagreed with a proposal to fund campaigns "entirely" with public money, *but*
- 60 percent agreed that there should be "some minimum level of public financing of political campaigns using tax dollars."[5]

These findings invite two comments. First, we have no way of knowing how representative these California opinions are of adults in the rest of the country. On the other hand, we have no evidence that they are atypical or idiosyncratic. And second, the public responses in six of these seven items run contrary to public policy in California. That state does not have any limit on individual, group, or PAC contributions, nor has it limits on candidates' receipts from PACs, on intercandidate transfers, or on candidate expenditures — and it has no limited ("minimum level") program of public financing.

Why then, both in state and in nation, do not the combination of reform leadership and mass public support lead to changes in policy on campaign finance? The answers to that question reveal a good deal about the special politics of campaign finance. To begin, while public opinion may be overwhelming and even emotional, it lacks the intensity or the salience for a place toward the top of most voters' list of priorities. Then, the public's preferred policy option (limits on expenditures) is not available; the Supreme Court ruled it out in *Buckley*. Moreover, the major political advantages in the new era of finance have accrued to the very people who must vote the changes: the incumbent legislators. And finally, the politics of campaign finance

[5]*The New Gold Rush*, 339–340.

embraces a cluster of issues and desiderata of daunting and cross-cutting complexity.

The defense of the status quo falls heavily to Republicans, both in the Congress and in the media and public outside of the capital. After an initial reluctance to take strong public stands, corporate, business, and association PACs have assumed an increasingly vigorous defensive posture. The relative silence of PACs generally disposed to Democratic candidates suggests again the overriding power of the party division on the issue.

II. Goals and Options

The politics of campaign finance is at its most explicit and operational in the politics of the regulation of campaign finance. Nothing activates and highlights the various interests and actors in a policy arena as effectively as a legislative proposal to bring about substantial change. These interests reflect different positions both on the political realities and on the quest for effective policy goals. Those observations are true of all policy conflicts, and campaign finance is different only because reform directly and personally touches those who define the political realities. The politics of campaign finance *is* virtually the politics of politics.

If one sat a group of experts and informed citizens down to design a system of campaign finance from scratch, there would be considerable agreement on a list of desiderata for that system. Ideally, the funding of campaigns should:

1. promote competitive choices in elections;
2. support (or at least not harm) the two-party system;
3. encourage a broad base of voluntary contributors;
4. limit the burdens of fund-raising;
5. provide enough resources for campaigns to communicate fully with voters;
6. protect freedoms of political speech, activity, and association;
7. ensure the accountability of sources and spenders;
8. limit the influence of contributors (of all or some kinds) on the candidates receiving their money; and

9. limit the amounts of money spent in the system. (This last criterion would be harder to frame and certainly would be more controversial.)

One might even be able to design a way of campaign finance — on some kind of tabula rasa — that would meet most or all of these goals. Unfortunately, though, we have a campaign finance system already full blown and firmly in place. Moreover, important interests are also in place and at risk with any proposal for change. Just a brief survey of these nine desiderata in the context of reform options in the late 1980s makes the realities terribly clear.

Promoting Competitiveness. If challengers are to be a real and credible alternative to incumbent officeholders, they must have the campaign resources with which to do so. Without competitive funding and competitive elections, a major assumption of representative democracy falters. In reality, the competitiveness of many congressional and state legislative elections has already disappeared as incumbents increase their funding at a faster rate than do their challengers. Proponents of public funding programs argue that they would assure funding (from part to all) for challengers. Those few proposals that do not also have expenditure limits (the so-called "floors without ceilings") address the issue of competitiveness. When one adds spending limits, however, the calculus changes (see "Limiting the Amounts of Money Spent" below). The politics of trying to achieve competitiveness is discouragingly clear; one is trying to convince legislators to make their political careers and futures less secure. It is not an easy or congenial task.

Supporting the Two-party System. For many Americans support for the two-party system is not far behind their loyalty to motherhood, the flag, and a favorite dessert. Support for the party system also has an elaborate justification rooted in the organization and representation of majorities within a large mass electorate. Fine, but the political realities of the 1980s include a great imbalance in the fund-raising capacities of the two parties. Not surprisingly, attempts to buttress the party role in campaign finance

— most often by raising or removing limits on party contributions and "on behalf of" spending — come almost exclusively from Republicans. The existing limits on the parties in the FECA are not especially generous, and they have already constrained national Republican committees. Again, the politics of trying to increase the party role are obvious; one is trying to convince the majority party in the Congress (i.e., the Democrats) to risk an even greater party disadvantage. The task is no easier than the last one.

Encouraging a Broad Base of Contributors. Broadening the base of contributors has at least two major justifications: encouraging citizen participation in a democracy and dispersing contributions to candidates in order to minimize the leverage of any one of them on a candidate. In reality American campaign finance has drawn on the voluntary contributions of some 10 to 15 millions of citizens, although the effect of the withdrawal of the income tax credit for contributions (1986 was the terminating year) may lower those totals. Proposals primarily from Democrats seek to restore it or expand it into a 100 percent tax credit. Opposition comes primarily from Republicans who argue on philosophical grounds that, however indirect, these are really public subsidies. On the other hand, attempts to raise the limit on individual contributions from the present $1000, even to restore it to its preinflation value, encounter Democratic claims that such a change would aid primarily the affluent.

Controlling the Burdens of Fund-raising. Although the point does not touch directly on the health of the democracy, its implications do. They suggest that officeholders ought not to be diverted from their responsibilities by the need to raise money for the next campaign. Nor should candidates of talent be deterred by the tasks of raising money or any candidates forced to leave the business of the campaign to find last-minute funds. Reformers address the issue chiefly with proposals for public funding that include spending limits — the public money is start-up or seed money for the inexperienced, and the spending limits control the amounts of money candidates have to raise. Public funding proposals draw opposition from those in the political center and right for administrative and philosophical reasons. Spending limits again threaten candidates who have to outspend opponents to overcome the advantages they have by reason of incumbency or party dominance.

Ensuring Campaigns that Communicate. The need for parties and candidates to inform the electorate in a campaign is obvious in the chain of choices in a representative democracy. Most assessments of the success of American campaigns as instruments of education and information are probably negative, but not many of those critics would ascribe the difficulty to *too little* campaigning. Those who do, however, do not make a trivial point.

> A typical $350,000 congressional campaign budget might buy about a dozen television exposures per household, or a targeted survey, mail or telephone packages designed to reach likely voters three or four times in a campaign. Is this too much to spend on politics? A few TV exposures or mailings do not let most challengers make much of a case against House incumbents.[6]

So, this criterion merges with the concern that there be resources enough to ensure competitive elections. Those concerned about it would raise contribution levels or even public funding programs without spending limits — or, in view of political realities, merely holding to the status quo.

Protecting Political Freedoms. Under the Constitution of the United States, securing this goal is the business of the Supreme Court now that the voluntary funding of campaigns enjoys the protections of the First and Fourteenth Amendments.[7] Whether one agrees with its definition of those rights and Congress's power to limit them is beside the point. The Court's decision in *Buckley* to hold unconstitutional — and thus eliminate from the list of policy options — any statutory limit on candidate expenditures, on the candidate's use of personal resources, or on any "independent" spending constitutes the single most important

---

[6]In the original the last sentence starts a new paragraph. Michael J. Malbin, "Public Financing for Congressional Elections Is Not the Answer: What's the Question?," *at Home with Consumers*, a publication of the Direct Selling Education Foundation (Dec., 1985).

[7]*Buckley v. Valeo* (424 U.S. 1, 1976).

constraint on policy-making about campaign finance. Conversely, the Court's willingness to accept spending limits if they are a part of voluntarily chosen public funding has "won" many new adherents for that option.

Ensuring Accountability. It is a premise, going back at least to the Progressives, that if one provides voters with information, they will act constructively on it. All strategies of disclosure, in fact, are rooted in accountability to a stern and potentially vengeful electorate. It is the major justification for the extensive reporting and publicity requirements in the FECA and much of the legislation of the states. (The rationale depends also on the presence of a viable and competitive electoral alternative, the point of the first of these criteria.)

FINE TUNING THE FECA

Some members of Congress try to eliminate avoidance or evasion problems with the FEC with bills that would tighten up some part or another of the FECA. H.R. 2464, introduced by Rep. Al Swift for himself and 10 other members in the 100th Congress, 1st Session, went (inter alia) after independent expenditures that are not fully independent by proposing the following addition to section 301(17) of the FECA:

An expenditure is not an independent expenditure if —
  (A) there is any arrangement, coordination, or direction with respect to the expenditure between the candidate and the person making the expenditure;
  (B) with respect to the election, the person making the expenditure —
    (i) is authorized to solicit contributions or make expenditures on behalf of the candidate or an authorized committee of the candidate;
    (ii) is an officer of an authorized committee of the candidate; or
    (iii) receives any compensation or reimbursement from the

candidate, or an authorized committee of the candidate; or

(C) with respect to the election, the person making the expenditure communicates with, advises, or counsels the candidate on the candidate's plans, projects, or needs relating to the election, including any advice relating to the candidate's decision to seek the office.

In fact, the major funding data of federal campaigns are now fully reported, except perhaps for the purposes of the expenditures. The public has information, probably too much of it, on the basis of which to act. The simplicity of the reporting-publicity-action assumptions fits less well as campaigning and its finance become more complex. Voters know about independent expenditures, but no candidates are responsible for them. Voters can hold only candidates responsible on election day. Then there are the instances in which no one is really sure who is responsible; bundling blurs the line between individual and committee (either party or PAC) responsibility, and soft money diversions go unreported and largely unknown. A good many of the less visible policy proposals focus on this issue: attempts to tighten specifications of which expenditures are truly independent, to force reporting of soft money transactions and to include bundled contributions within the contribution limits of the bundling committee (see box). The politics of these statutory changes are very specific. Independent spenders respond negatively to proposed constraints, bundlers fight limits on bundling, and so on. There are, moreover, partisan overtones. Democratic party committees have been more reluctant to disclose voluntarily their soft money diversions; Republicans, on the other hand, gain more support from bundling and independent spending. Finally, this criterion has another powerful side effect in policy-making: the avoidance of any reform that would divert more dollars into independent expenditures.

Limiting the Influence of Contributors. The debate begins with the inarticulate major premise behind the desideratum itself: that contributors have been or are capable of exerting objectionable ("excessive" by whatever standards) influence on candidates and subsequent officeholders who receive their contributions. Almost none of the policy debate centers on the influence of individual contributors or the parties; almost all of it centers on PACs. And so we have had repeated attempts to limit PAC contributions, either by lowering the statutory limits on their contributions (from $5000 to $3000 or less) or by placing a limit on the total PAC receipts a candidate for Congress can accept. Support for such measures comes largely from the political center and left, thus heavily from Democrats, reform organizations, and the media. That support is perhaps the clearest manifestation in the policy debate of the neo-Progressive view of power and privilege in American politics.

And finally one comes to the last criterion, the one that is in some ways the special one. Of all the nine rationales or desiderata, it is the only one that cannot be related easily to some of the premises of or assumptions about democracy. It, therefore, deserves more extensive consideration.

Limiting the Amounts of Money Spent. At one level of discourse about campaign finance, the complaint about "too much money" is simply a shorthand reference to many of the preceding criteria — too much money because it stifles competition, leads to undue influence, escapes accountability, becomes a burden in its raising, and so on. To that extent it is not a separate criterion. But it appears that for some Americans, there is too much money simply because there is too much. It is, however, a criterion without standards and without a calculus for determining how much is too much.

Indeed, by several of the most logical standards, American candidates are underspending. When one compares spending in American campaigns to that in other countries with free elections with the single metric of spending per voter (or citizen or resident), expenditures in the United States lag behind those in West Germany, Israel, and Ireland. If one includes the value of free radio and TV time, the cost is higher in Canada.[8] Alternatively, spending within the United States on other forms of per-

[8]See Howard R. Penniman, "U.S. Elections: Really a Bargain?," *Public Opinion* (June/July 1984), 51–53.

suasion, especially those of advertising, put campaign spending in a different perspective. Against the estimated $1.8 billion spent in 1984 for the campaigns of all candidates for all national, state, and local offices in the United States, the Big Three of American automobilia — Ford, Chrysler, and General Motors — spent almost $1.65 billion in advertising costs within the United States.

In truth, the determination to "do something" about spending levels reflects a mixture of concern about specific consequences of money and an emotional outrage reflecting highly personal judgments of "too much." For many individuals those judgments derive from experience with personal assets, tax liabilities, estate planning, the weekly or monthly budget, or checkbook balancing. Or they reflect either Progressivism's belief in the corrupting power of money of any kind or a distaste for campaigns and electoral politics generally.

Concerns about the levels of spending per se lead to proposals for limits on spending, which under the constraints of *Buckley* require voluntary public funding. (At least one state, Minnesota, has made the acceptance of spending limits a condition for granting tax credits to individual contributions to the candidate.) Opposition to spending limits in all their forms comes primarily from those concerned about competitiveness in elections and reflects the scholarly conclusions that a challenger needs usually to spend more to overcome the incumbent's advantages. In addition, Republican opposition reflects its struggle for more than a generation against a Democratic advantage in party loyalties in the electorate and Democratic majorities most of the time in the two houses of the Congress. Republicans need to spend more to overcome the Democratic superiority both in number of incumbents and in number of party loyalists among the voters. Expenditure limitations, which inevitably mean the same limits for incumbents and challengers, are, they think, "incumbent protection plans" and thus plans for the perpetuation of Democratic majorities.

So, there are at least nine different layers of policy contention, each with its different array of interests, its different coalitions and line-ups. The result is a dense and many-layered politics, all the more so because some of the criteria are conflicting. How does one achieve both competitiveness in elections and limits on spending? How can one place limits on the use of one's money while maintaining free political activity? And finally, to top off the complexity, there is over virtually every one of the nine desiderata an argument about the reality of the status quo. How competitive *are* congressional elections? How much influence in fact do PACs have over the recipients of their money? To what extent does the cost of a competitive campaign deny the polity able and even talented candidates? Whose reality is the credible "reality?"

Over all of these weighings and calculations, these matching of means and ends, there finally hangs the grim reality of the law of unanticipated consequences. Earlier attempts to reform the system of campaign finance have opened new routes or avenues for diverted streams of money. The largely unexpected growth of both PACs and independent spending after 1974 are the starkest of the reminders. Since much of the final business of hammering out reform proposals is the business of predicting the future of campaign finance under new constraints, a reformer has to be a confident, perhaps even foolhardy, prophet.

III. Reform after 1974: Public Funding

Successes in political reform often seem to follow a B movie script. A small band of devoted and zealous reformers work tirelessly, absorb repeated losses, don't give up when ordinarily reasonable people would, and triumph against all odds in the film's final heroic minutes. The script in campaign finance is far less dramatic. Reformers work sporadically, never really give up, absorb frustrating losses after smelling victory, and in the end never really succeed. The final result is that the legal environment of American campaign finance remains essentially where the Supreme Court left it after *Buckley v. Valeo*. There were additional legislative tinkerings in 1976 and 1979, but there has been no major legislative reshaping since 1974 and no major judicial redoing since 1976. Nor has there been much statutory or judicial change in the states since *Buckley*.

Even though the Congress and the courts have been inactive in reform, two great changes have nonetheless been wrought on the FECA. First, in reforming the federal income tax, Congress in 1986 dropped the tax credit for individual contributions. The impact of that change is yet to be measured. Second, inflation reduced the statutory limits on contributions by more than half between 1974 and 1986. The $1000 limit on individual contributions and the $5000 limit on PAC contributions, both passed in 1974, were worth $450 and $2252 in 1974 dollars some 12 years later in 1986.

Nonetheless, the failures and deadlocks in reform tell us as much about the politics of American campaign finance as would a string of successes — and reform, furthermore, is not permanently doomed. Its history post-1974 is, therefore, worth a short survey. Public funding comes first, and then private funding in the next section.

In deciding how to construct or reconstruct a tradition of campaign finance, one initially faces a fundamental choice: does one want a publicly funded campaign, or one relying entirely on voluntary contributions and spending, or a mixture of the two? The presidential campaign of 1988 will be the fourth election campaign covered by full public funding. The public treasury also provides part of the funds for eligible candidates seeking their party's presidential nomination. But campaigns for Congress and the overwhelming majority of state offices are entirely funded by nongovernmental sources. The Senate did indeed twice authorize public funding of congressional campaigns in the passage of the amendments to the FECA in 1974, but it lost out in the House-Senate conferences. Since then neither house has passed a proposal for public funding.

If one chooses the public funding option, framing a specific proposal involves a number of hard choices.

1. Is the program of public funding to include expenditure limits? The two are not inevitably linked, and there has always been minor but devoted support for ones without (the "floors without ceilings").

2. Is it to be partial or total? And if partial, for what sums or percentages of expenditures?
3. How is eligibility to be established? By right for the major party candidates? If so, what for other candidates? If not, then by some matching program in which public funds match private contributions, or by some demonstrated level of private support?
4. Inevitably the program will cover general election campaigns, but will it include primary campaigns too?
5. On what basis will the size of allotments and spending limits be drawn? Will candidates in all 435 House districts be treated equally, for instance, or will adjustments be made for the size of districts? And how is one to treat Senate campaigns from states as disparate as California and Delaware?

This list hardly exhausts the questions a bill drafter faces. For one it does not address the creation or delegation of administrative and supervisory authority.

Its supporters see public funding as the only way to rescue American campaign finance from its problems. It will provide a source of campaign funds untainted by the demands or expectations of the givers. It will provide the funds that challengers and other candidates need to run a competitive race. It will end the debilitating and distracting scramble for money by the candidates. And by reducing or eliminating the reliance on private funds, it will reduce or eliminate the problems of accountability for those funds. For those supporters who are attracted, post *Buckley*, primarily by the spending limits attached to public funding, the emphasis is primarily on ending fund-raising pressures and preventing the influence over elections and legislatures that derives from raising and spending campaign funds.

The opposition to public funding — at least in the latter 1980s — rests on both principled and pragmatic considerations. It offends the critics' conviction that government ought not to fund the dissemination of partisan political views and that it is unconscionable to make people support, through their taxes, political opinions and candidates they oppose. The pragmatic grounds are just as broad. Any use of public funds is one more claim on a federal budget already dangerously out of balance; it is a claim especially hard to grant when Congress cannot fund programs of needed human services. There will be arguments over equal or differential treatment in funding and spending standards; will the plan treat campaigning for the House in a few square miles of New York or Chicago the same as campaigning in half or all of a Western state? Are the arrangements for minor party and independent candidates fair? And then there are all the hesitations about administration and compliance — the audits, the rules and regulations, the burdens of reporting, the midcampaign disputes over eligibility for funds, the sheer administrative task of overseeing a complex program. Administering a public funding for presidential elections involves only one election race (two before the conventions), but there are 33 Senate races and 435 for the House every two years.

Since the early 1970s, Congress has seen a daunting variety of public funding proposals. The states have added to the variety, even adopting a few types. No one of them is in any way typical of the lot, but the most "possible" are perhaps typified by the Boren-Byrd bill (Sen. 2) of the 100th Congress (1987). Restricted to general election campaigns for the Senate, it would have created full public funding between the sums raised to establish eligibility and the stated spending limits. To be eligible for the public monies, candidates were to raise between $140,000 and $250,000, depending on the population of the state. Spending limits reflected a population-based formula and ranged from $698,750 for Vermont to $5.48 million for California.[9]

Public funding was only part of the Boren-Byrd package, but it was the most vulnerable part. The Senate Rules Committee reported it to the floor of the Senate on a party-line vote in spring of 1987; and after a Republican filibuster prevented consideration on the floor of the Senate, the authors recast the bill to eliminate the comprehensive public funding. By removing the sections most distasteful to the Republicans, they hoped at least to break the filibuster and bring a reform package to a vote. What was left did, however, have a kind of public finance. It was to be available to candidates whose opponents did not accept the voluntary lim-

---

[9]The bill also contained provisions beyond the public funding plan, most notably a series of measures to limit PAC involvement in Senate campaigns; they will be discussed later.

its on expenditures for which the new version provided. So, in such a public funding plan there would, ideally, be no public funding.

Beyond direct public funding, there are the indirect options. A good deal of the rest of the democratic world has for long provided candidates (or the candidates' parties) with free radio or television time or with access to the mails. The state of Oregon pays for a booklet, distributed by mail to all of its residents, that contains information on and statements by candidates for elective office. Such programs have the great attraction of being far less intrusive and far more easily administered than programs of direct public funding, and they have always had their advocates in Congress. In the 100th Congress, for example, Congressman Al Swift, a Democrat from Washington, proposed to extend reduced broadcasting and postage costs to House candidates who accepted a spending limit of $400,000 in an election cycle.[10]

The most successful of the recent indirect plans was that associated with two members of the House from New York: Matthew McHugh, a Democrat, and Barber Conable, a Republican.[11] They proposed an increase from 50 to 100 percent in the income tax credit for all individual contributions up to $50 ($100 for joint returns) — provided that the contribution was to a party committee or to a House or Senate candidate from the contributor's home state. Their plan thus would have ended the existing credit for contributions to congressional candidates from other states, to PACs, and to state and local candidates. The proposal passed the House as an amendment to the revision of the income tax statutes in December of 1985 on a 230–196 vote.[12] The majority was composed of 196 Democrats and 34 Republicans; the opposition included 146 Republicans and 50 Democrats.

In the final conference on the tax reform bills, the McHugh-Conable amendment was dropped. It probably suffered primarily because of philosophical objections to even indirect forms of public funding; it would also have sacrificed revenue at a time when Congress was attempting to pass a "revenue neutral" tax reform bill. Certainly the overwhelming Republican vote against

[10]H.R. 2464, 100th Cong., 1st sess.
[11]It appeared in its original form in H.R. 3737 introduced in Aug. 1983, the 98th Cong., 1st sess.
[12]The tax revision bill was H.R. 3838, 99th Cong., 2d sess.

it suggests a perception that, by reimbursing the small contributions of "little" contributors, it would have helped the Democrats more than the Republicans. (The fact that the idea seems to have emerged from the liberal Democratic Study Group in the House may have given extra credence to those suspicions.) In any event, the idea was attractive for opening up new funding sources, for leaving the choice of recipient to the contributor, and for avoiding the complicated administrative mechanisms that come with more direct subsidies. And it was the only substantial proposal for change in campaign finance to win the approval of even one house of Congress in the 1980s.

IV. Reform Attempts: Private Funding

On October 17, 1979, the House passed the Obey-Railsback Amendment to a budgetary authorization bill for the FEC. Of the 217 votes in its favor, 188 (87 percent) were cast by Democrats; Republicans accounted for 124 (63 percent) of the 198 negative votes. The amendment provided for reducing the PAC contribution limit from $5000 to $3000, for limiting to $70,000 the sum each House candidate could accept from PACs collectively, and for ending bundling by making the bundler count the bundled contributions against its contribution limit.[13] The Senate never acted on the amendment. But that threefold plan to reduce the PAC role has remained since 1979 the most powerful reform alternative to public funding.

THE VOICE OF A CRUSADER

In the 1980s no member of Congress has been more active in the cause of reforming the FECA era of campaign finance than Sen. David Boren, a Democrat from Oklahoma. A few of his views on the status quo and the reforming of it follow:

> Many of the sponsors of S.2, including myself, have had reservations about public financing of campaigns. Because of the court's

[13]It was an amendment to S. 832, 96th Cong., 1st sess.

decision [in *Buckley*], however, we included partial public financing only as a means to obtain voluntary spending limits. It is a reasonable price to pay to restore a system of grass-roots democracy.[14]

The money is no longer coming from small, individual donations from citizens at the grassroots in the way in which the political process ought to work in this government of the people and for the people and by the people. That is where the money should be coming from to finance campaigns; from that average citizen back home in the State or district that the Congressman or Senator is sworn to represent in the national interests.[15]

I see a trend under way that is going to destroy the democratic process if we do not do something about it. It is absolutely eroding the integrity of the election process, and if we cannot read in the 37 percent voter turnout in the last election alienation and deep concern on the part of the American people about what is going on in our political system, we have to be blind to what is going on in the hearts and minds of our own constituents.[16]

Obey-Railsback was reincarnated in the 1986 reform package devised by Sen. David Boren. (For a sampler of Boren's views on the reform of campaign finance, see box.) Again, PAC contribution limits were to be reduced to $3,000, and there was a very similar antibundling provision. Boren raised the receipt limit to $100,000 for the House (and $125,000 if the candidate had competition in both the primary and general election); a more complicated formula set the range of limits in the Senate from $175,000 to $750,000. (Boren's bill also contained other provi-

[14]David L. Boren, "It's Time to Cut PAC Power," *Washington Post* (June 30, 1987).
[15]"Should the Boren Amendment Approach To Curtailing PACs Be Adopted?," *Congressional Digest*, vol. 66 (Feb. 1987), 48.
[16]Excerpt from the *Congressional Record* of June 3, 1987, reprinted on "The Federal Page" of the *Washington Post* (June 24, 1987).

sions.) It passed the Senate in a preliminary vote on August 12, 1986, after two days of floor debate.[17]

The Senate passed the Boren amendment by a surprisingly wide margin, 69–30. There were, nonetheless, signs of the customary party division on these issues; 27 of the 30 dissents were Republican. But margin of preliminary victory notwithstanding, it never returned to the floor of the Senate for final consideration. The reason may very well have been in the amendment the Senate passed right after the Boren amendment. Sponsored by Sen. Rudy Boschwitz, Republican of Minnesota and soon to be chair of the National Republican Senatorial Committee, it prohibited all PAC contributions to parties and required that the parties disclose all soft money transactions — both moves that would embarrass or disadvantage the Democrats. The roll call on the bill was 58–42, with Republicans providing 51 of the "yes" votes and Democrats 40 of the "no" votes.[18] And so the two amendments died, "side by side" as if in a death pact.

The Boren bill reemerged in 1987 as a part of the Boren-Byrd bill, an omnibus measure that combined a limit on PAC receipts (the same $175,000 to $750,000 limits) with public funding, reduced limits on PAC contributions (down to $3,000) and limits on campaign spending from $950,000 to $5.5 million, depending on the population of the state. After the Republican filibuster of spring and summer in 1987 and after the dropping of the full public funding as a way of picking up support for breaking the filibuster, the limit on PAC receipts remained in the bill. Its constitutionality was uncertain, the Supreme Court never having decided the constitutionality of any kind of limit on receipts (as opposed to limits on contributions or expenditures). And its effect was uncertain, too. Throughout all of the debate, a note of concern sounded repeatedly that the "unused" PAC money would be diverted into independent spending.

Beyond the packages of limits on PACs, there is an almost limitless cafeteria of other options for altering and fine-tuning the voluntary portion of American campaign finance. Among the most persistent and viable of the recent ones are those that would

[17]It was passed as an amendment (based on his S. 1806) to a waste disposal bill (S. 655).

[18]The Boschwitz amendment was to the same waste bill, S. 655, on the same day, Aug. 12, 1986.

- redefine the "independent" in independent expenditures, usually specifying the presence of some individuals whose presence would reduce the independence of the spending (see preceding box);
- propose a constitutional amendment to guarantee Congress powers to regulate campaign finance fully, thus overturning the *Buckley* decision;
- provide free media time for a response to candidates whose opponents have been aided by independent spending, the purpose of the plan being to discourage the media from selling time or space to independent spenders in the first place;
- repeal the amendment to the FECA that permits members of the Congress elected before 1979 to make personal use of excess campaign funds; and
- end bundling by requiring committees that organize and transmit contributions to count those money totals in their own contribution limits.

Only congressional ingenuity limits the list. These and other proposals come and go, often a response to concerns and perceptions of the moment, yielding then to new attempts to deal with emerging concerns.

Again in 1987 the scenario ended without the triumph of reform and with a good deal of disillusionment and hardening of party positions. The Democratic compromise failed to end the Republican filibuster in the Senate for at least two major reasons. For one, public funding still remained, if only in a new guise as an enforcer, as a tool for making people do the right thing (i.e., accept spending limits) voluntarily. And, second, while the Republican rhetoric centered on the iniquity of using taxpayer money for campaigning, deep down they disliked the idea of spending limits just as much. Ultimately the separate financial conditions of the two parties and their partisans, just as much as separate political philosophies and worldviews, settled the matter. The Democratic leadership never broke the filibuster, and the Senate as a whole never considered a bill. The House, which had been waiting for the Senate to act, never brought a bill out of committee.

V. What Is To Be Done?

For a moment it may be useful to treat all of the pressures for re-form purely as a policy issue — as an issue of how best to heal whatever may be wrong with the campaign finance system. There are, of course, enormous political problems in dealing with any aspect of campaign funding; we have already identified most of them, and we will shortly return to them. But for a few paragraphs we look only at the policy question.

It is a commonplace belief now that "if it ain't broke, don't fix it." In campaign finance, however, there is no agreement as to whether it is broken; and even among those who think it is, there is great disagreement over *what* is broken. Large numbers of Americans and their opinion-makers agree that spending levels are too high. ("Obscene" is the adjective of choice.) They agree, too, that contributors exert too much influence over both elec-tion outcomes and elected public officials. At this point it makes little difference that they exaggerate the influence; the fact that they believe it makes it a powerful political reality. When mass beliefs bear on the very processes of democracy and the basic values of fairness and equality, as they do here, the cost of ignor-ing them is high. The risk is heightened political cynicism and the loss of political legitimacy.

And what is really broken? There is one important element of truth to the public's perceptions. Money does advantage the best financed campaigns and, conversely, disadvantage the im-poverished ones. As things have turned out, incumbents have parlayed their positions into campaign funding that swamps most challengers and adds to the decline of competitiveness in elections. Second, it now seems clear that the scramble to raise the ever greater sums of money seriously distracts officeholders from their public responsibilities and other candidates from the events and opportunities of the campaign. Some of the com-plaining, to be sure, is by candidates who find it all a demeaning nuisance and a source of stress and anxiety (very few warriors really enjoy an arms race), but the drain of time and energies is beyond question. Finally, there remain a number of the smaller issues — bundling and soft money typify them — that are embarrassing flaws in the system and, worse, additional invitations to cynicism and distrust.

While those might not have been the problems Congress foresaw when it wrote the FECA and its amendments in the 1970s, their regulatory regimen is still attractive. The Congress, as they say, got it right the first time with a comprehensive plan for all aspects of the campaign finance system. Part of that plan fell in *Buckley*, and one now confronts the problem of having legislative authority over only part of the system as one goes about prescribing for the ills of all of it. The impossibility of legislating candidate spending limits is constraining enough, but the worst of it is the constant fear that limits on contributions and receipts will drive undeployed money into unlimited (and "unlimitable") independent spending. With just a bit of invention, one can imagine double campaigns for public office — one contested by the candidates and the other by opposing and supporting groups spending to elect and/or defeat them.

The only direct solution is an overruling of *Buckley*. After the Court's brief hesitation over the independent spending clause in publicly funded presidential campaigns, it no longer seems in a mood to reconsider. There are a few members of Congress who favor a direct challenge to the Court: passing new expenditure limits, with a strong congressional finding of fact attached, in the hope that it would force the Court to reconsider. The only other alternative is a constitutional amendment overturning it. Amendments have been regularly proposed, but progress through the states would be slow. It would also face an opposition coalition of Republicans and civil libertarians. Proponents would bear the heavy burden of justifying legislative limits on First Amendment freedoms. That would not be an easy burden, even though one would be arguing interests no less than those of a healthy democracy enjoying the support of its citizens.

If *Buckley* stands and if limitations on levels of funding and spending are central to the problems with campaign finance, then how does one limit those expenditures? The preferred option of the Democrats and the reformers has been to attach the limits as a condition to the acceptance of public funding. That option involves complicated formulas and enormous problems of administration in hundreds of separate elections with more than a thousand candidates. To mention only one problem, it is not easy to be confident, on the basis of recent history, that the Congress is prepared to give the FEC either the authority or the resources to oversee such a program of public funding.

For the short run at least, expenditure levels attached to less intrusive programs bypass those legislative issues and administrative problems. The search for the perfect incentive goes on; it is one that costs nothing and attracts all candidates! Most recently, proposals for discounted mail and broadcast rates have been before Congress. So, too, has the "reverse gambit" that was the late summer compromise of 1987 — the threat of a candidate's opponent getting public funding if the candidate doesn't agree to spending curbs. My own preference would be for attaching spending limits to a revived, even augmented tax credit for individual contributors along the lines of the earlier McHugh-Conable proposal. In other words, candidates would have to agree to accept spending limits in order for individual contributors to their campaigns to take the tax credit. Such a plan would both encourage small individual contributions and probably assure a widespread acceptance of spending limits.

One last point about expenditure limits: they ought to be set fairly high, at least at a level close to the current norm. Why? Setting limits at the level of current practice — that is, to cap spending rather than roll it back — avoids creating a pool of unused political money that will seek an outlet. Relatively high limits will also minimize the problem of challengers struggling to overcome incumbents' advantages. Indeed, the decision to choose spending limits of any kind runs a risk of diminishing competition in elections. But what competition? It is hard to imagine incumbents being much more entrenched than they are in the limitless spending of the 1980s. Their superiority results primarily from causes beyond campaign finance and can be diminished only by changes or reforms outside of it.

Then, there is the agenda of "smaller" issues: bundling, soft money, genuinely independent spending chief among them. Small though they may be, they are hardly noncontroversial. They create windows of opportunity, and each of them admits more candidates or committees of one party than the other. Careful rewriting of the FECA could and should close them, for it is of such smaller matters that larger matters of trust, equity, and confidence are made.

That leaves only the question of a limit on PAC receipts. It is at the heart of the debate over the two realities in contemporary campaign finance. But aside from the fact that it is a solution for an exaggerated problem — and a quest for a scapegoat and a diversion from the real problems of campaign finance — there remain sobering questions about its consequences. First, there is the danger that PACs will move much more substantially into a strategy of independent spending. Moreover, a limit on PAC receipts will not affect all PACs the same way; for example, large and sophisticated PACs, especially those with early money, will be better positioned than smaller ones. There is also the possibility that PACs will perfect a kind of organized individual contributing, a bundling without the bundles or special delivery. And finally, a receipts limit would disturb the dispersed and to some extent countervailing nature of the PAC system.

Taking the policy problem as a whole, it is important above all to keep the supply of money and the demand for it in some reasonable balance. Limits on PAC receipts without spending limits put a balance in danger. On the one hand, we ought to avoid a sellers' market in which contributors are giving a scarce commodity for which candidates are tempted to bid. On the other hand, we ought to avoid adding to the power of the candidates in the relationship. The problem there is not with the power of all candidates, however, but the power of incumbent candidates. Power and resources among the contributors is dispersed; it is not dispersed among the candidates. But that problem, as we previously noted, lies in considerable measure outside of campaign finance.

VI. In Conclusion

The legislative stalemate over campaign finance is reminiscent of the stalemate over the electoral college. That issue also directly affects the fortunes and interests of the parties; and it, too, bears directly on matters of representation, democratic processes, and confidence in institutions of government. There too all sides argue about likely risks and dangers and about the accuracy of future scenarios under new rules. Has the electoral college advantaged the large or small states? What interests, regions, and parties has it helped? What is the likelihood of an election thrown into the House or an election in which a president is elected while losing the popular vote? In both instances there is also the specter of unforeseen consequences of changes in the status quo. And in both, repeated attempts at change have come to naught.

Perhaps such highly politicized aspects of the electoral processes are policy issues apart from others because of the immediacy of the political conflict and the difficulty of compromise or coalition. Perhaps in the absence of galvanizing events, they are especially prone to deadlock and inaction. Major change in the electoral college and campaign finance may well await a presidential election thrown into a lame duck House or another scandal of the proportions of Watergate. In campaign finance, at least, it is hard to see more than routine legislation emerging from the present political environment. Party lines are drawn on virtually every major proposal for reform, and some proposals indeed appear to have been framed precisely to play defensively on the partisan division. Even the minor issues easily become ones of party advantage — proposals to force reporting of soft money transfers, for example. And always it is the incumbent legislators who must vote changes in a system of campaign finance that has helped bring them unimagined political security.

It therefore seems likely that reform of the present American system of campaign funding will be possible — *possible*, not inevitable — under one of two circumstances. The first is the aftermath of a substantial catastrophe of some sort in campaign finance, one approaching the impact of the Watergate revelations that spurred the FECA amendments of 1974. (On that point it is perhaps worth remembering that nothing approaching such a scandal has happened in a period of unprecedented growth in the sums of money flowing in the system.) The second circumstance would seem to be the capture of the policy-making branches by one party — control of the presidency and enough seats in both houses of Congress to break a filibuster in the Senate and to pass legislation despite the straying of a few party mavericks.

Change, progress, and reform are, however, very perishable, very relative concepts. Different spans of time measure them very differently. In the short run, there has perhaps been no progress in regulating campaign finance; there certainly has been little change. But over the longer haul, say the last 40 or 50 years, the era of campaign finance post-1974 is — whatever one thinks of it — a considerable improvement over what preceded it. It has replaced the reign of the fat cats with what is very probably the broadest based system of voluntary finance ever devised for open, democratic politics. The old covert system of under-the-table transactions and endemic illegality has given way to a public, above board, fully reported one. Indeed, it is easy to imagine worse alternatives — and "easy" perhaps to produce them with misconceived change.

There is, however, no longer much public joy over the advances of the 1970s and 1980s. The "ideal" behind the FECA was a system depending heavily on the voluntary contributions of individuals, preferably small contributions from the constituency at which the campaign was directed. In such a grass-roots campaign finance, contributions would be relatively unencumbered by the demands or expectations of the contributor. It was a vision on which both members of Congress and reform groups could unite. The FECA did in fact succeed to a surprising extent in enthroning the small contributor, and it succeeded spectacularly in dispersing and fragmenting the available pool of political money. Yet, it has been an unheralded success, one overshadowed by the unexpected rise of PACs and parties and one largely unrecognized by the public.

Now even the partial triumphs of the FECA seem slowly to be slipping away. Not only is the share of funds contributed by individuals slowly declining, but independent spending and party "on behalf of" spending slowly assume a more important role. Even within the scope of individual contributions, the sums are getting larger and they come more frequently from outside the constituency. In a sense the individual contributors to candidates are becoming distant outsiders to the strategies of pursuing public office. Their contributions increasingly "cost" the candidate too much effort in the solicitation, and they often come late in the campaign. They are harder and harder to fit into the world of the streamlined, efficient, and fluent campaign.

Quite simply, campaign finance has been organized. PACs and parties bring all the advantages of political organization, not the least of which are expertise and strategic sophistication; their strategies mesh and interact smoothly with the strategies of candidates. They can relate their activity in campaign finance to other activities and strategies in the political process, and they can use their role in campaign finance as a way of getting cues and information to their attentive publics. The irony, of course, is that the newly powerful political organizations draw on individuals who are less political and less knowledgeable than the informed citizen of the textbooks. But it has always been that way, all the way back to the rise of modern political parties. It is in the nature of political organization.

APPENDIX A
A Note on Data

I. The Federal Election Commission

The major body of data for federal campaigns — those for Congress and the president — come from the reports that candidates, PACs, and party committees are required to make under federal law. Those reports have been gathered, reviewed, brushed up, aggregated, and published by the staff of the Federal Election Commission beginning with the 1976 election cycle.

The FEC data appear in a number of forms. Copies of specific reports by all files (mainly candidates, PACs, and party committees) are available on easy-to-access microfilm at the FEC or through its computer network. If one wants information or data about a specific transaction of a specific candidate, party committee, or PAC, these are the data one needs. But it is the aggregated data of the FEC on which this book, as well as scholarly research generally, relies; and it needs a fuller explanation.

As with all FEC reports, the aggregate totals are for the two-year election cycle. There is no attempt in federal reporting to separate, as some states do, the primary campaign from the general election campaign. Aggregate reporting begins about the 18th month of the election cycle (the end of June of election year), with interim reports on candidate, party, and PAC spending. There have also usually been end-of-October interim reports, either in full volumes or press releases. Final reporting for the entire cycle (that is, through the end of December of election year) has traditionally come in three stages. First, the FEC publishes summaries of major totals in a series of news releases (six to ten pages, usually) about six months after the election (in April or May of the following year). Second, full interim final volumes appear shortly thereafter; none were, however, published in 1987. And third, the final printed volumes and computer tapes become available about 12 months after the election. That third and final series of data is the one that all but the most impatient scholars use, and it needs some comment.

Users recognize the printed volumes of data by their standard format: wide pages, black spiral binding, and a bureaucratic blue cover. A full set for 1983–84 includes the following volumes:

1. *FEC Index of Independent Expenditures, 1983–1984* (published in July 1985). This volume lists the independent expenditures of individuals, groups, and committees both by the spender and by the candidate they are intended to support or oppose.

2. *FEC Index of Communication Costs, 1983–1984* (published in June 1985). As with the volume on independent spending, this one lists communication costs both by spender and by the candidate they are intended to support or oppose.

3. –6. *FEC Reports on Financial Activity, 1983–1984: Party and Non-Party Political Committees* (published in November 1985). These reports on party committees and PACs are divided into four separate volumes, the titles of which are:

   - VOL. I: *Summary Tables*
   - VOL. II: *State and Local Party Detailed Tables*
   - VOL. III: *Non-Party Detailed Tables (Corporate and Labor)*
   - VOL. IV: *Non-Party Detailed Tables (No Connected Organization, Trade/Membership/Health, Cooperative, Corporation Without Stock).*

   The format in each is similar: listings by individual committees, with extensive data on their receipts and expenditures, as well as some aggregate tables.

7. *FEC Reports on Financial Activity, 1983–1984: U.S. Senate and House Campaigns* (published in November 1985). The vol-

ume lists candidates filing reports, with extensive data on the receipts and expenditures of each; summary tables and data deal both with all candidates and candidates in the general election.

8. *FEC Reports on Financial Activity, 1983–1984: Presidential Pre-Nomination Campaigns* (published in April 1986). Data are reported generally by candidates for the party nominations. The late date of publication reflects the problems the FEC has in settling accounts and reports from the presidential primary period.

This series of reports has become the standard for the FEC, but it goes back only to 1978. Reporting for 1976 was understandably partial, and the printed volumes are organized differently. Even in 1978 the series has one lacuna; the FEC issued no final House and Senate volume for that cycle (number 7 above), and Interim Report Number 5 is de facto the final one on the transactions of House and Senate candidates. Since 1977–78, the formats of the volumes have stayed remarkably similar, making longitudinal studies and comparisons easy in most instances.

The computer tapes approximate the volumes on House and Senate candidates, and they too start with the 1977–78 cycle. For that election there are only two tapes available, one each for party and nonparty committees (PACs); the absence of a final report on House and Senate candidates explains the absence of that tape. Since the 1980 cycle, the FEC has issued three tapes for each cycle; in presidential years it adds a fourth for presidential campaign data. One file on each generally corresponds to the data of the printed volumes, but a second file on each goes beyond them to list specific contributions. The committee tapes list contributions to and spending on specific candidates by individual committee, and the House and Senate tape lists them by candidate. These are, then, very long files; the more than 3000 active PACs these days are reporting a total of more than 100,000 contributions in each election cycle.[1]

[1] On the FEC tapes see Clyde Wilcox, "Campaign Finance Data Available from the Federal Election Commission," *PS*, a quarterly publication of the American Political Science Association (Winter 1987), 75–78. Wilcox also describes the new FEC tape that brings together nonparty committee data from 1978 through 1984 in a format ideal for longitudinal analysis.

II. Data Consistencies and Inconsistencies

The more familiar one becomes with FEC data and with scholarship using it, the more aware one becomes of little differences in total sums or calculations deriving from them. In moments of despair, one gets the feeling that it is virtually impossible to match totals exactly. A part of the problem — small, one hopes — results from computational error. But the major part of it comes from the data themselves and, most often, from expecting exact correspondence when one shouldn't. The most common of these problems follow:

Data Changes over Time. The totals of the interim final reports and the news releases based on them are indeed interim reports. Totals change by the time of the final reports, and occasionally even after them. In fact, some of the totals for the 1975–76 cycle have been revised years after the fact; the FEC finally came to a revised conclusion about independent spending in 1976 (and in 1978 as well) in a press release of October 9, 1980. Happily, changes so long after the fact are rare.[2] This book, of necessity, relies on interim final totals for 1985–86.

Different Data Definitions. The FEC presents data on all candidates for Congress in a specific cycle; it also publishes and analyzes data for the general election candidates in that cycle (which data, however, include the primary campaign and all other dealings in the cycle). Confusion between the two universes is not uncommon. Similar confusions are possible, too, in two other pairs of data: total and net receipts, and total and net disbursements. Indeed, the FEC began in 1976 by publishing only the total figures, figures inflated by lateral transfers as money moves from one part to another of a reporting entity. It did not begin to publish net figures until 1978, all of which confuses any comparisons with 1976 data.

---

[2]For a reliable guide to early sources, see the full source notes to the tables in Joseph E. Cantor, *Campaign Financing in Federal Elections: A Guide to the Law and Its Operation*, report 86-143 of the Congressional Research Service (Washington, D.C.: Library of Congress, 1986).

Different Universes of Transactions. PACs report contributions to candidates, and candidates report having received contributions from PACs. The totals rarely agree. Why? There are a number of possible explanations. Simple clerical errors, overreporting, oversight, etc., may lead to different reports. So may the calendar; a contribution may be given in one cycle and received in another. But by far the most frequent explanation is differences in the universes of transactions. Candidates for the House or Senate report all the PAC contributions they received in the two years; all candidates report, therefore, all PAC contributions to them. The PACs, however, report all contributions made in the two years; that includes contributions to candidates in that cycle's election, but it includes more: contributions to candidates from the last cycle retiring debts, contributions to individuals who never became candidates (e.g., death intervened or their trial balloon was shot down), contributions to senators not up for reelection, and contributions to individuals whose spending total did not require that they report to the FEC.

Scholarly Procedures or Assumptions. Some of the disagreements between or among data are inevitably the result of different computations or assumptions that scholars make. How, for instance, does one compute the contributions candidates make to their own campaigns? The FEC does provide a single datum ("contributions from candidate"), but it does not include loans from the candidate. So, I have added "loans from the candidate" to "contributions from the candidate" and subtracted "candidate loans repaid." Other scholars may have used the single figure or some other calculation.

III. Miscellaneous Thoughts on FEC Data

It is not the purpose of this appendix to suggest that the data of the FEC are forbiddingly difficult, for they are not. They require of the user only care and a basic understanding of the structure of the data. The documentation is generally complete (although only barely adequate for some of the computer tapes). All in all, the data of the FEC, especially since the troubled cycle of 1976, present no great problems, except to those who are not confident with the definitions and categories of the FECA and other relevant legislation.

In fact, using the FEC data, one soon becomes aware of their strengths. Major series of data and major definitions have been carried through successive election cycles; that is, data "dead ends" are rare. (The size of the task did, however, force the FEC to shift from reporting on individual contributions of $200 or more to $500 or more; as of September 1987, it has not reported even on the $500 and greater contributions for 1986.) And both candidates and committees have fixed identification numbers, a regularity that facilitates research across election cycles.

Ultimately, the validity of the FEC data as measures of the campaign finance system depends on the validity of the concept behind the statutes. Some transactions have been exempted from reporting: for instance, the labor of volunteer campaign workers and expenditures for registering voters and getting them to the polls. Moreover, the data reflect the candidate-centered nature of the reporting; the sources of those candidate receipts is the most thoroughly documented aspect of campaign finance. By contrast, the reporting on the object or purposes of candidate expenditures or of committee expenditures, except those directly on a candidate, are thin and imprecise; and the FEC makes no attempt to break them into useful subtotals.

IV. The Other Reporters of Federal Data

Alexander Heard's *The Costs of Democracy* (Chapel Hill: University of North Carolina Press, 1960) summarized data, such as they were, through the 1950s. Herbert E. Alexander, primarily in his quadrennial volumes on the years of the presidential elections, mined reports of federal elections and put together the authoritative data from 1960 through 1976.[3] Data for 1972

---

[3]The volumes bear titles growing from a single formula: *Financing the 1960 Election* (Princeton, N.J.: Citizens' Research Foundation, 1962), *Financing the 1964 Election* (Princeton, N.J. Citizens' Research Foundation, 1966), *Financing the 1968 Election* (Lexington, Mass.: Lexington, 1971), *Financing the 1972 Election* (Lexington, Mass.: Lexington, 1976), and *Financing the 1976 Election* (Washington, D.C.: Congressional Quarterly Press, 1979). The series has continued through the 1984 elections.

and 1976 were also provided by Common Cause, and the FEC itself added partial data for 1976. The Common Cause data for the 1972 and 1974 congressional elections are certainly the most authoritative, and its data on the 1976 congressional elections help flesh out the FEC's first attempts.

Alexander's volumes and his other work (and the work of the Citizens' Research Foundation he heads) remain useful compilations and expansions on FEC data, especially in the presidential races and in state and local campaigns. His estimates of total spending in all campaigns — national, state, and local — in presidential years remain the most authoritative of such estimates. They have by now assumed the status of quadrennial benchmarks in American campaign finance.

Since the development of FEC data, Common Cause has assumed a role of supplementary data provider in two ways. Mining reports to the FEC, it often provides the first summaries of PAC, party, and candidate activity for an election cycle, often beating the FEC's first notice (in its news releases) by a month or so. The data are generally fairly accurate, but they add nothing except a little speed to the FEC summaries; they also furnish Common Cause the first opportunity to interpret the data. Second, Common Cause, again drawing on reports to the FEC, brings data together in special relationships, usually formed by the interests of PACs and some legislative connection: committee assignment, legislative voting patterns, or policy issues. They, too, provide an opportunity for Common Causes's interpretation and commentary.

V. Data from the States

Data from the states come almost exclusively from the reports of official state agencies. Since a number of states do not have agencies that publish collections or aggregates of data, the candidate and committee reports shout in a vacuum. Only rarely will enterprising reporters or public organizations publish state data in nonpublishing states. The law of available data is very much in force. An exemplary report such as *The New Gold Rush* on California's legislative campaign finance is possible, clearly, because the California Fair Political Practices Commission is probably the most effective state agency in making reports available and in publishing aggregate and collected data from them.[4] Table 9-5 indicates which states publish aggregate data.

Even among the states that do publish usable data — and, alas, even among the best of them — one finds a series of problems with published data that complicate, even thwart, the study of state campaign finance. It is inevitable that the states should do things differently; one takes that as a part of the bargain in comparative state studies. It is less inevitable, except for budgetary reasons, that they should do things in an unuseful way. But they do. Among the problems are these:

Partial Data. Undoubtedly for very practical reasons, a number of states report only contributions above a threshold level. California and New Jersey, two states with data far above the average in quality, report only totals of individual contributions above $100. One cannot, therefore, come to accurate totals of candidate receipts in these (and other) states.

Definitional/Conceptual Issues. As I already noted, different definitions from state to state are inevitable. They originate in different state statutes for the reports of financial activity, thus the categories of the data reflect those legislative categories. Nothing illustrates the point better than the definition of PACs. To begin, of course, the phrase "political action committee" is not used in federal statutes or in the data of the FEC; the "nonparty committees" are a statutory artifact, and so it is in the states. But they differ from state to state, most often because the state permits direct contributions by corporations and labor unions. In some states the confusion is exacerbated by state laws that have left categories of committees overlapping or unclear

---

[4]California Commission on Campaign Financing, *The New Gold Rush: Financing California's Legislative Campaigns* (Los Angeles: Center for Responsive Government, 1985). In addition to drawing on the tabulations of the FPPC, the Commission (a nongovernmental body) has contributed analysis of its own from reports filed and available with the FPPC.

and that force the data publishers into the use of omnibus residual categories.

Many of the states, indeed, publish data not by a category of political organization (as does the FEC) but by the nature of the political interest served. So, some states report contributions in aggregates by sectors of the economy or nature of the occupational/professional group. It is a way of organizing the data that facilitates attempts to relate money to legislative votes — but it does not facilitate comparison with federal data from specific kinds of political organizations.

Incomplete Descriptive Data. Working with the FEC data convinces one that there is a basic irreducible set of data about candidate finance that one must have just to explore the basic analytical questions. One ought to know about candidates, for example, whether they are Democrats or Republicans, incumbents or challengers (or open seat candidates), winners or losers, general election candidates or not. It is disturbing and frustrating to find state reports on candidate activity that do not disclose one or more of those facts about candidates whose financial transactions are described. To put it mildly, serious analysis is the loser.

In general, one gets the impression just from looking at the data of a number of states that they have been shaped more by Common Cause and/or investigative journalism than have the data of the FEC. State resources, rarely very ample, are clearly going into intricate breakdowns of the interests and activities of nonparty group contributors, often at the expense of other data about campaign finance. Data on other sources of contributions are often sketchy, and the data on the rest of campaign finance are, too. Some states do, however, provide one body of data that the FEC does not. Especially in one-party–dominant states where the decisions of the primary election are the locus of competition and an effective alternative, we have a useful separation of the campaign finance of primary and general elections.

VI. Finis

In order to master any body of data, one first must master the structure of regulation that produced it. There are more than adequate hints and references in this book for understanding the FECA and its aftermath at the national level. For the states, there is a handy overview of each state's structure readily available in James A. Palmer and Edward D. Feigenbaum, *Campaign Finance Law 86* (Washington, D.C.; National Clearinghouse on Election Administration of the Federal Election Commission, n.d.).

APPENDIX B
Tables of Statutory Limits and Sums

The first of these tables summarizes the assorted statutory limitations on contributions under the FECA. Had the Supreme Court not struck down the legislated limits on expenditures and on the candidates' use of their own money, the table would be far more complicated.

The second table summarizes the assorted limits and funding levels in the federally funded presidential campaigns, both in the primary period and in the postconvention general election campaign. Since all are indexed to the Consumer Price Index, their original statutory values and the 1984 equivalents are shown.

TABLE B-1
Contribution Limits under the FECA

Contributions from	To Candidate or Authorized Committee	To National Party Committee[1] per calendar year)[2]	To Any Other Committee (per calendar year)	Total Contributions (per calendar year)
Individual	$1,000 per election[3]	$20,000	$5,000	$25,000
Multicandidate committee[4]	$5,000 per election	$15,000	$5,000	No Limit
Party committee	$1,000 or $5000[5] per election	No Limit	$5,000	No Limit
Republican or senatorial campaign committee,[6] or the national party committee, or a combination of both	$17,500 to to Senate candidate per calendar year in which candidate seeks election	Not Applicable	Not Applicable	Not Applicable
Any other committee or group[7]	$1,000 per election	$20,000	$5,000	No Limit

[1]For purposes of this limit, each of the following is considered a national party committee: a party's national committee, the Senate campaign committees and the national congressional committees, provided they are not authorized by any candidate.

[2]Calendar year extends from Jan. 1 through Dec. 31. Individual contributions made or earmarked to influence a specific election of a clearly identified candidate are counted as if made during the year in which the election is held.

[3]Each of the following elections is considered a separate election: primary election, general election, run-off election, special election, and party caucus or convention that has authority to select the nominee.

[4]A multicandidate committee is any committee with more than 50 contributors that has been registered for at least six months and, with the exception of state party committees, has made contributions to five or more federal candidates. A candidate committee should check with the FEC to determine whether a contributing committee has qualified as a multicandidate committee.

⁵Limit depends on whether or not party committee is a multicandidate committee.

⁶Republican and Democratic senatorial campaign committees are subject to all other limits applicable to a multicandidate committee.

⁷Group includes an organization, partnership, or group of person.

Source: Federal Election Commission, *Campaign Guide* (Washington, D.C.: FEC, June 1985).

TABLE B-2
Subsidies and Limits in Presidential Funding (all dollar sums in millions)

		1974	1986
I.	*Subsidies*		
	Maximum in preconvention period	$10	$20.2
	General election, major party	$20	$40.4
	Party convention	$ 2°	$ 8.1
II.	*Limits on Expenditures*		
	Preconvention total	$20	$40.4
	Lowest state, preconvention	$ .2	$ .4
	Highest state, preconvention	16c/voter	$ 6.1
	National party (general election)	2c/voter	$ 6.9

°The original statutory provision in 1974 was $2 million; that figure was raised to $3 million in 1979 and $4 million in 1984, both times with the provision that the figure be indexed as of 1974.

(continued from page iv)
Henry Waxman." *The Wall Street Journal,* November 10, 1983. Reprinted by permission of The Wall Street Journal, © Dow Jones & Company, Inc. 1983. All Rights Reserved.

Maxwell Glen, "Spending Independently." *National Journal,* June 21, 1986. Copyright © 1986 by National Journal Inc. All rights reserved. Reprinted by permission.

Maxwell Glen, "Gaining Credibility." *National Journal,* December 20, 1986. Copyright © 1986 by National Journal Inc. All rights reserved. Reprinted by permission.

Maxwell Glen, "Early-Bird Fund Raising." *National Journal,* June 20, 1987. Copyright © 1987 by National Journal Inc. All rights reserved. Reprinted by permission.

Linda Greenhouse, "The N.R.A.'s Lobbying is as Effective as Ever." *The New York Times,* April 13, 1986. Copyright © 1986 by The New York Times Company. Reprinted by permission.

Alexander Heard, *The Costs of Democracy.* Reprinted by permission of the University of North Carolina Press.

Robert D. Hershey, "$22,000 Plus a Long List of Races Equals a Busy Session for One Committee." *The New York Times,* October 13, 1982. Copyright © 1982 by The New York Times Company. Reprinted by permission.

Paul Houston, "Outspent Senate Candidates Still Winners." *The Los Angeles Times,* November 6, 1986. Copyright, 1986, Los Angeles Times. Reprinted by permission.

Brooks Jackson, "Open Up Federal Campaign Finance." *The Wall Street Journal,* July 31, 1984. Reprinted by permission of The Wall Street Journal, © Dow Jones & Company, Inc. 1984. All Rights Reserved.

Brooks Jackson, "Loopholes Allow Flood of Campaign Giving by Business, Fat Cats." *The Wall Street Journal,* July 5, 1984. Reprinted by permission of The Wall Street Journal, © Dow Jones & Company, Inc. 1984. All Rights Reserved.

Elizabeth Kolbert, "Public Campaign Financing: Close but No Cigar." *The New York Times,* July 12, 1987. Copyright © 1987 by The New York Times Company. Reprinted by permission.

Bob Kuttner, "The Dukakis Money-Raising Machine." *The Boston Globe,* September 15, 1986. Reprinted by permission of the author.

J. Anthony Lukas, *Nightmare: The Underside of the Nixon Years.* Copyright © 1973, 1974, 1976 by J. Anthony Lukas. All rights reserved. Reprinted by permission of Viking Penguin Inc.

Congressman David S. Monson, "It was Conscience, Not NRA Money." *The Washington Post,* May 10, 1986. Reprinted by permission of the author.

Catherine Morrison, *Managing Corporate Political Action Committees.* Reprinted by permission of The Conference Board.

The New York Times, "Washington Talk," August 24, 1985. Copyright © 1985 by The New York Times Company. Reprinted by permission.

Larry J. Sabato, *PAC Power: Inside the World of Political Action Committees.* By permission of W. W. Norton & Company, Inc. Copyright © 1984 by Larry J. Sabato.

Burt Solomon, "Political Trawling Among Stockholders." *National Journal,* March 7, 1987. Copyright © 1987 by National Journal Inc. All rights reserved. Reprinted by permission.

Frank J. Sorauf, "Who's in Charge? Accountability in Political Action Committees." *Political Science Quarterly,* vol. 99 (Winter 1984-85). Reprinted by permission.

Phillip J. Trounstine, "Cranston Hits Democrats in Pocketbook." *San Jose Mercury News,* August 3, 1986. Reprinted by permission.

The Washington Post, "FEC Reports Fewer PACS in Late 1985," January 20, 1986. Reprinted by permission.

Warren Weaver, Jr., "Political Action Group Focuses on the Elderly." *The New York Times,* March 1, 1982. Copyright © 1982 by The New York Times Company. Reprinted by permission.

Index

399